A Study of Old English Literature

A Study of
Old English Literature

C. L. WRENN

Emeritus Professor of Anglo-Saxon
in the University of Oxford

NEW YORK

W · W · NORTON & COMPANY · INC ·

ISBN   0   393   09768   4

Library of Congress Catalog Card No. 68–10891
Printed in the United States of America

2 3 4 5 6 7 8 9 0

Contents

Preface

THE AIM OF THIS BOOK is to promote the pleasurable and profitable study of Old English (Anglo-Saxon) literature, primarily among university students both in the early phases and the more advanced stages of their work: but it is hoped also that it may interest nonspecialist educated readers. While seeking to cover the ground usually assigned to the historian and critic of its subject, it is somewhat impressionistic and at times individual in its choice of emphasis: and I have therefore described it as a "study" rather than by a more formally definite title. While it cannot claim to embody the results of anything like full research, I believe it may here and there suggest points of interest to the more mature specialist which have come to my mind as a result of over forty years of attempting to teach Old English to a wide range of university students.

As the book is intended particularly for students with some knowledge of Old English, and at least a little Latin, passages of illustration have usually been quoted in their original languages. But, since it is hoped that other readers may use the book, translations have been added for all verse passages, and for such prose citations as are not primarily given for illustration of their form and style. Where, however, prose is quoted specially for consideration of its form and style translation would have no real point, and has not been provided. All translations, unless otherwise stated, are my own.

The printing of Anglo-Saxon verse with a space between the half-lines to indicate the caesural pause, and the placing of the macron over vowels thought on etymological grounds to be long, I have avoided save in the chapter chiefly concerned with metre, where they are clearly helpful. These artificial devices were intended for the elementary student of the language rather than for the literary study of texts. I have, however, generally preferred to hyphenate compound words in excerpts from verse, as in my edition of *Beowulf*, but not in the prose passages. For it is important for the appreciation of the poetic vocabulary that the exact nature of all compound words should at once be realized.

The Select Bibliography, though aimed mainly at the less advanced student, provides within itself by reference to major bibliographies the means of answering all the scholar's needs: and the footnotes, which cover a fairly wide field, will at times be of some value to the specialist. While an index of both names and subjects is provided, I have not thought it necessary to add a glossary of proper names, since this would only be needed by the most elementary students.

Like everyone who works in a medieval field, I owe immense and various debts to a host of predecessors: but a more personal gratitude I owe to the late R. W. Chambers and C. T. Onions, and, among those still with us, to Kemp Malone and J. R. R. Tolkien. These have, especially in former years, given me not only the benefit of their writings but frequent personal guidance. To the Editors of *Anglia* I am particularly grateful for permission to reproduce from vol. LXXVI the substance of my paper "On the Continuity of English Poetry" which forms Chapter 2 of this study, and to Mr. M. B. Yeats and Messrs. Macmillan & Co. Ltd. for permission to quote from the poems "The Meditation of the Old Fisherman" and "When You Are Old" in the *Collected Poems of W. B. Yeats*.

C. L. WRENN

Oxford, 1967

Introduction

A PRELIMINARY NOTE on the terms of the title of this book and
on its intended scope seems desirable in view of the tendency to
vagueness or ambiguity in current English. The term 'Anglo-Saxon',
now often replaced among serious scholars by 'Old English', is perhaps preferable, since the historians have never abandoned it, as the
name for the Germanic inhabitants of Britain and their writings up
to the establishment of the Norman conquerors. The term 'English',
in the early spelling *Englisc*, was the regular native generic one for
language and people from the first incipient feelings of nationhood in
King Alfred the Great's time in the late ninth century. But because
of the immense changes in all aspects of the language since early
Norman times, it was found convenient from the middle of the nineteenth century to employ the term 'Old English' for language and
literature up to about A.D. 1100, thus keeping a suggestion of continuity for the whole civilization, and following 'Old English' with
'Middle' and 'Modern' English. But the dialect in which almost all
the 'Old English' literature has come down to us is a type of West-
Saxon, whereas our current literary forms are derived from a Midland or Mercian type which was, to judge by its surviving monuments,
almost non-literary. The term 'Anglo-Saxon', then, has the advantage
of traditional usage, while one recognizes the fact that Modern
English is not directly derived from the old language. It is, nevertheless, only a coinage of the early seventeenth century, though the
Elizabethans often used the term 'Saxon', as 'did many in the seventeenth and eighteenth centuries. The translator of the great antiquary
William Camden's *Britannia* (1610) rendered his Latin name for
the people *Anglo-Saxones* and his corresponding adjective *Anglo-
Saxonicus* as 'Anglo-Saxon': and this term remained in common use till
the mid-nineteenth century, since when it has been generally employed
interchangeably with the 'Old English' preferred especially by students
of the language. While 'Anglo-Saxon' is commonly preferred in this
book as the name of the English writings from their beginnings in the
late seventh century to about A.D. 1100, 'Old English' is sometimes
used interchangeably with it.[1]

The term 'literature' is here understood as covering the whole body

[1] For a discussion emphasizing the advantages of the term 'Old English' see
Kemp Malone, "Anglo-Saxon: a Semantic Study", *Review of English Studies* V
(1929), pp. 173–185.

of surviving writings of the Anglo-Saxon period. But since a good deal of this can only be of technical interest to the linguistic or historical scholar, the main emphasis throughout will be on 'literature' in the more restricted sense, implying those writings which are recognized as having permanent 'literary' value for such things as the evocation of beauty or other primarily aesthetic appeal.

As will be seen in the first chapter, there is a real continuity from Anglo-Saxon culture or civilization to our own; but so great have been the changes in the 'English' since Anglo-Saxon times that it must seem like a foreign tongue at first sight to those who do not study it specially.

The earliest attempts to express in written symbols the language which was to become the literary vehicle of Anglo-Saxon England were memorial inscriptions of magical import incised in runes. These runes (the word *rūn* originally meant a secret or mystery) were mostly angular or linear characters cut on stone, bone, or very hard wood, and were brought to England from the invaders' Germanic homelands at first as primarily magico-religious cult-symbols whose purpose was only secondarily linguistic communication. The oldest of these inscriptions dates back to the end of the fifth century, and was found in a pagan cemetery incised on a sheep's ankle-bone in an incinerary urn at Caistor-by-Norwich. After the conversion to Christianity, such inscriptions continued sporadically to be carved as memorials adapted to the attitudes of the new religion, though often retaining something of their auspicious implications, till the tenth century; and some forty of these have survived.[1] But the vernacular language was expressed from the seventh century onward in an alphabet adapted from the Latin script of the Irish missionaries. This alphabet, which has remained the basis of English orthography, at first ignored the runes entirely, as they were associated with heathen practices; but from about the mid-eighth century this Latin-based script was practically the only written form of Anglo-Saxon, adding, however, three symbols which pronunciation required, and which found no convenient Latin letters. These were two runes representing respectively the sounds of modern *w* and *th* (voiceless as in *thin*). Of these runic letters that for *w* (named *wynn* 'joy') has normally been printed since the early nineteenth century as *w*; but that for *th* (the rune þ, 'thorn') is still printed as þ. The third symbol, called *eth*, was made from the Irish/Latin shape of the letter *d* with a line at about 45° through its upper portion (written ð), and was originally meant for the voiced *th*-sound in modern *then*, though commonly employed by scribes in the same way as þ. This symbol continues to be normally printed as in the manuscripts.

---

[1] See C. L. Wrenn, "Magic in an Anglo-Saxon Cemetery", in *English and Mediaeval Studies Presented to J. R. R. Tolkien*, ed. Norman Davis and C. L. Wrenn (London, 1962), pp. 306–320. For a good introduction to runes see R. W. V. Elliott, *Runes* (Manchester University Press, 1959).

Though divided among a number of dialects, especially in early times, the language of Anglo-Saxon literature in the manuscripts in which nearly all of it is preserved is a kind of Late West-Saxon, which owing to the political dominance of Wessex became something like a universal literary language for the whole of England from the late ninth or early tenth century. As this was in effect a sort of *koinē* including some elements from other regions than Wessex, it may be called Classical Anglo-Saxon, as it is the vehicle in which nearly all the more significant literature has come down to us. This Anglo-Saxon, although it seems very far removed from our current English, in pronunciation, accidence, syntax, and vocabulary through the lapse of time and foreign cultural influences—especially French and Latin in the vocabulary—shows the same basic grammatical elements as modern English in its fundamental framework. It is easily recognizable as a member of the Germanic branch of the Indo-European family of languages. The following sentences, for example, can be turned into Anglo-Saxon with very little change in the actual words, though their sound, inflections, and to some extent their word-order seem at first strange, and here and there a word of foreign later importation has become a necessary replacement. Meanings, too, have sometimes changed in varying degrees.

Modern English	*Anglo-Saxon*
The hound might see a *very*	Se hund mihte seon an *swiðe*
little house in that land.	lytel hus in þam lande.
His teeth were sharp, and	His teþ scearpe wæron, and
he might bite *very* hard if	he mihte *swiðe* hearde bitan gif
he willed. His *master* was	he wolde. His *hlaford* wæs
the father of three sons and	se fæder þreora suna and
two daughters.	twegra dohtra.

Here the only distinctions in the words used are that modern English has lost *swiðe*, replacing it in the Middle English period by the French *very* (from *verai*, Modern French *vrai*); and the French *master* (from medieval *maistre*, modern *maître*) has replaced the Old English *hlāford* (which developed into our word *lord*).

These observations, however, are strictly only true of the simplest prose. For Anglo-Saxon verse had a very distinctive poetic diction inherited from an ancestral traditional vocabulary appropriate to war and leadership and heroism.

Since before the vernacular had developed into an effective literary medium for prose educated men (including one of the greatest Anglo-Saxons, Bede) inevitably expressed their thoughts in Latin, some account must be taken of the Latin writings of our period. Moreover, even learned poets or versifiers such as St Aldhelm and Alcuin in the eighth century wrote significantly in Latin. Yet, as the interest of our pre-Conquest Latin writings is not primarily literary, they will be treated only very briefly.

Because the book is intended principally for the literary student and educated general reader, rather than for the specialist in the Old English language or institutions, the major concerns will be with works of literary quality set in their cultural background. This means that, since Old English prose is mostly utilitarian or historical or translated from Latin, the emphasis will be on the poetry. Entirely non-literary utilitarian writings such as interlinear glosses on Latin, or charters, will be passed by, unless like some of the finer pieces of manuscript art they make aesthetic appeal of some kind.

An impressionistic and necessarily selective chapter on Anglo-Saxon culture generally, has been prefixed to the examination of its literature proper. To emphasize the significance of Anglo-Saxon poetry in the development of English thought and feeling as a whole—a fact most often neglected—a chapter has been devoted to the continuity from Old English poetry shown by types of thought and of form which have remained until our own times.

There is a growing use of 'Anglo-Saxon' as a very wide general term to describe the British and American peoples and those influenced by their ideas and institutions. This is especially common among political writers who employ such expressions as 'Anglo-Saxon Democracy' or 'The Anglo-Saxon attitude to life'. The student of English literature should only be concerned with this ambiguous usage to avoid it. It is to the products of the mind of the 'English'-speaking inhabitants of Britain before the Norman settlement that the term 'Anglo-Saxon' is properly applied by students of literature.

The superficially modern look of Chaucer's work, along with the apparent foreignness and remoteness of Anglo-Saxon as indicated above, still encourage the belief—though it is not seriously maintained by most responsible scholars—that the study of English literature must begin with Chaucer, with the implication that what went before Chaucer has little of properly literary importance or value. But Anglo-Saxon literature is in fact an all-important section of a continuing stream: and there is a sense in which the spirit which still animates English civilization has a derivative unity with Anglo-Saxon literature. Its study is part of that of the English developing *mind* in its wholeness. As R. W. Chambers put it, we may "dream of all our literature, whether in prose or verse, in modern English, in early English or in Latin, as the work of one spirit".[1] But Old English literature also merits full consideration in its own right, both for its intrinsic value and for its pleasure-content.[2]

[1] See *Man's Unconquerable Mind* (London, 1939), p. 17.
[2] The beginner in the study of Old English will find most convenient for an introduction to the language Henry Sweet's *Anglo-Saxon Primer*, revised by Norman Davis, 9th ed. (Oxford, 1953, and often reprinted since). This might be followed by Randolph Quirk and C. L. Wrenn, *An Old English Grammar*, 2nd ed. (London, 1957). For advanced study the authoritative work is A. Campbell, *Old English Grammar* (Oxford, 1959).

A Study of Old English Literature

PART I

GENERAL FEATURES

CHAPTER 1

Anglo-Saxon Culture

THE LEADING PLACE of Anglo-Saxon culture in medieval Western Europe is now coming to be regarded as an accepted fact. But the amazing variety of its heterogeneous elements—brought about by its extraordinary power of creative assimilation—has still to be realized, by the non-specialist at least.

In material culture, for example, one may think of the imported Byzantine silverwork in the seventh-century hoard discovered just before the last European war at Sutton Hoo, in Suffolk[1]; and the pair of silver spoons with the names Saul and Paul inscribed in Greek characters, which were part of the royal tableware of the king commemorated in that same Sutton Hoo ship-burial or cenotaph, are a most direct link between Anglo-Saxons and Byzantine Greeks. Or again, the general and sometimes marked influence upon Anglo-Saxon art from Byzantium, which runs all through the Old English period, deserves to attract more attention than it has received, despite its recent special emphasis by Mr Talbot Rice, author of the second volume of *The Oxford History of English Art* (published in 1952).

---

[1] *The Sutton Hoo Ship Cenotaph.* In July 1939 at Sutton Hoo there were discovered the outlines and nails of an Anglo-Saxon ship, together with treasures, in exquisitely worked precious metals and symbolic objects, which had been buried in the centre of the ship in a barrow 9 ft tall as part of the funeral rites of an East Anglian king of the later seventh century. These artefacts, the most important archaeological find in Britain of the century, are now preserved and exhibited in the British Museum. The best general account is in *The Sutton Hoo Ship-Burial: A Provisional Guide*, published by the British Museum, 1947, reprinted from 1951. There is an excellent bibliography of works on Sutton Hoo by Francis P. Magoun, Junior, in *Speculum* XXIX (1954), pp. 116–224, completed by Jess B. Bessinger, Junior, in *Speculum* XXXIII (1958), pp. 515–522. See also R. L. S. Bruce-Mitford, "The Sutton Hoo Ship-Burial: Recent Theories and Some Comments on General Interpretation", *Proceedings of the Suffolk Institute of Archaeology* XXV (1949), 1–78, and the 3rd edition of R. W. Chambers, *Beowulf: An Introduction* (Cambridge, 1959), pp. 508–523.

Thirdly, from the intellectual and spiritual point of view, one may think of the strong Byzantine influence on Anglo-Saxon Christianity, exemplified especially in the introduction into England of the ceremonies and doctrine of the Feast of the Immaculate Conception of the Virgin Mary. For it seems clear that this was essentially an Eastern and Byzantine contribution to Christendom brought to England by contacts with Greek monasteries in Rome, such as that effected when King Canute made his diplomatic pilgrimage thither in the year 1027.

But before going further, perhaps it should once again be explained that the term 'Anglo-Saxon' is here being used to mean the qualities of those Germanic invaders and their descendants, the 'Anglo-Saxons', who dominated Britain till the Norman Conquest, in the period from about the middle of the sixth to the third quarter of the eleventh centuries. One should entirely avoid the more loose and popular uses of the term 'Anglo-Saxon' which have become widespread throughout the world in the present century.

'Culture', too, is apt to be a vague and loose term on the one hand, or else a strictly technical expression in the language of a particular discipline (as it is, for instance, among the anthropologists). First, therefore, the term will here be limited as applied to the Anglo-Saxons to the kinds of things that may be known of a people of the distant past. That is to say that by 'Culture' is to be understood 'the expression of the mind of a people through its permanent monuments'. We can only know and speculate upon a people's culture through such lasting things as they have left behind.

One may perhaps make a very roughly convenient division of the culture we are to consider into (*a*) material—which, however, must be closely related to the aesthetic expression of a people's mind in forms of art; (*b*) intellectual; (*c*) moral; and (*d*) spiritual. In what follows, all of these cultural manifestations will be touched on, but chiefly the first, because the greatest discovery of our century in Anglo-Saxon material culture has been the finding of the Sutton Hoo ship-burial in 1939.

Broadly speaking, it is proper to think of European civilization as emanating from three main sources, which may fairly be termed respectively the Latin, the Greek, and the Islamic: and these belong, the first to Western Europe, the second to Eastern Europe, and the third to such centres of Islamic culture as flourished in medieval Spain, Persia, and Iraq. Now, in Western or 'Latin'-cultured Europe the Anglo-Saxons were the pioneers and leaders in such material arts as sculpture, metal-work, and textile embroidery throughout their history, as well as in penmanship and literature. They made, too, substantial contributions to the other divisions of culture, though their developments in science and philosophy were not especially outstanding; and indeed for these things and for some of the more purely spiritual aspects of thought Europe was to get its creative impulses largely from medieval Islam.

It is to some extent true that the dominating features of Anglo-Saxon culture survive as continuing influences on later Britain. These are, in general terms, the following: First, a love of ordered ceremony and ornament, which characterizes alike the elaborate and highly technical metre and diction of Old English poetry and the Anglo-Saxon material arts. Secondly, a genius for conserving while progressively developing a continuing tradition. This is seen, for example, in the fact that one can trace a continuing type of verbal formula from the letters of the later Roman emperors, through the epistle which King Alfred the Great sent to his bishops with his translation of St Gregory's *Pastoral Care* (a manual for bishops and their parish priests), on to the first royal proclamation made in English after the Norman Conquest, by Henry III in 1258, and right up to this day in the official 'letters patent' still issued by the British Queen. Thirdly, there is a very strong ethical consciousness which finds expression in constant moralizing, in and out of season (as it would seem to us moderns). This appears, for instance, in those frequent moralizing 'asides' which are so characteristic of Old English poetry. Finally, there is a quite remarkable power of adaptive assimilation of endlessly varied foreign materials and styles. There is, for example, something ultimately Greek or Byzantine in some of the Anglo-Saxon animal figures. This is noticeable alike in the Sutton Hoo treasures of the seventh century and in the illuminated manuscripts of the Winchester School in the reign of Ethelred the Unready.

Let us look now for a little at Anglo-Saxon material culture, and then touch very rapidly and summarily on others of its features.

The poet of *Beowulf*, the early eighth-century Anglo-Saxon epic, describing the ship-funeral of the first Danish king Scyld Scefing—who must, in so far as he was historical, have belonged to the fifth century—tells us how on the ship which bore the royal body out to sea

> þær wæs madma fela
> of feor-wegum frætwa gelæded.

There was a multitude of treasures and adornments, brought from far regions.

And the poet goes on to relate that

> þa gyt hie him asetton segen gyldenne
> heah ofer heafod

Furthermore they set high over his head a golden standard.[1]

Indeed, throughout the poem of *Beowulf*—the ideal Germanic hero in Old English pattern—there are descriptions of and allusions to the

---

[1] *Beowulf*, lines 36–37 and 47–48. All references are to the edition of C. L. Wrenn, 2nd ed. (London, 1958).

most magnificent and elaborate treasures, in precious jewels, metal-work, and tapestries. Until 1939 it had seemed to most students that the obvious love of such artistic treasures and the knowledge of how to provide them and enjoy them were an anachronism in such an early poem, treating of a still earlier age. Then suddenly, in July 1939, there was revealed the clear outline of a comparable ship-burial of a king of East Anglia late in the seventh century on the Suffolk coast at Sutton Hoo, with exquisitely made gold buckle and clasps, silver bowls, a royal purse whose frame was wrought with the finest art of the goldsmith and the jeweller, the framework of what has seemed to many to have been a royal ceremonial standard, and numerous other treasures testifying to the highest aesthetic development. Here, nearly a century before the composition of *Beowulf*, were in fact cultural monuments of the very type and quality described by the poet. The marvellous cloisonné work and niello inlaying of the Sutton Hoo treasures is, however, only the beginning of that leadership in such arts which Anglo-Saxon culture was to maintain till after the Norman Conquest.

But the Sutton Hoo find is rather a cenotaph than the commemora-tion of an actual burial, though in all respects, save only the presence of a corpse, it seems to resemble the ship-burial of the king Scyld in *Beowulf*; for the king commemorated with these ceremonial and symbolic treasures from among his choicest possessions on the Suffolk coast was probably himself given privately a Christian burial before the full pagan rites were thus observed by his ship being placed in a sandy mound and loaded at the centre with treasures representing the good life. This apparent blending of Christian and pagan ceremony and sacrament again reminds us of *Beowulf* with its Christian use of essentially pagan material; and one might almost say that the con-serving of pagan tradition with progressive Christian adaptation seen here in the Sutton Hoo finds is an essential and most characteristic feature of Anglo-Saxon culture as a whole. If there were any doubt as to the Christian element in Sutton Hoo, the pair of silver spoons inscribed with the names Saul and Paul respectively, already men-tioned as a Byzantine aspect of the treasures, would remove it; for such a pair of spoons could only be a reminder of the miracle which befell St Paul on the road to Damascus, when he was transformed from the Jew Saul to the Christian Paul. Such spoons would be a fitting gift to a king in honour of his baptism and reception into the Christian Church. One is reminded, too, by the wondrous bowls at Sutton Hoo of the precious goblets and pitchers which were among the dragon's hoard in *Beowulf*—which, like the ship-cenotaph, in-cluded a standard, "most glorious of symbols". That marked power of assimilating foreign ideas which characterizes Anglo-Saxon culture throughout is strangely seen in the occurrence of Byzantine work in the silver spoons and bowls blended with the inherited Roman design on the standard-holder (reminding us of a *vexillum*), the Frankish

Merovingian coins of gold found in the royal purse, and the gold and silver-work of the English smiths. Like the dragon's treasure in *Beowulf*[1] again is the suggestion of magic conveyed by the stag which surmounted the standard-holder: for the dragon's treasure, too, was in part

iu-monna gold, galdre bewunden,

gold of men of old time, encompassed with a magic charm.[2]

Indeed, the Sutton Hoo treasures embrace many aspects of Anglo-Saxon culture, and anticipate others. In one of the bowls, for instance, were found the remains of the upper portions of a harp—just the typical instrument with which the Old English poets accompanied the recitation of their lays, as described by Bede in his account of the first Anglo-Saxon Christian poet Cædmon, and in *Beowulf* itself. Attempts have been made to reconstruct this harp by adding its sounding-board so as to make it capable of music when played. But these efforts seem rather to suggest that it was in fact too small for use in accompanying poetic recitation in a large hall: and it is perhaps more satisfactory to regard it as primarily a symbolic harp. An Anglo-Saxon royal hero, like King Hrothgar in *Beowulf*, would be able to play the harp: and this little instrument, probably, was just a model to symbolize the noble art of harp-playing which a Germanic hero might expect to continue in the world after death; or such a harp may have been played by the king in more intimate private gatherings.

Naturally the textile and embroidery work which belonged to the royal Sutton Hoo treasures, such as that of the purse and the belt, have almost utterly disappeared with the passage of time: but in view of so many confirmations in these artefacts of the high aesthetic qualities of the artistic treasures described in *Beowulf*, one may well believe that such woven and embroidered materials were already a worthy anticipation of the glories of the St Cuthbert Durham stole of the early tenth century, and of the Bayeux tapestry by which Anglo-Saxon skill commemorated the Norman Conquest. In the hall of the king celebrated at Sutton Hoo in the seventh century there must have been examples of those tapestries mentioned as adorning Hrothgar's hall in *Beowulf*:

Gold-fag scinon
web æfter wagum, wundor-siona fela
secga gehwylcum þara þe on swylc starað.

Tapestries adorned in gold shone along the walls, many marvellous sights to every one of those who are wont to gaze on such things.[3]

---

[1] For the Dragon's Hoard, see *Beowulf*, lines 2752 ff., especially the references to the standard in lines 2767–2768 and 2776–2777.

[2] *Beowulf*, line 3052.

[3] *Beowulf*, lines 994–996.

The close relationship of the traditions of *Beowulf* to the Geats, the South-Swedish tribe of the period when the Anglo-Saxons were settling in Britain, is remarkably paralleled in the existence among the Sutton Hoo treasures of what seem to have been ancestral heir-looms of the East-Anglian king which were already of some antiquity when buried with his ship in the seventh century; for the portions of his helmet, shield, and sword which survive clearly suggest Swedish workmanship of the preceding sixth century. Or this again may be regarded as a sign of the breadth and assimilativeness of Anglo-Saxon culture. This receptivity to varied foreign artistic influences is further illustrated by the Frankish style of some of the cloisonné-work on gold: and perhaps even Celtic influence may be thought of when one looks at the animal figures in the Irish Latin Gospels in the Library at St Gall (Sankt Gallen) in Switzerland and compares them with those of some of the Sutton Hoo treasures. It is often assumed that the silver dishes and the pair of spoons at Sutton Hoo are simply Byzantine imports, especially in view of the large silver dish bearing the control stamp of the Emperor Anastasias I: but it may be suggested that it is possible that the spoons are in fact the work of Anglo-Saxon craftsmen who had the opportunity of modelling their skill and designs on originals from Constantinople. It is noticeable that the Greek letter for "L" in the name *Saulos* on one of the silver spoons is engraved turned upon its side; and this might perhaps mean that an English artist was imitating a Byzantine model with a certain amount of error through unfamiliarity with the Greek characters. The whole matter of Sutton Hoo has been most thoroughly surveyed in Charles Green's *Sutton Hoo: The Excavation of a Royal Ship-Burial* (London and New York, 1963).

The impressive effects of the gold, the garnet-work, and the mosaic seen on the Sutton Hoo buckle and clasps—with their suggestion of exquisitely graded and varied schemes of colour—may be compared with what the Anglo-Saxon poets frequently meant by their word *fag* (literally 'variegated in colour'), which they often applied in describing weapons and treasures in metal-work. The *Beowulf* poet again uses this same adjective to describe the traces of Roman tessellated paving from a Romano-British villa of long before, which could still be seen in the *fag flor* of a place of variegated colouring of Hrothgar's hall[1]: and this, like the Sutton Hoo treasures, reminds us of the Anglo-Saxon tendency to continuity and progressive conservatism of tradition; for the Oxfordshire village of Fawler, named *fag flor* in Anglo-Saxon times (as attested by a charter), was the place where fragments of Roman tessellated paving were in fact found in the middle of the last century.

The strong element of magic in Germanic pre-Christian religion exemplified in the use of runes—writing-symbols cut with straight lines in stone or hard wood—is implied to some extent, as

[1] *Beowulf*, line 725.

has been said earlier, in the Sutton Hoo finds. We see this first in the as yet little noticed set of half a dozen runes cut on one of thirty sheep's *astragali* or ankle-bones found in an urn at Caistor-by-Norwich, and dated by the experts at about A.D. 500. Here the runes are arranged in a confusing order so as to conceal the words from the ordinary observer. The six runes may be arranged so as to make the two words *næh*, 'near', and *hwær*, 'where'. But several other interpretations are possible: or they may be clearly cult-symbols.[1] Now within a couple of centuries of this magical use we find Christians using runes for commemorative inscriptions with that kind of assimilation of pagan elements which, as in *Beowulf*, is a general feature of Anglo-Saxon culture—including religious art.[2]

The next most outstanding example of this kind of heterogeneity of Anglo-Saxon culture is that group of inscribed and pictorially carved boxes or caskets of bone which includes the Franks Casket in the British Museum, the Mortain Casket from a church in Normandy, and the Brunswick (Braunschweig) Casket, now in the Brunswick Museum in Germany. Each of these shows carved or engraved designs of historical or legendary matters accompanied by what amounts to something like brief descriptive notes in runes: and they may well be regarded as having been employed—at least in their later Old English uses—as reliquaries for Christian saints.[3]

We find in the correspondence connected with the Anglo-Saxon mission on the continent of Europe in the third quarter of the eighth century that Bregowine, Archbishop of Canterbury, sent to the Bishop of Mainz *capsam unam ad officium sacerdotale fabricatam ex ossis*, 'a certain little box wrought out of bone for the business of a priest'.[4] Now, the Franks Casket, presented to the British Museum by one Franks who picked it up at a sale in France, is a little box made of whalebone; and on each side of it there are carved episodes from Christian history, from classical Roman history, and from Germanic heroic legend, with descriptive notes in runes. Here there meet in this little box elements from classical Roman, from pagan Germanic, and

---

[1] See R. Rainbird Clarke, *East Anglia* (London, 1960), p. 137, and Plate 43. See further in C. L. Wrenn, "Some Earliest Anglo-Saxon Cult Symbols" in *Franciplegius, Medieval and Linguistic Studies in Honor of Francis Peabody Magoun*, ed. Jess B. Bessinger and Robert P. Creed (New York, 1965), pp. 40–55.

[2] For the use of runes on objects of value, cf. *Beowulf*, lines 1687 ff., especially 1694–1698.

[3] For general discussions of these and related art-forms, see G. Baldwin Brown, *The Arts in Early England* V (London, 1921); and W. G. Collingwood, *Northumbrian Crosses of the Pre-Norman Age* (London, 1927). On Runes, see Helmut Arntz, *Handbuch der Runenkunde*, 2nd ed. (Halle/Saale, 1944). *Cf.* also Bruce Dickins, *Runic and Heroic Poems of the Old Teutonic Peoples* (Cambridge, 1915); also Maurice Cahen and Magnus Olsen, *L'Inscription Runique du Coffret de Mortain* (Paris, 1930). There is a good popular book, *Runes: An Introduction*, by R. W. F. Elliott (Manchester University Press, 1959).

[4] Quoted by Wilhelm Levison in his *England and the Continent in the Eighth Century* (Oxford, 1946), p. 41, note 5.

from Christian sources—Romulus and Remus the founders of Rome, the Adoration of the Magi, and a reference to the legend of Wayland, the magical Germanic smith (who is also indicated in a carving in the parish church at Leeds).[1] The Mortain Casket in a Normandy churchyard is quite clearly in origin a receptacle for the Holy Oil of Christian sacraments. Upon it is cut in runes the following inscription:

Good helpe Aeadan; þiiosne kiismeel gewarahtæ:

God help Aeadan: he wrought this *chrismale* [receptacle for the baptismal oil].

The Brunswick Casket is again clearly a reliquary, probably for an Anglo-Saxon saint, though the attempt to assign it to Etheldreda (or Audrey) of Ely (an abbess of the later seventh century) has not met with definite success, and indeed its runes have not been interpreted with any certainty.

The complete assimilation of pagan runic writing to Christian purpose is seen in the eighth century in the great Northumbrian pieces of sculpture which were among the cultural monuments that made the Anglo-Saxon age of Bede a creatively inspiring epoch for Western Europe. Some of these are completed by the addition of explanatory commemorative inscriptions like that on the Bewcastle Cross, in Cumberland, on which royal persons are celebrated, with an admonition to the people to pray for their souls. On the most famous of all these sculptures, the Ruthwell Cross in Dumfriesshire, in the Lowlands of Scotland, this use of runes reaches its highest artistic level: for here the sculptured figures from stories in the Christian Scriptures and traditions are given a wider significance by the addition of portions in runes of a Northumbrian poem expressing a dream-vision of the personified Cross of the Crucifixion which, in a later and expanded form made probably in King Alfred's reign, is one of the great religious poems of the English language. This is the *Dream of the Rood*,[2] preserved in the Vercelli Book copied in the late tenth century during the Benedictine Renaissance. A further notable instance of the use of runes for Christian purpose in a way which does not lose sight of their original magical properties is provided by the insertion of the name of the poet Cynewulf in each of his four surviving poems in runic characters, if we accept the view of some authoritative scholars that the purpose of using these runic names was to ask for the prayers of the readers or hearers of the poems for

---

[1] The best technical exposition of the Franks Casket is still that of Arthur Napier in *An English Miscellany Presented to Dr. F. J. Furnivall* (London, 1901). For general discussion see G. Baldwin Brown, *op. cit.* VI (London, 1930), and R. W. V. Elliott, *op. cit.*

[2] For almost all the Old English poems subsequently mentioned, reference is made to *The Anglo-Saxon Poetic Records: A Collective Edition*, ed. G. P. Krapp and E. van K. Dobbie, 6 vols. (New York and London, 1931–53). This will be abbreviated as ASPR. For *The Dream of the Rood* see ASPR II, pp. 60 ff.

the poet Cynewulf by name[1]; and the way in which these runes are arranged—sometimes so as to utilize the words which are their Old English names and sometimes merely as letters—suggests that to the poet they still had auspicious qualities descended, as it were, from their original Germanic magical properties. It is generally agreed that in this eighth-century renaissance, the Age of Bede, England showed a pioneering leadership of Europe in sculpture which was largely maintained till the coming of the Normans.

The astonishingly delicate metal-work of the Sutton Hoo buckle and clasps was the forerunner of a continuing superiority among the Anglo-Saxons in such spheres of art: and the other periods of renaissance, the ages of Alfred the Great and of the Benedictine saints of the later tenth century, produced comparable features. King Alfred's Jewel, now in the Ashmolean Museum at Oxford, with its exquisite enamel-work, is an outstanding example; and here once again there is perhaps a connection between material art and letters. For it seems not unlikely that this famous incomplete piece of gold and enamel-work may have been the base of that *æstel* or book-mark which King Alfred sent to each of his bishops along with the gift of a copy of his translation of the *Pastoral Care* of St Gregory. This apparently gold and bejewelled bookmark was worth, the King tells its recipients in his accompanying letter, the sum of fifty *mancuses*—using here the Latin form of an Arabic measurement which was becoming common in western Europe.[2] This sum would be something like £900 in our currency in economic value. King Alfred spent, according to his biographer Asser, one-sixth of his revenue on the upkeep of artificers of all kinds[3]; and like the Northumbrian kings of the Age of Bede, Offa of Mercia, Athelstan, and Edgar, he was both a great patron of art and a believer in encouraging it for his educational purposes. King Alfred's reign may also remind us of how widespread in Anglo-Saxon England were artistic products. The sculptured stone slab at the church of Codford St Peter, in Wiltshire,[4] which is one of the great pieces of religious art of its time, was made in his kingdom of Wessex, as was also the Minster Lovell Jewel. Nor did the artistic impulses illustrated by such monuments lose their power before the Norman Conquest; for William of Normandy's chaplain, William of Poitiers, has left on record the astoundingly abundant and impressive artistic treasures of every kind which King William removed from Anglo-Saxon abbeys and churches to make as gifts to similar institutions in his own Normandy.

[1] See K. Sisam, "Cynewulf and his Poetry", in *Studies in the History of Old English Literature* (Oxford, 1953), p. 23.

[2] King Alfred's Prefatory Epistle to his Old English version of St Gregory's *Cura Pastoralis* can conveniently be found in H. Sweet's *Anglo-Saxon Reader*, 13th ed. (Oxford, 1954).

[3] *Asser's Life of King Alfred*, ed. W. H. Stevenson (Oxford, 1904), p. 87.

[4] D. Talbot Rice, *English Art, 871–1100*, vol. 2 of *The Oxford History of English Art* (Oxford, 1952), p. 17.

Work in ivory (walrus is often used for smaller or less formal objects) was continuously on a high level throughout the Old English period, though only that of the later half has survived effectively. But one can see a continuity, with a developing elaboration and skill as more and more foreign motives are assimilated, from the whalebone box of the Franks Casket to the highest artistic achievements of the best crucifixes and bishops' pectoral crosses of the later Benedictine Renaissance. This type of art has naturally some affinities with that of the illuminating of manuscripts: and this too shows both a long history of development and extremes of artistic excellence in its greater phases. Beginning with Latin Psalters and Gospels and culminating in more elaborate ceremonial service-books and works of education in the Winchester School of the late Old English period, we find among the Anglo-Saxons the evolution of a native hand-writing under Irish influence, and a supremely beautiful native type of manuscript illumination. This latter shows, as do most Old English arts, the assimilation and 'Englishing' of all sorts of foreign ideas, as well as elements that suggest some continuity of tradition extending far back into the days of Roman Britain. The outstanding work in initial letters, in animal figures and in scroll-designs as well as the complete full-page pictures which often appear in later Old English manuscripts, is well known; nor is there space here to dwell on such elaborate and exquisitely detailed masterpieces as those of the Winchester School, exemplified in *The Benedictional of St Æthelwold* transferred from Chatsworth to the British Museum in 1959. One of the greatest achievements in illuminated manuscripts is the Latin Lindisfarne Gospels of the eighth century. The fact that St Dunstan was himself a skilled practitioner of all the arts emphasizes the cultural achievement and character of his age. And perhaps its attitude to art in general may be symbolized by the picture of St Dunstan himself prostrate at Christ's feet which is included in a manuscript in the Bodleian Library, and is stated by its scribe to be *de propria manu S[an]c[t]i Dunstani*—'from St Dunstan's own hand'.

Reference has been made at the beginning of this chapter to that love of ordered ceremony and delicate sense of decoration which is a characteristic feature of Anglo-Saxon culture, and which has in some measure persisted in Britain to this day. This quality may be seen in all the varied types of material culture already touched upon. It is seen in the harmonizing of motives of differing foreign origin into artistic wholes of ordered coherence. But it appears too in the care and effectiveness of religious ceremonial and liturgy, such as the elaborate ritual of the services for Palm Sunday which was devised by the English Benedictines of the late tenth century, and is still often followed. It must always be borne in mind that all forms of Anglo-Saxon culture, whether pagan or Christian, are intimately related to religion; yet always the natural tendency is towards ordered conceptions with a strong sense of fitness and continuity. Sudden spiritual inspirations, therefore, are scarcely to be looked for: and even the great Old English missionaries who carried their religion and education over half Europe were powerful rather as practical organizers and devisers of workable religious methods than primarily spiritual teachers. Similarly, the qualities of Anglo-Saxon literature point to the same gifts for ordered ceremonious arrangements and balanced types of ornamentation which have been emphasized. Such considerations may now lead us to look very briefly at the intellectual contributions and achievements of the Anglo-Saxons.

Apart from their magnificent achievements in poetry, permanent intellectual work of the Anglo-Saxons lies mainly in three fields: those of historiography, prose-literature, and education; and like the arts hitherto discussed, they are especially noticeable during the three great periods of creative development, the eighth century, the age of King Alfred, and the Benedictine Renaissance most conveniently linked with the name of St Dunstan, who died in the year 988.

The creative work of Bede in the writing of the first really scholarly history in post-classical Western Europe is well enough known. But his great *Church History of the English People* [*Historia Ecclesiastica Gentis Anglorum*], though written in Latin, is very English in those features of order, continuing tradition, love of moralizing, and capacity for assimilating fully varied external material which may be taken as general characteristics of the Anglo-Saxon mind.[1]

At the other end of the eighth century Alcuin, the learned and orthodox Englishman from the School of York, the organizer of education and doctrine in Charlemagne's Frankish empire, was not so much a creative originator as the careful and practical exponent of what Matthew Arnold was to call "the best that is known and thought in the world". He wrote theological works to confute heresies, reorganized the text of the Latin Bible and the Western Canon of the Mass; he planned education for the nobility. But while the results of his work largely remain as permanent parts of Christian use (though Alcuin's part is seldom remembered), it must be said that his work was valuable practically rather than in any fuller sense. Even his prayers, such as that which he made to begin the service of the Holy Communion, and which is still in use, *Deus cui omne cor patet*, are effective working devices rather than anything newly created. Yet he manages to say exactly what most effectively expresses the human needs of the people.[2]

Again, the work of the Benedictine saints, Dunstan, Oswald of Worcester, and Æthelwold in the later tenth century, was essentially in directions of ordered ceremonial, practical working compromise,

[1] The best edition of Bede's *Historia Ecclesiastica Gentis Anglorum* is in Charles Plummer's *Venerabilis Bedae Opera Historica*, 2 vols. (Oxford, 1896). There is a useful translation by A. M. Sellar (London, 1907).

[2] For Alcuin's work, see Eleanor Duckett, *Alcuin, Friend of Charlemagne* (New York, 1951).

and the organizing of adapted continuing tradition. Yet in reorganizing and disciplining the Anglo-Saxon Church of their time these men did also revitalize it, and through it the whole of the Anglo-Saxon culture. They encouraged all the arts—including even to some extent that of poetry; and it will be admitted by all that theirs was the great age of Anglo-Saxon art. It was the age which excelled at once in all the arts—of metal-work and enamel, sculpture, ivory-work, book-production and manuscript-illuminating, architecture, liturgy, and prose-composition in the vernacular. It was truly an age of renaissance; but a renaissance need not be an age of originality, provided that it has that kind of *élan vital* which can give it vigorous new life.[1]

Indeed, most of the intellectual aspects of Anglo-Saxon culture are derived rather than original, practical rather than creative. This is generally true of Old English prose. The astonishing thing is that the Anglo-Saxons were the pioneers in Western Europe in the making of a prose in the vernacular, long before other peoples had got beyond the Latin of the Church. King Alfred's own prose is effective rather than literary, practical rather than aesthetically attractive. But with the Benedictine Revival of the age of St Dunstan and Ælfric, we have in Anglo-Saxon a prose that aims consciously at rhetorical effects and aesthetic satisfaction—a prose which could produce a really agreeable version of a Greek romance in the tale of *Apollonius of Tyre* in a style that gives secular pleasure as well as ethical 'uplift'. Old English poetry, which naturally was far older than its prose, is the carrying on and enlarging of a common Germanic tradition: but the prose is in some degree a new factor in European vernacular literature created at a remarkably early date by the Anglo-Saxons.

It is in no way surprising that Anglo-Saxon literature, coming as it did soon after the acceptance of Christianity, should be fundamentally religious, and that this should in general take markedly didactic forms; but the especially strong ethical consciousness which characterizes Anglo-Saxon culture becomes apparent from the love of moralizing which seems to us moderns to intrude so constantly even in secular and heroic poetry. A striking instance of this appears near the beginning of *Beowulf*. The poet, having mentioned the glorious fame of Beowulf, the Danish king of the Scylding dynasty, solemnly turns aside to the audience to point out the proper way for a prospective king to be brought up and to behave:

> Swa sceal geong guma gode gewyrcean,
> fromum feoh-giftum on fæder bearme,

---

[1] For the Benedictine Renaissance in general, see J. Armitage Robinson, *The Times of Saint Dunstan* (Oxford, 1923). *Cf.* also S. J. Crawford, *Anglo-Saxon Influence on Western Christendom* (London, 1933); and R. W. Chambers, *England before the Norman Conquest* (London, 1926). See generally also Dom David Knowles, *The Monastic Order in England*, 2nd ed. (Cambridge, 1963).

þæt hine on ylde eft gewunigen
wil-gesiþas, þonne wig cume,
leode gelæsten; lof-dædum sceal
in mægþa gehwæm man geþeo(ha)n.

Thus should a young man bring it about by his virtue, by liberal gifts of wealth while he is still under the protection of his father, that in his old age willing comrades may remain with him, if war should come, that they may aid their prince. In every tribe a man should prosper through deeds worthy of praise.[1]

A king, that is to say, should provide his son who is to succeed him with the means of being liberal to a band of followers of his own—the prince having thus a *comitatus* or group of voluntary companions under his leadership even while he is still under his father's tutelage, so that when at last he does become king he will already have gained a trusty band ready to give him loyal service if war should come. Or again, the poet of the exiled *Wanderer* in the Exeter Book joins the two main sections of his poem by a set of what are termed 'gnomic verses'—groups of familiar proverbs and platitudes which all the audience must have known by heart almost from their infancy. What must appear to the modern reader like mere platitudinous moralizings, then, seems to have pleased the Old English audiences; for one cannot believe that poets of the high quality and skill that produced *Beowulf* and *The Wanderer* would have introduced such moralizing matters unless they had been sure that their hearers would have found pleasure as well as edification in them. In other words, it would seem that the Anglo-Saxons found aesthetic satisfaction in the repetition—even in the best poems—of obvious ethical matters.

It is very difficult to distinguish a purely spiritual aspect of Anglo-Saxon culture from the intellectual; for—apart from a number of visionary experiences such as we find among any people in the early days of their conversion to a new religion—the practical turn of mind of the Anglo-Saxons seems to have precluded the development of what may perhaps be termed the expression of higher spiritual experience. England had to wait for impulses from abroad for such things. Though the whole of their culture was throughout permeated by religion, the theology of the Anglo-Saxons was mainly derived or secondary. It consisted for the most part in expressing in the vernacular the accepted ideas of the orthodox Christian Fathers, Augustine, Gregory, and Jerome; and in the development of a language—most effectively in the time of the Benedictine Renaissance —capable of expressing clearly and simply these ideas. Its aims were strictly practical; and King Alfred's selection of a famous manual for bishops and parish priests for his first attempt at translation from

[1] *Beowulf*, 20 ff.

Latin into the vernacular was characteristic of the Old English attitude.

But there is one exception to the above generalization. This is in the formulating by an Englishman shortly after the Norman Conquest of that doctrine of the Immaculate Conception of the Blessed Virgin Mary which was, so much later, to become a Catholic dogma. No doubt the English genius for ordered ceremony, which as already remarked found its outlet in contributions to the liturgies and ritual of the English Church, was the first cause of the appearance in England, long before it was known anywhere else in Western Europe, of the Feast of the Conception of the Blessed Virgin Mary. Essentially Eastern in origin, this Feast, with its ceremonies, was probably brought to England through King Canute's visit to Rome early in the eleventh century. Its implied doctrine that the Virgin herself had been conceived without taint of that original sin which is held by theologians to be essential to human nature was not accepted at once. But Eadmer, who was St Anselm's chaplain before the close of the eleventh century, set himself to explain and justify in simple language this philosophical doctrine. There were at the time many fantastic tales of miracles and marvels which were supposed to require and confirm the doctrine; but the Anglo-Saxon Eadmer, in his Latin treatise on the Conception of the Blessed Virgin Mary, *Tractatus de Conceptione Sanctae Mariae*, set himself to show that, for an ordinary Christian of simple and humble piety, the belief was implied clearly in the Scriptures themselves, and needed no miraculous tales or later authorities to justify it. He said that if John the Baptist and Jeremiah were "holy from the womb", as the New and the Old Testaments declare, then it would be both natural and reasonable for an ordinary pious believer to assume that at least the same must be true of the Virgin Mary, who was the very receptacle and chosen vehicle of the humanity of Christ. It was just the quite natural belief of those 'especially in whom there flourished a pure simplicity and very humble devotion towards God': *praecipue in quibus pura simplicitas et humilior in Deum vigebat devotio*. Discarding all the legends and apocryphal writings, Eadmer set up what one might call the interior miracle as against the external. Now, though Eadmer wrote all this in Latin, this attitude of his, with its practical working simplicity in religious matters, was characteristically Anglo-Saxon. It shows a turn of mind which to some extent has remained a feature of the English way of thought.[1]

---

[1] Eadmer's *tractatus* is in Migne, *Patrologia Latina*, Vol. 159, columns 301–318; and for a more modern edition see *Eadmeri Monachi Cantuariensis tractatus de conceptione sanctae Mariae*, ed. H. Thurstan S.J. and T. Slater S.J. (Freiburg, 1904). For valuable studies of the origins and history of the Feast in Britain, see the following: A. W. Burridge, "L'immaculée Conception dans la Théologie de l'Angleterre Médiévale", *Revue d'Histoire Ecclésiastique* XXXII (1936), pp. 570–597; H. Francis Davis, "The Origins of Devotion to Our Lady's Immaculate Conception", *The*

There is one religious poem, *The Dream of the Rood*, which seems to be an outstanding original creation, with its anticipation of the later medieval use of the dream-vision and of personification and its simple allegorical implications. It stands, however, alone, with its method in some respect looking forward in West European poetry to the thirteenth-century French *Roman de la Rose* and its multitude of followers; but probably its qualities are rather those of a nameless Anglo-Saxon poet of superb genius than characteristic of Anglo-Saxon culture in general. Other allegorical elements—and these do occasionally appear in Old English literature—are derived or translated from Latin Christian sources.

Enough has now been said to explain the suggestion that Anglo-Saxon culture shows in general the four characteristics (among others) of love of ordered ceremony and delicate sense of ornament, assimilative receptivity of foreign influence, a sense of continuity in conserving tradition, and delight in moralizing.

It was said at the beginning of the chapter that the term 'culture' had been taken to include the mind of a people as represented by its surviving monuments; and the suggestions so far made have come principally from one set of archaeological remains and from Anglo-Saxon art and literature. No attempt has been made to deal with Anglo-Saxon institutions such as the Laws, from which so much of the typically English common law has developed. Still less has any effort been made to reconstruct anything of the ways of Anglo-Saxon daily life. From archaeology one may learn something of the earliest English houses, with some aids from charters and other documents. From modern methods of aerial photography one may construct something of the Anglo-Saxon system of agriculture. From manuscript illustrations and carvings and sculptures we might deduce a good deal concerning the clothes that people of various ranks wore. Or one might explore the relationship between Anglo-Saxon architecture and Romanesque church-building. However, it has seemed best to limit discussion to those aspects of culture of which one may be able to form some fairly definite impressions, rather than to attempt to cover so vast a field. It should not in any way be assumed that the general characteristics here mentioned are the only notable ones, or that they can be regarded as even a fair—still less a properly classified—summary. The impressionistic method seemed on the whole the most convenient in a short space. With the lately quickened interest in archaeological remains, the immense value of archaeological treasures is beginning to be realized by the public. It will now be appreciated that there is an overwhelming significance in the Sutton Hoo ship-cenotaph and its treasures, and why it has been made the centre-piece of this chapter. It is for England the great archaeological

Dublin Review, Vol. 228, No. 465 (1954), pp. 375–392; S. J. D. Van Dijk, "The Origins of the Feast of the Immaculate Conception", *ibid.*, Vol. 228, No. 465, pp. 251–267, and No. 466, pp. 428–442.

discovery of our present century. It changes so much in the poem of *Beowulf* from poetic fantasy to historic reality, and it links Anglo-Saxon culture even with that of Byzantine Constantinople through its silver bowls and spoons.

The fact that Anglo-Saxon culture retained its vitality right up to and beyond the Norman Conquest is proved by the Bayeux tapestry, which is but the world-famous exemplar of the skill and beauty of that *opus Anglicanum*, 'English work', which was valued so highly throughout Europe long after the coming of the first Norman invaders. And it is perhaps fitting to end with illustrating once more this feature of vital continuity in a progressively adaptive and receptive tradition, which is a fundamental Anglo-Saxon characteristic.

Late in the Old English period there was composed a poem in which each of the runic letters is given explanations or descriptions of the meaning of its name. Of the runic symbol called *TIR*, which is the letter "T"', the poet says:

TIR biþ tacna sum:

T is a most important symbol.

Now, the shape of the Germanic runic "T" seems clearly to be derived from a Greek *TAU* (T). But the name of the rune, which means in Old English 'glory', is clearly a confused descendant of some form of the great Germanic ancestral deity's name which is represented in normal Anglo-Saxon as *Tiw*, whose name survives in many place-names where heathen worship lasted long after the conversion to Christianity, as well as in the modern *Tuesday*. This god Tiw, who appears as *TIR* in the name of the T-rune, is in fact that deity mentioned by Tacitus in his *Germania* in the form *Tuisco* or *Tuisto* as the divine ancestor of all the Germanic tribes. And naturally this rune *TIR* is especially auspicious and helpful in warfare, with its shape like the head of an arrow or javelin. Thus in this late Old English sentence we see ancient classical and Germanic cultures blending in a late form which still preserves the sense of pre-Christian magic: and the name of the ancestral Germanic deity has passed from a personal being to that glory in war which his memory could still provide. Nearly five centuries after the cutting of the secret magical runic words on the sheep's knuckle-bone at Caistor-by-Norwich, the memory of the auspicious deity of the T-rune was still living in this strong, simple verse.[1]

[1] The most efficient work containing the historical background of this chapter is Peter Hunter Blair, *An Introduction to Anglo-Saxon England* (Cambridge, 1956). This includes a workmanlike Select Bibliography. *Cf.* also Dorothy Whitelock, *The Beginnings of English Society*, vol. 2 of *The Pelican History of England* (London, 1952).

CHAPTER 2

On the Continuity
of English Poetry[1]

IN ANY EARLY LITERATURE poetry must be—both intrinsically and extrinsically—more important than prose. It also invariably develops far sooner and more rapidly. It seems appropriate, therefore, to devote a chapter to the continuing links of Anglo-Saxon poetry with modern English literature through the Middle Ages and the Renaissance. More especially did it seem right to emphasize verse in this matter of continuity in view of Chambers's definitive work on prose—for it will be observed that the title of this chapter is taken from a deservedly famous essay of one of the greatest of English literary scholars: *On the Continuity of English Prose*, by the late R. W. Chambers.[2] Indeed, Chambers had before his death projected a parallel essay for English poetry, which he did not live to prepare for publication.

Dryden's familiar statement that Chaucer was "the Father of English Poetry", made some two hundred and seventy years ago, though scarcely now echoed by any who have direct knowledge of earlier English literature, is still implicit in most textbooks that purport to cover the whole history of the subject. There is the famous denial of "Q" that *Beowulf* could have any relationship whatever with the poetry of our century; and a recent *Illustrated History of English Literature*, that of A. C. Ward, in effect rules out pre-Chaucerian poetry primarily because of its lack of continuity with what followed. While the question of continuity in prose could at least be clearly examined, as Chambers's essay has magnificently shown, poetry presents a far more complicated and difficult collection of material. Moreover, even Chambers found difficulty in avoiding some confusion between a continuity of thought and one of language; and the mid-twelfth-century *Peterborough Chronicle* is in fact far nearer to prose of our day in style and language than are the religious writings of the next century, on which he laid so much emphasis. For our tradition descended from the East rather than the West Midland region, as far

---

[1] The substance of this chapter appeared in *Anglia* LXXVI.
[2] *On the Continuity of English Prose from Alfred to More and his School:* first printed in *Harpsfield's Life of More*, ed. E. V. Hitchcock (EETS 186: London, 1932); separately reprinted (Oxford, 1957).

as language is concerned, though in the matter of thought there are marked links with the latter.

One of the most obvious and significant difficulties in treating of continuity in English poetry is the fact of the revolutionary effects of popular printing. Milton was probably the last great poet who deliberately wrote to be read aloud or recited. Printing had transferred poetry from the ears of an audience to the eyes of the reader—a fact which fundamentally changed its form and appeal. It will be clear, on the other hand, that prose literature would naturally have been far less subject to the effects of printing, though by no means immune. But enough has been said to indicate both the difficulty of the subject and the need for a discussion of it in particular poetic continuity.

Two rough methods of approach seem to suggest themselves at once. One might try to look into matters of continuity for English poetry under such heads as form, matter, and thought-process. Or again, one might consider the whole canvas of poetry in England through the ages, and seek to determine what qualities had been carried over from one age to the next. Let us see if some pursuance of these two lines of study might lead to a worth-while general impression.

Four general features of Old English culture, and therefore of its poetry, may be broadly listed as remarked in the preceding chapter:

- (*a*) a love of ordered ceremony and ornament;
- (*b*) a genius in the conservation of tradition;
- (*c*) gnomic moralizing, and
- (*d*) a remarkable power of adaptive assimilation.

Now, from a superficial glance at our poetry it would appear that all these features have in some measure been retained. Nevertheless, such elements of continuity are largely hidden from the view of the ordinary literary critic unacquainted with the earlier parts of English poetic technique, through two special causes. First, almost any poetry older than that of Chaucer—and even much of that contemporary with him written outside his own poetic tradition—can only be approached by such critics through the medium of so-called translations; and these for the most part can convey little more than the subject-matter. Indeed, Old English poetry is so much more intimately related to its special qualities of technique and language than is that of later periods that only a somewhat close study of its actual form can render its aesthetic features even to a limited extent transferable to the modern mind. That complete fusion and harmony of form and matter which is proper to great poetry, too, must almost inevitably be missed by the modern critic: and without its subtle shapes and meanings Old English poetry will scarcely seem poetry at all. Closely related to this kind of difficulty is the second cause of the inability of the modern to see any worthy continuity. This is what may be called the heresy of the subject-matter: that is, the judging of a poem by its subject-matter alone. Chaucer, for instance, is so often discussed as if he had written in prose, and *Piers Plowman* is criticized merely as if Langland had intended only to provide what in current jargon we term a 'social document'. Still more easily is such a poem as *Beowulf* read in translation as if it were nothing but a collection of tales of monsters and monstrous adventures. Barriers of language there must inevitably be in the study of a poetry with so long a history as that of England, covering as it does nearly thirteen centuries from the work of its first recorded poet Cædmon to our own day. But this kind of difficulty is especially marked in a culture whose thought and language have been so deeply—and at times suddenly—receptive of foreign influences. Yet such barriers of language are in some ways less profound than barriers of thought which exist—not only merely in Britain but throughout Western Europe—between one age and another.

Such obstacles as these barriers of language and thought—but even more, perhaps, this 'heresy of the subject-matter' which has been touched on above—make it a thing of extreme difficulty to grasp any concept of poetic continuity for England, since they appear to render it well-nigh impossible (in Matthew Arnold's phrase) to 'see it steadily and see it whole'. There is indeed great value as a safeguard against the heresy of the subject-matter in remembering Coleridge's saying that "the *immediate* object of poetry is pleasure, not truth". The *immediate* (as distinct from any deeper or more remote or ultimate) object of most Old English poets was the pleasurable entertainment of their audiences; and to a more limited extent this applies also to Middle English poetry. That is to say—among other things—that if the poem did not manage to afford pleasure *through its actual sounds* to its hearers it had not attained the poet's object, his *immediate* object.

R. W. Chambers, in an unpublished address to the Medieval Society at Oxford, suggested that Western European culture seemed in many ways to divide itself historically into three. These were first the *medieval period* in its widest sense, covering an epoch from the break-up of the Western Roman Empire to the time of the Tudor sovereigns; secondly the *modern age* in its widest sense, beginning with the sixteenth and seventeenth century Renaissance (if one may be old-fashioned enough to use a now outmoded term), with its rise of capitalism, individualism, national consciousness, etc., and ending with the reign of King Edward VII and the outbreak shortly after of the World War of 1914–18. Since that point, when the 'modern age' as thus defined may be said to have closed, Chambers regarded us all as being in an 'age of transition', whose characteristics are of necessity complex, fluctuating, and unclassifiable. St Francis of Assisi, he said, would have understood the thought of St Augustine of Hippo and the

Church Fathers of the early fifth century equally with that of Thomas More, who was the last great Englishman before the modern age: or again the Elizabethans would have been as well intelligible to the English Victorians. The members of the new Royal Society founded in London in 1662, however, would have found even Thomas More using a different language and thought-process; and our literary students of today quite fail to share common ground in basic thought-patterns with even the Victorian men who thought and wrote little more than sixty years ago. If this is anything like true, it follows that the student of earlier English poetry must learn not only a partly new language and a quite strange poetic technique of metre and diction, but also must acquire new ways of thinking and imagine new fundamental values. The student of medieval literature needs, therefore, not merely that "willing suspension of disbelief for the moment which constitutes poetic faith" (in the words of Coleridge), but must go further and seek to acquire imaginatively or simulate mentally an actively sympathetic belief in the postulates and assumptions of that 'Catholic' religious faith which both founded and dominated almost the whole of medieval poetry.

Bearing in mind, then, the above, and similar difficulties and barriers, we may well lose heart and ask whether indeed there can be any hope of discerning poetic continuity at all in so extended and vast a literature as English. But here Aristotle's famous description of poetry as being 'more philosophical and more nobly serious [φιλοσο-φώτερον καὶ σπουδαιότερον] than history' may suggest that the struggle is worth-while, and some result at least not improbable. Are there not, in other words, some basic thoughts and feelings in mankind which to some extent transcend the barriers of time and place and culture — some things which we may count upon finding in the poetry of *any* language above the most primitive? Is there not something, for instance, common in basic thought and feeling between the Old English exile's 'elegiac' meditation in *The Wanderer* and Gray's *Elegy*, or between the Old English sadness of *The Seafarer* and these lines of W. B. Yeats?

> You waves, though you dance by my feet like children at play,
> Though you glow and you glance, though you purr and you dart,
> In the Junes that were warmer than these are, the waves were more gay,
> *When I was a boy with never a crack in my heart.*[1]

Or one may compare the gnomic religious moral exhortations which so often end Old English poems, such as *The Wanderer* and *The Seafarer*, with Chaucer's lines in which he finally meditates hortatively on the tragedy of the loves of Troilus and Criseyde:

> O yonge, fresshe folkes, he or she,
> In which that love up groweth with youre age,

[1] *The Meditation of the Old Fisherman*, stanza 1.

Repeyreth hom fro worldly vanyte,
And of youre herte up casteth the visage
To thilke God that after his ymage
Yow made, and thinketh al nys but a faire
This world, that passeth soone as floures faire.[1]

But it may be said such 'continuity' is but general to most poetry, and is scarcely peculiar to English. Let us then, even with this vague beginning, look further for something more positive and defined.

But first another (though negative) type of thought-barrier must be touched on. Old English poetry has only the slightest treatment of love, and that almost impersonal, in the so-called *Wife's Lament*, *The Husband's Message*, and the fragment (also in the Exeter Book) *Wulf and Eadwacer*. As a poetic theme love is practically alien to the Germanic, and therefore to the Anglo-Saxon genius. For, as we learn very early from Tacitus's *Germania*, marriage is a practical, not an emotionally egocentric affair with the ancient Germanic peoples from whose stock the Anglo-Saxons had sprung, and among whom, he tells us, *Sera iuvenum venus*—young men's falling in love comes late.[2] It was not, indeed, till the contacts with Latin Romance civilization of the twelfth century that English poetry began to assimilate and take to itself something of that 'Latin' attitude towards love which has been productive of so much that is most purely poetical in the English lyric throughout its subsequent history. We must not, therefore, look for much continuity in love-poetry earlier than the twelfth century; though even here we should not forget that in Old English poetry *freond* may mean a *lover* and not merely a *friend*, as in prose and in the later language: so that when the 'Wife' in *The Wife's Lament* says that *frynd sind on eorþan* she is thinking that there are *lovers* in the world.[3]

Another question that may be asked before approaching our subject more narrowly is this: how far may poets of various periods be assumed to have had acquaintance with the work of their predecessors? Shelley, in his Preface to *The Revolt of Islam*, said that "A person familiar with nature, and with the most celebrated productions of the human mind, can scarcely err in following the instinct, with respect to selection of language, produced by that familiarity". Now, in this context "the most celebrated productions of the human mind" will mean primarily for the poet the best poetry of his forerunners. For the poet, in using language, is—consciously or unconsciously— influenced by the shades of meaning, the connotations and associ-

---

[1] *Troilus and Criseyde* V, 1835 ff., in *The Complete Works of Geoffrey Chaucer*, ed. F. N. Robinson, 2nd ed. (London, 1957). All references to Chaucer are to this edition.

[2] *Germania*, Cap. XX, 3; *cf*. Caesar, *De Bello Gallico*, Lib. VI, 24, 4.

[3] *The Wife's Lament*, line 33. ASPR III, p. 211. There is a convenient translation in N. Kershaw, *Anglo-Saxon and Norse Poems* (Cambridge, 1922).

ations, and the suggestive qualities of all the poetry he has ever read or heard: nothing is entirely lost that has ever entered the poet's mind. When Wordsworth, for example, wrote that little poem on the death of Lucy which Raleigh has supposed to illustrate the application of his theory of poetic language as set forth in his Preface to the *Lyrical Ballads*[1] he has been touched in concluding his second stanza by the subtle linguistic tone of Milton's *Paradise Lost*.

> A slumber did my spirit seal;
> I had no human fears:
> She seemed a thing that could not feel
> The touch of earthly years.
>
> No motion has she now, no force;
> She neither hears nor sees;
> Rolled round in earth's diurnal course
> With rocks, and stones, and trees.

Now in the use of the word *diurnal* in the penultimate line, while there is no precise echo of any *specific* passage of Milton, there is held a clear yet subtle suggestion of the linguistic atmosphere of *Paradise Lost*. Every poet—though in an infinite variety of degree—cannot but show some kind of continuity from his predecessors: and so we might suppose that it should be possible in some way, however slight, to discern a kind of continuous chain of links from one poet to another throughout English poetic history. Thus, for example, the Old English poet of *Andreas* saturates himself with echoes of *Beowulf* and of traditional heroic formulae, and the much later author of *Judith* has clearly felt in some degree the same influences: and even across the vast mutations of the Norman Conquest one can feel in the very tone of the homiletic moralizing of the late twelfth century *Poema Morale* something as it were 'tradited' from Hrothgar's moving sermon in *Beowulf* (1724 ff.). As late as the thirteenth century we find a religious poet who uses the new style and tone of his age describing the Mother of Christ in an alliterative traditional phrase which must have been of the diction of common Germanic poetry before the Anglo-Saxons ever came to Britain:

Bricht in bure and eke in halle[2]

for this epithet *bricht in bure* (bright in bower) is identical with the *björt í búre* of the Old Norse *Poetic Edda*, and must have been a common poetic inheritance of the Germanic peoples. In the metre and style of Gerard Manley Hopkins—to come to times near our own

---

[1] Sir W. Raleigh, *Wordsworth* (London, 1903), p. 111.
[2] From No. 61 (line 3) in Carleton Brown, *English Lyrics of the Thirteenth Century* (Oxford, 1932). *Cf.* The Poetic Edda, *Goðrúnarkviða hin forna*, line 2.

—one can easily hear something that the rhythms and diction of
Piers Plowman did to the poetic mind of a modern Jesuit.

Yet no one has told us clearly what predecessors in poetry influenced
Chaucer. In the West of England we can trace something of a
continuity in rhythm and diction from Old English through such a
poem as *Sir Gawain and the Green Knight* to Northern and Scottish
poetry of the Early Tudor period: but in the East the continuity eludes
us. What poetry had Chaucer read? How much nearer to our language
and poetic forms does he seem than any one of his contemporaries in
the traditional and conservative West Midlands! Though the old
notion that Chaucer's influence had moulded the English language
has long rightly been discarded, he may yet be properly regarded as
the 'father' of *modern* English poetry in as much as it was he more than
any other who acclimatized metres and a poetic pattern of a common
medieval Latin and French poetic diction in England. Through the
'aureate terms' of the fifteenth century, thence through Spenser and
Milton, we can trace the establishment in poetic convention of some
of those stock phrases against the use of which Wordsworth rebelled.
But between Chaucer and Old English poets it is hard to see any
connection which could properly be termed continuity, though with
some of his predecessors as far back as the thirteenth century he
seems to show some acquaintance. For example, the new and magical
set of ideas connoted by the romantic word 'Faerie' had made its
entry into English poetry through French Breton lays: and in fact
Spenser's famous phrase "lond of Faerie" is first recorded in the
Middle English Breton lay of *Sir Orfeo*.[1] Now, the romantic appeal
of this idea is clearly heard in the midst of the satiric realism of
Chaucer's *Sir Thopas*. For suddenly, as he begins his comic encounter
with Sir Thopas, the giant exclaims from his forest lair:

> "Heere is the queene of Fayerye,
> With harpe and pipe and symphonye,
> Dwellynge in this place."[2]

And Chaucer has, too, probably read his great Northern or West-
Midland contemporary the poet of *Sir Gawain and the Green Knight*.
For not only is there an echo of the description of King Arthur's
feast from *Sir Gawain* at the beginning of his *Squire's Tale*, but after
describing the knight on the steed of brass in a way calculated to
remind us of the entry of the Green Knight into King Arthur's hall,
Chaucer tells his audience that this knight's demeanour was such

> That Gawayn, with his olde curteisye,
> Though he were comen ayeyn out of Fairye,
> Ne koude him nat amende with a word.[3]

[1] *Sir Orfeo*, ed. A. J. Bliss (Oxford, 1954), line 562.
[2] *Sir Thopas* 814–816.
[3] *The Squire's Tale*, 95–97.

Nevertheless, it probably remains true that one cannot reach back from Chaucer to any point of poetry before the Norman Conquest, except in that general kind of continuity of tradition in thought which has already been touched upon as a feature extending throughout the Middle Ages, and for the occasional use of some traditional popular alliterative phrase. Twice, indeed, Chaucer makes use of a free kind of alliterative rhythm for the express purpose of describing battles—once in the great tournament in the *Knight's Tale*,[1] and once in the account of the battle of Actium during the treatment of Cleopatra in *The Legend of Good Women*.[2] This deliberate use of the traditional type of metre, however, does not look back to the poetic diction which went with it in Old English times, nor is the alliteration near to the Old English type in anything more than a very general sense:

> The helmes they tohewen and toshrede;
> Out brest the blood with stierne stremes rede;
> With myghty maces the bones they tobreste.
> He thurgh the thikkeste of the throng gan threste;
> Ther stomblen steedes stronge, and doun gooth al.[1]

In the forms of poetry, then (as distinct from matter and thought-pattern), it seems we must admit a gap in the East of England in our poetic continuity, and in this regard almost be prepared to think of Chaucer's work as ushering in a new age. But because modern literary English is largely based upon an Eastern type of language, the continuity will also cease in the West and North of England from the sixteenth century, when the dialects of those areas cease to have a separate literary existence, though some continuity will remain in Scotland in so far as a Scottish literary dialect may be held to have remained alive till at least the time of Burns.

Let us now, having dealt with these preliminary matters, look a little more narrowly at the question of continuity from the several points of view of form, subject-matter, and thought-pattern.

Broadly speaking, it may be said that English poetry during its medieval period exchanged the herioc and primarily Germanic diction which is the characteristic of Old English or Anglo-Saxon for one (which has remained in common use since Chaucer's days) which is a kind of Englishing of a common European diction of largely Latin origin. The sounds of the language too (and to some lesser extent its shapes) have greatly changed since Middle English times. If, then, we are to consider that external continuity in English poetry which relates to its *forms*, we should look for it in such matters as rhythm, metre, stress-patterns, etc. For the basic grammatical structure of English has not changed, despite multifarious changes in meaning and the vast overlaying of its vocabulary with words of mainly

---

[1] *The Knight's Tale*, 2609 ff. [2] *The Legend of Cleopatra*, 635 ff.

Romance origin; nor has its system of stress altered fundamentally. The metre has passed from one which was primarily dependent upon stress and that kind of internal rhyming of the initial sounds of words which we call alliteration to one which is partly syllabic, but yet retains a good deal of the older stress patterns; and the rhyming of final syllables has generally replaced internal alliteration. Despite the tendency of the schoolmasters to scan modern verse as if it consisted of the quantitative iambs, trochees, and dactyls of Latin and Greek metre, the patterns of ordinary English metres are mainly a matter of stress which is variable in the ratio of number to the line, rather than purely of syllable. The opening lines, for example, of Chaucer's Prologue to the *Canterbury Tales* show considerable variation in the number of emphatic syllables to the line, though the number of syllables is more constant without being at all rigid:

> Whan that Áprill with his shóures sóote
> The dróghte of Márch hath pérced to the róote,
> And báthed évery véyne in swích licóur
> Of which vertú engéndred is the flóur;
> Whan Zéphirus éek with his swéete bréeth
> Inspíred hath in évery hólt and héeth
> The téndre cróppes, and the yónge sónne
> Hath in the Rám his hálve cóurs yrónne,
> And smále fóweles máken mélodýe,
> That slépen ál the nýght with ópen ýe
> (So príketh hem natúre in hir coráges);
> Thanne lóngen fólk to góon on pílgrimáges.

It will be noticed if this passage is read aloud how the stresses vary in number, as well as that there is a relative freedom in the syllabic pattern which is not so remote from that of older English. Though Chaucer's contemporary Langland was using a free variety of the traditional alliterative metre inherited from the oral traditions of earlier times, it will again be noticed how his syllabic pattern, despite the adherence to alliteration, seems partly to look forward to modern rhythm:

> In a somer seson whan soft was the sonne,
> I shope me in shroudes as I a shepe were,
> In habite as an heremite unholy of workes,
> Went wyde in this world wondres to here.
> Ac on a May mornynge on Maluerne hulles
> Me byfel a ferly, of fairy me thoughte.[1]

It has often been remarked that English metre combines elements from both Germanic and Latin Romance sources: and a comparison between the two passages just cited—the one from Chaucer and the

---

[1] *Piers Plowman*, B version, Prologue 1–6.

other from his West-Midland contemporary Langland—brings this
out clearly. Again, in the metre of another of Chaucer's contemporaries, the poet of *Pearl* and of *Sir Gawain and the Green Knight*, one
can see the old alliterative internal rhyming of the initial sounds of
stressed syllables combined with modern final rhyming in a stanzaic
pattern, and in *Pearl* in a shorter line than that of Anglo-Saxon.
Listen to the opening stanza of *Pearl*:

> Perle, plesaunte to Prynces paye
> To clanly clos in golde so clere,
> Oute of oryent, I hardyly saye,
> Ne proued I neuer her precios pere.
> So rounde, so reken in vche araye,
> So smal, so smoþe her sydeȝ were.
> Queresoeuer I jugged gemmeȝ gaye,
> I sette hyr sengeley in synglere.
> Allas! I leste hyr in on erbere;
> Þurȝ gresse to grounde hit from me yot.
> I dewyne, fordolked of luf-daungere
> Of þat pryuy perle wythouten spot.[1]

But in fact the device of combining final rhyme with alliteration had
been practised in Anglo-Saxon times, both sporadically and in such
a full-length piece as the *Rhyming Poem* of the Exeter Book, whose
didactic style and method anticipate a good deal of the more moralizing religious lyric poetry of the thirteenth century.

The truth is probably, however, simply that the main patterns of
stress in English have continued with relatively little change all
through its history. Now, since the prosodic patterns of Old English
poetry were primarily a selection of the more dignified and emphasized
patterns of actual speech, continuity in form for English poetry, in so
far as we may be sure of observing it, must be regarded as very
largely due to a fundamental continuity in the actual stress-patterns
of the language. Yet the changes in metre touched upon in the foregoing remarks can be seen to overlap and to merge to some extent
into one another. Moreover, though alliteration has long since disappeared from poetry as an integral part of its form, poets have until
our own time continued to use it on occasions as a means of special
aesthetic effect—apart from the survival of some alliterative phrases
in common speech to this day. Thus, for instance, Swinburne often
made deliberate use of alliteration as one of the artistic devices in
what one might call his more merely musical verse, such as his
Dolores. Here we find such lines as

> For the crown of our life as it closes
> Is darkness, the fruit thereof dust:

---

[1] *Pearl*, ed. E. V. Gordon (Oxford, 1953), lines 1–12.

or again in a more obvious strain,

> Could you hurt me, sweet lips, though I hurt you?
>   Men touch them, and change in a trice
> The lilies and languors of virtue
>   For the raptures and roses of vice.

One may conclude, then, that despite the changes of sound and meaning and choice of words on the one hand, and the partial re-orientation of the metre on the other, there is a real continuity in form, though of a limited kind. *Piers Plowman,* as illustrated by the opening lines of its Prologue already quoted, looks back to *Beowulf* in its metre; for these lines keep the rules of Anglo-Saxon verse-structure in rhythm and alliteration well. But they at the same time look forward also, even to our own days, in their shorter lines and partially syllabic pattern. Incidentally, it may be added that these particular lines show no actual difference in choice of words from the modern, apart from changes of meaning: and they would be quite intelligible to any educated English hearer of today if one read them in our contemporary pronunciation.

Let us now look for continuity in subject-matter.

Of the four characteristics of Anglo-Saxon culture which were mentioned earlier in this chapter, two have made for continuity in form of poetry—namely, its capacity for ordered ceremony and ornament and that for conservation of tradition. A third, its power and adaptive assimilation of heterogeneous material from outside, has probably had an influence against continuity. But in the study of continuity of *matter*, the love of moralizing which is so marked a feature of Anglo-Saxon poetry has on the whole remained constant: so that it may be said at the outset that there is a continuing didactic strain throughout English poetry. Especially has this moralizing taken the form of the casual elegiac meditation on mortal transitoriness and death. Compare this famous passage from an Anglo-Saxon poem *The Wanderer,* for example, with the still more famous soliloquy of Macbeth on life and death. Here are the two passages:

> "Hwær cwom mearg? Hwær cwom mago? Hwær cwom maþþum-gyfa?
> Hwær cwom symbla gesetu? Hwær sindon sele-dreamas?
> Eala beorht bune! Eala byrn-wiga!
> Eala þeodnes þrym! Hu seo þrag gewat,
> genap under niht-helm, swa heo no wære."

A rough rendering of this is

> "Whither has gone the steed, whither the man who rode him?
> Whither has gone the lord who rewarded with treasure?
> Whither have gone the sittings at the feasting? Where
> are the revellings in hall? Alas for the shining goblet,

alas for the warrior in his armour! Woe for the glory of the prince!
How that time has passed away, grown dark 'neath the shades of
night as if it had never been."[1]

And Macbeth's meditation:

> To-morrow, and to-morrow, and to-morrow,
> Creeps in this petty pace from day to day,
> To the last syllable of recorded time;
> And all our yesterdays have lighted fools
> The way to dusty death. Out, out brief candle!
> Life's but a walking shadow, a poor player
> That struts and frets his hour upon the stage,
> And then is heard no more.[2]

Why is it that Gray's *Elegy Written in a Country Churchyard* is perhaps the best known of all English poems? Is it not—partly, at least—
because it expresses just this type of moralizing? In the more personal
modern idiom made possible by the juxtaposition of the Germanic
and Latin Romance civilizations, there is an essential similarity with
W. B. Yeats's free rendering of the French "Sonnet pour Hélène" of
Ronsard, beginning "When you are old and grey". And it will be
noticed if one compares the French original with the Englishing of
Yeats how he uses the French poem to some extent in its general ideas
and setting till he comes to the final couplet, but then turns away to
a quite different sombre meditation. Ronsard ends his poem with the
admonition of the lover to his lady:

> Vivez, si m'en croyez; n'attendez à demain;
> Cueillez dès aujourd'hui les roses de la vie.

For this Latin sentiment inherited from Catullus, Yeats substitutes:

> And bending down beside the glowing bars,
> Murmur, a little sadly, how Love fled
> And paced upon the mountains overhead
> And hid his face amid a crowd of stars.

Old English poetry had been basically religious—and this has remained true to some extent of English poetry throughout its history,
whether the religious quality were specifically Christian or not. All
the secularizing influences from the Renaissance onward have not—
at least till our own age of transition—prevented a continuity in this
fundamental feature. Old English poetry lacked mysticism; and this
was supplied from the continent of Europe through Richard Rolle of
Hampole in the fourteenth century, and remained one of the English
poetic elements. We see it in the so-called metaphysical poets of the
seventeenth century, in Wordsworth, or in Yeats: and it continued

---

[1] *The Wanderer*, 92 ff. ASPR III, p. 136.
[2] *Macbeth*, Act 5, Sc. 5, line 19 ff.

in our own days in T. S. Eliot. One must, of course, always remember
Eliot's despairing reflection when contemplating the problem of
poetic language:

> For last year's words belong to last year's language
> And next year's words await another voice.[1]

Mysticism, like love, had to wait for the coming to England of new
cultural streams from Europe; but once received into the poetic mind
of the country, it too has preserved something of continuity.

Another aspect of subject-matter which has remained and multi-
plied from Old English poetry throughout English poetic history is
the simple expression of natural pleasure in external nature. It is
much the same in the opening lines of *Piers Plowman* already quoted,
in the more personal expression of Chaucer's Prologue to the *Legend
of Good Women*, in Elizabethan lyrics, or in Browning's

> Oh, to be in England
> Now that April's there,

from his *Home Thoughts, from Abroad*. Even Gerard Manley Hopkins, who seems to have anticipated much that was strong in the
poetry of the last half-century, with all his special complex sensitivity
and gnarled tricks of language, can show the same fundamental
approach to nature-poetry in his *Harry Ploughman*. Not only does his
delight in so narrowly observing the physical qualities of the ploughman look back to Middle English in its use of 'sprung rhythm' and
queerly archaic vocabulary, but the basic feeling for natural beauty
is yet of that simple kind which Chaucer shared with Langland.

Now this simple kind of nature-poetry already existed to some
extent in Anglo-Saxon times, though for the most part it was the more
startling and impressive natural phenomena that appealed sym-
bolically to the Old English poets, much as they did to Thomas
Hardy. Yet just as one may hear the poets of the thirteenth century
echoing the moralizings of *Beowulf* or of Cynewulf, so too that same
century produced simple lyrics of joy in nature which only enlarged
something already felt by some Anglo-Saxon poets. In *Beowulf*,
when winter has passed and spring brings the breaking of the ice in
the Northlands, the poet tells us:

> Holm storme weol,
> won wið winde; winter yþe beleac
> is-gebinde, oþðæt oþer com
> gear in geardas, swa nu gyt do-ið,
> þa ðe syngales sele bewitiað,
> wuldor-torhtan weder. Ða wæs winter scacen,
> fæger foldan bearm.

[1] *Four Quartets* (London, 1944), Little Gidding II.

The sea boiled in storm, fought 'gainst the wind; winter had enclosed
the waves with a binding of ice, until another Spring came to the
dwellings of men, just as it still does now—those gloriously bright
seasons which continuously carry out their cycles. Then had winter
gone hurrying away; and earth's bosom became fair.[1]

It is at least arguable that there is a real continuity between such a
passage and the well-known spring-song from the thirteenth-century
lyric in the Harley collection *Lencten is come wiþ Loue to toune*, where
indeed the very expression *to toune* means literally "to the dwelling"
and serves to fill out the line in precisely the same way as the corresponding *in geardas* of the *Beowulf* passage. In the devotional poem to
the Blessed Virgin Mary called *On God Ureisun of Ure Lefdi* in MS.
Cotton Nero A XIV Paradise is described very simply in terms of
familiar earthly nature in words that almost seem to echo the Anglo-
Saxon poem of *The Phoenix*:

> þer ðe neure deað ne com, ne herm ne sorinesse.
> þer bloweð inne blisse blostmen hwite and reade;
> þer ham neuer ne mei snou ne uorst iureden;
> þer ne mei non ualuwen, uor þer is eche sumer;
> Ne non liuinde þing woc þer nis ne ȝeomer.

There where neither death nor injury nor sadness have come.
There blossoms bloom in bliss, both white and red; there neither
snow nor frost may be felt by them, nor may any of them grow
yellow and wither: for there it is eternal summer; and no living thing
there is feeble or grieved.[2]

The Old English poem on *The Phoenix*, though largely a free adaptation from a Latin original, here shows its poet's own pleasure in
just the same *simple* things of nature:

> Ne mæg þer ren ne snaw,
> ne forstes fnæst, ne fyres blæst,
> ne hægles hryre, ne hrimes dryre,
> ne sunnan hætu, ne sincaldu,
> ne wearm weder, ne winterscur
> wihte gewyrdan, ac se wong seomað
> eadig ond onsund. Is þæt æþele lond
> blostmum geblowen.

There is no disaster may be caused by rain or snow, nor by the
breath of frost, nor the blast of fire, nor the fall of hail nor hoar-
frost, nor the sun's heat nor lasting cold, nor hot tempests nor storms

---

[1] *Beowulf*, 1131 ff.
[2] *On God Ureisun of Ure Lefdi*, 36 ff. This poem and the *Poema Morale* are
included in *Selections from Early Middle English*, ed. J. Hall (Oxford, 1920).

of winter. But the whole region remains blessed and healthful.
That excellent land is filled with blossoms in bloom.[1]

For this continuing poetic approach to Nature one might compare
Hopkins's *Heaven-Haven*:

> I have desired to go
> Where springs not fail. . .

But enough has been said to show that there is at least some clear
continuity in the subject-matter of English poetry from the times of
the Anglo-Saxons onward, and not merely from Chaucer's day: and
it would scarcely be profitable to attempt anything like a complete
picture or a thorough examination. The heroic and didactic themes
of Old English poetry have long been exchanged for others; but these
strands of continuity remain.

It is not easy to feel at all sure of how much continuity there may
be in thought-processes, in so far as these may be distinguished from
subject-matter. Diction, word-meanings, and the background of
thought have changed in the course of the ages, and vast new fields of
thought and the vocabulary to express them have come into English.
The substitution of printing, too, for manuscript—with its con-
sequential replacing of audiences by readers—must certainly have
entailed profound changes in mental approach. Many will also feel
that there has been since the "Age of Enlightenment" and its consequences a contracting of spiritual capacities in those who now read
what poets write. For instance, the allegory, which was so fundamental an expression for the Middle Ages for realities beyond the
world of matter, has long ceased to be an effective or properly intelligible vehicle for poetry, though some types of symbolism have
increased. The allegoric method which seemed necessary and natural
to Langland had been used by the Anglo-Saxons: and indeed some of
its devices, such as the dream-vision and the personification of objects
had been magnificently employed in the Old English *Dream of the
Rood* in a way which looks forward to the medieval *Romance of the
Rose* and its numerous offspring. But already Langland's more profound spiritual quality makes the allegory of Chaucer seem to be
merely external where Langland's is integral; and with Spenser there
is something clearly self-conscious in the allegoric devisings of the
Faerie Queene.

That magical, mysterious kind of imaginative thought which came to
English poetry through the French of the Celtic Breton lays was in
some sense a contribution of the Celtic mind to English, and there is
no clear sign of it among the Anglo-Saxons: so that here again we
must think of continuity only since the thirteenth century. The
imaginative gift of 'Faerie' to English poetry is, therefore, only another instance of that multitudinous enlargement of English poetic

---

[1] *The Phoenix*, 14 ff. ASPR III, p. 94.

thought which seems to have been a continuous process from the earliest Saxon times up until the beginning of our age of transition.

Thought-process, like intonation in a language, cannot be expressed with any real clarity; and for this reason it must not be pursued at all narrowly. In the great poetry form and subject-matter are inseparably integrated; and it is the poet's thought-process which makes this integration. One cannot often make a clear division between form, matter, and thought—at least, in the work of great poets. Consider, for example, these single lines, the one from Chaucer's *Troilus and Criseyde* (in the passage already quoted), and the other from Hamlet's words to Horatio:

> Repeyreth hom fro worldly vanyte:
>
> Absent thee from felicity awhile.[1]

This latter, it is worth remarking, was chosen by Matthew Arnold as an example of the kind of single line which might be used as a touchstone for detecting really great poetry, or poetry in the 'grand style'. Now, the pattern of these two single lines is identical in syllable and stress; and their style seems also to be exactly alike. Wherein, then, lies the difference? Or would Matthew Arnold—who does not seem to have paid much attention to Chaucer's poetry outside of *The Canterbury Tales*—have recognized the line from *Troilus and Criseyde* as having the same great qualities as that from *Hamlet*? If so, perhaps he would not have denied his quality of "high seriousness" to Chaucer. But what, then, is the distinction between the two single lines? Their matter is very similar. Must it not therefore lie somewhere in difference of thought-process? But here is intended only an illustrative puzzle, not a solution.

It is natural that the greatest gaps in continuity of ways of thinking should have some relation to the great division between the medieval period and the modern epoch which ended when our present transitional period began: so that here the Renaissance will probably turn out to be the rough dividing-line. After the Reformation, and all that went with it in Western Europe, even the texture of men's thoughts changed so profoundly that, for example, men of Dryden's age could not in general understand the thought-processes or the metre of Langland, or even of Chaucer. Whereas in the things which belong to language and subject-matter there is a continuity of many kinds easily to be noticed in English poetry from Chaucer onward—thus bridging to some extent all the revolutionary happenings of the sixteenth and seventeenth centuries—the changes in ways of thinking, the intellectual and especially the spiritual climate, had been so transformed in the Tudor period that those deeper aspects of thinking and feeling in which the poet deals must of necessity show far less 'patternable' and far more uncertain threads of continuity than either

[1] *Hamlet*, Act 5, Sc. 2, line 361.

external form or actual subject-matter. Moreover, as has been seen,
one can scarcely effectively separate for the purposes of such an
investigation the processes of thought from those of choice of subject-
matter.

Impressionistically, however, one may safely say that T. S. Eliot in
fact incurred that debt to the thought of the 'metaphysical' poets of
the seventeenth century which he himself acknowledged; or that Mr
Ezra Pound has acquired something—however tenuous or miscon-
ceived—from direct reading of Anglo-Saxon poetry such as that which
produced his new poem erroneously called a translation of *The
Seafarer*. But such things are to be regarded as instances of poets
deliberately looking back rather than as examples of continuity. It is
nevertheless true, as already remarked, that a strong capacity for
conserving traditional ways of thinking, as well as of forms, is a definite
English characteristic inherited through the ages from the Anglo-
Saxons; and neither the Reformation nor the Cromwellian Rebellion
of the seventeenth century was able to change the fundamental
English preference for gradual rather than sudden change, for incomplete rather than consummated revolution. But because of the
absence of sufficient written poetry between the Norman Conquest
and Chaucer, we are not able to say anything of thought-continuity
in that period, though the gap suggested by the jejune written
monuments may in fact be illusory. Nevertheless, at least from the
thirteenth century onward examples of thought-continuity can be
found, though the process may be uneven and obscure.

One may now, perhaps, be in a position to ask what are the aspects
of English poetry that have endured continuously through the ages.
Clearly the longest threads are of outward form, in the survival of
something of the syllabic structure and stress-patterns of Anglo-
Saxon poetry to this day, despite changes of every kind that have
made its language unintelligible except to the student or really keen
amateur. Though our chief metres and to some extent our poetic
diction go back only to Chaucer, there is yet this kind of continuity
from the days of Cædmon. Subject-matter too has in some ways
bridged the ages, though the Anglo-Saxon poets had their Germanic
practical independence of love and mysticism. The moralizing of the
poet of *Beowulf* in Hrothgar's simple but profound and moving
homily of farewell to Beowulf[1] is matter so often echoed by the
religious lyric poets of the thirteenth century, and yet would have
seemed entirely natural to Gray (who had, however, some knowledge
of the older poetry). Poets have continued, however inhibited by the
vicissitudes of reform and revolution, to express their simple pleasures
in natural objects in a way that the poet of *Beowulf*, Langland, Milton,
and Wordsworth could all have shared. Nor have the elegiac tones
of the Anglo-Saxon poets ceased to have parallels throughout

[1] *Beowulf*, 1700 ff, especially 1724 ff.

English poetic history. Because of the English capacity for adaptive assimilation of new material, much, on the other hand, has come into English poetry in the process of time that cannot be seen at all in its earliest phases. But such new foreign material or method, once accepted, has usually remained as a source of a continuity thereafter unbroken.

In this chapter the attempt has been made to indicate some of the threads of differing kinds that may be seen running throughout English poetry from the seventh to the twentieth century. And of one thing at least the reader will be convinced—that there is a sense in which English poetry, from *Beowulf* to T. S. Eliot, is a whole, and that there is value in trying to look at it as a whole—that the concept of continuity suggested by R. W. Chambers is worth exploring.

CHAPTER 3

Form and Style in Anglo-Saxon Literature

IT WILL HAVE BECOME CLEAR from the preceding chapters that the special and individual qualities of Anglo-Saxon literature must chiefly be looked for in its forms and styles. While in much of its substance this literature conforms to general tendencies in medieval European writing, its methods of presenting this common type of subject-matter both give it its lasting value and furnish the modern student with his principal difficulties through a kind of aesthetic remoteness. Centuries before the rise of a vernacular prose in any other Germanic language, Old English had advanced far in literary prose in the more mature writings of King Alfred, and had developed some outstanding prose-styles in the later period of the Benedictine Revival in the hands of Ælfric, Wulfstan, and the author of the romance of *Apollonius of Tyre*. In verse, while sharing a common Germanic type of rhythm, metre, and poetic diction, it had been by a long way the first in the field in point of time, and had quickly developed separate qualities of high poetic potentiality. It is, so to speak, a law of nature that the oral making of verse arises early in the history of a people's culture, whereas prose can only develop in a relatively maturing state of civilization when the art of writing, as distinct from oral tradition, has begun to serve utilitarian and didactic purposes. Religion, magic, the natural rhythms of work and of the seasons, all ask for poetry and song or chant from virile human beings in a natural state of living; while the writing of prose normally comes much later as the result of deliberate and conscious effort. It follows, therefore, that it is in their poems that men develop most fully and naturally the inner and individual qualities of their language, and that aesthetic excellences, if found at all, are to be sought in the verse rather than the prose of an early stage of literature. For these and similar reasons, then, verse rather than prose must receive the first and more considerable attention of the student of Old English literature.[1]

Throughout the Old English period the basic patterns of its verse—

[1] *Cf.* H. M. and N. Chadwick, *The Growth of Literature*, Vol. I (Cambridge, 1932).

its metre, rhythm, and diction—remained constant, though there were developments in licence and innovation, especially in its later phases. As time went on, the rules of alliteration and stress—the two fundamental principles—tended to relax, and to some extent rhyme and assonance were blended with alliteration; while some of the verbal machinery of heroic oral formulaic tradition,[1] designed for the description of noble warfare, was replaced by conventional formulae appropriate to religious or hagiographical matters. Yet almost the whole of the poetry, whether fragmentary or complete, heroic or homiletic, popular, learned, or aristocratic, has come down to us in one and the same metre and diction throughout.

What then is known for certain, and what may be inferred, of this metre and diction? Poetic vocabulary and style were exceptionally remote from those of ordinary speech, as well as from those of more formal prose, though the rhythm was the result of an apparently unconscious selection of rhetorically emphasized speech-patterns. From descriptions and references concerning the techniques of Old Icelandic poetry, such as Snorri Sturluson's thirteenth-century treatise and the poetic *Edda*,[2] we are able to reconstruct much of the rules which must have governed earlier common Germanic verse: but in Old English itself there exists nothing but a few slight and doubtful references to poetic technique.

That the *scop*[3] or poet accompanied his recitations in early times on the harp is attested by Bede's famous account of Cædmon,[4] and this is borne out by a number of casual allusions in *Beowulf* and other poems,[5] as well as by the preservation of the small model of a royal harp in the Sutton Hoo collection. To such external evidences must be added the primary internal evidence of the basic material patterns demonstrated through a thorough statistical survey of

---

[1] See Francis P. Magoun, Junior, "Oral-Formulaic Character of Anglo-Saxon Narrative Poetry", *Speculum* XXVIII (1953), 11, 446 ff.

[2] A convenient volume, which includes Snorri's work on the poetic art, is *Edda Snorra Sturlusonar*, ed. Guðni Jónsson (Reykjavík, 1949). For the Poetic Edda see the edition of Finnur Jónsson, *Sæmundar-Edda, Eddukvæði* (Reykjavík, 1926).

[3] *Scop* is the regular Old English word for 'poet'. It can hardly be etymologically related to the verb *scieppan* (pret. *scōp*) 'to create', but seems to belong rather to the group represented by Old Norse *skop*, 'mockery' (Old High German *scoph*, etc.) From the idea of satirical verse the word may have come to be applied to all kinds of poets. Cf. *scoff*.

[4] *Historia Ecclesiastica* IV, 24, where the Latin *cantare* is rendered in the Old English version *be hearpan singan*.

[5] E.g. *Beowulf* lines 89–90 and 2458–2459, *Seafarer* line 44, and especially *The Fortunes of Men*, 80 ff. (ASPR III, p. 156):

> Sum sceal mid hearpan æt his hlafordes
> fotum sittan, feoh þicgan,
> ond a snellice snere wræstan,
> lætan scralletan sceacol, se þe hleapeð,
> nægl neomegende; biþ him neod micel.

Beowulf, first by Sievers in 1885, and studies of the rhythm of the corpus poeticum.[1]

Old English had a fairly elaborate system of metrical patterns and a poetic diction inherited and developed from a common Germanic tradition. This tradition continued to be based on the assumption of oral recitative, and hence made much use of those formulaic devices which in most languages serve to aid the memory of the reciter.[2] The scop, or composer and reciter of poetry, was probably originally an aristocratic warrior reciting with an inherited accepted technique to a trained and receptive audience of the same type as himself. For the most part the surviving verse is aristocratic in tradition, implying a high degree of inherited culture and technical knowledge in poet and audience. That there was also a more popular or 'folk' poetry we know from Bede's account of Cædmon: for here we learn that a peasant cultivator might have been expected to declaim in the *convivia* of his fellows when the harp would be passed round to each in turn for a recitation. One may speculate on this more popular poetry, which would have been less technical than what has survived; but since it did not generally, as it were, get itself written down, our comments on metre must perforce be confined to what may be inferred from the corpus poeticum extant. The miracle of the poet Cædmon which Bede meant to convey was, not that a herdsman suddenly could make poetry (since that would have been quite natural in the Northumbria of those days), but rather that an ignorant peasant should in a single night acquire the power of expressing a given subject in the aristocratic rhythm and poetic diction which only years of absorption of inherited tradition and training could be supposed to have rendered possible.[3] Cædmon had in his remembered vision achieved the revolutionary miracle of applying to the new Biblical material the traditional aristocratic heroic metrical technique, and the traditional heroic diction of pre-Christian times, with its formulaic vocabulary which had developed for the description of the heroism of war.

What then is the rhythm and diction of this poetry? Its two basic principles of metre are those of stress or emphasis in the construc-

---

[1] See the two long articles "Zur Rhythmik des germanischen Alliterationsverses" in Paul-Braune's *Beiträge zur Geschichte der deutschen Sprache und Literatur*, X (1885), and the later work *Altgermanische Metrik* (Halle, 1893), which is the basis of most accounts of his five-type theory. He modified his views in favour of a more musical outlook, but with a very personal attitude, in *Ziele und Wege der Schallanalyse* (Heidelberg, 1924) and in "Zu Cynewulf" in *Neusprachliche Studien, Festgabe für Karl Luick* (Vienna, 1925). A convenient English account of the 'orthodox' view of Old English metre is in J. Schipper, *A History of English Versification* (Oxford, 1910), a translation of his *Grundriss der englischen Metrik* (Vienna, 1895). For an able defence of Sievers's types with a modern approach, see A. J. Bliss, *The Metre of Beowulf* (Oxford, 1960).

[2] See Magoun, *op. cit.*

[3] See C. L. Wrenn, "The Poetry of Cædmon", *Proceedings of the British Academy* XXXII (1946), pp. 277–295.

tion of the patterns of its half-line, which is the metrical unit, and secondly of alliteration, or the rhyming of initial sounds internally, as the method of uniting the two half-lines in the ears of their hearers. A selection of the speech-patterns felt to be suitable for poetry, somewhat formalized by the needs of rhetorical emphasis, seems to be what lies behind the half-line; and Sievers in 1885 demonstrated by a statistical study of *Beowulf* that these stress- or pitch-patterns are in fact five basic combinations of stress or lift of the voice, half or secondary stress or half-lift, and unstressed syllables in which the voice is sunk or dropped. It is now clear, as J. C. Pope has very fully demonstrated,[1] that Sievers's classification of five types of half-line— which is still found the most widely convenient for the student— is inadequate because it ignores the musical side of the verse, and confuses grammatical with metrical quantity, thus encouraging a purely artificial and less natural method of reciting. Nevertheless, Sievers's five types are in fact a correct description of the metrical patterns, and remain the generally accepted basis of metrical textual study. Certainly an Old English poem was musical in its nature, as is suggested by such terms for it as *leoð*, 'song'; and a true method of reciting must imply conscious recognition of the tempo of music. It is also true that musical pitch and stress-emphasis are inevitably confused in the traditional Sievers notation. But the accompaniment by the harp, which Pope found necessary to explain, producing what he regarded as a proper musical notation for *Beowulf*, is something too remote from practical demonstration to be called into use; and the Sutton Hoo harp, when reconstructed by the addition of its missing soundboard, gives forth a scarcely adequate sound. No doubt, when the essential patterns are grasped and the alliteration which 'rhymes' the two halves of the line is fully brought out in reading or reciting, the verse of *Beowulf* can be made to approximate to what was intended in effect, though without the key to its finer music it must sound unduly formalized, like the iambs and trochees of modern English verse as described in older text-books.

One may think of a syllable as having degrees of 'emphasis' (the usual sense of 'stress'), 'pitch', or height of musical tone, and 'duration,' or length of time in utterance. Emphasis and pitch generally go together, and may for practical purposes be taken as coinciding. Duration frequently corresponds with stress, but by no means invariably: a stressed syllable is commonly but not necessarily 'long'; but an unstressed syllable may be 'long' historically, and a 'short' syllable may be the root-syllable of a noun or other naturally emphatic word, and therefore carry the main stress. Metrically, a stressed and a high-toned syllable are conveniently to be taken as the same thing, and the term 'lift' (Sievers's *Hebung*) will be used for

---

[1] J. C. Pope, *The Rhythm of Beowulf* (Yale Univ. Press, 1942). This outstanding and thorough work includes a review of all the important previous theories, as well as providing a new and valuable application of musical notation to the poem.

it in what follows. Such lifts or primary stresses naturally occur in formal or rhetorical speech on the root-syllables of nouns and adjectives, and may in appropriate contexts fall also on finite verbs. They may also arise on strongly emphasized pronouns and adverbs, but not otherwise on these last two. Prefixes are naturally weakly stressed or low-toned, unless they dominate the meaning, as in such a word as *únriht*, 'wrong'. Prepositions and conjunctions, as well as adverbs and pronouns not specially emphatic, are normally part of the 'drop'. Any number of unstressed syllables, from one upward, are taken together metrically as an unstressed or low-toned group, and will be termed a 'drop' (Sievers's *Senkung*). The second element of a normal compound word of noun + noun or noun + adjective naturally has a 'lift' on its root syllable which is less in force than that on the root-syllable of the first element which takes a strong or primary stress. This lesser yet marked stress is termed a 'half-lift' (Sievers's *Nebenton*). It may be seen clearly by comparing such a pair of Modern English words as 'sheep-dog' and 'sheepish'. Here 'dog' is less emphatic than 'sheep', yet it retains a good deal more force than the final syllable of 'sheepish' because it is still felt to be to some extent meaningful. A few syllables which form the second elements of words in Old English also may be regarded as half-lifts, because they retain something in meaning which is distinctive: such are *-ing* in the patronymics like *æðeling* and *Scēfing*, and the *-end-* in present participles. But any half-lift may count also as either full lift or mere drop if in a given context the metrical pattern requires it. Thus, for instance, in the half-line *Oft Scýld Scēfing* in *Beowulf*, line 4, the two lifts are on the root-forms of the two nouns *Scyld* and *Scēf*, and the *-ing*, though grammatically a 'long' syllable and normally a half-lift, is only the drop. Finite verbs, too, may take the *half-lift* on their root syllables, especially in types D and E. Sievers divided each half-line into two 'feet', doubtless under classical influence; and this is often quite artificial and musically unnatural, especially in compound words occurring in types B and C. Yet his arrangement is often convenient, and is still commonly accepted. In what follows Sievers's five-type classification is taken as the basis, though somewhat simplified and modified so as to avoid the danger of confusing quantity of syllable with stress.

Taking the acute accent as the mark of the lift, the grave for half-lift, and using the sign × for each of the syllables that form the drop, we get the following five patterns or types for the half-line. For each the simplest example is given in Old English, followed by Modern English approximate renderings designed to show the positions of the stresses: for generally the stress-patterns of Old English still survive today. While the Old English 'quantity' is indicated where it is historically 'long', it is to be remembered that it is always stress or pitch, not length of syllable, which determines the metrical pattern, so that a 'long' syllable often will form a drop.

or part of a drop. All the examples are taken from *Beowulf*.[1] A vertical line divides the 'feet'.

Type A ´ x | ´ x *lángĕ | áhtĕ*   'lóng hĕ rúled thĕm' (31)

Type B x ´ | x ´ *hĭe wýrd | fŏrswéop*   'thĕm fáte dĕstróyed' (477)

Type C x ´ | ´ x *ŏn Fréan | wǽrĕ*   'iñ Gód's kéepiñg'   (27)

Type D ´ | ´ \ x *swȳn | éal-gỳldĕn*   'bóar áll-gòldĕn'   (1111)

or   ´ | ´ x \ *Fórð | néar ǽtstŏp*   'fórth néarĕr wènt'   (745)

Type E ´ \ x | ´ *Héngĕstĕs | héap*   'Héngĕst his tróop'   (1091)

While the division of each half-line into 'feet' in the above simple basic examples does not markedly cut across the natural divisions of speech as a rule, in such a B-type half-line as *ǽt his sélfĕs hám* (1147) it will be seen at once that the notation x x ´ | x ´ suggests a quite absurd division of *selfes* which puts each of its syllables into separate feet. But though Sievers's method does sometimes completely fail to agree with the nature of speech and the music of poetry recited to the harp, his five patterns do—since they are a true description of the facts, even if crudely indicated—aid the beginner in recognizing the rhythm of Old English verse as well as serving as a guide in textual criticism. But the student, having learned the main features of the rhythm by these formal aids, will quickly learn to read Old English verse with appreciation by putting stresses and pitch in the places which seem to come naturally in formal rhetorical utterance.

A few more general pointers may be added for the beginner.

(*a*) The drop may consist of more than one syllable, as in *ðŏnnĕ swéordă gĕlác* (1040) in type B with two-syllabled drops; or *ín ùnder éoderas* (1037) in type A with again two-syllabled drops, but with the foot-division quite inappropriately applied between *under* and *eoderas*. Here, of course, the adverb *in* is emphatic, and therefore stressed.

(*b*) When the lift is on the light or short syllable because it bears the main stress (as in a noun or adjective), this light syllable may combine with an immediately following light syllable to form in the pattern of the half-line a heavy beat or lift consisting of the two syllables 'slurred' together so as to carry the weight or duration of one heavy or long syllable. This use of two light syllables when the first bears the natural main stress as the lift Sievers termed 'resolution' (*Auflösung*), and described the two syllables as being 'resolved' (*aufgelöst*). This 'resolution' or 'slurring' (Henry Sweet's term) is seen in the first lift of *Scĕdĕ-làndŭm ín* (19), which is in Type E with the first lift resolved, and may be expressed in the notation ´x x \ x | ´

---

[1] *Beowulf*, ed. C. L. Wrenn, 2nd ed. (London, 1958).

(*c*) An extra-metrical syllable from the point of view of the above patterns is often found at the beginning of the half-line. This has been compared to a musical 'grace-note', and is termed an 'anacrusis' (Sievers's *Auftakt*). An example of a type A with ana-crusis is *ic̆ þǽt gĕhȳrĕ* (290), which may be expressed symbolically as x | ⁄ x | ⁄ x .

(*d*) While the first three types are 'equal-footed', consisting re-spectively of two feet in falling rhythm, two in rising rhythm, and of one foot in rising and one in falling rhythm, the remaining types D and E are 'unequal-footed', consisting of one heavy syllable or resolution in one foot, and three varied syllables—lift, half-lift, and drop—in the other. It is chiefly in compound words that types D and E will most naturally occur, since secondary stress is regular in the second member of the most frequent kinds of compounds.

(*e*) There must normally be two lifts in each half-line, and the two halves are rhymed together internally by alliteration, which must fall on at least one lift in each. This alliteration will fall on those of the four possible lifts which naturally bear the stronger emphasis—nouns, for instance, being generally preferred to verbs, and so on. But the emphasis required by a given context may cause a verb to carry the alliteration in preference to a noun, as in the line (A and B)

Gĕfĕng þā bĕ́ éaxlĕ   —nălăs fŏr fǽhŏĕ́ mēarn.

Then he seized her by the shoulder: he cared not for hostility (1537)

where the emphasis is more on the act of the *seizing* of the monster's shoulder by Beowulf than on the particular part of her body that was held.

(*f*) The first lift of the second half of the line, termed, from the Icelandic *höfuð-staf*, a "head-stave," determines the sound which is to bear the alliteration; and with it may alliterate one or both of the lifts in the first half-line. Every consonant alliterates with itself, except that the sound-groups represented by *sc*, *sp*, and *st* are felt each to form one unit, and therefore may only alliterate respectively with themselves—*sc* only with *sc*, *sp* only with *sp*, etc. *Scip*, 'ship', may not therefore alliterate with *sāwol*, 'soul', but only with words of the same initial sound, such as *scēap*, 'sheep'. But vowels—since all have the same initial glottal stop breathing in common—alliterate with one another quite indiscriminately, as in the line

ángăn éafĕrắn.   Hĭm ŏn éaxlĕ lǽg (1547)

(*g*) In 'scanning', first find the lifts, beginning with the first (or head-stave) of the second half-line, so as to check the alliteration. These are found conveniently by looking for nouns, adjectives, finite verbs, in that order; and then if necessary considering whether pronouns or adverbs are sufficiently emphatic to bear the lift. Thus in *sȳ̈ð̈ð̈an ǣrest wéarð* (6) there are no nouns or adjectives, and the lift must be placed on the finite verb *wearð*. But since this can only be the second of the two, the adverb *ǣrest* is to be examined to see whether it bears enough emphasis naturally; and it clearly does so, and therefore takes the first lift. It is to be remembered that diphthongs, whether long or short historically, are always metrically one and not two syllables; so that this half-line is of type Bxx/|x/, supplying incidentally yet another example of the foot-division falling unnaturally between the two syllables of *ǣrest*.

(*h*) A syllable which normally takes the secondary stress may count in a given metrical context as also either a full lift or as a drop or part of a drop. Thus in the phrase *in geár-dà̈gŭm* (1), the half-lift would come in prose on the penultimate syllable -*dag*: but here the pattern of the C-type half-line requires something like the notation x/|/x, as if the two elements of the compöund *geár-dagum*, being separately meaningful, could be taken separately in the scansion. Or again, in *hŭ̈ ð̈å̈ æ̈p̈ël̈ín̈g̈ås̈* (3), we have a C-type half-line (with resolved first lift), though the element -*ing* originally bore the secondary stress. The notation would be xxẍx|/x. In *Öft Scýld Scëf̈ing*, on the other hand, as has been indicated earlier, the -*ing* forms the drop of another C-type half-line.

(*i*) Elision may occur if the metrical pattern requires it, when a word ending in a vowel-sound is immediately followed by one beginning with a vowel. For example, *méodo-sètla oftëah* (5), which is a type E half-line with resolved first lift, and the last syllable of *setla* elided with the first of *oftēah*:{ẍx\x|/.

(*j*) The *drop* in types D and E may be disyllabic, as in *éald énta gewèorc* (2774), which is D /|/xx\ , or *Wélàndes gewéorc* (455), which is E/\ẍx|/.

(*k*) In type E the first *lift* may be expanded by the addition of an extra light syllable after it so as to give /x instead of / . Examples are *wínter ȳþe belëãc* (1132), D /x|/xx\ ; or *fífel-cÿnnes éard* (104), which is E/x\x|/.

(*l*) The Old English poet may gain some stylistic variation by lengthening either or both half-lines with the addition of an extra lift or foot occasionally, in the so-called 'lengthened verses' or *Schwellverse:* e.g., *The Battle of Maldon* 1, *hët þå̈ hýssä̈ hwǽnë̈*, which may be regarded as a lengthened A type, / x|/ x|/ x rather than B x x/ | x ẍx since it naturally has three beats rather than two.

(*m*) The poet of *Beowulf* sometimes used older forms of words which had later been contracted to a lesser number of syllables, though it is not certain how far such uncontracted forms were archaisms and how far they were still in use in his time.

Metrical patterns clearly show that uncontracted forms must be read or recited in some half-lines, and it is probable that later poets still retained the choice between some uncontracted archaic forms permitted in poetry and the normal contracted words, according to the needs of their metre. Such fuller uncontracted forms, modernized by the scribes of the extant manuscripts, must be 'restored' or indicated by the editors to make the texts metrically intelligible. Thus, for instance, in *Beowulf* 1644 the half-line *ðā cōm ín gān* of the manuscript must be read with the older uncontracted form of the infinitive, *ga-an*. It then becomes a C-type half-line *ðã̈ cõm ín gá-ãn*. Similarly 512, *þā git on súnd rēon*, will only become metrically intelligible if we restore the fuller form *rēowon*, so that the half-line becomes *þã̈ git õn súnd rēowõn*, type C; so too 539, *þā wit on súnd rēon*. It is usual to write a circumflex accent over the vowel or diphthong to be metrically 'uncontracted', as *dôn* when it is metrically to be read as *dō-ãn*, or *gân* for *gá-ãn*: but it is perhaps better to write out the fuller forms as an aid to recitation.[1]

The following is a full indication of the scansion of *Beowulf* 1357b to 1376a, with the alliterating sounds italicized. It is the description of the mere in which dwelt Grendel and his mother.

> B Hie *d*ȳgĕl lónd
>
> D *w*arigĕaðˇ, *w*úlf-hlèoþŭ̈, A *w*índigĕ næssã̈s,
>
> D *fr*ĕcnĕ̈ *f*én-gĕlâd, B ðæ̈r *f*ȳrgĕn-strēam
>
> B ŭndĕr næssã̈ gĕnìpu A *n*iþer gĕwïtĕ̈ðˇ,
>
> A *f*lód ŭndĕr *f*óldã̈n. C Nís þæ̈t *f*éor hĕonŏ̈n
>
> A *m*íl-gĕméarcĕ̈s, C þæ̈t se *m*ĕre stándĕ̈ðˇ;
>
> C ófĕ̈r þǣm *h*óngiãðˇ A *h*ríndĕ̈ bĕarwã̈s,
>
> D *w*udu *w*ȳrtŭm fæst A *w*æter ófĕrhélmãðˇ.
>
> B þæ̈r mæ̈g *n*íhtã̈ gĕhwæ̈m E *n*iðˇ-wŭndŏr sĕon,
>
> A *f*ȳr ŏn *f*lódĕ̈. C Nŏ̈ þæ̈s *fr*ód léofãðˇ
>
> A *g*umĕna bĕarnã̈, C þæ̈t þŏnĕ grúnd wíte.
>
> C Ðĕ̄ah þĕ *h*æ̈ðˇ-stàpã̈ A *h*úndŭm gĕswéncĕ̈d
>
> D *h*ĕorot *h*órnŭm trùm A *h*ólt-wŭdŭ sécĕ̈,
>
> A *f*éorrã̈n gĕ*f*lȳmĕ̈d, C ær hĕ̈ *f*éorh sélĕ̈ðˇ,
>
> A *á*ldŏ̈r ŏn ófrĕ̈, C æ̈r hĕ̈ *í*n *w*íllĕ̈,
>
> A *h*afelã̈n hȳdã̈n. B Nís þæ̈t *h*ĕoru stŏ̈w:
>
> B þŏnŏn *ȳ*ðˇ-gĕblónd A *ú*p ãstìgĕðˇ

---

[1] See *Beowulf*, ed. Wrenn, pp. 31 ff.

A wón·tō wólcnum,   C þŏnnĕ wínd stýrĕþ
A lāð gĕwídru,   C ŏð þæt lýft ŏrýsmāþ,
A rŏderăs rĕotāð.

They dwell in a secret land, where there are wolf-haunted slopes and wind-swept headlands, perilous paths over the marshes where the stream from the mountains goes down deep beneath the mists of the cliffs as water flowing under the earth. It is not far from thence measured in miles that there stands a lake, over which there hang thickets covered in hoar-frost. Trees firmly rooted overshadow the mere. There each night is to be seen a horrible wonder, a fiery light on the water. There lives not one of the children of men who is wise enough to know its depth. Even though the stag strong in his antlers should seek that forest when hard pressed by the hounds from afar he flees, he will first give up his life and power of living on the bank rather than enter the lake to hide his head. That is not a pleasing place from whence the swirling of the waves rises up darkly to the skies when the wind stirs up hateful storms until the air grows suffocating and the clouds weep.

The metre described in the foregoing outline is that employed for Old English poetry of every description throughout. It is, as might be expected, treated with increasing freedom or licence in technique in its later period, though instances of entirely 'correct' versification are to be found right up to the time of the Norman Conquest. Within this system—which at first view might seem likely to produce monotony—there are almost limitless varieties of style which are frequently related to changes in feeling, tone, or subject-matter.

The use of lengthened verses for stylistic effects has already been mentioned. A remarkable example of this is in *The Dream of the Rood*, 40 ff.

Gestāh hē on géalgan hēanne,
mōdig on mánigra gesýhðe,   þā hē wólde máncyn lýsan.
Bífode ic þā mē se béorn ymbclýpte.   Ne dórste ic hwæðre būgan tō
éorðan,
féallan tō fóldan scēatum,   ac ic scéolde fǽste stándan.

He climbed up on to the high gallows, valiant in the sight of many, when he was about to redeem mankind. I trembled as the hero embraced me. Yet I dared not bend down to the earth nor fall to the surface of the ground, but I was forced to stand fast.

These seven half-lines may all be described as lengthened A types, some with and others without anacrusis. The same poem provides other examples; and it is remarkable that the lengthened verses just quoted occur in the earlier Northumbrian Runic inscription on the Ruthwell Cross as well as in *The Dream of the Rood*, which is in some respects an expansion of the poem of the inscription or a completion of it. These lengthened lines, then, belong to earlier as well as to later Old English poetry. Another striking instance of their use is the epilogue to *The Wanderer* (111 ff.), which is again a series of three-beat half-lines indicating a deliberate and weighty change of style:

Swá cwæð snóttor on móde; gesǽt him súndor æt rúne. etc.

Thus spake the wise in heart as he sat apart in privacy.

The fact that the so-called *Genesis B* is characterized by for the most part exceptionally long half-lines of three or even four beats is a special instance of foreign influence from a very closely related language: for this piece is based on a close rendering of an Old Saxon poem itself characterized by the same prolongations of the normal metrical patterns.

Old English metre naturally lends itself to what in later verse is termed *enjambement*, or the linking of lines and series of lines in sense-units such as sentences and verse-paragraphs, with "the sense variously drawn out from one verse into another" in Milton's famous phrase. The structure is almost invariably strophic, and arrangements such as stanzas are scarcely known. The fact that the device of the refrain may have been in use for certain sorts of lyric poetry—though not in the surviving records—is, however, suggested by the poem called *Deor* in the Exeter Book; for this series of philosophical reflections of a displaced scop appears in divisions of varying length separated in something like stanzaic manner by the refrain

þæs oferéode; þísses swá mæg.

That was got over: so may this be.

There is, too, the suggestion of a possible refrain in that fragment of a love-poem (found again in the Exeter Book) which is known as *Wulf and Eadwacer*.

The sporadic use of internal rhyme in combination with the normal alliterative metre to join the two half-lines appears in Old English poetry in single lines, and more rarely in short continuous passages. Thus, for instance, in *The Battle of Maldon*, a poem from the close of the tenth century, we find (271) the line

ǽfre embe *stunde* hē sealde sume *wunde*

and again in the same poem (282)

Sībryhtes *bróðor* and swīðe mænig ōþer.

Earlier, in *The Phoenix* (53–55), there is a short continuous passage in which internal rhymes and assonances occur as a stylistic device in describing the 'earthly paradise'; and the epilogue to Cynewulf's

Elene, in which he expresses his own personal feelings and divine hopes, begins with 17 lines of internal rhyme or assonance combined with alliteration. The fact that the idea of a whole poem in internally rhyming alliterative metre had occurred to at least one poet before the Norman Conquest is shown by the so-called *Rhyming Poem* in the Exeter Book. Though it is not clear whether this piece of religious edification is of the middle or later period of Old English poetry, it anticipates a Middle English development which found its supreme achievement in *Pearl*.[1] This use of the Leonine[2] rhyme may have been first suggested to monastic writers by the common practice in Latin hymns. The influence of the Old Norse practice of blending rhyme and alliteration in elaborate stanzaic structures in Skaldic poetry, which has been suggested in explanation of the quasi-stanzaic structure of *Deor*, and for the form of *The Rhyming Poem*, could only be credible if both these poems were certainly known to be quite late. The opening lines of the epilogue to Cynewulf's *Elene*, moreover, belong to a time certainly earlier than the Norse settlements. Here are the opening lines:

> þus ic frod ond *fus*   þurh þæt fæcne *hus*
> wordcræftum *wæf* ond wundrum *læs*,
> þragum *þreodude* ond geþanc *reodode*
> nihtes *nearwe*. Nysse ic *gearwe*
> be ðære rode *reht*, ær me rumran *geþæht*
> þurh ða mæran *mæht* on modes *þæht*
> wisdom *onwrah*. Ic wæs weorcum *fah*,
> synnum *asæled*, sorgum *gewæled*,
> bitre *gebunden*, bisgum *beþrungen*,
> ær me lare *onlag* þurh leohtne *had*
> gamelum to *geoce*, gife *unseoce*
> mægencyning *amæt* ond on gemynd *begæt*,
> torht *ontynde*, tidum *gerymde*,
> bancofan *onband*, breostlocan *onwand*,
> leoðucræft *onleac*, þæs ic lustum *breac*
> willum in worlde. (lines 1236 ff.)[3]

Thus I, aged and ready to depart because of this deceitful bodily frame, wove with skilful words and wondrously gathered matters, from time to time pondered and sifted them in my thought in stress by night. I had no just knowledge concerning the Cross until divine

[1] *Pearl*, ed. E. V. Gordon (Oxford, 1953).

[2] Hexameters, or alternating hexameters and pentameters, in which the word before the cæsura rhymes with the last in the line were termed 'Leonine', apparently after a none too clearly identified versifier, Leo, in the early Middle Ages.

[3] The rhymes, near-rhymes, and assonances of this passage were somewhat obscured by the rewriting of Cynewulf's Anglian original in the usual classical Anglo-Saxon of the late tenth-century Vercelli Book. They have therefore here been restored to their probable Mercian forms to make them clear.

wisdom in glorious might revealed a more spacious counsel in the thoughts of my heart. I was guilty in deeds, chained in sins, tormented by griefs, bitterly bound and thronged about by cares, until the all-powerful King gave me instruction in glorious wise when I was old, as an aid; gave me a gift of grace which was not subject to sickness. He measured it out to me and poured it into my mind; he disclosed to me something glorious; from time to time enlarged my ken; he unbound my body, unloosed the secrets of my breast. He unlocked in me the power of poesy, so that I enjoyed pleasures in the world.

Poetry arose from the selective need to express natural feelings in relation to the lives of poet and audience. Because for the most part we possess only poetry of aristocratic heroic living in the earlier period, and later that of Christian belief and feeling expressed in an inherited traditional language which had first grown up near to pagan heroic times, it follows that its language, like its metre, was primarily a selection of the speech of 'real life'. But this language, which had originally expressed the best moments of the lives of Germanic heroes, had especially to express orally such things as the magic and religion which had been indicated by the mystery-symbols of runes scratched on stone or hard wood or metal: it had to express the life of war, and of the social graces, the love of beautiful treasures and of noble speaking. Later it had to express in a written medium, which yet inherited many of the forms proper to oral tradition or spoken verse, heroic matters from the Bible and from the lives of Christian saints. Now, this select language for selected themes must perforce have grown up in vital relationship with the needs of oral transmission and mnemonic recitation. Hence it must quickly have become distinct in choice of words and diction from speech, formalized in habit, and abounding in convenient mnemonic formulae such as those to be found in other orally transmitted poetry, like the earlier European ballads, described by F. P. Magoun, junior, as furnishing "the oral-formulaic character" of Old English narrative verse.[1] The Old English scop, originally an aristocratic warrior among others of his class trained in the oral traditions of verse-craft, conventionally employed forms of words developed for recounting heroic events in which he himself might be supposed to have shared: and these forms were passed on to be employed as part of the accepted machinery of Christian verse-making. It is only to be expected, therefore, that the diction of Old English poetry is very much apart from that of prose, that it is highly conventionalized and traditional, and that it abounds in 'oral-formulaic' inherited phrases.

Andreas, a heroic hagiographical poem of the earlier ninth century, begins with exactly the same exordial formula in only slightly changed words as does *Beowulf*:

[1] *Op. cit.*

Hwæt, wé gefrúnan on fýrn-dàgum
twélfe under túnglum tír-éadige hǽleð,
þéodnes þégnas.

Truly we have heard tell of twelve glorious heroes in days of yore beneath the stars; noble retainers of a prince.

Such forms of opening for heroic poems, and the poetic epithets conventionally applied to famous heroes, may easily be paralleled in the heroic verse of many languages.[1] What then are the more special characteristics of Old English poetic diction?

Old English poetic diction developed from a common Germanic pattern, and the same descriptive and figurative epithets and phrases occur in the verse of other Germanic languages—in the Old Norse *Edda* and the Old High German *Hildebrandslied*. But we are here concerned only with Old English. Its abundance of descriptive and figurative words and phrases as poetic names for persons or things— termed *heiti* by the Icelandic writers—is fairly obvious and expected. To speak of one's home as *hæleða ēðel*, 'native land of heroes', or of the royal residence as *medu-ærn*, 'mead-building' or 'dwelling in which mead is drunk', does not seem very surprising for a poet in the given environment; but it is when such descriptive and figurative names take the special form as the 'kenning' that we have the really outstanding and special quality of Old English poetic diction set before us.

The kenning is so named from the Icelandic term. As distinguished from other poetic namings of persons and things such as the *heiti* or descriptive figurative appellation, it may be broadly defined as the poetic expression in a periphrasis of a person, thing, or thought by means of a condensed or implicit simile, usually in the form of a compound. Such compounds commonly consist of a basic word and a defining word. For example, a frequent kenning for 'the sea' is *hron-rād*. Here the basic word is *rād*, 'riding-place', and the defining word is *hron*, 'whale'. The sea, then, is spoken of as 'the riding-place of the whale': and we have a condensed or implicit simile of the whale 'riding' over the sea like a great steed on a vast undulating plain. Similarly, a ship is described as *mere-hengest*, 'sea-horse', and an arrow as *hilde-nǽdre*, 'battle-serpent'.[2] Other kennings are: *swan-rād* for 'sea' (literally 'swan's riding-place'), *mere-hrægl* for 'sail' (lit. 'sea-garment'), *freoðu-webbe* for 'woman' (lit. 'weaver of peace') and *hilde-lēoma* for 'sword' (lit. 'light of battle').

The kenning reached extremes of complexity and elaboration in the later Skaldic verses of Norse court-poets, and this makes it seem

---

[1] See W. J. Entwistle, *European Balladry*, 2nd ed. (Oxford, 1952).

[2] For a full study of the Old English kenning with a survey of previous work on it see Hertha Marquardt, *Die altenglischen Kenningar, ein Beitrag zur Stilkunde altgermanischer Dichtung* (Halle, 1938).

likely that its origin was in part connected with courtliness of language. The kenning may perhaps look back also to the kind of magico-religious matters and taboos expressed in early runes. One may compare the Old Slavonic loss of the simple word for a *bear* apparently for fear of ill-omen: the only modern Slavonic word generally used is that of the type of Russian *med-ved* (lit. 'honey-eater').

The abundance of descriptive periphrastic compounds in Old English poetry, other than kennings properly so called, is one of its most marked features—often conjoining elements of vocabulary which in prose are known only as individual words. This poetry is also characterized by a vast number of what appear to be synonyms, though on closer examination each word or phrase will be found to have retained some slight nuance of its meaning from earlier semantic history. Already by the time of the poet of *Beowulf* many words which had once held distinct individual meanings had, in the course of frequent use, lost their edges or boundaries as it were, and fallen together—hence the oft-repeated statement that Old English poetry had a large number of synonyms for 'warrior', for example, and for 'sea'. While it is true that such a group of words as *beorn*, *freca*, and *wiga* may each often be fairly rendered as 'warrior', all of these terms still retained something of individual connotation or suggestion or subtle association for the ears of both poet and hearers. Such words must inevitably lose in meaning-content when translated into a language relatively much poorer in concrete words. *Beorn* originally meant 'bear', *freca* 'wolf' ('the greedy one'), and *wiga* 'fighter'. There are in fact no synonyms in the strict sense of the term in Old English poetry. However, it is doubtless true that poets often found it convenient to have a choice of words and phrases of approximately the same meaning—near-synonyms—which could be drawn upon according to the needs of the rhythmical pattern and of alliteration. In *Beowulf* 2336

Wédera þíoden,   wrǽce leórnode,

The prince of the Geats planned vengeance

Wedera may have been substituted for the simple *Gēata* because of the need of the alliteration for a noun beginning with *w*. The Danes (*Dene*) in *Beowulf* are variously expressed in the compounds *Beorht-Dene*, *Ēast-Dene*, *Gār-Dene*, *Hring-Dene*, *Norð-Dene*, *Sūð-Dene*, and *West-Dene*: and it is clear that the choice between the first-elements or 'defining words' of these compounds has often little or no relation to meaning but is dictated by the needs of alliteration. In *Beowulf* 116, for example,

hēa[ha]n húses,   hū hit Hríng-Dène,

the Danes are called *Hring-Dene* because *h* is the alliterating letter and this is the only one among the poet's collection of words for

'Danes' that begins with an *h*. At the same time it is likely that the poet did also often choose his compound proper name for the sake of an element in its meaning, as in *Beowulf* 1,

Hwæt wē Gār-Dèna   in geár-dàgum,

where the warlike qualities of the *Dene* are suggested by the element *gār*, lit. 'spear'.

It seems certain that some traditional forms were archaic even as early as the time of the maker of *Beowulf*. The natural tendency of poetry to retain archaic words and phrases would be especially strong in the scop of an aristocratic community. One type of such archaism was the use of traditional compound words of which the general sense was well apprehended by poet and audience, while the exact meaning of its first element was no longer understood. For example, the word *regn-heard* (*Beowulf* 326) clearly has something like the sense of 'mighty, powerful' as applied to 'shields' (*rondas*), but the element *regn* has little force beyond that of a general intensive. Now, the older meaning must have been nearer to 'wondrous hard' or 'magically hardened', for *regn* is the same word as the Norse *regin*, 'the gods', well known from *ragnarök*, so that a still earlier meaning of *regn-heard* is likely to have been 'tempered by the gods'. By the time of the *Beowulf*-poet, however, this ancient word *regn* had become absorbed in its homophonic prose counterpart *regn*, 'rain'; and the same poet uses the adjective *scūr-heard* at line 1033 in a similar sense to *regn-heard*, which suggests that to him these two words were pretty well interchangeable epithets. If 'rain-hardened , why not 'shower-hardened'?

Old English poetry shows an amazing number of words that occur only once in its whole corpus—the 'once said' words, or ἅπαξ λεγόμενα. Many of these, however, may be only apparently or accidentally unique, in view of the fragmentary nature of the surviving poetic records, and of the known fact that much that once existed has been lost through such causes as the dissolution of the monastic libraries, fire, and neglect. Almost any piece of Old English verse has its unique words and phrases. Some of these may once have been common, while others are the deliberate acts of individual poets. Yet one can never discriminate between what may be termed the merely accidental or apparent uniqueness and the true uniqueness.

It may fairly be said that the kenning, the heiti, and other descriptive and figurative periphrases are all modes of poetic 'variation'. A specially favoured stylistic device is what is termed 'parallel variation'—that is, the repetition in different words of the same thing or thought in consecutive half-lines, often in a second half-line followed by a first. A very plain instance of this is in *Beowulf* 1273–1274:

ðȳ he þone feónd ofercwóm,
gehnǽgde hélle-gàst.

Therefore he overcame the fiend, laid low the spirit of hell.

Or again in lines 714–715 Heorot is described in consecutive half-lines as *win-reced*, 'wine-mansion', and as *gold-sele gumena*, 'gold-hall of men'. This parallel variation is, of course, not peculiar to Old English poetry, but is used in a freer form sometimes in prose: yet its presence in verse is both marked and a recognized convention. It is often linked with the use of traditional formulae of the type already noticed, as in *Beowulf* 258–259:

> Him sē ýldèsta ándswáròde,
> wérodes wísa, wórd-hòrd onléac

The senior leader of the troop made answer, unclosed the treasury of his words.

Here *word-hord onlēac* is a formulaic phrase from oral tradition, forming a parallel variation on *andswarode*.[1]

At first sight Old English poetry, with its innumerable periphrastic compounds and descriptive epithets, its kennings and parallel variations, may seem expansive in style. But the fact is that this kind of diction does for the most part, and fundamentally, make for stylistic compression rather than expansiveness. This becomes clear at once to anyone who tries to translate it while carefully preserving its full content of meaning. Consider, for example, such compounds as *bān-hūs*, 'body', *woruld-candel*, 'sun', and *gold-wine*, 'gold-friend'. Each of these condenses into a single two-element compound a whole range of poetic description which would have to be greatly expanded in modern prose translation if all its nuances and associations of meaning were to be fully expressed. *Bān-hūs* is the timbered building of the body in which the spirit resides; *woruld-candel* compares the sun to a vast candle which illumines the whole world; and *gold-wine* (a specially frequent poetic *heiti* or name for an esteemed lord) is the king or ruler who shows his love for his retainers by exercising the heroic virtue of treasure-giving. The highly charged phrase *wintres wōma*, 'terrifying sound of winter', in *The Wanderer* line 103 implies so much more than can be translated; for the poetic word *wōma*, which originally seems to have meant 'sound' or 'noise', has acquired connotations of terror in its poetic semantic development with the suggestion of a phantom: so that *wintres wōma* includes among other things in this passage something like 'the terrible crashing of the winter's wind'. Or again in lines 61–62 of the same poem a poetic periphrasis for death compresses a moving yet familiar scene into the two words *flet ofgēafon*, literally 'have quitted the floor':

> hū hī fǽrlìce flét ofgéafon,
> mŏdge mágu - þègnas

[1] For an excellent study of parallel variation see A. Brodeur, *The Art of Beowulf* (University of California Press, Berkeley, 1959).

How suddenly the proud and valiant retainers have quitted the floor of the banqueting-hall of this life.

For the word *flet* at once calls up the image of a noble hall where the ruler feasted and gave out treasure and heard poetry with his retainers. The compound adjective *winter-cearig* in line 24 of *The Wanderer* implies both that the poet is sad (*cearig*) because of the cold of *winter* and that his gloom is deepened by thoughts of oncoming old age (*winter* in the sense of 'year').

wód winter-ceàrig ofer wáþema gebínd

might literally be rendered 'went, winter-sad, across the binding-together of the waves', but how little this would convey of the full poetic content of this most compressed line! *Waþema gebind* is something like 'the freezing sea': for there was an ancient Germanic folk-idea of the frozen sea as being bound with ropes, so that the poet of *Beowulf* could speak (lines 1609–1610) of God the Father 'unwinding the ropes of water' when describing the breaking of the ice in spring on a northern sea:

ðonne fórstes bénd Fǽder onlǽteð,
onwíndeð wǽl-rápas:

When the Father unlooses the bonds of the frost, unwinds the ropes of the sea.

Now, to bring out the full meaning of the line from *The Wanderer* in modern prose one would have to expand it into something like this: 'I journeyed, wretched with the cold and filled with sadness at the thought of oncoming old age, across the ice-cold expanse of the ocean-waves'. The poet is rowing; and hence the sea must be ice-cold rather than actually frozen. But such a rendering misses the poetry.[1]

It will be appropriate to conclude this exposition of metre with some references to the development of prose generally, especially in its relations with verse in matters of style, rhythm, and the employment of alliteration.

Prose, the language of speech, ordinary life, and utility, did not attain to written literary form till a good deal later than verse in Old English. Indeed, any aesthetic interest in it as a form of art developed only incidentally, it would seem, under the influence of men educated in the discipline and tradition of Latin rhetoric at the time of the Benedictine Renaissance in the late tenth century. The primary function of poetry was pleasure or entertainment; and though for the most part only that of the aristocratic kind has survived, it must

---

[1] For an especially valuable essay on diction entitled "On Translation and Words", by J. R. R. Tolkien, see the 'Preliminary Remarks' to C. L. Wrenn's revised edition of John Clark Hall's prose translation of *Beowulf*, 2nd ed. (London, 1950). A useful essay on 'The Translator's Task in *Beowulf*' by Edwin Morgan is prefixed to his verse translation of *Beowulf* into Modern English (The Hand and Flower Press, Ashford, Kent, 1952).

have existed also for the people generally. This last point is made certain by Bede's story of Cædmon; and there are popular elements occasionally to be recognized, such as the repetitive formulae of some of the *Charms* and elements of folk-tradition in the *Maxims* or *Gnomic Verses*, and in *Riddles* like that of the Man in the Moon. Poetry was for entertainment; prose later for information and edification. Yet there is one probable exception to this generalization in the apparent accidental preservation in the *Anglo-Saxon Chronicle* under the year 755 of a saga-like piece from oral tradition, interpolated by a scribe who, one may imagine, had heard this vivid and dramatic account of the slaying of King Cynewulf of Wessex and its avenging recited in some village. This *Chronicle* entry for 755, with its allusive and selective manner, its emphasis on the dramatic highlights of the tragic situation, and its abrupt transitions from direct to indirect speech, reminds one of the Old Icelandic saga-style, and may suggest that England had once a traditional style of oral prose for historical narrative in some ways parallel to the saga-style of ancient Iceland. The relatively early coming of Latin-Christian culture to England was perhaps unfavourable to the development as written literature of this form of art; whereas in Iceland, to which Christianity came only some four centuries later, the saga had taken too firm root for it to fail to get into writing when the new culture made this possible.[1]

There is, however, a special form of loosely rhythmic alliterative prose which arose in England apparently as a way of rendering edification—or instruction receivable as entertainment—to people who were accustomed to hearing verse-recitations but were not ready for literary prose. This alliterative prose, in which irregular lines occur roughly stressed like verse and having alliteration on some of their strong stresses, was deliberately employed by the great literary homilist Ælfric for his *Lives of Saints*. It serves, in a sense, to bridge the gap between the natural earlier poetry and the later educative prose. The following lines, for example, open Ælfric's *Life of Saint Oswald the King*, with the alliterating letters in italics and lines separated as in verse:

> Æfter ðan ðe *A*ugustinus   to *E*ngla lande becom,
> wæs sum *æ*ðele cyning,   *O*swold gehaten,
> on Norðhymbra *l*ande,   ge*l*yfed swyðe on God.
> Se *f*erde on his iugoðe   fram his *f*reondum and magum
> to *S*cotlande on *s*æ,   ond þær *s*ona wearð gefullod,
> and his geferan *s*amod   ðe mid him *s*iþedon.[2]

---

[1] See C. E. Wright, *The Cultivation of Saga in Anglo-Saxon England* (Edinburgh, 1939). *Cf.* C. L. Wrenn, "A Saga of the Anglo-Saxons", *History* XXV (1940), pp. 208–215.

[2] The full text of this homily is in *Ælfric's Lives of Saints*, ed. W. W. Skeat (EETS 114: London, 1900), II, pp. 124 ff., and in Sweet's *Anglo-Saxon Reader*, 13th ed. (Oxford, 1954), pp. 75 ff.

This may be roughly rendered so as to indicate its general quality:

> After Augustine to England came, there was an upright king called
> Oswald in the Northumbrians' land who believed in God. This man
> fared in his youth from friends and kinsfolk to Scotland by sea, and
> soon was baptized; and his comrades joined in this, journeying with
> him.

Poetry also left its mark in the prose of more rhetorical homilists
such as Wulfstan in the early eleventh century in the occasional
use of alliteration as a deliberate stylistic device; and the mnemonic
advantage of alliterative pairs of words of related meaning probably
accounts for their frequent use in Old English *Laws*. The phrase
stric ond steorfa, 'plague and pestilence', for instance, occurs in the
Laws of Canute as well as in Wulfstan's famous *Sermo ad Anglos*.[1]

Occasionally writers of the Benedictine Renaissance, like Ælfric
and Wulfstan in their sermons, and the writer of the romantic tale
of *Apollonius of Tyre* (who rendered a Latin version with real literary
skill), used deliberate rhetorical devices as conscious literary artists.
There is also some element of the aesthetic in the choice of the semi-
metrical alliterative prose style and the use of alliterating pairs of
words just mentioned. In general, however, it must be said that verse
was primarily an art aimed at pleasurable instruction through
entertainment, whereas prose was rather a slowly manufactured
utilitarian practical means of communication, in which literary qualities were for the most part late, sporadic, and secondary accretions.

Apart from the odd survival of a sort of oral prose in the *Chronicle*
for 755, and the late homiletic alliterative semi-versified prose described above, there are broadly four main types of prose style in
Old English. There are (*a*) the merely elementary and utilitarian
formulaic manner of early laws and charters and of the early
Chronicle; (*b*) the straightforward and efficient narrative style evolved
by King Alfred in his more mature writing, and in the historical
narrative manner of the *Chronicle* of his times; (*c*) the type of translation from Latin, which is so close and literal as to be unnatural in
syntax and often unclear, such as the prentice hand of King Alfred
in his version of St Gregory the Great's *Pastoral Care*, and (*d*) the
consciously literary and often rhetorical writing of the Benedictine
Revival—of Ælfric, Wulfstan, the author of *Apollonius of Tyre*,[2]
and the Chronicler for the reign of Ethelred the Unready. Of these,
while the second is effective and sometimes promising as a medium
of narrative, only the last is properly to be described as literary.

Of the elementary earlier style the entry for the year 678 in the

---

[1] *Sermo Lupi ad Anglos*, ed. Dorothy Whitelock (Methuen's Old English
Library, 2nd ed. London, 1952). It is also in Sweet, *op. cit.* pp. 82–89.

[2] *The Old English 'Apollonius of Tyre'*, ed. Peter Goolden (Oxford English
Monographs, Oxford, 1958).

Parker Manuscript of the *Chronicle* may serve as a sufficient example:

> Her oðiewde cometa se steorra, and Wilfred biscop wæs adrifen of his biscopdome from Ecgferþe cyninge.

> In this year the star comet appeared, and Bishop Wilfred was driven out from his diocese by King Ecgfrith.[1]

The straightforward effective style of the Alfredian Renaissance may be seen in the King's own rendering of Orosius' *Historiarum adversum Paganos Libri VII* where the Latin is generally effectively rendered. But in the same king's earliest work, and in that of his contemporary translator Bishop Wærferth, the weaknesses and at times unintelligibility resulting from too literal a following of the Latin constructions may be frequently seen. In the version of Bede's *Historia Ecclesiastica* of King Alfred's reign (probably mainly by Wærferth, or under his direction) the penultimate sentence of Bede's account of Cædmon reads as follows in the Old English:

> And seo tunge þe swa monig halwende word on þæs Scyppendes lof gesette, he þa swylce eac þa ytemestan word on his herenesse hine sylfne seniende and his gast in his handa bebeodende betynde.[2]

Literally translated, this would be:

> And *that tongue which* had composed so many healthful words in praise of the Creator, *he* then likewise also concluded his last words in His praise, crossing himself and commending his spirit into His hands.

This anacoluthic sentence at once becomes clear when one looks at the Latin:

> *Illāque linguā quae* tot salutaria verba in laudem Conditoris composuerat, ultima quoque verba in laudem ipsius, signando sese et spiritum suum in manus eius commendando, clauderet.

The translator has wrongly taken the ablative case of *illāque linguā quae*, 'with that tongue which', as a nominative, and so rendered it by *seo tunge*. Similar syntactic muddles could be cited from this version and from King Alfred's rendering of the *Pastoral Care*.

The conscious art acquired by skilful use of lessons learned from Latin orators and historians was applied to Old English prose by Ælfric. He it was too who first made Old English prose fully able to express with agreeable clarity the matters of philosophy and theology which the Benedictine reformers needed to make intelligible in the vernacular; and Ælfric's contemporaries in varying degrees showed

---

[1] *Two of the Saxon Chronicles Parallel,* ed. Charles Plummer (Oxford, 1892), I, 38. There is an excellent translation of the whole *Chronicle*, with apparatus, by G. N. Garmonsway (Everyman's Library 624, London, 1954).

[2] See the text in Sweet's *Anglo-Saxon Reader*, 13th ed., p. 46 and notes p. 208.

the capacity to devise a literary prose which could harmonize native modes of thought and expression with Latin rhetorical features. The art of prose rhythm was practised in strikingly different ways by both Ælfric and Wulfstan, as well as by several anonymous homilists.[1] Rhetorical and semi-poetical passages occur in the *Chronicle* for this period, as well as examples of sustained literary prose which combine natural gifts with a definitely conscious aesthetic art. The following passage from Ælfric's homily on the *Assumption of St John* shows the artistic style of the later period at its best:

> Nacode we wæron acennede, and nacode we gewitað. Þære sunnan beorhtnys, and þæs monan leoht and ealra tungla sind gemæne þam rican and ðam heanan. Renscuras and cyrcan-dura, fulluht and synna forgyfennys, huselgang and Godes neosung sind eallum gemæne, earmum and eadigum: ac se ungesæliga gytsere wile mare habban þonne him genihtsumað, þonne he furðon orsorh ne bricð his genihtsumnysse. Se gytsere hæfð ænne lichaman, and menigfealde scrud: he hæfð ane wambe, and þusend manna bigleofan: witodlice þæt he for gytsunge uncyste nanum oðrum syllan ne mæg, þæt he hordað, and nat hwam.

This passage when rendered literally goes easily and eloquently into Modern English:

> Naked we were born, and naked we shall depart. The brightness of the sun and the light of the moon and of all the stars are common to the mighty and to the lowly. Showers of rain, marriage at the church-porch, baptism and the forgiveness of sins, going to Mass and God's visitation, are common to all, both the poor and the wealthy: but the unhappy miser desires to have more than will be enough for him, when he does not enjoy even his sufficiency without anxiety. The avaricious man has one body and manifold garments; he has one belly and the nourishment of a thousand men. Truly that which because of the vice of greed he cannot give to others, that he hoards up, and knows not for what.[2]

Within these broad types of Old English prose-style there were of course some individual qualities and personal characteristics, such as the mixture of traditional Latin epistolary formula and personal idiom of King Alfred's famous letter prefixed to the copies of his version of the *Cura Pastoralis* sent out to his bishops, and the original interpolations in a more native yet undeveloped style which he inserted into his rendering of Orosius. But such matters belong to the treatment of separate authors.

---

[1] See Angus McIntosh, "Wulfstan's Prose", *Proceedings of the British Academy* XXXV (1949), 109–142. There is a useful account of Wulfstan's style in *The Homilies of Wulfstan*, ed. Dorothy Bethurum (Oxford, 1957), pp. 87–98.

[2] From Sweet's *Anglo-Saxon Reader*, 13th ed., p. 61.

CHAPTER 4

Latin Writings in Britain

FOR THE STUDENT of Anglo-Saxon literature, it is obvious that the Anglo-Latin writings of the period can have only an indirect and secondary interest. Yet because of the light these may throw on Anglo-Saxon thought, the dominant influence of the Latin culture of the Church, and sometimes their direct influence on Old English writers themselves, they cannot be entirely omitted. It was, of course, the immense and fundamental influence of Latin thought in the formation of Anglo-Saxon civilization that made it possible for Anglo-Saxon England to play the leading part it did, as explained in Chapter 1, in the development of that medieval Christendom which laid the foundations of our surviving heritage of Western European culture.[1] But most of the written Latin monuments, classical and medieval, were produced on the Continent. The Latin writings from Britain proper, though often of real historical importance, can, with the outstanding exception of the work of the Venerable Bede, scarcely claim to be literature in any strict sense of the word. Confining our record, therefore, to Latin writings of the Anglo-Saxon period made in Britain, what then is important in their significance to the literary historian?

The earliest writer in Latin whose work falls within the Anglo-Saxon period is a West of England monk named Gildas, a Briton who still thought of himself as a Roman citizen (*civis*) and wrote a vehement religious tract for the times somewhere about the middle of the sixth century. This book, commonly entitled *De Excidio et Conquestu Britanniae*, is a bitter homily, often in epistolary form, addressed to contemporary British or Welsh kings, chastizing them for their wickedness, and including the Church leaders and nobility in violent and florid rhetorical denunciation backed by much Scriptural citation. But, as the only text which offers, though almost inadvertently, some historical account of England between the coming of the Anglo-Saxons and the middle of the seventh century, Gildas, as the one fitful dark-age historical light, has received much attention, though this is not for his literary merit. Writing during the period (some half-century) of comparative peace after the British victory of Mons

---

[1] *Cf.* S. J. Crawford, *Anglo-Saxon Influence on Western Christendom* (London, 1933). For some valuable detailed studies of Anglo-Saxon influence in Europe see Wilhelm Levison, *England and the Continent in the Eighth Century* (Oxford, 1946).

Badonicus, Gildas, probably from the safe distance of Brittany, could threaten contemporary notables with a final overthrow by the heathen barbarians unless they repented: and in illustrating his furious argument he preserved many historical traditions of real value.

But Gildas is significant not only for the historian; for, while influencing Bede through his material, he was also evidently read and admired by later Anglo-Saxon churchmen. For instance, Archbishop Wulfstan of York, in a famous sermon declaimed in the early eleventh century, cites Gildas as a wise historian when he draws a parallel between his own times of corruption and Viking warfare and those of the British monk.[1] Gildas had knowledge of some Latin literature, both classical and Christian, as well as of the Bible. His Celtic type of Latin learning reminds us that there were still some traces of Latin civilization at the time of the early Saxon settlements, and may be in some sort a link with that other Celtic culture from Ireland which was soon to be a great formative force in the making of Anglo-Saxon civilization.

Gildas also wrote Latin verse in the normal rhythmic lines, often with rhyme or assonance. One of these, the famous *Lorica* prayer, was widely known and perhaps imitated by Old English writers. It shows the Celtic fondness for out-of-the-way words; and in its use of internal rhyme may possibly look forward to the kind of Old English Leonine verse mentioned in the previous chapter as illustrated by the Epilogue to Cynewulf's *Elene*. But the practice of combining internal rhyme of rhythmic verse with alliteration, probably derived from Irish types, does not become fully effective till a little later, in the poems of St Aldhelm. There is a good modern translation of Gildas's chief work as *De Excidio Britanniae*, edited by Hugh Williams in the Cymmrodorion Records Series, 1899.

In a tenth-century manuscript of Aldhelm's prose treatise for nuns, *De Laudibus Virginitatis*, there occurs a mixed Anglo-Saxon and Latin poem in praise of St Aldhelm, which is an excellent reminder of his immense reputation in Old English times, and of the character of his writings.[2] His book is here made to speak the lines:

> Þus me gesette sanctus et iustus
> beorn boca gleaw, bonus auctor,
> Ealdelm, æþele sceop, etiam fuit
> *ipselos* on æðele Angolsexna,
> byscop on Bretene. *Biblos* ic nu sceal,
> *ponus* et pondus pleno cum sensu,
> geonges geanoðe geomres iamiamque,
> secgan soð, nalles leas, þæt him symle wæs

[1] See "Sermo Lupi ad Anglos" in *The Homilies of Wulfstan*, ed. Dorothy Bethurum (Oxford, 1957), p. 274, lines 176 ff.
[2] ASPR VI, p. 97.

euthenia oftor on fylste,
æne on eðle ec ðon ðe se is
yfel on gesæd.

Thus it was that a saintly and righteous good author, a man skilled
in books, a noble poet Aldhelm who was also eminent in the land of
the Anglo-Saxons, composed me. He was a bishop among the Britons.
Now, as a book I must, with the sadness of recent sorrow, speak the
truth, no falsehood, relate his toilsome and weighty work in its full
sense. I must relate that he always had abundance of help and fame
in his own country, more often indeed than one of whom evil is
spoken.[1]

And this obscure and learned panegyric goes on for another four and
a half lines with increasing difficulty. The larding of the Latin with
Greek words here italicized, and the very strange syntax, are characteristic of the Irish-influenced Latin writings of this period, and very
much of Aldhelm himself; but the blend of English and Latin recalls
the fact that St Aldhelm was reputed a most skilful poet in Anglo-
Saxon as well as Latin. The matter truly indicates that he was also
regarded as a saint, and that in his final bishopric of Sherborne he
ruled over Britons, since there was a large West British or *Dumnonian*
element in the population of this diocese in its earliest period.

Aldhelm lived from about 640 till 709, and marks the first high
florescence of Latin learning in Wessex. After training under the
Irish saint and scholar Maeldubh at Malmesbury Abbey, Aldhelm
made two stays at Canterbury, where Abbot Hadrian, under Archbishop Theodore, had made possible a true cultural renaissance with
the aid of first-hand knowledge of Latin and Greek, both classical
and patristic. Later he taught, achieving great fame, as Abbot of
Malmesbury, which his beloved Irish teacher had founded. Indeed,
the name 'Malmesbury' appears in Anglo-Saxon documents in
varieties of the two forms *Aldhelmesburg* and *Maeldufesburg*, thus
commemorating both the Irish saint and his English disciple.[2] The
establishment of Archbishop Theodore and his outstanding helper
Hadrian at Canterbury in 668 was the most decisive happening for
education, and therefore indirectly for literature, in Anglo-Saxon
history. Aldhelm, with a background of Irish Latin learning dis-
ciplined and broadened by his sojourn at the Canterbury school,
naturally became the outstanding cultural influence in Southern
literature, as Bede was to be in the North, though he was far inferior

[1] For the Greek words here roughly rendered by Latin letters, see Dobbie's
notes to this piece in ASPR VI, p. 194. The translation here offered is necessarily
somewhat free.

[2] See *Malmesbury* in the *Oxford Dictionary of English Placenames*, ed. Ekwall,
4th ed. (1960). For some further detail on the connection of Aldhelm with Malmesbury *cf.* C. L. Wrenn, "Saxons and Celts in South-West Britain", *Transactions of
the Honourable Society of Cymmrodorion*, Session 1959, p. 43.

to Bede as thinker and scholar. We know nothing of the basis of his great reputation as a vernacular poet, since none of his poetry has survived. But King Alfred is said to have greatly preferred Aldhelm as a poet, and William of Malmesbury, writing early in the twelfth century, records a vivid memory of St Aldhelm standing on a bridge, reciting Anglo-Saxon poems accompanied by his harp, thus attracting men to God by traditional Germanic means.[1]

It is, then, only from his Latin writings that we can know Aldhelm at first hand. Of these, some of his letters are of importance to the historian; but only one, his large epistle addressed to a Northumbrian king Aldfrith under the name of Acircius, a miscellaneous treatise largely treating of metrics, concerns us here. This work, written in a difficult and otiosely learned style, discusses the hexameter in particular, and illustrates that special interest in Latin metrics which characterized the first phase of Anglo-Saxon learning, and was shared by both Bede and Alcuin. But this *Epistola ad Acircium* is principally interesting to the literary student for its inclusion of the century of *riddles* or *aenigmata*. These versified Latin riddles were most influential for vernacular poetry, as may be seen from their adaptation or imitation in some of the riddles of the Exeter Book; but they are also extremely valuable in their own right for the light they throw on Anglo-Saxon daily life, and on the high level which this culture had reached in Wessex of the late seventh century.[2] As poetry, however, Aldhelm's riddles are more ingenious and cleverly learned than strictly literary. No. 35, on the *lorica* or corslet, in the Exeter Book is freely translated from Aldhelm; as is also No. 40, which is the longest of all, and is a protracted discourse on Creation and the aspects of nature rather than a riddle. It is little more than an Englishing of Aldhelm's *Aenigma De Creatura*. That Aldhelm's *Lorica* aenigma was highly esteemed is suggested by the fact that its Anglo-Saxon rendering appears not only in the Exeter Book, but also a second time in eighth-century Northumbrian dress in a Leiden University MS version now known as *The Leiden Riddle*. There was a special interest for the early learned Anglo-Saxons in riddles, grammatical problems, metrics, and generally learned puzzles; and the age of Bede produced a good deal of ingenious Latin writing: but this is hardly literature. Archbishop Tatwine of Canterbury produced a collection of *aenigmata* in the Aldhelm manner early in the eighth century; and a certain Abbot Eusebius of Wearmouth completed the set to make a century. With regard to the influence of Aldhelm on Anglo-Saxon verse, the most striking thing is the Irish-suggested blend of alliteration and internal end-rhyme which he and others of

---

[1] In his life of St Aldhelm included in Book 5 of his work on the English bishops *Gesta Pontificum Anglorum*, ed. N. E. S. A. Hamilton (Rolls Series, London, 1870), pp. 330–344.

[2] There is a convenient edition of these Riddles by James H. Pitman, *The Riddles of Aldhelm* (New Haven, 1925), which includes a translation.

his time cultivated; for this practice probably lies behind the use of
Old English Leonine rhymes which developed in later times. Here is
a fair specimen of Aldhelm's verse of this type:

> En vehebant volumina numerosa per agmina
> multimodis et mysticis elucubrata normulis,
> quorum auctori *aius* adesse constat alitus;
> quae profetae, apostoli doctiloqui oraculi
> indiderunt pergaminae almo inflati flamine.[1]

Here the language is simpler than is common with him; yet even in
this short passage we find a Latinized Greek word, *aius* = *hagios*, 'holy'.
The authenticity of the above lines as Aldhelm's work has of late been
questioned, and they have been attributed to his royal pupil Æthel-
wald of Mercia; but they are exactly in the manner of that Aldhelmian
group of Anglo-Saxon Latin practitioners of rhythmic metre combined with alliteration and internal rhyme which characterized the
period and influenced vernacular verse later.

Aldhelm's most considerable poem is his famous *De Laudibus
Virginum*, which puts into hexameters his prose work on the same
theme, with many more examples. It was regarded as almost a text-
book for religious, and was for long quoted and glossed. But Aldhelm's tumescent style and deliberate flourishing of learning lack
literary merit, though his verse, being restrained by his feeling for
grammar and the discipline of the alien hexameter, is less obscure and
tedious. It is, indeed, as a cultural inspiration that Aldhelm is important; as the chief labourer in the field which Theodore and Hadrian
had planted. His aim was to combine ecclesiastical with literary
culture, to make the Anglo-Saxon Church employ fully the literary
arts which were necessary to the proper handling of the Bible; and to
direct the nascent literary art into ecclesiastically desirable channels.
This is true of his work for Latin. No doubt the same principles
guided his vernacular poetry, of which we can only now catch
memories. It is tantalizing indeed that St Aldhelm may well have
been a slightly earlier Anglo-Saxon poet than Cædmon, and yet that
we possess not even one line of his native verse. Aldhelm stands out
as the most distinguished product of the early Canterbury school,
who became a focus for that civilizing classical and patristic Latin
culture which had almost disappeared from the rest of Europe. As
Ernst Curtius puts it:

> It (the work of Aldhelm) is the first expression of the new Christian
> culture of England, which arose between 650 and 680 after the conver-
> sion of the Anglo-Saxons, and in which not only Irish and Roman

[1] Quoted in F. J. E. Raby, *A History of Secular Latin Poetry in the Middle Ages*
(Oxford, 1934), I, p. 173.

but also Graeco-Oriental (Theodore of Tarsus and the African Hadrian) influences mingled with British and Anglo-Saxon culture.[1]

At the time when Theodore of Tarsus was being commissioned in Rome as Archbishop of Canterbury a young Northumbrian monk, an aristocrat, happened to be there seeking to enlarge his scholarship, and it was the meeting of Theodore and this monk, known as Benedict Biscop, that gave the original impetus to the development of that Northumbrian 'golden age' of which Bede was the greatest product. Benedict Biscop, returning to England with Theodore, studied under him and Abbot Hadrian, worked for a time as Abbot of the Canterbury monastery, and then founded the monastries first of Wearmouth and then of Jarrow as its sister house. These linked monasteries quickly became centres of the most learned and cultured scholarship in Europe; and Benedict Biscop, on repeated travels to Rome and other Italian towns, immensely enriched his houses with libraries of Latin and Greek learning, sacred and also secular, and by his immense interest in the material arts also gave a great impetus to that flowering of all aspects of then known art which was to make his Northumbria the leader of Europe in arts as well as in letters. It was under Benedict Biscop, and then his pupil and successor Ceolfrid as Abbot of Jarrow, that Bede received his education. This meant that Bede gained the nearest possible thing to a full liberal education then obtainable in Europe. Born in 673, Bede spent his whole life as a Benedictine monk in his beloved monastery of Jarrow, leaving it only for short visits, between the age of seven and his death on May 27th, 735. Always fully carrying out his duties as a monk, the *opus Dei*, he devoted all the rest of his time and immense intellectual energy to reading, teaching, and writing. He produced works on grammar and metre, commentaries on books of the Bible, scientific treatises on chronology, medicine, astronomy, and meteorology, lives of saints, and poems including a set of hymns. But it was in his last years that he completed what may still fairly be called a great work of historical scholarship in his *Ecclesiastical History of the English People* [*Historia Ecclesiastica Gentis Anglorum*], finished in the year 731.[2] His reputation throughout the Middle Ages and beyond covered all kinds of learning, both for his writings and as a teacher; but today it is his *Historia Ecclesiastica* that still maintains his name as one of the master-minds of Europe.[3]

Only five lines of Anglo-Saxon verse, generally known as *Bede's*

[1] E. R. Curtius, *European Literature and the Latin Middle Ages*, translated by W. R. Trask (London, 1953), p. 457.

[2] The most convenient edition is that in the Loeb Classical Library by J. E. King, which includes a competent translation: *Baedae Opera Historica* (London, 1930). Charles Plummer's edition of the Latin text remains the best: *Bedae Opera Historica* (Oxford, 1896). There is a useful translation also in Everyman's Library 479.

[3] *Cf.* R. W. Chambers, "Bede", Annual Lecture on a Master Mind, *Proceedings of the British Academy* XXII (1936), pp. 129–156.

Death-Song,[1] remain of Bede's vernacular writings, though we know from a Latin letter of his disciple Cuthbert that he was dictating his translation of St John's Gospel at the time of his death.[2] It is therefore only as an Anglo-Latin writer that we may now consider him. The vernacular poem has little more than historical interest, as it shows only the same rather stiff competence as does his Latin verse.

Bede was primarily a teacher, providing books for learners and scholars, and in no sense did he ever aim at literary art. But such is the pleasing simplicity, clarity, and grammatical superiority of his prose style that at least his narrative and historical works can be read with some aesthetic satisfaction. He habitually spoke, wrote, and taught in Latin all his life, so that there is a natural ease and directness in his prose which contrasts markedly with the rather 'showing-off' style of St Aldhelm, who perhaps wished to demonstrate that he could equal the Irish Latinists in stylistic learning. On the other hand, Bede's interest in metre, which produced his treatise *De Arte Metrica*, was due mainly to the value he set on the study of Latin metre as a necessary aid to the discipline of the effective use of that language. Bede was not, in any strict modern sense, an original thinker, yet he was clearly creative in presenting in his *Historia Ecclesiastica* the basic features of scientific historiography in a way unequalled between classical times and the Renaissance. He consulted all available authorities at first hand from all parts of the country and beyond, as well as traditions and direct memories handed down by authenticated persons. He carefully mentions his authorities and his methods of consulting them. His friend Albinus, a learned product of Theodore's Canterbury school, for instance, was made to check all the Southern material as indicated in Bede's preface: and a priest (afterwards archbishop) named Nothelm, who visited Rome, authenticated and copied under Albinus's direction all the relevant Papal documents, such as those of St Gregory the Great, who had sent out the mission of St Augustine. A draft of the *Ecclesiastical History* was read and criticized by the antiquarian Ceolwulf, King of Northumbria. In the same way, when preparing his account of St Cuthbert of Lindisfarne —a shorter version in prose and another expanded into verse—he consulted people who had personally known the saint, and had everything checked by monks from Lindisfarne.[3]

Bede's primary interest was the story of the conversion of England to Christianity, and the personalities of the chief actors in that heroic history, so that his *Historia Ecclesiastica* becomes vivid and moving from the account of the arrival of St Augustine's mission onward.

[1] *Bede's Death-Song*, included in the *Epistola Cuthberti de Obitu Bedae*, is fully studied in E. v. K. Dobbie, *The Manuscripts of Caedmon's Hymn and Bede's Death Song* (New York, 1937).

[2] This is included in the editions of Bede's historical works already noted, of both Plummer and King. The latter provides a translation.

[3] See *Two Lives of St. Cuthbert*, ed. Bertram Colgrave (Cambridge, 1940). This includes a translation.

The numerous short lives of saints which consequently occupy so much of the book, though they necessarily imply acceptance of the faith and outlook of the age, show the same care in authenticating stories of supernatural happenings and miracles. While holding implicitly the faith in miracles of a good Catholic, he shows himself, in Dryden's words on Chaucer, "a perpetual fountain of good sense." But there are at least two other ways in which Bede made remarkable historical advances. He first applied the new chronology invented by the sixth-century Dionysius Exiguus by which all matters are dated from the year of Christ's Incarnation, as they still are. Secondly, he first expressed and implied the idea of an English nation which included Angles, Saxons, and Jutes. Indeed, his chosen title, *Historia Ecclesiastica Gentis Anglorum*, implies that he thought of the English (*Angli*) as one nation (*gens*). While using Continental authorities, such as the Spaniard Orosius, for the early pre-conversion period of English history he also sometimes shows that he had examined the work of the British Gildas for its occasional glimpses of earliest Anglo-Saxon history. The same qualities as historian, though sometimes obscured by the method of hagiography then universally accepted, are exemplified in Bede's account of the abbots of Wearmouth-Jarrow, the *Vitae Beatorum Abbatum*, and the prose life of St Cuthbert: and many of his letters giving advice and theological or historical information at request are agreeable and forceful in style. An example of this is Bede's letter sent to Egbert on his taking up duty as Archbishop of York.[1]

Bede's scientific work is best illustrated in his treatise on times and seasons and natural phenomena, *De Temporum Ratione*, which supplies matter scientifically in advance of the age and shows the breadth of its author's interests in chronology and meteorology. But this, like his work of natural history, *De Naturis Rerum*, falls quite outside of literary study. Similarly, Bede's numerous exegetical theological writings must be omitted. An attractive, if somewhat imaginative and speculative, study of all aspects of Bede, at once scholarly and for the general student, is included in Eleanor Duckett's *Anglo-Saxon Saints and Scholars* (New York, 1947). For the literary historian, however, there is one chapter of the *Historia Ecclesiastica* which is of special importance: the account of the first Anglo-Saxon poet whose name can be linked with known work—Cædmon, whose revolutionary influence as a pioneer was touched on in the preceding chapter. This passage, IV, 24, well illustrates Bede's simple and attractive manner and the quality of his Latin. But it also shows his literary sensitiveness in refusing to attempt an exact rendering of Cædmon's *Hymn* into Latin while providing its sense and matter. The impossibility of translating the best poetry literally from one language into another without loss is emphasized here:

[1] Text in Plummer, *op. cit.* There is a good translation in *English Historical Documents*, ed. Dorothy Whitelock (London, 1955), I, pp. 735 ff.

Neque enim possunt carmina, quamvis optime composita, ex alia in aliam linguam ad verbum sine detrimento sui decoris ac dignitatis transferri.

As a hagiographer Bede, within the limitations of the thought-patterns of his time, writes often well, though his prose life of St Cuthbert 'is outdone by the work on this theme of a Lindisfarne monk.[1] The making of Latin lives of saints became from this time on a very considerable monastic industry in which the eighth century often did well. Notable, besides the anonymous life of St Cuthbert, is, in a far less restrained style, that of St Wilfred of York by Eddi (Eddius).[2] Many of Bede's short lives incorporated in his *Historia Ecclesiastica* were later translated into Old English. Among the best are those of St Oswald of Northumbria and St Chad of Mercia. One hagiographical work stands quite apart from the rest: a life of St Gregory the Great by an unknown monk of Whitby, written about the end of the seventh century. This, of which there is as yet no satisfactory edition, is almost certainly the oldest piece of writing produced in England by an Anglo-Saxon. It is quite individual in its arrangement, is in very poor Latin, but it embodies what seem to be oral traditions of St Gregory and the conversion of England through his initiative and that in particular of King Edwin of Northumbria.[3]

Bede's correspondent Egbert, Archbishop of York, through setting up a school of Christian Latin learning at York which in time outshone Wearmouth-Jarrow, came to be the teacher of the greatest scholar of his time, Alhwine (Latinized as Alcuin), who inspired directly what is often called the Carolingian Renaissance, which re-established learning on the European continent and revitalized education. Anglo-Saxon life and the work of Anglo-Saxons on the Continent between Bede and Alcuin (the name by which he is universally known) may be followed in generally effective and readable medieval Latin in the numerous letters which were exchanged between the ecclesiastical leaders of Anglo-Saxon England or between them and their European colleagues. Bede's own letters already mentioned may best be followed by the reading of those of St Boniface, the Devon scholar who did such great practical work as missionary to the Germans.[4] Alcuin himself was no inconsiderable letter-writer.

[1] See Bertram Colgrave, *op. cit.*

[2] Bertram Colgrave, *The Life of Bishop Wilfrid by Eddius Stephanus* (Cambridge, 1927). This contains text, translation, and notes.

[3] See Bertram Colgrave, "The Earliest Life of St. Gregory the Great, written by a Whitby Monk", in *Celt and Saxon, Studies in the Early British Border*, ed. Nora K. Chadwick (Cambridge, 1963), pp. 119–137.

[4] St Boniface's letters are conveniently available in translation in Ephraim Emerton, *The Letters of Saint Boniface* (Columbia University, 1940). Some of the more important in translation are included also in *English Historical Documents*, op. cit., along with other Latin letters of special interest to Anglo-Saxon students in the section *Early Correspondence*, pp. 727 ff.

Born in the year of Bede's death, 735, Alcuin received his training in his native York, and became a teacher in that famous school when he was about thirty, and later its head. In later life he became the Emperor Charles the Great's principal educator, about 782; and spent nearly all the remainder of his life first at Charlemagne's palace, where he set up an educational centre, and from 796 at the monastery of St Martin at Tours, of which he had become Abbot. Here he had his great school and library. His death was in 804.

It cannot be said that Alcuin is important in the history of literature in the strict sense; yet as an educationist of dominant influence on Western medieval culture, and as a practical theologian who has left permanent effects on the text of the Latin Bible and the liturgy of the Church, he has at least indirectly a place as a formative literary power. His Latin prose is generally straightforward and clear in the many manuals and 'helpbooks' he produced for his students. His verse is fairly correct on classical lines, but seldom suggests a poet any more than does Bede's. He dealt with grammar and rhetoric, but mainly with Biblical exegesis and the confutation of current heresies. Probably the most interesting thing about Alcuin is that his is the first recorded example in England of a vocation to the teaching profession; and his most valued work was the building up of schools of learning, first at York, and later at Charlemagne's capital Aachen and at his great monastery of St Martin at Tours. His interest in Anglo-Saxon education was kept up after he had taken up work on the Continent by a wide correspondence with English colleagues and students, and occasional visits to his native York. Following on the practical work of St Boniface and his associates, Alcuin was able to forward as a practical administrator and adviser every aspect of the Carolingian Renaissance. But this is a matter which does not belong to the present chapter.

Apart from his educational work, the two outstanding contributions of Alcuin of profound significance are his share in the revision of the text of the Vulgate Bible[1] and his work on the revision of the Gregorian Sacramentary, which is the basis of the Mass to this day. His other theological writings retain no importance; but his work on the Bible text and on the liturgy is characteristic of the practical gifts of the best Anglo-Saxon scholars, who generally made but little contribution to philosophy of any kind. Today Alcuin's prayer, as noticed in Chapter 1, is still most widely used—*Deus, cui omne cor patet*—and this still opens the Communion service in the Anglican Prayer-book and those of its affiliation: "O God, to Whom all hearts be open." This prayer has true literary quality, blending brevity, economy of language, and dignity. Alcuin's other lasting contributions to liturgy were the introduction of the practice of chanting the Nicene Creed at Mass and the establishment of the Festival of All-

---

[1] *Cf.* Edward K. Rand, "A Preliminary Study of Alcuin's Bible", *Harvard Theological Review* XXIV (1931).

Saints—both ideas probably brought from Ireland via England. Though in later life a *de facto* prince of the Church, he remained only in deacon's orders—a fact which confirms the impression of humility made by his writings. Today his most interesting writings are his letters,[1] filled with practical advice and progressive ideas on education and Church organization, and his poem on the holy men of York Minster, *De Pontificibus et Sanctis Ecclesiae Eboracensis Carmen*.[2] The best of his few lives of saints is that of his kinsman St Willibrord, the apostle of the Frisians. This, following the example of both Aldhelm (in his prose and verse treatises *De Laudibus Virginitatis* and *De Laudibus Virginum*) and Bede (with his dual treatment of St Cuthbert), Alcuin wrote in both a prose and a metrical version.[3] Alcuin's finest purely literary work would undoubtedly be his *Contention between Spring and Winter* [*Conflictus Veris et Hiemis*], if its authenticity as his work could be established. This is a graceful poetical exercise in that debate-literature which was a feature of Roman schools of rhetoric, and it is historically significant as the earliest example of this type in England. It has a pastoral setting, reminding one of classical verse-contentions, and is concerned especially with the cuckoo, *Cuculus*, and as the harbinger of spring it is handled in a way somewhat parallel to its treatment in such Anglo-Saxon poems as *The Seafarer* and *The Husband's Message*.[4]

In some of his poems addressed to his friends and pupils, as in some of his familiar letters, Alcuin shows that he could write gracefully and with a light touch in familiar style. A favourite pupil, one Dodo whom he playfully used to call Cuculus, and who had apparently left his studies for Bacchus and other pleasure-givers, has a charming little poem addressed to him, in which he is referred to as the cuckoo who departs before the summer is fulfilled:

Heu cuculus, nobis fuerat cantare suetus!
  quae te nunc rapuit hora nefanda tuis?
Heu Cuculus, cuculus, qua te regione reliqui,
  infelix nobis illa dies fuerat.
Non pereat cuculus, veniet sub tempore veris,
  et nobis veniens carmina laeta ciet.

[1] See Rolf B. Page, *The Letters of Alcuin* (London, 1909). A few of Alcuin's letters are translated in *English Historical Documents*, op. cit., pp. 774 ff. For the complete text of Alcuin's letters see *Monumenta Germaniae Historica, Epistolarum*, Vol. IV.

[2] Alcuin's poems are in *Monumenta Germaniae Historica, Poetae Latini Aevi Carolini*, Vol. I, ed. Dümmler, and Vol. IV, ed. Strecker. The *De Pontificibus et Sanctis Ecclesiae Eboracensis Carmen* in Vol. I, pp. 169 ff.

[3] *Vita Sancti Willibrordi* is in *Bibliotheca Rerum Germanicarum*, ed. Jaffé, Vol. VI, *Monumenta Alcuiniana*, pp. 35 ff. It is translated in A. Grieve, *Willibrord* (London, 1923), pp. 99 ff.

[4] See *Mon. Germ. Hist. Poetae Lat. Aevi Carolini*, I, pp. 270 ff. An attractive and accurate rendering of this poem by Professor William Alfred of Harvard is in the volume of studies in honour of F. P. Magoun (New York, 1965), pp. 17–18.

Alas, cuckoo who was wont to sing to us, what horrible hour has
ravished thee from thy people? O cuckoo, cuckoo, it was an unhappy
day for us in whatever place I left you. May the cuckoo not perish.
He will come back with the season of spring, and returning to us will
recite joyful songs.[1]

For the student of Anglo-Saxon poetry Alcuin has a special
interest, like Bede, for a reference in one of his letters to native
English lays. Addressing the monks of Lindisfarne at the close of the
eighth century, Alcuin rebukes them for listening to heroic lays such
as that about Ingeld, accompanied by the harp, when they ought to
be hearing in their refectory a reader declaiming sermons of the
Fathers.[2] Evidently Anglo-Saxon secular poetry was being recited in
traditional style in some Northumbrian religious houses when Alcuin
wrote. No doubt it was to this and similar practices that we owe the
preservation of *Beowulf*. The Abbot of Tours poses in this letter the
rhetorical question "Quid Hinieldus cum Christo?" He claims that a
religious house is too narrow to hold both Germanic hero-kings and
the King of Kings. Alcuin's denial of the place of a pagan Germanic
hero such as Ingeld, whose story is allusively told in *Beowulf*,[3] had in
fact been largely answered by Cædmon's application of the traditional
heroic poetic technique to Christian purposes, as described by
Bede.

There is excellent documentation and a bibliography of Alcuin
in Eleanor Duckett's *Alcuin, Friend of Charlemagne* (New York,
1951).

The age of Alfred, so important in the history of Anglo-Saxon
prose, produced one piece of Latin prose which may be said to have
made literary history. This was the biography of King Alfred,
written soon after the year 893 by Asser, the Welsh monk from St
David's who became the King's Latin teacher, adviser on Welsh
affairs, and Bishop of Sherborne. Inspired, it would seem, by Einhard's Life of Charlemagne, *Vita Caroli Magni*,[4] one of the greater
products of the Carolingian Renaissance, Asser produced the first
biography of a secular notable known in England. Einhard had
conscientiously followed in the steps of the Roman Suetonius's "Lives
of the Emperors"—*De Vita Caesarum*; and there had been some
Irish secular lives of military heroes which Asser could have known
also. But his vivid if over-laudatory pictures of Alfred's personality,
and intimate glimpses of his daily life, may be said to mark the beginning of the literary art of secular biography in England. The Latin of
Asser is generally simple and sometimes vivid.[1] Not only is its matter

[1] The poem is admiringly examined by F. J. E. Raby, *op. cit.* I, pp. 184–186.
[2] Text in *Monumenta Germaniae Historica, Epistolarum* IV, p. 183.
[3] Cf. *Beowulf*, lines 2024 ff. and *Widsith*, lines 45–49.
[4] There is a translation in A. J. Grant, *Early Lives of Charlemagne* (London,
1926).

basic for the history of its period, including some otherwise unobtainable information about Alfred's dealings with the Welsh princes, but it is in itself not without literary merit. In particular, its account of King Alfred's education, his special zeal for Anglo-Saxon poetry, and his ways of studying, are of real value to the historian of English vernacular literature. Asser's style has been called pretentious and verbose: but in fact it compares favourably with most writing of his time, though it is very unequal. The combination of biographical matter with Latin renderings of annals from a lost version of the *Anglo-Saxon Chronicle* gives the whole an awkward shape, and Asser seems to have left his book unfinished. The authenticity of the work has been lately doubted, and it has been attributed to a time a century or more later.[2] But even if the generally accepted view that it is (apart from obvious interpolations) the genuine work of Bishop Asser should have to be modified, its value to the student of literature would remain. King Alfred mentions Asser as one of his helpers for Latin in the Preface to his translations of St Gregory's *Pastoral Care* and William of Malmesbury speaks of Asser as having helped Alfred in translating Boethius. Moreover, both the *Anglo-Saxon Chronicle* and the *Annales Cambriae* record Asser's death. Here is Asser's account of how King Alfred first came to learn Anglo-Saxon poetry by heart, which may serve to illustrate him at his best:

> Cum ergo quodam die mater sua sibi et fratribus suis quendam Saxonicum poematicae artis librum, quem in manu habebat, ostenderet, ait: "Quisquis vestrum discere citius istum codicem possit, dabo illi illum". Qua voce, immo divina inspiratione instinctus Alfredus, et pulchritudine principalis litterae illius libri illectus, ita matri respondens, inquit: 'Verene dabis istum librum uni ex nobis, scilicet illi, qui citissime intelligere et recitare ante te possit?' Ad haec illa, arridens: 'Dabo,' infit, 'illi'. Tunc ille statim tollens librum de manu sua, magistrum adiit, et legit. Quo lecto, matri retulit et recitavit.[3]

It is significant in this famous Chapter 23 of Asser that the boy Alfred, who could not read till he was twelve, being *illiteratus*, as Asser puts it, was attracted by the beauty of an illuminated initial capital at the beginning of the book of poems which his mother

[1] *Asserius De Rebus Gestis Ælfredi* is most thoroughly edited by William H. Stevenson as *Asser's Life of King Alfred* (Oxford, 1904). There are translations by A. S. Cook (Boston, 1906) and by L. C. Jane with Introduction and Notes (London, 1926).

[2] See V. H. Galbraith, *An Introduction to the Study of History* (London, 1964), Part 3.

[3] Text from W. H. Stevenson's edition of Asser, *op. cit.*, p. 28. *Cf.* his important notes, pp. 221 ff., in which he emends *et* of the penultimate line to *qui*. This chapter 23 is translated in *English Historical Documents* I, *op. cit.*, p. 266.

showed him, and that, having the work read aloud to him by his teacher, he then learned it by heart and recited it. The rather hagiographical tone, which may remind us a little of Bede's account of the poet Cædmon, is of course inevitable at this time.

In reviewing the great men of tenth-century Anglo-Saxon England, J. Armitage Robinson, in the Preface to his authoritative *The Times of St Dunstan*, observes, "We could wish to know more of these great men: but our records are very scant. They were men of acts, not of words: and they left little or nothing in writing."

Indeed, the period between Asser and the Norman Conquest is not from the point of view of Latin literature in Britain notable for originality or memorable aesthetic quality. Latin, being the language of the Church and all its administration, of all higher education and usually of legal charters, continued to produce writings of many kinds increasingly. There is no falling off, but rather increase in quantity, but scarcely anything in itself, apart from some of Ælfric's Latin, of any outstanding permanent value. The impulse given by King Alfred's translations of standard Latin works into the vernacular never failed, though it naturally fluctuated with changes in political and social conditions. During the time of the Benedictine Renaissance of the late tenth and early eleventh centuries Latin writings became, of course, more abundant and of better technical quality: yet the literary work produced by this great age was in strength and originality one of Anglo-Saxon prose, which at this time reached a level of conscious literary art. Further, the art of vernacular translation from Latin considerably improved and enlarged its scope. The Norman Conquest made no break in continuity as regards Latin writing in England, but it was not till the twelfth century that Latin literature began again and at a much higher level to produce work that was creative and had aesthetic appeal.

The leading makers of homilies of the Benedictine period, such as Ælfric and Archbishop Wulfstan, wrote in Latin, of course, as well as in English. But their Latin was usually for purely practical and teaching purposes. Ælfric wrote the Preface to his *Latin Grammar*[1] in both Latin and English. His most important work of practical education was this *Grammar*, which is an outstanding work of its kind, intended for the teaching of Latin in monastic schools. Written in Anglo-Saxon with explanations of all the Latin technical terms of grammar, it provides for the first time in a European vernacular native but new-fabricated grammatical terminology. Of special interest is his *Colloquy*,[2] which provides simple conversation-pieces in the form of dialogues between teacher and pupil, treating of the ordinary happenings of rustic daily life and occupations. This

---

[1] See *Ælfrics Grammatik und Glossar*, ed. Julius Zupitza (Berlin, 1880).
[2] Ælfric's *Colloquy*, ed. G. N. Garmonsway, 2nd ed. (London, 1947).

Colloquy affords excellent illustrations of the familiar use of colloquial Latin, with parallel Anglo-Saxon renderings.

The continuity of Latin hagiography at a fairly even level through and beyond the Norman Conquest is well illustrated by the constant writing of Latin lives of saints, which went on side by side with the increasing provision of vernacular translations of such works. Ælfric's life of his Winchester mentor, St Æthelwold, *Vita Sancti Ethelwoldi*,[1] is a first-class piece of Latin hagiography, as well as being of historical importance. The life of St Oswald of Worcester[2] written by a monk of Ramsey who may have been Byrhtferth, the learned scientific teacher who wrote the vernacular *Manual*, is in rather high-flown and verbose Latin, but is of special interest for its account of the coronation of King Edgar in 973; for its author was himself present at this historic ceremony in Bath, of which he gives a detailed account. Upon this rests our knowledge of the first fully ritual and sacramental coronation liturgy in Britain, a liturgy which is the foundation of the English coronation service to this day.[3] A good example of the continuing vitality of Latin hagiography in England after the Conquest is the work of Eadmer, who was St Anselm's chaplain and disciple. He was an Anglo-Saxon monk, born about 1060. Like Ælfric a century earlier, he wrote, about the year 1120, a life of his own beloved master St Anselm, in vivid and pleasing Latin. In fact his *Vita Sancti Anselmi*[4] is one of the best of its kind written by an Anglo-Saxon. Historically valuable also, and again in direct and agreeable Latin, is his account of the chief historical events between 1066 and 1120: *Historia Novorum in Anglia*.[5] Eadmer is also worthy of especial mention for his clear and well-argued little theological treatise on the doctrine of the Immaculate Conception,[6] which, as explained in Chapter 1, is the first known reasoned defence of its subject, and shows the Anglo-Saxon ability to present theological matters in simple and direct style, of which Ælfric had given so many demonstrations.

Throughout this period the growing need of the Church for Latin books of all kinds brought about a multiplication of improving Latin manuscripts, and the art of the scriptorium produced some works of the highest quality. St Dunstan was a great promoter of artistically attractive Latin texts, of which the famous *Benedictional*

[1] See *Chronicon Monasterii de Abingdon*, ed. Joseph Stevenson (Rolls Series, London, *Rerum Britannicarum Medii Aevi Scriptores*, 1858, Vol. 2, pp. 255–266.

[2] See *The Historians of the Church of York and its Archbishops*, ed. J. Raines (Rolls Series, London, 1879), II, pp. 399–475.

[3] See L. B. Wickham Legg, *English Coronation Records* (London, 1901). *Cf.* P. E. Schramm, *A History of the English Coronation*, translated by L. B. Wickham Legg (London, 1937).

[4] See *Eadmeri Historia Novorum in Anglia*, ed. M. Rule (Rolls Series, London, 1884), pp. 303–440.

[5] *Op. cit.*, pp. 1–301.

[6] *Eadmeri Tractatus de Conceptione Sanctae Mariae*, ed. H. Thurstan and T. Slater (Freiburg, 1904).

of *St Æthelwold* and the *Bosworth Psalter* are among the finest examples. England before the Norman Conquest had become notable
for its book production. In the period of Ælfric, too, there were laymen who could read Latin and even seek its culture, such as Ælfric's
friend Æthelweard, an ealdorman of the South-west. This Æthelweard even attempted composition, or at least translation, in Latin.
Some years before his death in 998 he made his Latin *Cronicon*,
which is a history of England made largely from a lost version of the
Anglo-Saxon Chronicle with some additions as far as the death of
Edgar in 975.[1] Its Latin is at once ambitious and extremely inaccurate, and William of Malmesbury thought it, as contrasted with the
pleasurable style of Eadmer's *Historia Novorum in Anglia*, best passed
over in silence. However, there can be little doubt that, at the time of
the Norman Conquest, England was far more advanced in the arts
engendered by Latin culture than were her conquerors, though for a
time Anglo-Saxon Latin writings were no longer creative or
original.

Looking back at the Latin writings of the Anglo-Saxon period,
from the point of view of style, two influences stand out: that of the
Hisperica Famina and that of the Vulgate Bible. The strange collection of rhythmical and often poetic prose which was produced,
probably in the west of Britain in the sixth century, and known as
Hisperica Famina,[2] is characterized by the use of learned and obscure
vocabulary, such as Greek and even Hebrew words among many rare
Latin terms. In describing aspects of the life of a student, it shows
itself the product of a secular school of Celtic Latin learning (some
think it originated in Ireland rather than Britain), and its obscure but
at times poetical and eloquent style is clearly of just the type which
lies behind much of the writing of Gildas, St Aldhelm, and Alcuin,
and can still be seen in some of the Latin charters of King Athelstan
as late as the early tenth century. But the dominant stylistic model in
the best of the Latin writers, beginning with Bede, was that of the
Vulgate. This influence of the Latin of the Bible was what one would
expect in view of the medieval canons of literary criticism. Clarity,
and the conveying of facts and meanings in a style both natural and
pleasing (the aim of St Jerome), was the aim alike of Bede and of
Ælfric two and a half centuries later; and the letters of the Church
leaders of the Benedictine Revival again illustrate these qualities. The
Irish liking for the enigmatic naturally influenced early Anglo-Saxon
Latinists educated in an Irish-inspired tradition, as did the Celtic
love of combining internal rhyme with alliteration in rhythmic Latin
versifying. Yet it was the dominating teaching-position of the Vulgate
which triumphed in the end—especially in Latin prose. Asser, as a
Welshman, might indulge at times in stylistic obscurity apparently

---

[1] There is an excellent edition with translation by A. Campbell in the Nelson
Mediaeval Series (Edinburgh and London, 1962).
[2] *Cf.* F. J. E. Raby, *op. cit.*, I, pp. 167–169.

for the sake of effect; but, as the example quoted earlier in this chapter shows, he could also write with relatively simple agreeableness.

Finally, it should be remembered that, though the influence of Latin on Anglo-Saxon linguistically was never very great, the effects of Latin Christian culture on patterns of thinking were profound.

PART II

POETRY

CHAPTER 5

Germanic Heroic Tradition

ALTHOUGH ALMOST ALL the surviving Old English poetry appears only in manuscripts of the late tenth or early eleventh centuries, there is included in this corpus a group of fragmentary short pieces which contain material going back to heroic traditions brought from the Continental homes of the Anglo-Saxon settlers in Britain (as does *Beowulf*), presenting echoes of a way of life belonging to the age of the Germanic migrations, before the fundamental effects of Christian and Latin contacts. These poems, which link Anglo-Saxon culture with its Germanic places of origin, embody the oldest expression of the Germanic heroic spirit in Anglo-Saxon. Some of them also tell us of the life and poetic art of the Old English verse-reciter, called in his own language a scop. The group, which includes pieces of varying date, character, and homogeneity, comprises *Widsith*, the *Finn Fragment*, *Waldere*, *Deor*, and *Wulf and Eadwacer*.

These earliest Old English remains of Germanic heroic verse, though occasionally touched by the fact that their authors and audiences were already Christian-influenced, preserve much of the culture described by Tacitus in his *Germania*,[1] an account of the Germanic tribes written near the close of the first century, with its emphasis on the basic Germanic values—loyalty to chosen aristocratic leaders even to death and beyond, the sacredness of the ties of kinship, the supreme duty of avenging a slain leader, and a deep devotion to a type of naturalistic religion which derived heroic rulers from the gods through carefully remembered genealogies. We first learn of these ancient Germanic heroic lays—from which the earliest strata of Anglo-Saxon verse are ultimately derived—in Tacitus's *Germania*. In his third chapter he tells us that these ancient lays, *carmina antiqua*, are the sole means of handing down—orally, of course—the tribal historical and legendary traditions; and that they record how the hero-god, "bravest of all men", whom he calls by the

[1] Ed. J. G. C. Anderson (Oxford, 1938).

Roman name Hercules, was once among them. They celebrate in ancient lays, he says, the founder of the whole Germanic race Tuisto, their principal deity and founder who was sprung from the earth:

> Celebrant carminibus antiquis, quod unum apud illos memoriae et annalium genus est, Tuistonem deum terra editum.[1]

As they are about to go into battle, we are told in the same chapter, the Germani, singing war-songs of Hercules, chant a kind of declamation or war-cry which they themselves term by the probably onomatopoeic word Latinized as *barritus*. This *barritus* inflames the minds of the warriors to war; and by its varying tones the fortunes of the impending battle may be discovered by divination. In this recitation, "harshness of sound and a kind of rhythmic rising and falling are especially aimed at, as the sound of the voices is made to swell out more fully and with more powerful weight through the repercussion caused by placing men's shields in front of their faces". The passage is worth quoting in the original, because the reference to the rising and falling rhythm apparently implied by the words *fractum murmur* would seem to anticipate that rhythm which is basic to all early Germanic verse and is the foundation of Anglo-Saxon verse-patterns:

> Adfectatur praecipue asperitas soni et fractum murmur, obiectis ad os scutis, quo plenior et gravior vox repercussu intumescat.

Some three centuries later than Tacitus the Goths, the most widely famous in verse of all Germanic peoples, are described in the *Latin Anthology* in a little piece entitled *De Conviviis Barbaris*, apparently by some Roman poetaster compelled to attend a banquet of the by then ruling Goths and to listen to their heroic poetry. Blending the important ill-spelled Gothic words with his Latin, he speaks of the cries of the men in greeting or health-drinking:

> Inter *eils* goticum *scapia matzia ia drincan*:
> non audet quisquam dignos edicere versus.[2]

While the Goths are saluting each other with healths, they make poetry, eat and drink: no one dare recite worthy verses.

One may imagine the Roman, with perhaps some fine set of verses concealed in his toga, listening to these sounds he would consider barbarous, when he would so gladly have produced his own elegant Latin poem. This little epigram is our first definite glimpse of the manner of reciting Germanic poetry in peacetime. Just as in *Beowulf*, at a banquet given by the king or leader to his noble retainers or comitatus, the Gothic equivalent of the Anglo-Saxon scop recited in the great hall as the warriors feasted. It is the way in which they

[1] *Germania*, III.
[2] From the *Anthologia Latina*, quoted in Stamm-Heyne's *Ulfilas*, ed. Ferdinand Wrede (Paderborn, 1920), p. xvii.

share to a varying extent in these Continental traditions of the heroic history and legend from the migration periods of the fourth, fifth, and sixth centuries that gives a certain community of tone to the otherwise somewhat heterogeneous group of short poems with which this chapter is concerned. They are what remains, in fragmentary and allusively incomplete form, of material from Germanic heroic story which the Angles, Saxons, and Jutes must have brought to Britain from their homelands, with an already established tradition of metre, diction, and style. But this material and the outlook in which it is expressed is properly to be regarded as Germanic rather than English. For the Germanic peoples had thought of themselves as based upon the idea of the clan, not in any sense of nationality. Even as late as *Beowulf*, in which the characters of the stories which make up the poem are of differing Germanic tribes—Danes, Geats, Swedes, etc.— the outlook is still mainly Continental Germanic, though fundamentally touched by Christian culture. Of the five pieces especially now to be discussed, three, *Widsith*, *Deor*, and *Wulf and Eadwacer*, are in the Exeter Book, a kind of anthology of short, mostly lyric, poems copied at the close of the tenth century. The other two, *The Finn Fragment* and *Waldere*, each found on odd sheets of parchment, are again of approximately the same date in their surviving forms. Yet there is considerable disparity in their probable dates of origin. Moreover, the heroes touched on in these poems came originally from the different Germanic peoples, and none of them are in fact English. Nor did they originate from the Anglo-Saxon homelands for the most part. Weland, the magic smith illustrated in *Deor*, was of South German origin, while Eormanric and Theodoric, who appear in this poem, were Goths. The characters of the love-story implied in *Wulf and Eadwacer* are of no known provenance. Finn was a Jutish king of the Frisians, though Hengest of this story may be identified with the Hengest who led the invasion of Britain in English historical tradition. The Guthhere of *Waldere* is probably originally the king of the Burgundians better known as Gunther. Some of these characters are found again in *Beowulf*, such as Weland, Eormanric, Finn, and Hengest.

The longest but also the oldest of our poems is *Widsith*, which is 143 lines in the Exeter Book. First put together in the late seventh century—that is to say, in the earlier years of the age of Bede—it appears in its surviving shape in the usual classical Anglo-Saxon of the Benedictine Renaissance period, since its unique copy was made, like those of the rest of the Exeter Book poems, in one of the leading cultural centres of Wessex (thought to have been Glastonbury, where St Dunstan had done his first pioneering work). Like other Old English poems, it owes its title to its editors: but in this case the title is clearly most appropriate. For the poem is a deliberate presentation of the ideal scop in his life and work by means of a fictitious hero-poet who is given the symbolic name of *Widsith*, 'far traveller'. This imaginary scop Widsith, while describing his marvellous skill in the art of the poet, provides a kind of historical and legendary conspectus of notable characters and events of that Germanic heroic tradition which the Anglo-Saxons had inherited, and still cherished in their edifying entertainments in their mead-halls. The poet seems to have based his work primarily on three of those mnemonic metrical lists of notables and famous tribes which had been handed down from more ancient times, and still survived or were imitated in Old Icelandic literature of as late as the thirteenth century, and which were termed *thulas*. With the Norse word *þula* one may perhaps compare the term *þyle*, often translated 'spokesman', applied in *Beowulf* to Unferth, who was among other things a kind of 'remembrancer' at the court of King Hrothgar of the Danes. The Latinized tribal names in the list given in Chapter 40 of the *Germania* may be a relic of such an ancient thula.

In *Widsith*, in addition to a prologue to introduce the scop Widsith, and an epilogue of concluding general observations, each of nine lines, the poem proper consists of one long speech of the scop himself of probably rather less than 120 lines—which falls clearly into three parts—with a few more that seem to have been interpolated as later additions. The poem proper is thus in three divisions—or *fitts*, as the Anglo-Saxons called them—each consisting of a thula followed by narrative or comment glorifying the poet in his far-flung journeys and his service to noble rulers, or treating of Germanic history or legend. These ancient lists are formulaic in character, and in an older type of metre than the scop's own material. Dealing respectively with kings, tribes, and notables from the Germanic fourth to sixth centuries, they follow respectively these more or less set patterns. The first are of type 'Attila ruled the Huns, Eormanric the Goths': the second 'was with the Huns, the mighty Goths, the Geats and the South Danes'; and the third 'I visited Wulfhere and Wyrmhere'. There are episodes touching on famous heroes well known otherwise in Old English poetry, such as Eormanric the historical Gothic king of the later fourth century, Offa the Angle ruler who was an ancestor of King Offa, the great ruler of Mercia, and Ingeld of the Heathobards, who is referred to in *Beowulf* and was the subject of a lost lay celebrating his tragic part in a notorious blood-feud. Eormanric of the fourth century and the last Lombard king, Alboin (here called Ælfwine), alike played a part in the life of this ideal and so long-lived imaginary poet.

Here is the Prologue, followed by a modern rendering:

> Widsið maðolade, word-hord onleac,
> se þe monna mæst mægþa ofer eorþan,
> folca geond-ferde; oft he on flete geþah
> mynelicne maþþum. Him from Myrgingum
> æþele onwocon. He mid Ealhhilde,

fælre freoþuwebban forman siþe
Hreð-cyninges ham gesohte
eastan of Ongle, Eormanrices,
wraþes wærlogan. Ongon þa worn sprecan.

Widsith, who of men had traversed most of the tribes and peoples throughout the earth, opened the treasure of his words, and spoke. Often had he received delightful treasure in halls. His lineage was from among the Myrgings [a Saxon tribe dwelling to the south of the river Eider]. On his first journey he sought the home of the glorious king Eormanric who was a foe to traitors, with his gracious consort Ealhhild, weaver of peace, travelling east from the land of the Angles. Then he began to utter an abundant speech.[1]

After some introductory lines of gnomic character the first division of the poems begins with the first thula at line 18. Beginning with Attila of the Huns, this list of rulers continues for eighteen lines. Then the poet treats in his own style of episodes of Offa the Angle and of the blood-feud which ended the glory of Heorot, Hrothgar's wondrous hall which is the scene of Beowulf's earlier exploits, and refers to the tragedy of Ingeld. Offa is most highly praised, as indeed are all the notable rulers visited by Widsith. But the special glorification of Offa, since he was the ancestor of the great Offa of Mercia of the later eighth century, may point to a Mercian centre for the completed composition of the poem. Some boasting by the imaginary scop of the many places he has visited, the vastness of the material he has collected for his poetry and the immense esteem in which he has been held, leads to the second thula at line 57 with this time the slightly varied formula as in:

Ic wæs mid Hunum and mid Hreð-gotum, etc.

I was with the Huns and with the noble Goths.

This extends for some 30 lines: and then Widsith returns to the praise of the great Gothic Eormanric with which he had begun (lines 88 ff.) and of the generosity to the scop of both the Ostrogothic king and his queen in recognition of his outstanding skill.

The second and third thulas are joined by a passage in which Widsith describes how he and a companion scop sang before the Court of Eormanric to the accompaniment of the harp so as to win the very highest praise; and this passage (lines 103 to 108) may serve as an example of the poet's own style at its best:

Ðonne wit Scilling sciran reorde
for uncrum sige-dryhtne song ahofan,

[1] This translation, and in fact the whole treatment of the interpretation of the poem, is based on the most thorough and convincing edition, by Kemp Malone in the series *Anglistica*, Vol. XIII (Copenhagen, 1962), which presents a fuller re-examination of the material in his edition of *Widsith* (London, 1936).

hlude bi hearpan hleoþor swinsade;
þonne monige men modum wlonce
wordum sprecan, þa þe wel cuþan,
þæt hi naefre song sellan ne hyrdon.

When Scilling and I with clear voices raised our joint song before our victorious lord, loudly sang a melody with harp accompaniment, there were present many men proud in heart who were skilled in such arts, who declared with emphasis that never had they heard a better poem.[1]

After a third thula with the formula *Ic sohte* of some dozen lines (112 to 124), Widsith ends his speech with more general reflections on his triumph as a singer and a little of that moralizing in which the Anglo-Saxons found pleasure.

The Epilogue to the whole poem, its final nine lines, rounds it off symmetrically in relation to the Prologue of identical length. Having introduced the poem with some account of the imaginary scop Widsith, the poet ends with an edifying piece of moralizing on the life of minstrels in general:

> Swa scriþende gesceapum hweorfað
> gleo-men gumena geond grunda fela,
> þearfe secgað, þonc-word sprecaþ,
> simle suð oþþe norð sumne gemetað
> gydda gleawne, geofum unhneawne,
> se þe fore duguþe wile dom aræran,
> eorlscipe æfnan, oþ þæt eal scæceð,
> leoht ond lif somod; lof se gewyrceð,
> hafað under heofonum heah-fæstne dom.
>
> (lines 135–144)

So it is that the minstrels among men move about as their fates determine through many lands. They utter their needs, speaking words of thanks. Always, South or North, they meet with someone who is able to value poetry, who will not be niggardly of gifts. This man will raise up his glory before his noble retainers and perform deeds of valour, until all passes away, light and life together. He who does deeds worthy of praise shall receive beneath the skies the most exalted fame.

Widsith has often been regarded as of little literary merit, but chiefly valuable for its historical and traditional material, which often markedly aids the study of *Beowulf* and other heroic poems. The thulas, which the poet probably found ready to hand as an inheritance from an older and cruder style, must have given aesthetic pleasure to

---

[1] On the special significance of this passage see Kemp Malone's Commentary in his edition, *op. cit.*, p. 51. *Cf.* also C. L. Wrenn, "Two Anglo-Saxon Harps", *Comparative Literature* XIV (1962), pp. 119–128.

an aristocratic audience steeped in Germanic lore: and the gnomic and moralizing passages again are of a quality which the Anglo-Saxons evidently found aesthetically agreeable. The careful construction and the contrasting styles and rhythms of the thulas, the poet's own reflections and narratives, can in any case still give pleasure of a properly literary kind to the student who can get something like the 'feel' of the language and the sounding rhythm of its lines. There is truth, if also some exaggeration, in Kemp Malone's words of appreciation:

> We have in our poem, indeed, a little masterpiece in structure and style. As a stylist our poet is notable above all for his success in making the complex seem simple. His elaborate periods are so cunningly wrought that the unwary reader marks neither the artifice nor art, or hears at most a flow of words as limpid as a folk-song's. Conventional stylistic devices are not wanting, it is true; but these (like those found in a folk-song) by virtue of their very familiarity and obviousness only add to the effect of simplicity at which the poet is aiming throughout.[1]

Although *Deor*—or *Deor's Lament*, as it is sometimes called—is probably of considerably later date than *Widsith*, it should properly be grouped with the other pieces of Germanic tradition dealt with in this chapter rather than with the elegiac group with which it has also some affinities. For it is parallel with *Widsith* in that it treats of a fictional scop and part of his life-story: but at the same time it deals also with a number of characters from ancient Germanic history and legend. It shares in some degree with the fragmentary *Wulf and Eadwacer*, also in the Exeter Book, the use of the lyric refrain—a device unknown in Anglo-Saxon poetry apart from these two pieces. It may not be entirely accidental, then, that in this anthology of lyric poems the Exeter Book *Deor* is immediately followed by *Wulf and Eadwacer*. Until lately it was thought that *Deor* was unique in being arranged in stanzaic form; but the discovery some twenty-five years ago of an Elizabethan transcript of a poem now known as *The Seasons for Fasting* made from one of the Cotton manuscripts burned in 1731 has provided us with an example of a much longer stanzaic piece of verse. This latter is a versified homily of 230 lines divided into stanzas of eight lines each: but its division into stanzas is not specially marked in the manuscript as the scribe of *Deor* has done, nor is its stanzaic structure combined, as in *Deor*, with the repetition of a terminal refrain.

Deor is divided in the Exeter Book into groups of lines, marked off as if stanzas by the use of initial capitals to begin each, and each, except the sixth (lines 28 to 35) concluded with an identical line which is commonly regarded as a refrain. These groups of lines are

---

[1] Kemp Malone, *op. cit.*, p. 76.

of unequal length, varying from three to eight, but the sixth group, lacking the refrain, is not separated from the seventh in the manuscript, and in it the otherwise regular special sign placed at the end of each group-refrain does not appear. The irregularity thus arising has caused many to suspect the sixth group as a later interpolation, especially because its homiletic tone does not, to a modern reader, accord with the rest of the poem, and because its presence either makes the poem end with one vastly long stanza or otherwise upsets its schematic structure by providing a stanzaic group without a refrain. But the presence in *Deor* of such a homiletic moralizing passage at the end of a set of *exempla* of unfortunate Germanic notables, and preceding the poet's final meditation on his own private misfortune, is not in fact inappropriate in an Anglo-Saxon poem: its Christian tone too would not seem inconsistent to an Anglo-Saxon audience with the traditional matter of the rest of the poem.

An evidently imaginary scop with the probably symbolic name of Deor ('noble', 'excellent', etc.), here following something like the literary device of *Widsith*, cites in five successive stanzas examples of famous Germanic characters who suffered heavy disasters which could yet be overcome. Weland the magic smith, the noble lady Beaduhild ravished by Weland in revenge for her father's barbarous cruelty to him, and an unknown woman Maethhild whose love brought sorrow—these three are from ancient Germanic legend. The fourth and fifth stanzas treat of Theodoric, the historical Gothic king of the late fifth and early sixth century, and of Eormanric, ruler of the Ostrogoths, also historical, the same who is so much admired by the poet of *Widsith*. An apparent period of exile is implied as Theodoric's misfortune, and the sufferings of his subjects under his tyranny explain the presence of Eormanric. The sixth group of lines, noticed above as suspected unnecessarily to be a later pious addition, runs on in the manuscript into a final group in which the scop Deor tells the story of his own misfortune. One cannot be certain whether, in view of the manuscript failure to mark off the sixth group, we should think of the whole passage from line 35 to the final refrain of line 42 as forming all one long stanza, or whether, as is usual among editors, the two groups should be taken as separate. In the former case the poem will divide itself into six parts, the five *exempla* of misfortune overcome, and a final homily and personal reflection by the author.

Inevitably the details of the legendary and historical Germanic characters referred to in the poem cause difficulty in interpretation, though the language is very simple in itself. For the poet, as always in this kind of composition, could assume that his audience was very thoroughly acquainted with the ancient traditions he used: so that his manner is always very allusive, and to a modern reader tangential. The final group of the poem from line 35 may best serve to indicate the quality of this poem, whose literary merits are considerable:

Þæt ic be me sylfum secgan wille,
þæt ic hwile wæs Heodeninga scop,
dryhtne dyre, me wæs Deor noma.
Ahte ic fela wintra folgað tilne,
holdne hlaford, oþþæt Heorrenda nu,
leoð-cræftig monn lond-ryht geþah,
þæt me eorla hleo ær gesealde.
þæs ofereode; þisses swa mæg!

(lines 35–42)

This it is that I may say concerning myself: that for a time I was the scop of the Heodenings, beloved by my lord: my name was Deor. During many winters I had a fine position as a retainer and a gracious lord: until now Heorrenda, a man skilled in poesy, has received the grant of land that was legally mine which the protector of men had aforetime given to me. That grief was overcome: so may this be.

The exact meaning of the refrain

þæs ofereode; þisses swa mæg

is still in doubt. The usual translation is some variation of 'That was overcome; so may this be.' But if the poem is of relatively late date, as some think despite its subject-matter, the refrain might plausibly be rendered 'Time has passed on from that: so it will from this.' *Ofer-eode* might mean either 'got over', used impersonally with *þaes* as genitive of reference or respect—'it was got over in respect of that'; or, if *þæs* were taken as a temporal adverb, *ofer-eode* could be rendered 'passed over'—'it [time] passed on after that'. Either way the verb in the preterite, *ofer-eode*, must be taken impersonally, and its infinitive *ofergan* must be assumed to be implied after *mæg*. *Mæg* in later Old English is sometimes used as a simple auxiliary for 'will'. One could render the refrain, therefore, either as 'that was overcome [or got over]; so may be this', or 'Time has passed on from that; so it will from this'. The word *þisses*, parallel to *þæs*, may be either genitive of reference or a genitive used adverbially of time. This question of the exact interpretation of

þæs ofereode; þisses swa mæg

is important, because the interpretation of the whole basic spirit or philosophy of the poem to a considerable extent depends on how this refrain is taken.[1] Is the poet saying that as the misfortunes of his five Germanic notables were overcome, so too may be those of others, like his own? Or is it rather to be regarded as a stoical statement that

[1] A recent attempt to take the refrain as pointing to the poem having been originally some kind of formulaic charm seems far-fetched.

time settles all troubles—it will be all the same, so to speak, in a hundred years?

This so-called refrain is in fact rather a repetitive emphasis of the moral of the poem than a lyric refrain in the more technical sense—introduced, it would seem, to drive home the lesson of the piece rather than for any metrical aesthetic purpose.

Evidence as to the date of first composition of *Deor* is not sufficient for definite conclusion. Occasional Alfredian forms among the normal late tenth-century classical Anglo-Saxon of the Exeter Book show that the poem existed as early as King Alfred's time, when it must have been copied. The references to the Gothic ruler Theodoric (Theodric) puts the earliest limit in the sixth century. The tone of the poem perhaps best fits a date in the eighth century, but some features in it, notably what look like affinities with the courtly or skaldic poetry of Iceland, would preclude a date much before the end of the ninth century. Shortly before 900 seems the most probable date on the whole.

Apart from its historical importance for its ancient Germanic traditional material, *Deor* has its place in the story of the development of English metre. For though, as has been said, there is at least one other poem written in stanzas (though it is probably late), and something like the use of a lyric refrain appears in *Wulf and Eadwacer*, *Deor* alone artistically blends a structure of stanzas whose varying length creates stylistic aesthetic value with the use of a strikingly impressive refrain the ambiguity of which may set the listener thinking.[1]

The little fragment usually known as *Wulf and Eadwacer*, which immediately follows *Deor* in the Exeter Book, gets its title from the names of its two characters, whose actions in a triangular love-tangle are referred to in passionate lyric verse by the speaker of the piece, evidently a woman. Nothing is known of Wulf, apparently the lady's lover, nor of Eadwacer, who seems to be her husband. But she and they seem clearly to be the actors in some remembered old Germanic story: and it is for this reason, and because of the use of a refrain which reminds one of *Deor*, that this obscure yet intensely moving fragment of nineteen lines is placed here in the group of poems of Germanic tradition. The lady and her lover Wulf (the name may imply that he has been outlawed) are on separate islands, kept apart by her cruel husband. Either the lady's own people or even the fierce inhabitants of Wulf's desolate island might have received him: but they cannot come together ever. She sits in tears and misery, comforted by the embraces of Eadwacer which give her some pleasure yet are hateful to her. It is doubting thoughts of her love, not hunger,

[1] For an excellent appraisal of *Deor*, see the edition of Kemp Malone (London, 1933). In this edition, contrary to most received opinion, Theodoric is taken to be the Frankish king, not the Goth.

that make her miserable. Wulf will carry their wretched offspring (it
is not clear who is the father) to the forest. This allusive and incomplete love-poem may, like *The Wife's Lament*, be a survival of Germanic folksongs once sung by women, as Kemp Malone suggests in
his paper "Two English *Frauenlieder*"[1]: and certainly the simplicity
of its very direct language and the musical element in its verse would
support this view. It is, at any rate, the most passionate lyric cry of
the heart that has survived in Anglo-Saxon. The following text
with a rendering, which is based on Kemp Malone's translation,[2]
will give some idea of its quality. The words of the refrain are
italicized:

> Leodum is minum swylce him mon lac gife;
> *willað hy hine apecgan, gif he on þreat cymeð.*
> > *Ungelic is us.*
> Wulf is on iege, ic on oþerre.
> Fæst is þæt eglond, fenne biworpen.
> Sindon wælreowe weras þær on ige;
> *willað hy hine apecgan, gif he on þreat cymeð.*
> > *Ungelic is us.*
> Wulfes ic mines wid-lastum wenum dogode;
> þonne hit wæs renig weder ond ic reotogu sæt,
> þonne mec se beadu-cafa bogum bilegde,
> wæs me wyn to þon, wæs me hwæþre eac lað.
> Wulf, min Wulf, wena me þine
> seoce gedydon, þine seld-cymas,
> murnende mod, nales mete-liste.
> Gehyrest þu, Eadwacer? uncerne earne hwelp
> bireð Wulf to wuda.
> þæt mon eaþe tosliteð þætte næfre gesomnad wæs,
> uncer giedd geador.
> > (ASPR III, 179–180)

It is to my people as if one should have made a gift to them if *he*
[*Wulf*] *should come into danger, they will take him in* [*as if he were a
gift*]: *it is not like that with us.* Wulf is on an island: I am on another.
That island where he is is as a fortress surrounded by fen: and there
are fierce men there. *If he should come into danger, they will take him
in: it is not like that with us.* I thought of my Wulf and his far journey-
ings with doubts in my heart. When it was rainy weather [the floods
of my tears], I sat in sadness, and it was then that the bold warrior
[Eadwacer] would enfold me in his arms: and from that I had some
joy but it was yet hateful. Wulf, my Wulf: it is hopes of thee and
thy seldom coming that have caused my sickness; my grieving

---

[1] See *Studies in Old English Literature in Honor of Arthur Brodeur* (University
of Oregon, 1963), pp. 106–111.
[2] *Op. cit.*, p. 108.

heart, not by any means lack of food. Dost thou hear, O Eadwacer? Wulf shall bear our wretched whelp to the forest. That which was never joined together may easily be torn asunder—our song together.

Metrically *Wulf and Eadwacer* is a unique curiosity. Its structure, in so far as this can be determined from its incomplete state, is not really stanzaic, though the use of the refrain may suggest this. On the other hand, the refrain consists of a line and a half, unlike that in *Deor*, which is a normal line, and its occurrence only twice makes it hardly a refrain in the usual sense, though it clearly adds to the lyric effect of the whole. This poem and *The Wife's Lament* are the only love-poems in Anglo-Saxon, the gnomic verses in the Exeter Book on the love of the Frisian sailor and *The Husband's Message* being not enough to come properly within this category. But of the two *Wulf and Eadwacer* comes much nearer to that kind of romantic love-lyric which began to flower in England under direct Continental influence from the twelfth century onward. In this respect, then, also it is unique. As has been said already, the egocentric expression of love did not normally find a place in ancient Germanic culture. This love-poem is certainly, as it seems, popular in origin, rather than courtly. Its simple, almost naked expression of passion lacks any of the sophistication of the poetry of 'courtly love'. The fact that it is placed in the mouth of a woman, too, would support the view that it sprang rather from popular than from courtly culture. The date of its composition, as with so many Old English poems, cannot be determined more than very roughly. Its language suggests an Anglian origin, and that there was a copy of it in existence as early as about A.D. 900 is indicated by some Alfredian forms.

Its allusively referred-to story, however, is clearly from the Germanic heroic age, in which it finds several partial parallels. All the very slender corpus of Anglo-Saxon love-poetry, as will have been noticed, survives only in the Exeter Book anthology of lyrics. We cannot be sure whether this fact is accidental.

Two short and incomplete poems, *Waldere* and *The Finn Fragment*, may be considered together: for their tone and background are much more obviously Germanic heroic in character, with their emphasis on war and the duties of the Germanic comitatus, loyalty and the blood-feud. Both are portions of lost longer poems: *Waldere* of a probably epic poem of considerable length, and *The Finn Fragment* of a heroic lay. Both, with an older approach than *Beowulf*, show something of the sheer joy of battle, with plenty of simple and vivid direct speeches of warlike boasting: but *The Finn Fragment* is too short and incomplete to show much purely literary quality. Yet, as Charles Kennedy says, "the story [of Finn] is so vividly told, and the dramatic situations are so typically Germanic, that the description of the bitter hall-fight at Finnsburg reads like tribal tradition authentically grounded in tragic event".[1] The eighty lines in two disparate fragments of *Waldere*, and the forty-eight of *The Finn Fragment*, are the most spirited and dramatic expression of tragic conflict that have survived in Anglo-Saxon from material of the ancient Germanic world.

Waldere (*Waldhere*), two quite separate fragments of verse in the usual Anglo-Saxon of the later tenth century discovered on two leaves in the Royal Library at Copenhagen in 1860 is all that remains of a late copy, going back probably to an original as old as the eighth century, of a romantic heroic poem which must have been at least as long as 1000 lines. It is the earliest Old English poetry which touches romance: and, like Spenser of his *Faerie Queene*, its maker might have said "Fierce warres and faithfull loues shall moralize my song." It tells, with the usual assumption that the audience is already very familiar with its story, allusively and dramatically, a tale which we can only partially piece together from later versions, of the flight of the betrothed lovers Waldere, or Walter the Gothic prince of Aquitaine, and Hildegyth or Hildegund, a Burgundian princess, from the Court of Attila the Hun, where they had long been hostages. Taking valuable treasure with them, the fugitives are intercepted and attacked by a certain king Guthhere or Gunther and his doughty followers. Waldere faces overwhelming odds and is victorious single-handed, after some dramatic exchanges between him and Guthhere, to whom he had offered a gift of treasure and peace which had been rejected. The lovers, according to the earliest other version of the tale *Waltharius* in tenth-century Latin hexameters, then journey home to Aquitaine and find marriage and long prosperity.[2]

Almost the whole of *Waldere* is in direct dramatic speech: a stirring exhortation by Hildegyth to her warrior to fight well and win in a right cause which God will decide justly, and an exchange of challenging speeches between Waldere and Guthhere in which weapons and armour are especially praised. Famous Germanic characters are named—Weland the magician smith and maker of the noblest weapons, and Theodoric the Goth, both of whom had their part in *Deor*. The heroic personified swords with names of especial power which appear to have been characteristic of heroic poetry find a place here with Mimming, the most famous work of Weland, given by Theodoric to Widia (Wudga elsewhere in Old English heroic verse),[3] the Gothic hero Vidigoia, and now possessed by Waldere. In a warrior Hagena, who had been the companion and friend of Waldere at Attila's Court, but was also the vassal of Guthhere, we

---

[1] See Charles W. Kennedy, *The Earliest English Poetry* (New York and London, 1943), p. 41. In this first-rate literary study will be found admirable verse renderings of select passages from most of the best Anglo-Saxon poetry.

[2] For a full and well-documented account of *Waldere* and its probable sources and analogues, see the edition of F. Norman (London, 1933).

[3] See *Widsith*, line 124.

glimpse in the poem that tragic conflict of loyalties in a noble hero which appears again in the story of *The Finn Fragment* and of the Finn episode of *Beowulf*. For it seems that this Hagena, loyal to his great friend Waldere, is forced by his duty to his lord, Guthhere, to act against Waldere, though he seems to have refused to share in the attack on him. Mention is made of Attila the Hun as already indicated, also referred to in *Widsith*: and it may be that the Guthhere of our poem is the famous Guthhere the Burgundian named in *Widsith* and as Gunnarr in Old Norse tradition.

Despite the extremely difficult and inevitably disrupted reconstruction of the story of which this is but two disjointed fragments, the poem still has in its vivid and moving dramatic speeches an appeal which makes one deeply conscious of how great is the loss of the epic of which we have here two pieces both stirring and poetical. The poem must from linguistic evidence have been in existence by King Alfred's time, and its tone and style suggest the *Beowulf* period or a little later. Its definitely Christian references to God in otherwise Germanic heroic surroundings would seem, perhaps, to point to a clerical maker. Yet it is especially the unexpected romantic appeal of this tale of true love—implied, of course, rather than told—that will be most remembered. However, *Waldere* contrasts markedly with *Wulf and Eadwacer*, for it is a tale of exciting adventure in fighting, in which the love interest is merely implied, not expressed. Waldere and Hildegyth are, like the married couples of the Germani as described by Tacitus, comrades in toil and in fight whose relationship is practical.[1] Here are the opening lines of the first fragment of the poem. Waldere, feeling the effects of a long day's combat, is exhorted by Hildegyth to a supreme effort of battle as his enemies are approaching again to attack:

> . . . . Hyrde hyne georne:
> "Huru Welandes worc ne geswiceð
> monna ænigum ðara ðe Mimming can
> heardne gehealdan; oft æt hilde gedreas
> swatig ond sweord-wund secg æfter oðrum.
> Ætlan ord-wyga, ne læt ðin ellen nu gyt
> gedreosan to-dæge, dryhtscipe. . . . .
> . . . . Nu is se dæg cumen
> þæt ðu scealt aninga oðer twega,
> lif forleosan, oððe langne dom
> agan mid eldum, Ælfheres sunu."
>   (lines 1-11, ASPR II, 4-5)

---

[1] Cf. *Germania*, op. cit., Chapter 18: "Ne se mulier extra virtutum cogitationes extraque bellorum casus putet, ipsis incipientis matrimonii auspiciis admonetur venire se laborum periculorumque sociam, idem in pace, idem in proelio passuram ausuramque."

Eagerly she heard him. "Truly Weland's work [the sword] will not fail any of the men who have the ability to wield Mimming the mighty. Oft in battle has fallen one warrior after another, bloody with wounds from that sword. O bold warrior of Attila, do not yet let thy valour and manly might fall away this day. Now is the day come that thou indeed must do one of two things, o son of Ælfhere: either lose thy life or gain eternal glory among men".

Both *Waldere* and *The Finn Fragment* still retain something of the ancient Germanic joy in battle—a quality which has been almost lost by the time of the *Beowulf* poet. Though they both seem to date from about the *Beowulf* period or even a little later, they have preserved this more primitive heroic zest as *Beowulf* has not.

In the year 1705 George Hickes included in his famous *Thesaurus* of ancient northern languages a fragment of forty-eight lines of a most vivid and dramatic poem treating of a tragic feud between Danes and Frisians, in which the leader of the Frisians was Finn, centred on Finn's fortified dwelling which the poet calls Finnsburh.[1] This heroic piece, in which the ancient Germanic battle spirit and loyalties are tragically glorified, is commonly included as an appendix in editions of *Beowulf*, under such titles as *The Fight at Finnsburh* and *The Finn Fragment*. It was evidently part of a lay, of which our *Fragment* occurred near the beginning, and another version of a later portion is found as an episodic lay recited by King Hrothgar's scop in *Beowulf*.[2] Hickes says that *The Finn Fragment* was printed by him from a single isolated folio which he found in a volume of homilies probably thirteenth-century, in the Archbishop of Canterbury's London palace at Lambeth.[3] The text, copied apparently somewhat freely by Hickes in 1705, has never been traced, so that his printed version remains the only authoritative source. This presents, with Hickes's own errors, what looks like an eleventh-century version. The story, of which an early part is told by *The Finn Fragment*, can, with the aid of the so-called 'Finn Episode' in *Beowulf*, be reconstructed hypothetically with some plausibility but without certainty: it is naturally the subject of much disagreement in its details.

A long-standing feud between Danes and Frisians had been seemingly settled by a marriage between Hildeburh, a princess of a tribe closely connected with the Danes, and Finn, who, while himself a Jute, ruled the Frisians from his palace of Finnsburh, situated just outside of Friesland. The tribe of the Hocingas, to which Hildeburh belonged, may have been ethnically Jutes yet subjects of the Danish king. Thus this marriage could have been the easier to arrange because both Finn and Hildeburh were of Jutish origin, though members of quite separate groups. The fact that the feud which was

---

[1] See *Linguarum Vett. Septentrionalium Thesaurus* (Oxoniae, 1705), Vol. I, pp. 192–193.
[2] See *Beowulf*, lines 1068–1159.   [3] Now known as ms. Lambeth Palace 487.

to break out again many years after this reconciling marriage would be between warriors who were on either side both Jutish, and were brought to renewed fighting by the supreme duty of revenge, would add tragic poignancy to the tale. For the obligation to avenge a slain leader, a matter of comitatus loyalty, took, in the Germanic code, priority over the loyalty of blood-relationship. When Hildeburh's sons were grown enough to bear arms an occasion arose when her brother Hnæf, leader of the 'Half-Danes' (a name by which her Jutish people were known) visited her and her husband King Finn, accompanied by sixty warrior retainers. These guests, sleeping in the hall of Finnsburh after being well entertained, were suddenly attacked by night by Finn's men and Hnæf, as well as his sister's sons, along with many warriors on both sides, was slain. But Hengest, who succeeded Hnæf as the leader of the Half-Danes (referred to as Danes), had by then got himself with his men into some strongly protected position from which they could not have been dislodged save with more loss of Finn's Jutes than he could risk. So Finn accepted a truce apparently proposed by Hengest, that both sides should have a great ceremonial funeral for their dead, and then Hengest and his men would, at least for the winter (which was fast approaching), become Finn's followers. Finn promised them excellent treatment as members of his comitatus, equal to what he gave to his own Frisian warriors. Hengest's motive appears to have been revenge, which could be more surely carried out if he gained a respite by this postponement. Some think that there was a profound struggle in Hengest's mind, torn between the heinousness of taking service with Finn, the head of the people who had slain his own leader Hnæf, and the basic Germanic duty of exacting vengeance for Hnæf. After spending the winter with Finn, who is not supposed himself to have been responsible for the initial outbreak of the fighting, Hengest, egged on also by some of his followers, plans deliberately for vengeance, thereby ignoring the new loyalty to Finn which his joining his comitatus implied. The fight is renewed by some of Hengest's men acting apparently as *agents provocateurs*, and Finn and all his men are slain. Hildeburh, also perhaps glad of this vengeance though distraught with the conflicting loyalty to her husband Finn, is carried by the victorious Danes back to her homeland.

This tragic tale, so vividly illustrating conflicting Germanic heroic loyalties, is evidently told in its original lay to an audience entirely familiar with its subject-matter. Only the crises, the highlights and dramatic moments, are touched upon, and this very allusively. Hence the unravelling of the details must remain a kind of jigsaw puzzle to us today. The original lay of the *Fight at Finnsburh* must have been much older than the *Fragment*: and later parts of it are treated in a seemingly somewhat more advanced style in the 'Finn Episode' of *Beowulf*. Yet while the style and tone of the *Fragment* suggest an early date, the occasional irregularities of its metre would point to

a later period. The appearance of Hengest in it may mean that it is
the one poem of the ancient Germanic tradition which would have
had a specifically English interest. For this Hengest has been plausibly
identified with the Hengest who was a leader of the first Anglo-Saxon
invasion of Kent according to the *Anglo-Saxon Chronicle*.[1] Both Finn
and Hnæf are mentioned in *Widsith* (lines 27 and 29), which suggests
that their story was well known on the Germanic Continent as well
as in England. Most of the *Fragment* is in dramatic direct speech:
but here in lines 34 to 42 is a piece of heroic narrative showing the
earliest expression of the Germanic spirit at its best and most moving:

> Hræfen wandrode
> sweart ond sealo-brun. Swurd-leoma stod,
> swylce eal Finns-buruh fyrenu wære.
> Ne gefrægn ic næfre wurþlicor æt wera hilde
> sixtig sige-beorna, sel gebæran,
> ne nefre swetne medo sel forgyldan,
> ðonne Hnæfe guldan his hæg-stealdas.
> Hig fuhton fif dagas, swa hyra nan ne feol,
> driht-gesiða, ac hig ða duru heoldon.
>   ASPR VI, 4.

The raven, black in its dark shining coat, flew hither and thither. The
gleaming of the swords made it seem as if all Finnsburh were on fire.
I have not heard of sixty victorious warriors bearing themselves
better and more honourably in battle; and never did men better requite their leader for the sweet mead-drink than Hnæf's noble
warriors then. For five days they had fought, in such wise that not
one of his comrade retainers had fallen: but they held the door.

Besides the 'Finn Episode', there are echoes of other ancient
heroic lays in *Beowulf*, notably one dealing with Sigemund the dragon-
slayer, of which the material is found more fully in Old Norse Eddaic
verse and prose.[2] There is also allusively echoed a lay of Ingeld of the
Heathobards, who married the Danish king's daughter to end a feud,
much as Hildeburh had married Finn: and with the same tragic
result. This last-named lost lay[3] is that against the recitation of
which in monastic refectories Alcuin had protested with his famous
rhetorical question "Quid Hinieldus cum Christo?" But of the echoed
lays in *Beowulf*, only the tale of Finn has left us a separate part of a
distinct poem in *The Finn Fragment*. The tragedy of Ingeld, like that
of Finn, also found its place in *Widsith* (lines 45–49).
    It is not surprising that *The Finn Fragment* and *Waldere*, like all
the pieces dealt with in this chapter, should be short or fragmentary,

---

[1] See *Beowulf*, ed. C. L. Wrenn, pp. 52–53.
[2] See *Beowulf*, lines 874–898, and the explanations in the edition of Wrenn,
pp. 55–56.
[3] See *Beowulf*, lines 2024–2069.

since they are echoes of that Germanic heroic tradition which was being replaced by a more consciously Christian didactic poetry. For in the religious houses, which were the only centres of culture where writing or copying could normally take place, this kind of verse—which no doubt had first flourished in oral tradition—had little chance of being written down unless it appeared to have possibilities of edification. Nor, even if written down, would it be likely to survive after it ceased to appeal to the clerics, the only educated people who wrote. Parchment, being scarce and valuable, was felt to be needed for more serious purposes. Indeed, sometimes parchment on which secular heroic verse had been copied seems often to have been used for writing more edifying matter in palimpsests over what had been there, or even for binding religious codices thought to be of permanent use. Both *The Finn Fragment* and *Waldere* seem to have survived by some fortunate accident only, though in fragments, because one of the folios of each was preserved for use in binding. Even *Beowulf* may owe its survival only to the fact that it could be read in the spirit of Christian moralizing and symbolism. Losses arising from such inevitable changes of interest centred in monasteries must account for the extreme paucity of the literary remains in Old English of the traditions of the ancient Germanic heroic ages. Much too of what did survive was likely to have been lost in the devastations of the monasteries by Viking plunderers, William the Conqueror's laying waste of the North as a result of its rebellion, and finally by the effects of the dissolution of the religious houses with their libraries under Henry VIII and Edward VI. But from what has survived of earliest heroic verse we may gather much of the quality of the first Anglo-Saxon culture. Moreover, something of its spirit and outlook was carried forward right through the Anglo-Saxon period, as the noble expression of the ancient heroic spirit in *The Battle of Maldon* at the close of the tenth century suggests. The revolution by which the ancient technique of verse was adapted to Christian subject-matter—which is associated with the name of Cædmon—carried with it echoes of the Old Germanic spirit, which are to be met with even in specifically Biblical and hagiographical verse such as *Judith* and Cynewulf's *Elene*.

CHAPTER 6

Cædmon and the Christian Revolution in Poetry

APART FROM CASUAL MENTION of nuns with poetic gifts, we have only three names with which we may connect the 30,000 or more surviving lines of Anglo-Saxon verse: Cædmon, Aldhelm, and Cynewulf. Of these, St Aldhelm, whose Latin work was described in an earlier chapter, has left only a great reputation but no writings as a vernacular poet. We have (apart from the tradition of his standing on a bridge leading to Malmesbury to attract the people of the later seventh century by reciting Anglo-Saxon poems) only the evidence recorded by William of Malmesbury of St Aldhelm's immense reputation, at least in Wessex: but that this should have continued till as late as the early twelfth century, when William of Malmesbury wrote his *Gesta Pontificum Anglorum*, is significant. No less a judge of Anglo-Saxon poetry than King Alfred is here said to have stated in his lost *Handboc* that Aldhelm surpassed all others in any age in ability to compose poetry in his native language:

> Aldhelmus nativae linguae non negligebat carmina, adeo ut, teste libro Elfredi (manuali libro sive handboc) nulla aetate par ei fuerit quisquam poesim Anglicam posse facere.

From Cynewulf we have the four so-called signed poems with his name in runes to attest authorship. Yet of his life we know nothing beyond what may be doubtfully inferred or conjectured from the texts. Only of Cædmon have we an authentic picture of both his life and his personality, thanks to Bede, and at least one authentic poem, the nine-line piece known as *Cædmon's Hymn*. In the first part of Chapter 24 of the fourth book of his *Historia Ecclesiastica Gentis Anglorum* Bede gives a careful and detailed account of Cædmon and of the miracle which he believed he had thoroughly authenticated, by which this illiterate herdsman in a vision was granted the gifts of the finest poetry. Since this account by Bede is the first piece of genuine literary history we have, and because Cædmon's work and influence were of pioneering revolutionary effect for Anglo-Saxon poetry, it will be worth so much space to repeat, in translation from Bede's Latin, the oft-told story of Cædmon's poetic awakening.

> In the monastery of this abbess [St Hild] there was a certain brother specially distinguished by divine grace because he was accustomed to

making poems fitting to religion and piety. This he did in such wise that, whatsoever he had learned from divine Scriptures through interpreters, this he himself after a short time would bring forth in his own tongue—that is, the language of the Angles—composed in poetic words with the greatest sweetness and moving quality. By these poems of his the minds of many were often enkindled to the despising of the world and to the longing for the heavenly life. Yet indeed there were others after him among the people of the Angles who strove to make religious poems: but none was ever able to match him. For himself had learned the art of poesy not through men nor taught by a man: but he had received the gift of song freely by divine aid. Wherefore he could never make anything of frivolous or vain poetry, but only those verses which belong to piety, which were becoming to that religious tongue of his. In fact he had been settled in the secular way of life until he was of advanced age [*provectioris aetatis*]: and he had not at any time learned anything of poems. Hence it was that sometimes when at a party [*convivium*] when it had been decided for joyful entertainment that all in turn must recite verses to the harp's accompaniment [*cantare*, which the Alfredian translation renders *be hearpan singan*], he when he saw the harp getting near to himself would arise from the midst of the feast and go out and walk back to his house. [Here the Alfredian version adds that it was from a feeling of shame, *for scome*, that he did this]. When on a certain occasion he had done this, and leaving the house where the party was held had gone out to the cattle-pens, as their care had been assigned to him for that night, and when there he had at the normal time given his limbs to sleep, a certain man was standing by him in a dream and, greeting him and calling him by his name, said: "Cædmon, sing me something." But he in answering said: "I do not know how to sing: for it was just for this reason that I came away from the feast and departed hither, because I could not sing." Again he who was talking with him said: "Yet you *can* sing to me." "What," said Cædmon, "must I sing?" Then the other said: "Sing of the beginning of created things." Now when Cædmon had received this answer, immediately he began to sing verses in praise of God the creator which he had never heard, of which this is the sense [*quorum iste est sensus*]: 'Now we must praise the Author of the Kingdom of Heaven, the might of the Creator and the thoughts of His mind—the deeds of the Father of glory. [We must sing] how he who is eternal God, the Author of all marvellous things, was manifest: he who first created heaven as a roof-covering for the sons of men, and then as almighty guardian of mankind made the earth.' This is the sense but not the actual order of the words [*hic est sensus, non autem ordo ipse verborum*] of what Cædmon had sung while sleeping. For poems, however excellently composed, cannnot be translated word for word from one language into another without damage to elegance and dignity. Now when he had risen from his sleep, he retained in his memory everything which he had sung while sleeping. And to these verses he quickly added more in the same rhythm and metre [*in eundum modum*] in words of a poem worthy of God.

When morning had come, he went to the steward who was his chief and showed him what sort of gift he had received. He was then conducted to the Abbess and commanded to show what he had dreamed in the presence of many learned men and to recite the poem: so that by the judgment of everyone it might be tested of what kind or from whence had come what he had related. And it seemed to them all that it was a grace from heaven and granted by God. Then they expounded to him a discourse of sacred history or doctrine, and commanded him, if he could, to render this into the melody of poetry [*in modulationem carminis*]. So he, when he had finished these matters, went away: and in the morning he came back and produced it composed as had been ordered in the most excellent poetry. Wherefore the Abbess, immediately embracing the grace of God in the man, instructed him with a proposal that he should abandon the secular habit and take that of a monk. So she added him, with his goods, after receiving him into the monastery, to the company of the brethren: and she commanded that he should be taught the whole sequence of sacred Scripture. Now he, taking all that he could learn by hearing, retaining it in his mind, and turning it over like a clean beast ruminating [*quasi mundum animal ruminando*], converted it into the sweetest poetry. Indeed by the sweetness of its melody he made his teachers in their turn become his listeners. Now he sang of the creation of the world and of the origin of the human race and the whole narrative of Genesis, concerning the going out from Egypt of the Israelites and their entry into the land of promise. He sang about very many other historical parts of sacred Scripture, about the Incarnation of the Lord, His Passion, Resurrection, and Ascension into heaven, about the coming of the Holy Ghost and the teaching of the Apostles. Likewise he made many songs of the terror of Judgment to come and the horror of the punishment of hell and the sweetness of the heavenly kingdom. But furthermore he made very many other compositions concerning divine blessings and judgments, by all of which he sought to turn men's minds from delight in wickednesses, and indeed to stir them to the love and skilful practice of good deeds. For he was a most religious man who subjected himself with humility to the disciplines of monastic rule. But against others who wished to act otherwise he was aflame with fervid zeal. Hence it was that he closed his life with a beautiful ending.

Bede concludes his account of Cædmon with a vivid and moving narration of a saintly death.

Bede was careful to state, it will have been noticed from his account of Cædmon's first poem, that he had only given the Latin sense of the *Hymn*, not its exact words: and his reference to the order of the words is clearly an indication that Cædmon had used the Old English alliterative style in his metre. From the Anglo-Saxon version of this chapter of Bede, made in King Alfred's reign perhaps by Bishop Waerferth at his bidding though preserved only in later manuscripts, it is clear that *Cædmon's Hymn* was carefully cultivated as a text of sacred tradition. For here the Alfredian version does not merely translate the Latin of the poem from Bede, but quotes it in a West-Saxon form of the actual verses which agrees substantially with eighth-century Northumbrian versions of the same *Hymn*. Moreover, that there was a vernacular tradition of Cædmon's life and of his *Hymn* handed down to King Alfred's time is suggested by a number of slight variations in the translation from the Latin, which are deliberate and not due to error. Thus, as will have been seen, Bede's word *cantare*, 'to sing', is rendered as *be hearpan singan*, indicating that recitation of poetry to the accompaniment of the harp was meant. Again, it would seem that the Anglo-Saxon translator knew the detail that it was from a feeling of shame, *for scome*, that Cædmon fled from the demand that he should recite. Bede's word *convivium* too is Englished, as it were, as well as translated by the Alfredian version's term *gebeorscipe*, which means literally 'drinking of beer together': and this would be the natural kind of party for the herdsman Cædmon to have attended. In the *Hymn* itself the Alfredian version differs in one remarkable way from both Bede's Latin and the early eighth-century Northumbrian texts. Whereas in the Latin rendering heaven was created as a roof-covering 'for the sons of men', *filiis hominum*, and the two earliest Northumbrian texts which were copied in as additions to Bede's Latin have 'for the children of men', *ælda barnum*, the other two Northumbrian copies have 'for the children of earth', *eordu bearnum*, which suggests that against the Biblical phrase 'children of men' used in the earliest versions of the *Hymn* there was a different oral tradition favouring 'children of the earth'. Now, the West-Saxon versions of *Cædmon's Hymn*, quoted as the original poem itself as against Bede's Latin general sense, show the same variety of text here: those manuscripts which are complete translations of Bede into Old English having *eorðan bearnum*, while other copies of the vernacular *Hymn* inserted into later Latin manuscripts have *ylda bearnum*.[1] It may be, then, that an orally transmitted version of the *Hymn* with a somewhat differing tradition existed, both in Northumbrian and in West-Saxon. Another small but possibly significant difference between Bede's Latin and the Alfredian version of the biography of Cædmon is that while the Latin describes the herdsman as being in secular life till he was of 'advanced age', *provectioris aetatis*, the Old English has *gelyfedre yldo*, which literally should

---

[1] For a complete transcription of all the seventeen manuscripts of *Cædmon's Hymn*, with a full examination and classification of the texts, see Elliott van Kirk Dobbie, *The Manuscripts of Cædmon's Hymn and Bede's Death Song* (New York, Columbia University Press, 1937).

mean 'of weakened or infirm old age'. The Abbess St Hild ruled the joint house at Whitby for monks and nuns from A.D. 658 to 680: so that we are able to fix very closely the date of Cædmon's *Hymn* when he was of advanced or infirm old age, since it must have been between these dates.

Before proceeding to further discussion of the *Hymn*, it will be well to quote it in its earliest known form in the Northumbrian dialect, which was near the actual language in which the poet himself must have dictated it to the monks of Whitby. For this first-known Anglo-Saxon poem, in a manner quite without parallel save only for *Bede's Death-Song* (to be noticed later) exists in no less than seventeen copies, dating from the earlier eighth to the later fifteenth centuries: and it must therefore be regarded as a very specially venerated work. The almost invariable situation of Old English poems, including *Beowulf*, is that they have survived each in only one unique copy.

The two earliest manuscripts of *Cædmon's Hymn*, known respectively as the Moore Manuscript and the Leningrad Manuscript of Bede, since they are copies of the full Latin text of the *Historia Ecclesiastica* into which the vernacular poem is inserted, are dated to within sixty to eighty years of Cædmon's miracle—the Moore at A.D. 737 and the Leningrad, with less confidence, at 746. The Alfredian Bede, which includes a West-Saxon reproduction of the *Hymn* in lieu of translation, survives only in copies of the tenth century or a little later, though its archetype was made at the close of the ninth. But the remarkable agreement in wording generally between the closely similar Moore and Leningrad Northumbrian copies on the one hand and the late West-Saxon texts on the other goes to emphasize the great care which must have been bestowed on the preserving of this most valued poem, as well as to confirm our confidence in its authenticity. The Moore Manuscript of Bede gets its name from Bishop Moore of Norwich, who bought it in France at the close of the seventeenth century and bequeathed it to Cambridge University Library, where it remains. The Leningrad Manuscript of Bede, now in the Public Library in that city, was acquired—by the Russian aristocrat collector Pyotr Dubrovsky—in a sale of some books from the library of the Benedictine monastery of St Germain-des-Prés on the suppression of that house in the French Revolution, and was bequeathed to the State. The best text of the Anglo-Saxon Bede is in MS. Bodleian Tanner 10, probably written in western Mercia in the tenth century. Of the early Northumbrian texts of the *Hymn*, the Moore is to be preferred for reproduction here, as it has some archaic forms lacking in the Leningrad Manuscript of Bede (with which it very closely agrees) that seem to look back directly to Cædmon's own linguistic practice. Here is the Moore text:

Nu scylun hergan hefaenricaes uard,
metudæs maecti end his modgidanc,

uerc uuldurfadur, sue he uundra gihuaes,
eci dryctin, or astelidæ.
He aerist scop *aelda barnum*
heben til hrofe, haleg scepen;
tha middungeard moncynnæs uard,
eci dryctin æfter tiadæ
firum foldu, frea allmectig.

This may be fairly literally translated thus:

Now ought we to praise heaven's kingdom's guardian, the might of the Creator and the thought of his mind, the works of the Father of glory. (We should sing) how he, the eternal Lord, set up a beginning for every wondrous thing. He who is the Holy Creator designed heaven as a roof for the children of men. Then mankind's guardian, the eternal Lord, almighty ruler, afterwards made the earth for men.

The Alfredian version of the *Hymn*, taken from the Tanner text, runs thus:

Nu sculon herigean heofon-rices weard,
meotodes meahte and his mod-geþanc,
weorc wuldor-fæder, swa he wundra gehwæs,
ece drihten, or onstealde.
He ærest sceop *eorðan bearnum*
heofon to hrofe, halig scyppend;
þa middan-geard mon-cynnes weard,
ece drihten, æfter teode
firum foldan, frea ælmihtig.[1]

It will be noted that these two texts exemplify respectively the literary tradition of Northumbria *ælda barnum* (WS. *ylda bearnum*) as against a probable equally ancient oral tradition of WS. *eorðan bearnum* (Northumbrian *eordu* or *eorðu barnum*).

Since its first printing under the editorship of Junius in 1655 at Amsterdam, the manuscript of Biblical poems now catalogued as Junius 11 in the Bodleian Library has been associated with the name of Cædmon erroneously, and is still often referred to as 'The Cædmon Manuscript'. It contains four poetical paraphrases or free adaptations of matter from Genesis, Exodus, and Daniel, with a piece of mainly New Testament material known as *Christ and Satan*. This fourth poem, rather disconnected in narrative, treats of the lamentations of the fallen angels expelled from heaven, Christ's descent into hell after the Crucifixion with his Resurrection and presiding at the Last Judgment, and finally with Christ's temptation in the wilderness. The four poems are obviously of differing authorship and origin, and

---

[1] Both texts in ASPR VI, pp. 105, 106.

none can with any plausibility be attributed even remotely to Cædmon save a few fragments of Genesis. But the correspondence in theme between these pieces taken together—extending as they do from the creation of the world to the Last Judgment—with those assigned by Bede to Cædmon's treatment, together with some common stylistic features, naturally led their first editor to assign all to Cædmon. But the title *Junius Manuscript*—since Junius was the undoubted producer of the *editio princeps*—is now the most acceptable, and is employed for the first volume of *The Anglo-Saxon Poetic Records*.

Beyond what Bede tells us, and the evidence as to his date, we have no certain knowledge of Cædmon save the nine lines of this *Hymn* and what may be inferred from them. Yet, in view of the considerable agreement between Bede's account of Cædmon's other many works and the contents of the so-called *Cædmon Manuscript*, MS. Bodley Junius 11, it was but natural that his authorship of the early Biblical poems there preserved in late tenth-century copies should have been assumed until the coming of a more scientific scholarship. Indeed, the Dutch Anglo-Saxonist Junius, who produced the first printed edition of these texts from Amsterdam in 1655, had given great impetus to this assumption by entitling his book "Cædmon the monk's poetical paraphrase of Genesis, etc.": *Cædmonis Monachi Paraphrasis Poetica Genesios ac præcipuarum Sacræ paginæ Historiarum . . . Anglo-Saxonice conscripta*.

Yet a closer examination of the four poems of the Junius Manuscript makes it clear that they are each by different authors. For though all share those qualities of style and diction which are first adumbrated by the authentic *Cædmon's Hymn*, they all differ from it in tone, method, and treatment very markedly. *Exodus* is an epic, though incomplete, which shows the unities of action, place, and time, taking as its central theme the crossing of the Red Sea by the Israelites and ending with the utter destruction of the Egyptians: but it is in no sense a paraphrase of the Biblical narrative, and is extremely individual in vocabulary. Whereas *Genesis* of this manuscript is a very free heroic paraphrase of the Old Testament account as far as the sacrifice of Isaac, *Exodus* shows a unique use of metaphor reminding one indeed of modern poetry, with an exciting vigour of vivid presentation unparalleled in Anglo-Saxon poetry. The third piece, following *Genesis* and *Exodus*, is a free paraphrase of the Book of *Daniel*, ending incompletely with Balshazzar's Feast: but its style is not like that of *Genesis* except in a general way. The fourth piece is rather a triple group of poems than a single composition, though it goes under the somewhat loose title *Christ and Satan*. It treats as mentioned above, first of the lamentations of the rebel angels after their fall, then of some events in the life of Christ including the 'harrowing of hell' and ending with the Last Judgment, and then finally with the Temptation in the Wilderness which was later to be the subject of Milton's *Paradise Regained*. Here again the treatment and style are different from those of the other poems in the Junius Manuscript: and it seems to most readers that each of the three parts of *Christ and Satan* also differs from the others.

The poems of the Junius Manuscript, then, do in a way treat of themes of man's history from the Creation to the Last Judgment, as Bede's statement would lead us to expect. But only here and there in the Genesis poem are there apparent traces of the authentic Cædmon. Sir Israel Gollancz, who edited the facsimile of the Junius Manuscript with an elaborate Introduction, went so far as to end his discussion of *Genesis* with these words: "*Genesis A* may I think have the same ascription as the Hymn. PRIMO CANTAVIT CÆDMON ISTUD CARMEN." The Latin words are those added in the Moore Bede to its copy of the Northumbrian *Hymn*.[1] In particular, there are several formulaic phrases of Old English religious verse which are first found in the *Hymn*, and then in *Genesis*, notably *frea almihtig*, which occurs many times in *Genesis*. As we have it the so-called *Genesis A* or *Elder Genesis* of the Junius Manuscript seems to contain the mixed work of several redactors: but some 54 lines have been held to show authentic Cædmon.[2]

Into the Junius Manuscript poem of *Genesis* a quite different and much superior Genesis piece has in some way not yet clear been interpolated. This passage of some six hundred lines (235 to 852) is an account of the rebellion of Satan and his angels and of the fall of man evidently composed as late as the closing years of the ninth century: and it is therefore known as Genesis *B* or the *Later Genesis*. *Genesis B* is a translation or close adaptation made in the reign of Alfred the Great of an early ninth-century Saxon poem. Its author evidently was familiar with both Old Saxon (the language spoken by Saxons who had remained in their German homelands) and with the English vernacular. In fact, so close are parts of *Genesis B* to fragments of the original Old Saxon poem found in the Vatican that the virtues of the poem must be held to be those of the Old Saxon poet rather than his translator-adapter. *Genesis B* shows a quite unusual subjective interest and a vivid presentation of the personalities of Satan and of Adam and Eve. It is a true Germanic heroic poem, glorifying the comitatus spirit exemplified here in Satan and his followers: yet its treatment of Eve shows a 'human interest' of the kind that still has its appeal today. *Genesis B* is a magnificent addition, partly overlapping the *Genesis A* account of all the Fall, much of which is missing. It is part of a literary masterpiece of unique quality. Along with the *Exodus* poem, it furnishes almost all that is of

[1] See *The Caedmon Manuscript of Anglo-Saxon Poetry, Junius XI in the Bodleian Library, with Introduction by Sir Israel Gollancz* (Oxford, for the British Academy, 1927), p. cvi. For full discussion of Cædmon's share in *Genesis*, see *ibid.*, pp. xlviii–lxviii.

[2] See E. Sievers, "Cædmon und Genesis", *Britannica, Max Förster zum sechstigsten Geburtstage* (Leipzig, 1929), pp. 57–84.

permanent poetic appeal in the Junius Manuscript. Here are parts
of two of Satan's speeches by way of illustration.

(Satan is speaking of hell, into which God has thrown the defeated
rebels.)

> "Is þæs ænga styde ungelic swiðe
> þam oðrum ham þe we ær cuðon,
> hean on heafon-rice, þe me min hearra onlag,
> þeah we hine for þam al-waldan agan ne moston,
> romigan ures rices. Næfð he þeah riht gedon
> þæt he us hæfð befælled fyre to botme,
> helle þære hatan, heofon-rice benumen;
> hafað hit gemearcod mid mon-cynne
> to gesettanne. Þæt me is sorga mæst,
> þæt Adam sceal, þe wæs of eorðan geworht,
> minne stronglican stol behealdan,
> wesan him on wynne, and we þis wite þolien,
> hearm on þisse helle. Wa la, ahte ic minra handa geweald
> and moste ane tid ute weorðan,
> wesan ane winter-stunde, þonne ic mid þys werode . . .
> Ac licgað me ymbe iren-benda,
> rideð racentan sal."

(lines 356–372)

"This narrowly confined region is most unlike to that other home high
in heaven's kingdom which we knew aforetime, which my Lord had
granted to us though we could not keep possession of it by striving
after our realm. Yet he has not done right in felling us to the fiery
depths of hell's heat, bereft of the heavenly kingdom; and he has
planned to settle it with the race of man. This it is which is the
greatest of griefs to me, that Adam, who was made from earth, must
hold possession of my mighty seat and dwell in joy, whilst we endure
this torment and injury in this hell. Alas for woe! Had I but the power
to use my hands, might for one brief hour be out of this place, then
I, with this band of followers, would . . . But bonds of iron are fast
about me and I am weighed down with ropes of fetters."

(Then Satan exhorts his comitatus to supreme effort in the traditional
heroic language.)

> "Gif ic ænegum þægne þeoden-madmas
> geara forgeafe, þenden we on þan godan rice
> gesælige sæton and hæfdon ure setla geweald,
> þonne he me na on leofran tid leanum ne meahte
> mine gife gyldan, gif his gien wolde
> minra þegna hwilc geþafa wurðan,
> þæt he up heonon ute mihte
> cuman þurh þas clustro, and hæfde cræft mid him
> þæt he mid feðer-homan fleogan meahte,
> windan on wolcne, þær geworht stondað

Adam and Eue on eorðrice
mid welan bewunden, and we synd aworpene hider
on þas deopan dalo."

(lines 409–421)

"If I in times past have given princely treasures to any retainer in
days when we dwelt in happiness in that noble realm, and each of us
had power and freedom of place, then such an one could not requite
me with benefits and with deeds at a more longed-for time: if any of
my followers would be among those who agree to this, namely that he
should fly out from thence, make his way through these dark prisons,
that he might have power in himself to fly with Weland's coat of
feathers, go whirling along the clouds to where there stand Adam and
Eve created in the kingdom of earth encompassed with riches, whilst
we are hurled down hither into these deep valleys."

It will now be clear that the poems in the Junius Manuscript show
only traces of Cædmon himself in *Genesis A*. The rest of its contents
are, however, 'Cædmonian' in two ways: their subject-matter taken
as a whole does very roughly correspond with works by Cædmon
which Bede tells us he made, and, though their several styles and
treatments are not those of the poet, they yet all share that adaptation of the Germanic heroic diction which is first known to have been
employed in the *Hymn*. Of the five poems (counting *Genesis A* and
B as two) of the Junius Manuscript, *Genesis A* is most Cædmonian,
and is a free and often paraphrasing adaptation of Scriptural narrative:
Daniel though its treatment is quite different and it includes apparent
interpolations in lyric manner of the prayer of Azarias and the song
of the Three Children, again freely paraphrases the Vulgate. *Exodus*
and *Genesis B* stand really quite apart, as they are original and creative
in treatment, though their basic material is Biblical. *Christ and Satan*
is the least Cædmonian of the codex, for its treatment is that of a
series of lyrical and dramatic passages often seeming to be reminiscent
of the Cynewulfian poems, and more in the homiletic manner of the
late eighth century, without anything like the same direct dependence
on Scripture to be found in the other Cædmon poems. Moreover,
the second part of *Christ and Satan*, which deals with the Harrowing
of Hell and the Resurrection and the Last Judgment, is like a poetical
Easter homily rather than a Biblical story: and it here contrasts with
the more Cædmonian poems in using material from the New Testament, whereas they employ only the Old. *Christ and Satan* is an
example of that second phase of Christian poetry in the Anglo-Saxon
period which passes from Old Testament themes proper to a lyric
and homiletic handling of matter from the New Testament and the
Fathers. One might, then, say that *Christ and Satan*, which shares
something of the basic Cædmonian manner with a definitely Cynewulfian treatment (Part I shows parallels with *Guthlac A*), is a kind
of bridge between the school of Cædmon and that of Cynewulf. It

has some vivid dramatic moments, but is not especially outstanding as a poem or group of poems. Only *Exodus* and *Genesis B* are truly memorable as poetry. *Genesis A* has nevertheless a definite historical interest because of its apparently genuine echoes of the authentic Cædmon.

What, then, was the nature of that fundamental development in Anglo-Saxon poetry which may be called the Cædmonian revolution? First of all it is natural to ask what was the happening described by Bede which he and the Whitby monks and St Hild regarded as a miraculous intervention of divine Providence. The nine lines of the *Hymn*, even when judged in the light of Old English poetic performance as a whole, will scarcely seem in themselves of supreme excellence. The 'miracle', it may be suggested, was rather of a more technical kind than will appear at first sight to the modern reader. The making of verses was evidently quite commonplace among the Northumbrian peasants such as those with whom Cædmon shared that so significant *convivium*, or *gebeorscipe*: so that his companions seem naturally to have expected that the cow-herd could have taken his part at reciting to the harp when his turn came round. Monastic scriptoria, concerned primarily with matters of edification, inevitably failed to preserve the peasant type of verse which must have been freely made and handed down in oral tradition, though possibly some traces of this may have indirectly survived here and there in ballads of a much later date. The thing which astounded his hearers when Cædmon recited his *Hymn* was that a peasant, lacking entirely that kind of upbringing and training which could have given him the ability to employ the essentially aristocratic technique of the Germanic heroic diction and style, should suddenly have produced a poem in which all this 'educated' technique was demonstrated with exact correctness. For the Anglo-Saxon peasant versification (perhaps the ancestor of *Piers Plowman*) would have been far freer and much less elaborately technical than the Anglo-Saxon poetry we know, and its diction could not have had the obviously aristocratic character we associate with that language. As was said earlier, what Cædmon did was—so far as we know, for the first time—to apply the whole technical apparatus of that Germanic heroic poetry which the Anglo-Saxons had brought with them from their Continental homelands to a specifically Christian version of the story of Creation.

When Hrothgar's scop in *Beowulf* sang to the harp his lay of the Creation,[1] whether or not his author actually was consciously echoing Cædmon, he was certainly using the new style created by Cædmon's poetic revolution—what Humphrey Wanley called the *stilus Cædmonianus*. The vernacular poems of St Aldhelm, evidently admired by King Alfred, must have been recited at about the same time as Cædmon's miracle: but as we can know nothing directly of them, *Cædmon's Hymn* is properly to be taken as the first example of the

[1] *Beowulf*, lines 90–98.

new application of traditional Germanic pagan technique to Christian themes. In its nine lines there are nine words which seem to have belonged always to the traditional aristocratic poetic vocabulary, whose application in the new field may be called revolutionary. Such are *metod*, 'Creator', with its association with the act of measuring or apportioning; *wuldor*, 'glory', in the poetic name for God as *wuldor-fæder*, 'father of glory'; and *ælda*, in the phrase *ælda barnum* (West-Saxon *ylda bearnum*), 'children of men'. This last, obviously suggested by Scripture in its new use, recurs as clearly a formulaic expression in *Beowulf* 70, as *yldo bearn*. Parallels have been found in the folk-traditions of several countries to the general picture of an unlettered peasant suddenly becoming a poet, and the tale of Cædmon was perhaps imitated in the accounts prefaced much later to the Old Saxon ninth-century poetic Gospel harmony known as the *Heliand*. The appearance, too, of supernatural aid in a dream or vision is a central element in folk-tradition, even as far afield as Uzbekistan, in Central Asia. But such parallels from folklore do not affect the basic fact of the Cædmonian poetic revolution. The *Hymn*, indeed, may still seem to a modern reader to exhibit qualities of balanced and rhythmic grandeur in a poetic appeal. Cædmon may be said, in fact, to have preserved for Christian poetic art the great verbal inheritance of pagan Germanic heroic poetry, so that in Old English verse always after that the heroes of the new culture, whether Biblical or hagio-logical, would be presented in the linguistic garb and in the sentiment of Germanic heroic tradition. Very soon after Cædmon we find Christ presented in the poems of the Ruthwell Cross runic inscription and its later expansion *The Dream of the Rood* as a truly heroic Germanic warrior with his disciples as his loyal comitatus. In the Cædmonian poems of the Junius Manuscript we find Moses in *Exodus* as a warlike leader of sea-rovers as he crosses the Red Sea; and Christ forcibly removes the souls of the good from Satan's imprison-ment in *Christ and Satan* again in heroic diction. In first applying the pagan discipline of Germanic tradition, language, method, and style to the matter of Latin Christian culture, Cædmon—or at least the Cædmonian style which flourished in his followers—set the whole tone of Anglo-Saxon poetry.[1]

By applying the technique of secular traditional heroic poetry to Christian subject-matter and edification, Cædmon and those who followed him had indeed found an answer to Alcuin's objections to the preserving of elements of the pagan Germanic tradition which had produced lays such as that of the Heathobard warrior prince Ingeld. For to his famous rhetorical inquiry "Quid Hinieldus cum Christo?" it could in effect be answered that the new Cædmonian poetry made the heroic diction of Ingeld labour in the service of Christ. The Old Testament poems of the Junius Manuscript, corres-

---

[1] On the Cædmon question generally *cf.* C. L. Wrenn, "The Poetry of Cæd-mon", *Proceedings of the British Academy* XXXII (1946), pp. 277–295.

ponding as so much of them do with the lectionary readings required between Septuagesima and Easter, may well have been put together as suitable reading in refectory at a religious house: and *Christ and Satan*, the rather later verse which seems to have been added after the Old Testament compilation had already been planned, again may be regarded as having Easter Day as its centre, though with a homiletic approach.

It is clear that the Old Testament poems—by far the larger part of the Junius Manuscript—present an incomplete carrying out of a careful and elaborate plan, perhaps made under the patronage of a certain Ælfwine, probably the head of a religious house, whose name in a medallion portrait appears below a large illustration on page 2. Illustrations were evidently planned for the whole Old Testament series, though only the first two-thirds of *Genesis* have them—the rest being indicated by blank spaces which should have been filled by the artist commissioned for this purpose, who was a man of considerable skill and imagination. Moreover, the Old Testament pieces are all copied by the one scribe, and the whole series divided into continuously numbered sectional or 'fit' passages, suggesting that it was considered here as a whole and not as individual poems. *Christ and Satan*, copied in three rather later hands and termed *Liber II* by its last scribe, seems to have been added later to the original scheme of the book, in which the Old Testament pieces would have become *Liber I*. This added matter has its own separate sectional divisions. No other of the four major Old English verse manuscripts shows comparable careful planning: and the Junius Manuscript alone was devised with provision for full illustrations.

Of all these Cædmonian poems, *Exodus*, as has been indicated, is the most signalized by epic heroic features, though, like the other pieces in this manuscript it is incomplete and shows lacunae. It opens with the regular formulaic beginning for a heroic poem, one of exactly the same type as the exordium of *Beowulf*:

> Hwæt! We feor and neah gefrigen habað
> ofer middan-geard Moyses domas,
> wræclico word-riht, wera cneorissum, etc.

Now indeed we have heard tell far and near throughout the world of the judgments of Moses, his wondrous proclaiming of the law to the tribes of men.

Genesis, *Exodus*, and *Daniel*, though of diverse authorship, all probably date in their original forms from the age of Bede, a time when something like a 'school of Cædmon' might have been expected to have existed, especially in Northumbria. *Genesis*, by far the largest though nevertheless unfinished, covers, including the later interpolated *Genesis B*, 2936 lines. *Exodus* and *Daniel* cover only 590 and 764 respectively.

With the loss of St Aldhelm's vernacular poems there disappeared the last chance of finding any poetry actually composed by a contemporary or near-contemporary of Cædmon. But in the age of Bede, the great flowering-time of Northumbrian art, there is one versifier in the vernacular whose name we know. For Bede, though normally concerned only with the academic art of Latin metre, has left us one little Anglo-Saxon epigram. This, because of its authorship, merits special notice. It is known as *Bede's Death-Song*.

A monk, Cuthbert, later Abbot of Wearmouth-Jarrow, and one of Bede's disciples to whom he seems to have dedicated his treatise *De Arte Metrica*, wrote in a letter to one Cuthwine a vivid and justly famous eye-witness account of Bede's last days and of his death. So much was this letter, known as *Epistola Cuthberti de Obitu Bedae*, valued through the Middle Ages that there are still nearly 50 copies of it surviving.[1] In no less than 29 of these there was included or added, sometimes in Northumbrian and sometimes in West-Saxon, this Anglo-Saxon five-line epigram on death which, as Cuthbert tells his correspondent, Bede recited along with many passages from the Scriptures shortly before his end. The Anglo-Saxon text of the poem follows immediately after this statement:

> Et (canebat) multa alia de Sacra Scriptura, et in nostra quoque lingua, ut erat doctus in nostris carminibus.

Here is the oldest of the Northumbrian versions from a ninth-century manuscript in the library of the Benedictine house of St Gall in Switzerland:

> Fore there neidfaerae naenig uuiurthit
> thoncsnotturra, than him tharf sie
> to ymbhycggannae aer his hiniongae
> huaet his gastae godes aeththa ylfaes
> aefter deothdaege doemid uueorthae.[2]

Before the inevitable journey no one will be wiser than he need by considering, before his departure, what will be adjudged to his soul of good or evil after his death-day.[3]

The description by Cuthbert does not state explicitly that Bede was himself the author of the little piece he recited; and it has of late been suggested that he recited (*canebat*), since he was skilled in our poems (*doctus nostris carminibus*), a poem he knew from memory. But the

---

[1] For the full text of Cuthbert's letter see Dobbie's study of *Cædmon's Hymn and Bede's Death Song*, op. cit., pp. 117 ff.

[2] MS. St Gall 254, as in ASPR VI, p. 107. The second word in line 1 is taken as *there* as by Dobbie in his earlier work of 1937 (op. cit.) as against the *thaem* of ASPR.

[3] Translated by C. T. Onions in Sweet's *Anglo-Saxon Reader*, 13th ed. (Oxford, 1954), p. 223.

existence of so many copies of the poem, extending in date from the ninth to the sixteenth centuries, would seem to imply a deep-seated tradition that the *Death-Song* is in fact the work of the Venerable Bede himself: and the Latin context certainly is consistent with this most widely accepted view. The piece is decidedly Cædmonian in style, and its literary quality seems neither better not worse than that of *Cædmon's Hymn*: but to ascribe it to Cædmon, as Bulst has sought to do, is unnecessary speculation.[1] The epigram is just what one would have expected of Bede, with all the care and attention fixed on technical correctness and on the wisdom of its statement. But the *Death-Song* may have another and quite different importance. For without it, and Cuthbert's statement that Bede was skilled in "our poems" (that is, vernacular poetry), we should not have known that he was interested in the poetry of his native tongue besides his special concern with Latin versifying as an academic discipline.

Apart from the basically important *Cædmon's Hymn*, which belongs to the time of Bede's infancy or a little earlier, the other poems discussed, with the exception of the later *Christ and Satan* and *Genesis B*, may properly be said to have been originally composed in the age of Bede. This period of literary history, which roughly covers the first half of the eighth century, was indeed something of a golden age, not only of English Northumbrian art, but also of Anglo-Saxon poetry. *Genesis A*, *Exodus*, and *Daniel*, in their original forms, seem clearly to belong to this period: but it is probably true too that much of the best of Anglo-Saxon poetry, including its greatest product, *Beowulf*, originated in the eighth century—especially in its earlier years. As has been shown in the preceding chapter, the older poems of Germanic heroic tradition belong to this age (*Widsith* may be of a rather earlier date). Some of the best pieces in the Exeter Book, the so-called elegiac poems, are commonly attributed to the eighth century. The fragmentary verses of the runic inscription on the Ruthwell Cross in Dumfriesshire—definitely Northumbrian, of the age of Bede or at any rate of the eighth century, and possibly as early as Cædmon's time—are part of what must have been one of the greatest religious poems of the language, as is indicated clearly by its later expanded form in *The Dream of the Rood*. But it is not possible, especially in view of so much uncertainty of dating and of the relatively large quantity of poetry attributable in origin to the age of Bede or a time later in the eighth century, to treat of these poems in any way chronologically. While bearing in mind probable order of composition, it has seemed best to treat Anglo-Saxon poetry as representing various types or genres: so that other poems which may seem historically to belong to the period of this chapter must be dealt with chiefly in subsequent ones. *Beowulf*, alike for its intrinsic excellence as the greatest long Anglo-Saxon poem and for its historical importance, will provide the matter of the next chapter.

[1] *Zeitschrift für deutsches Altertum* LXXV (1938), pp. 111–114.

CHAPTER 7

Beowulf

Beowulf[1] is the editorial title of the long heroic poem which is the supreme monument of the Anglo-Saxon poetic genius in view of its size and sustained high quality, although it may be thought to have been surpassed in individual excellences by parts of some of the shorter quasi-lyrical pieces—notably *The Wanderer* and *The Seafarer*. As this title suggests, it is a poetic presentation in a full background of a man Beowulf as the ideal example of the Germanic heroic culture discussed in Chapter 5, treated for a Christian audience with an implicit symbolism of the conflict of *humanum genus* with the powers of evil.

Beowulf himself is at once the ideal Germanic hero—in so far as this can be assimilated in a Christian tradition—and the source of poetic entertainment in a dramatic story as enjoyed by an eighth-century audience, and copied in its surviving form for the pleasure and edification of a monastic cultural centre in the later age of the Benedictine Revival. While it is a thoroughly Germanic poem, yet presented by a Christian to Christians, it has several levels of meaning, though it could clearly be enjoyed simply as an entertainment without consciousness of these. It has, for instance, implications of the hero's fights as symbols of the human conflict resulting from original sin, and there are elements comparable with aspects of the heroes of Spenser's *Faerie Queene* and with Bunyan's *Pilgrim's Progress*. It dramatically presents the moments of high adventure and of tragedy in the life of Beowulf, illustrating them by means of parallelism and contrast and a kind of tragic irony through allusive echoes of Germanic heroic lays (now lost) and historic traditions well known to its auditors. It has something of the depth and tone of an epic, but has not the form and construction which that ancient classical term now suggests. It presents a universally appealing tragedy of the human predicament through Germanic history, legend, and folklore in a style and diction which sustains the best qualities of what may be termed Classical Old English poetry throughout its more than 3000 lines. Its title was given in England by Kemble in his edition of 1833: for, as usual, the manuscript has no heading.

[1] For literary study of the poem with minimal apparatus see the edition by C. L. Wrenn (London, 1958). For the fuller technical examination *cf.* R. W. Chambers, *Beowulf, an Introduction to the Study of the Poem*, 3rd ed., with Supplement by C. L. Wrenn (Cambridge, 1963).

The poem seems to have been put together in Anglian territory, either in the Northumbria of the age of Bede or in Mercia near the close of the eighth century in the period of Offa, the great king of the Mercians. It was built up from traditional Germanic material of history, legend, and folklore in a Christianized Old English cultural environment. Though some of this material was probably known from traditional lays, the structure of the poem shows a deliberate and highly developed art in which the variety of episodes and digressions, so foreign to the epic traditions of Greece and Rome, vividly enhances and heightens the poetic effectiveness of the simple central narratives. The apparently advanced sophisticated culture of the life shown in the poem, and the interest in the Danish royal family in whose service the hero performs his adventures, have suggested relatively late dates for the composition of *Beowulf* as we have it.[1] But, on the other hand, the parallels between the treasures of the highest craftsmanship and art discovered at Sutton Hoo in 1939 and material described in *Beowulf* have seemed to some to point to an earlier date, when the memory of such a ship-cenotaph as that of Sutton Hoo would still have been fresh.[2] From the point of view of such chronology as may be indicated by comparison with other Old English poetic monuments, *Beowulf* seems, from its tone, to be a little later than the originals of the Cædmonian Old Testament poems treated in the preceding chapter, but also somewhat earlier than work of the Cynewulf School, in some of which—notably *Andreas*—*Beowulf* is distinctly imitated or echoed.

The sole surviving manuscript, in which *Beowulf* was copied along with *Judith*, belongs to the end of the tenth century or the beginning of the eleventh. Though written in the usual Classical Old English or late West-Saxon which was the literary *koinē* of the period, *Beowulf* is exceptionally well preserved as a text, despite the transfer from its presumed original Northumbrian or Mercian dialect.[3] The Beowulf Manuscript, as it is generally called—originally a separate book containing three prose pieces as well as *Beowulf* and *Judith*—was bound up early in the seventeenth century with a twelfth-century manuscript containing principally King Alfred's adaptation of St Augustine's *Soliloquies*. Its fly-leaf shows the signature 'Laurence

[1] The most recent full discussion of the date is Gösta Langenfelt, "Beowulf och Fornsverige: ett forsök till datering av den fornengelska hjältedikten" (*Ortnamnssälskapets i Uppsala Årskrift*, 1961–1962), Part 1, pp. 35–55, and Part 2, pp. 23–38.

[2] *Cf.* C. L. Wrenn, "Sutton Hoo and Beowulf" in *Mélanges de Linguistique et de Philologie Fernand Mossé in Memoriam* (Paris, 1959), reprinted in a handy collection of essays on *Beowulf*, *An Anthology of Beowulf Criticism*, ed. Lewis E. Nicholson (University of Notre Dame Press, 1963), pp. 311–330.

[3] There is a facsimile of the manuscript, with transliteration, by Julius Zupitza (EETS 77: London, 1882): this was revised with new collotype photographs by Norman Davis (EETS 245: London, 1959). The fullest study of the manuscript is in the introduction by Kemp Malone to *The Nowell Codex, Cotton MS Vitellius AXV*; volume XII in the series *Early English Manuscripts in Facsimile* (Copenhagen, Baltimore, and London, 1963).

Nouell', that of Lawrence Nowell, Dean of Lichfield, dated 1563: and this well-known Anglo-Saxonist may well have been concerned with its re-discovery after the dissolution of the monasteries. In the library of Sir Robert Cotton (who died in 1631) the combined manuscript was catalogued from its position on a case surmounted by the bust of the Roman emperor Vitellius as Vitellius A XV. Hence, when the Cotton collection passed to the British Museum it continued to be known as MS. Cotton Vitellius A XV. This Beowulf Manuscript is one of the four basic manuscripts of Old English poetry.

Beowulf is, as has been indicated, basically a Germanic rather than an English poem in subject-matter. Yet its tone implies much that is characteristic of Anglo-Saxon civilization at its height. Moreover, though its main material is Scandinavian, it does include two, or possibly three, characters closely connected with Britain. These are Offa the Angle king, ancestor of the great Offa of Mercia who reigned in the later eighth century, Hengest the Jute, who seems to embody traditions of the historical Hengest who was a first leader of the Germanic invaders in the middle of the fifth century, and Finn (mentioned also in *Widsith*), whose name occurs in Anglian genealogies. For this last may possibly be linked with the leader in the Finn episode of our poem. It has often been remarked too that the heroic spirit displayed by Beowulf himself is, as it were, clearly echoed in the poetic story of the last stand of Byrhtnoth of Essex against the Vikings described in the late Old English poem *The Battle of Maldon*: for Beowulf's last tragic fight with the dragon parallels Byrhtnoth's fatal conflict in showing the Old English heroic spirit reaching its height in the moment of the final facing of impossible odds.

The plot of *Beowulf* is a simple, disjointed tale of conflicts between the hero and supernatural monsters of evil. In his confident youth Beowulf overcomes the demon monsters Grendel and his mother. Then, after fifty years of noble rule over his people, the Geats of South Sweden, he faces in heroic old age a fire-breathing dragon which is destroying his country, and slays it while himself receiving his death-wounds, exulting in his heroic past life and in the noble memory he will leave with posterity. To the modern reader this is— at least, at first sight—a trivial plot for a great heroic poem; nor can he share in the immense aesthetic pleasure which the Old English audience must have derived from its 'grand style', rhythm, and noble traditional diction. Such a poem inevitably must suffer from the modern tendency to judge of a piece of literature from its ideas and subject-matter alone, forgetting that harmony of form and matter which we may easily recognize in great poems whose language and thought-pattern are still understood with relative ease. Historically *Beowulf* is, of course, of the first importance as a monument of Anglo-Saxon culture whose influence can also be traced to some extent throughout the Anglo-Saxon period. But its rhythm is also still that of English speech, though its diction seems remote: and there are

many passages which, even in translation, may still move the reader
as great poetry should. Indeed, such reading may well suggest to
reluctant students that it would be productive of true literary pleasure
to make a close study of it in the original.[1] The best translation for
the appreciation of *Beowulf* as a poem is that of Charles W.
Kennedy (New York, 1940), who conveys as much as possible of its poetic
impression in a rendering into alliterative verse. The art of translating
it has been admirably discussed in a preliminary essay to Edwin
Morgan's verse translation (Hand and Flower Press, Aldington, Kent,
1952).

Beowulf, though having its place in the continuity of English
poetry, as shown in Chapter 2, is in no sense a 'national epic'. Its
place in world literature can hardly be assessed, therefore, compara-
tively, nor is it, save in very general terms, to be compared with the
Aeneid or the *Iliad*—still less with the *Chanson de Roland* or the
Finnish *Kalevala*. But it is the earliest outstanding heroic poem in
the Western post-classical world: and its importance is as much for
its intrinsic merits as a poem as for its obvious historical value. It includes examples in individual passages too of all the best qualities to
be found in the various genres of Old English poetry—heroic, lyrical,
elegiac, descriptive, and homiletic. Some passages, like so many of
its traditional phrases, are formulaic inheritances from the Germanic
past. Such is the epic-type opening of the poem, a formal call to the
audience to concentrate attention on a basic theme, which is paralleled
in other Germanic poetry and occurs frequently in Old English epic
pieces such as *Exodus*, Cynewulf's *Elene* and *Andreas*. Here are the
opening lines of *Beowulf* followed by a fairly free prose rendering:

> Hwæt we Gar-Dena in gear-dagum
> þeod-cyninga þrym gefrunon,
> hu ða æþelingas ellen fremedon.
> Oft Scyld Scefing sceaþena þreatum
> monegum mægþum meodo-setla ofteah;
> egsode Eorle, syððan ærest wearð
> feasceaft funden; he þæs frofre gebad:
> weox under wolcnum, weorð-myndum þah,
> oðþæt him æghwylc þara ymb-sittendra
> ofer hron-rade hyran scolde,
> gomban gyldan: þæt wæs god cyning!

Indeed we have heard of the might in days of yore of the kings of the
people of the warlike Danes, how those noble princes wrought deeds
of valour. Often did Scyld Scefing deprive troops of his foes in many
a tribe of their mead-benches. He it was who struck terror into the

---

[1] There is a fairly accurate prose translation by J. R. Clark Hall with introduction and notes by C. L. Wrenn and a notable preface by J. R. R. Tolkien. There is
also a rendering with useful apparatus by David Wright in the Penguin series
(London, 1957).

men of the Heruli from the time when he had first been found destitute and helpless. For that he found consolation: for he prospered exceedingly under the skies, honoured in men's memories, until every one of those who dwelt around him across the sea, the path of the whale, was forced to obey him and to pay him tribute. That indeed was a good king.

In this rough prose translation, which is yet as close to the original as is compatible with current English, as in the other renderings which illustrate this chapter, a style is sought which suggests the aristocratic nature of the audience and their love of traditional language by the use of a somewhat old-fashioned tone, with occasional archaisms and traditional poetic expressions. The audience, having been recalled from the pleasures of the festive banquet by an appropriate sign from the king or chief and the utterance of the above formulaic summons by the scop, are ready to listen to the heroic narrative enhanced by the gently dovetailed accompaniment of the harp.

This beginning, reminding us as it may of the *Aeneid* and the *Iliad*, is followed by a moving and meditative account of the final departure of the founder of the Danish kingdom's greatness in a mysterious ship-burial rather reminiscent of that of Sutton Hoo (lines 32–52). This, with the initial lines, forms the introduction to the poem, whose narrative then begins. The end of the poem too is a description of the funeral rites of the hero himself, and a brief word of praise for his glorious life. The increasingly tragic tone of the whole is thus emphasized and given form by its beginning and ending with the enigma of death.

Having set forth the lineage and background of the great Danish king Hrothgar in whose service the hero's first two adventures are to take place, the poet describes the noble new hall with gold-adorned roof named Heorot, which became the seat of what has been called "the great Arthurian court of the North", and how its highly civilized happiness is suddenly ended by the deadly nightly attacks of the demon-monster Grendel, whose envy and hatred have been aroused, since he is descended from Cain the first murderer. Beowulf, a young prince of the South-Swedish tribe the Geats, arrives at Heorot to seek the adventure of slaying Grendel, accompanied by a small chosen comitatus. His generous reception in courtly manner by the aged and intensely grieved Hrothgar is followed by a very brief but vividly dramatic picture of Grendel's visit to the hall of sleeping warriors at night where Beowulf awaits him. Here is the beginning of the description of the fight with Grendel with a portrait of the monster:

> Ða com of more under mist-hleoþum
> Grendel gongan, Godes yrre bær;
> mynte se man-scaða manna cynnes

sumne besyrwan in sele þam hean.
Wod under wolcnum, to þæs þe he win-reced,
gold-sele gumena gearwost wisse,
fættum fahne. Ne wæs þæt forma sið
þæt he Hroþgares ham gesohte.
Næfre he on aldor-dagum ær ne siþðan
heardran hæle heal-ðegnas fand.
Com þa to recede rinc siðian
dreamum bedæled. Duru sona onarn
fyr-bendum fæst, syþðan he hire folmum gehran:
onbræd þa bealo-hydig, ða he gebolgen wæs,
recedes muþan. Raþe æfter þon
on fagne flor feond treddode,
eode yrre-mod; him of eagum stod
ligge gelicost leoht unfæger.
Geseah he in recede rinca manige,
swefan sibbe-gedriht samod ætgædere,
mago-rinca heap. Þa his mod ahlog;
mynte þæt he gedælde, ær þon dæg cwome,
atol aglæca, anra gehwylces
lif wið lice, þa him alumpen wæs
wist-fylle wen. Ne wæs þæt wyrd þa gen,
þæt he ma moste manna cynnes
ðicgean ofer þa niht.

(lines 710–736)

Then Grendel came walking from the moor mid the mist-covered
slopes: he bore in himself the wrath of God. That wicked worker
of harm meant to ensnare one of the race of men in that high hall.
Beneath the skies he advanced till he could very clearly discern the
mansion for the wine-drinking, the hall of men decked out with gold
plating. That was not the first time that he had sought out Hrothgar's
dwelling. Never in the days of his life, before or since, did he meet
with noble guardians of the hall with tougher fortune. Now this
warrior, bereft of joys, went journeying to the building. Instantly
its door, though firm in its fire-tempered steel girders, fell in the
moment he touched it with his hands. Then intent on battle and
swollen with rage as he was, he tore open the entrance to the hall.
After that speedily the fiend stepped along the floor with its tessellated
paving, furious in heart. From his eyes there shone a horrifying light
most like to a flame. In that hall he perceived many of the warrior
retainers sleeping all together, a band of kindred men. Then it was
that his heart laughed aloud. It was the horrible demon's purpose
that he should sever, before the dawn of day, the life from the body
of every one who was there, since there had come to him hopeful
expectancy of a banquet of slaughter. But it was not at that time his
fate that he should devour during that night more of men.

Beowulf's victorious fight with Grendel, like most things of the kind in Anglo-Saxon poetry, is described very briefly, with a few sweeping strokes which kindle the imagination in a vividly memorable picture, despite the absence of that "particularity" and "awareness of the contemporary scene" which T. S. Eliot would require. For in Germanic literature it is not till the making of the Old Norse sagas some centuries later that we find anything of vivid personal physical detail in the dramatic presentation of the characters. We do not know what Beowulf is supposed to have looked like, nor the exact physical appearance of the monsters in the poem: yet we are made intensely to perceive alike the heroic qualities of Beowulf and the shattering terror of Grendel and his mother.

After the first victory, the poet gives us moving descriptions of the triumphant rejoicing which followed in Hrothgar's court. There are sports and pastimes and entertainments by the scop singing appropriate lays of victorious heroes. But the basic and increasingly tragic tone and atmosphere of the poem are yet here suggested by two evidently traditional lays which are emphasized in recitation. The lay of Sigemund, who slew a dragon whose death brought a curse on his slayer (lines 864–898), thus shows a kind of tragic irony in foreshadowing Beowulf's own victory over a treasure-guarding dragon whose magical spell was connected with his own death in that fight. For the audience know full well the traditional legend of Sigemund and his treasure-guarding dragon, even as this lay is being recited in glorification of Beowulf's slaying of Grendel. Again, the longer episode of Finn (lines 1063–1159) in describing from an older lay the deadly feud between Danes and Frisians parallels events in royal Danish history which, as the audience know, are to take place later with devastating tragedy. The marriage between a Danish princess and Finn, ruler of the Frisians, aimed at healing a long-standing bitter feud, ended after some happiness in the breaking out anew of the old quarrel and a holocaust of tragedy: and so, too, as the audience know, will it happen to Hrothgar's glorious hall. For Heorot was to be destroyed when a feud between Hrothgar's Danes and the tribe of the Heathobards, which Hrothgar had sought to heal by giving his daughter in marriage to Ingeld, ruler of the enemy people, was later to be rekindled, and to result in the total destruction of Heorot by fire. This kind of tragic anticipation in irony in the Sophoclean sense had already been suggested by the poet in an early description of the splendours of Hrothgar's hall:

> He beot ne aleh, beagas dælde,
> sinc æt symle. Sele hlifade
> heah ond horn-geap, heaðo-wylma bad,
> laðan liges; ne wæs hit lenge þa gen,
> þæt se ecg-hete aþum-swerian
> æfter wæl-niðe wæcnan scolde. (lines 80–85)

He [Hrothgar] did not belie his boastful promise: for he shared out treasure of twisted gold at the banquet. The hall, with its spaciously wide gables, towered high into the air. It was to await the furious surging of hateful flame: but not yet was the time at hand that the embattled hatred between son-in-law and father-in-law was to break forth because of a slaughterous enmity.

And after the festive triumphing in the hero's victory over Grendel is to come the terror of the deadly onset of Grendel's mother—a monster even more mysteriously terrifying than he. Returning to his home in a supernaturally lighted cave-dwelling under an incredibly deep black mountain lake, Grendel lies mortally wounded from the effects of Beowulf's tearing off his arm and shoulder, and he dies, thus stirring his demon-mother to revenge. She, from the lair which she had shared with her son in the demon-haunted lake, attacks Heorot with a slaughter which includes Hrothgar's favourite noble; and it is thus that Beowulf goes to the haunted mere to seek out the female monster who is even more potent than Grendel. Anglo-Saxon nature-poetry, in its often almost Hardyesque subjective gloom, is seen at its finest in this description of the mere where the monsters and many other demons dwelt.

> Hie dygel lond
> warigeað, wulf-hleoþu, windige næssas,
> frecne fen-gelad, ðær fyrgen-stream
> under næssa genipu niþer gewiteð,
> flod under foldan. Nis þæt feor heonon
> mil-gemearces, þæt se mere standeð
> ofer þæm hongiað hrinde bearwas;
> wudu wyrtum fæst wæter oferhelmað.
> Þær mæg nihta gehwæm nið-wundor seon,
> fyr on flode. No þæs frod leofað
> gumena bearna þæt þone grund wite.
> Ðeah þe hæð-stapa hundum geswenced,
> heorot hornum trum holt-wudu sece,
> feorran geflymed, ær he feorh seleð,
> aldor on ofre, ær he in wille,
> hafelan hydan. Nis þæt heoru stow;
> þonon yð-geblond up astigeð
> won to wolcnum, þonne wind styreþ
> lað gewidru, oðþæt lyft ðrysmaþ,
> roderas reotað.
>
> (lines 1357–1376)

They live in a land of mysterious secrecy, slopes haunted by wolves, wind-swept headlands, a terrifying region which crosses the fenlands where the mountain torrent goes deep down neath the mist-covered rocks, in a flood under the earth. It is not far from thence in measured miles that there stands the mere, above which there overhang thickets of bushes covered in hoar-frost: and the water is shadowed above by densely-rooted forest. At that place every night is to be beheld a mysteriously terrifying sight, fire upon the water. There is none of those wise in age among the children of men who knows its depth. Even though the stag who traverses the heath strong in his horns may seek the forest when hard pressed by hounds from afar in flight, he will give up his life on the mere's bank before he will dive in to hide his head. That is not a place of pleasantness. From there the swirling of the waves rises up dark beneath the clouds when the wind stirs up horrible storms, till the air becomes choking mist and the skies weep.

The poet has here succeeded in creating the atmosphere he needs.

After this second slaying of a monster, Beowulf, welcomed back by his almost desparing comrades, decides to return to his own country, since now finally Heorot is purged of all evil and terror; and his triumphal return voyage to Geatland and his own king Hygelac is described. But in taking an affectionate farewell of the wise and patriarchal Hrothgar, Beowulf is given a magnificent homiletic oration at the final banquet (lines 1700–1784) in which are combined general moralizing of the kind dear to an Old English audience, praise of the hero about to depart, and advice as to his conduct through life. Having admonished Beowulf to take to heart the exemplary fate of Heremod, one of Hrothgar's least admirable predecessors, the king adds a homily of some forty lines which is complete in itself and Christian in tone. This is sometimes thought to be artistically superfluous and taken to be a later Christian interpolation: but its literary quality is so outstanding, and indeed in accordance with the genius of the poet, that it should be accepted as genuine. Moreover, there is realism in making the aged king become so carried away with his moralizing that he continues—from some points of view, too long. Here is part of this poetic sermon, probably unmatched in its kind:

> "Wundor is to secganne,
> hu mihtig God manna cynne
> þurh sidne sefan snyttru bryttað,
> eard ond eorlscipe; he ah ealra geweald.
> Hwilum he on lufan læteð hworfan
> monnes mod-geþonc mæran cynnes,
> seleð him on eþle eorþan wynne
> to healdanne, hleo-burh wera;
> gedeð him swa gewealdene worolde dælas,
> side rice, þæt he his selfa ne mæg
> for his unsnyttrum ende geþencean.
> Wunað he on wiste, no hine wiht dweleð
> adl ne yldo, ne him inwit-sorh
> on sefan sweorceð, ne gesacu ohwær

ecg-hete eoweð, ac him eal worold
wendeð on willan. He þæt wyrse ne con,
oðþæt him on innan ofer-hygda dæl
weaxeð ond wridað, þonne se weard swefeð,
sawele hyrde; bið se slæp to fæst,
bisgum gebunden; bona swiðe neah,
se þe of flan-bogan fyrenum sceoteð.
Þonne bið on hreþre under helm drepen
biteran stræle—him bebeorgan ne con—
wom wundor-bebodum wergan gastes."

(lines 1724–1747)

"A wondrous thing it is to speak of, how almighty God in the spacious-
ness of his thought assigns to the race of men prudence, territory and
noble quality. He it is who has power over all things. Sometimes He
permits the working of the mind of a man of famous race to wander
in pleasure, grants to him in his own country to possess earthly joy
and a protecting fortress of warriors. He awards to him thus limited
regions of this world in a spacious kingdom, so that he himself,
because of his ignorance, has no power to meditate upon his end. He
lives in abundant pleasure; nor do sickness or old age in any wise
afflict him, nor does the malice of grief bring gloom to his heart, nor
is there anywhere strife or warlike enmity displayed against him. But
for him the whole world goes in accord with his desire. He knows not
the most evil thing that is to come, till within him a deal of over-
weening pride grows up and flourishes. For it is then that the guardian
protector of his soul is sleeping. Too deep is that sleep when he is
bound round with worldly cares. Now very near approaches the
slayer who shoots with deadly aim from his bow with an arrow.
Then is the man smitten with a bitter dart in his breast, neath his
protecting armour. He cannot save himself. He is smitten by the
mysterious crooked promptings of the accursed spirit."

On returning home to his own king and people, Beowulf is much
glorified: and the episodic account of Offa, King of the Angles, is
introduced for the purpose of emphasizing the hero's wondrous early
life by its parallels with that of the great Angle king who was the
ancestor of the historical Offa of Mercia. For like Beowulf, Offa[1] had
been sluggish in his youth, and had at first seemed unpromising (lines
2183 ff.). This account of Beowulf's home-coming serves to link the
two contrasting parts of the whole poem—the stories of Beowulf's
glorious conquest of Grendel and of his mother and the tragic fight
of his old age fifty years later with the dragon. Beowulf has become
the ruler of his people, the Geats; and it is to save them from the
dragon that he enters his last fight, knowing that it must end with
his own death. Since *Beowulf* is a poem displaying in balanced contrast

---

[1] On Offa see R. W. Chambers, *op. cit.*, pp. 31 ff., and cf. *Widsith*, lines 35 ff.

the glories of its hero—joyful in his youth and tragic in his experienced old age—its tone and style change after the introduction of the dragon (line 2210). This change, and the fact that the dragon—a treasure-guarding creature in a burial-mound, from out of folklore—is so different in nature from Grendel and his mother has led some critics to reject the unity of the poem and to separate in origin the accounts of Beowulf's first two victorious fights from that of his last and fatal one. But like Beowulf's earlier monster foes, this dragon, however it differs in origin from them, seems to symbolize the super-natural power of evil. Viewed as a picture of the high moments in a whole heroic life, with its inevitable tragic ending in accord with Germanic heroic tradition, the dragon-story is necessary and artis-tically fitting in the poem as conceived: and the change in the style and tone may be looked upon as true decorum.

It is in this last portion of the poem, naturally, that there chiefly occur those lyric and elegiac passages which may be compared with such pieces as *The Wanderer* and *The Seafarer*. Here is one of these, in which the last survivor of a glorious royal line utters his thoughts on placing his ancestral treasures in the burial-mound where the dragon later ruled over them:

> "Heald þu nu, hruse, nu hæleð ne mostan,
> eorla æhte! Hwæt hit ær on ðe
> gode begeaton. Guð-deað fornam
> feorh-bealo frecne, fyra gehwylcne
> leoda minra, þara ðe þis lif ofgeaf,
> gesawon sele-dream; nah, hwa sweord wege,
> oððe feormie fæted wæge,
> drync-fæt deore; duguð ellor scoc.
> Sceal se hearda helm, hyrsted golde,
> fætum befeallen; feormynd swefað,
> þa ðe beado-griman bywan sceoldon;
> ge swylce seo here-pad, sio æt hilde gebad
> ofer borda gebræc bite irena,
> brosnað æfter beorne; ne mæg byrnan hring
> æfter wig-fruman wide feran
> hæleðum be healfe. Næs hearpan wyn,
> gomen gleo-beames, ne god hafoc
> geond sæl swingeð, ne se swifta mearh
> burh-stede beateð. Bealo-cwealm hafað
> fela feorh-cynna forð onsended!"
> (lines 2247–2266)

"Hold thou, O earth, since men now may not, the possessions of noble warriors. Truly it was in times of yore that excellent men got them from thee. Death in battle, the terrible destroyer of life, has carried off every one of the men of my people, those who have given up this life. They have seen the ending of their joyful revelries in hall. I have no one who may bear a sword or polish the noble cups and drinking-vessels of plated gold. All the fine company of noble warriors have hastened away to another world. The strong helmet adorned with its plating of gold is to be stripped of that gold. Those who once were wont to embellish the war-helm are sleeping in death. The battle-armour, too, which once endured the bite of iron weapons in the fighting mid the crashing of breaking shields, rots along with its warrior owner: nor may the linked mail journey far and wide with the war-leader beside heroes. Not at all is there the joyous sound of the harp, the happy music of melodious wood. There is no fine hawk whirling through the hall in flight, nor any swift steed with hooves ringing on the streets of the citadel. Wicked slaughter has sent many of mortal men on their journey hence."

After the fatal fight of the hero with the dragon whose treasure bore a deadly curse on him who should take the hoard, the poem ends with a description of Beowulf's funeral rites and final words of praise for the ideal king. It closes in a funeral elegy as it had begun, thus emphasizing the tragic shape of the whole. It is significant that the poet's final words in praise of Beowulf by emphasizing his gentleness clearly suggest how Christianity had touched this embodiment of the noble Germanic heroic culture:

> cwædon þæt he wære wyruld-cyninga,
> manna mildust ond mon-þwærust,
> leodum liðost ond lof-geornost.
> (lines 3180–3182)

Men said that he was, of the kings of this world, the mildest and most gracious of men, the gentlest to his people and the most eager for praise.

In some respects *Beowulf* is indeed a vast and episodically complex elegy for its hero,[1] and there is some fittingness in the title which Grundtvig, its first Danish translator, gave to it as *Bjovulfs-Drapen*, 'Heroic poem in praise of Beowulf', in 1861.

As has been remarked, the text of *Beowulf* managed to survive during the two or three centuries that must have elapsed between its first writing down and the copying of it in the later 'Classical' or West-Saxon dialect with relatively very little corruption or loss. It remains, therefore, the best and fullest source for our appreciation of the potentialities and varieties of the Anglo-Saxon alliterative metre. Throughout all its extent of over three thousand lines there are very few indeed that are not metrically satisfying: and though a modern reader might well expect monotony in so long a poem whose

---

[1] For the view of the meaning and structure of the poem here generally followed, see J. R. R. Tolkien, "Beowulf, the Monsters and the Critics", *Proceedings of the British Academy* XXII (1937), pp. 245–295. *Cf.* for the interpretation of the episodes Adrien Bonjour, *The Digressions in Beowulf* (Oxford (Blackwell), 1950).

basic rhythm is never changed, this does not occur. For within the constant metrical framework there is always variation of style and tone to suit the changing nature of the subject-matter; and there are endless subtle devices within the rhythm—in the use of the longer or extended line, an occasional internal Leonine rhyme, in strange uses of parallel variation, and in the grouping of lines in verse-paragraphing.

As has been mentioned earlier, Anglo-Saxon poetry depended very much for its success on its aesthetic appeal to the *ears* of its hearers. Though we may not, even after prolonged study, be able to catch all the nuances of its music, nor even the exact pronunciation intended when the poem was copied as we have it—still less the sounds which its original composer used in the Northumbria or Mercia of the eighth century—the interested student, having grasped the basic features of the metre, may gain genuine poetic pleasure from the form and style of *Beowulf*. Especially needful, however, for this kind of literary enjoyment is the recitation or reading aloud of the text. For this purpose the use of gramophone records which reproduce recitations by competent scholars will be found to be an invaluable aid.[1]

Besides being the earliest monument of its kind in Western Europe, and in its own right a great poem (though the degree of this greatness must always remain a matter of opinion and taste), *Beowulf* retains those wider interests which its earlier students may be thought to have emphasized sometimes disproportionately: it is a basic document for the historian, the archaeologist, and for the linguistic study of the development of English.

Though most of its characters, including that of Beowulf himself, seem to belong to that traditional Germanic heroic material which is often inseparable from legend or mythology, it does contain elements of authentic and verifiable history. Hygelac, the King of Geatland, in Sweden, who is Beowulf's kinsman and ruler, finds mention in authentic historical writings which show him to have rashly invaded the Franks and Frisians about the year A.D. 520, and thereby met his death—an event which is said in the poem to have ultimately led to Beowulf's ascending of his people's throne. This great disaster to the Geats, repeatedly referred to allusively (lines 1202 ff., 2363 ff., 2910 ff.) is used by the poet subtly and admirably in the art of tragic atmosphere. This external evidence of the date of the historic Hygelac makes it clear that the events of the poem, in so far as they can be thought of as related to fact, took place in the latter half of the fifth century. The Geats themselves are known to history: and that they, along with the Swedes and the Danes, were of special interest to the Old English aristocracy is suggested by their mention together in

---

[1] *E.g.*, Charles W. Dunn, *Early English Poetry* (New York: Folkways FL 9851, 1958). J. C. Pope and Helge Kökeritz, *Beowulf and Chaucer* (New Haven (Whitlock), 1955). J. B. Bessinger, *Beowulf, Cædmon's Hymn and Other Old English Poems* (New York: Cædmon TC 1161, 1962).

Widsith.[1] Here the traveller speaks of having been "with the Swedes,
the Geats and the South-Danes." The late fourth-century Gothic
ruler Eormanric, so famous elsewhere in Germanic tradition, is referred to in line 1201.[2] The Sutton Hoo finds of armour and weapons
of Swedish workmanship may again point to English royal interest
in Scandinavian ancestry.[3] The account of the wars of Geats and
Swedes which occupy much of the later portion of *Beowulf*, and
which seem to have had some special appeal to the poet and his
audience, also show names and events which are vouched for by some
external historical evidence. Most scholars believe that the Continental Germanic material in *Beowulf* was brought over by the Anglo-
Saxon invaders, though the poem as a whole, with its Christian
implications, could scarcely have been composed before the beginning
of the eighth century.

For the archaeologist *Beowulf* is of outstanding importance. The
poet was evidently a man of Christian education with strong antiquarian interests, who while picturing many details of eighth-century
English aristocratic society at the same time often deliberately looked
back to the Germanic heroic age. Thus for instance the ship-funeral
at the beginning of the poem and the account of Beowulf's own pagan
funeral rites remarkably parallel features of the Sutton Hoo finds:
yet at the same time there are other elements in these descriptions
which suggest confusion between earlier and later practices. Heorot,
Hrothgar's magnificent hall, again may remind us by its name of the
royal symbol of the stag found surmounting the mysterious piece of
metal framework which apparently carried a standard or other kingly
symbol of the seventh-century East Anglian ruler. Much too is to be
learned of weapons and armour from the archaeological study of
Beowulf.

The language of *Beowulf* as we have it in its late revision must conceal much of the linguistic detail of its original. Yet its metre and
formulaic phraseology clearly look back to a pre-Christian past. It is
in *Beowulf* that we have a storehouse of those traditional Germanic
poetic formulae which must have been something like the stock-in
trade of the earliest Anglo-Saxon scop.[4] Moreover, as has been
indicated earlier, it is in *Beowulf*, even in its redaction of the late
tenth century, that we have the primary document for the study of
the basic principles of Anglo-Saxon metre.

The spirit and diction of *Beowulf* are, at first sight, the same as
those of the fragments from heroic tradition discussed in Chapter 5.
Whereas, however, those poems are but surviving fragments, *Beowulf* has the magnitude, the completeness, and the depth of an epic,

[1] Line 58.
[2] Eormanric appears in *Widsith*, lines 8–9, and in *Deor*, lines 21–23.
[3] See R. W. Chambers, *op. cit.*, pp. 508–523 and 612–613.
[4] *Cf.* Francis P. Magoun, junior, "Oral-formulaic Character of Anglo-Saxon
Narrative Poetry", *Speculum* XXVIII (1953), pp. 446 ff.

and is a whole consciously expressing the fulfilled artistic conception of its maker. Of late critics have tended to emphasize its Christian appeal and even to discern in it elements reminiscent of lives of saints or of the type of symbolism in allegory descended in Christian culture from such Latin poets as Prudentius.[1] Such views are to some extent the natural reaction from the earlier emphasis on the poem's pagan Germanic qualities. Yet some symbolic interpretation of the basic Christian conflict between good and evil, light and darkness, there undoubtedly must have been present in the minds of its auditors.[2] But because the poet has achieved a harmony between his form and his matter, between the traditional Germanic culture of the past and the Latin-Christian civilization of his own outlook, we still may feel that *Beowulf* is an artistic unity in a great poem, despite apparent discrepant features in its structure.[3] It is, too, a poem of dramatic speeches and of action rather than of characterizations: yet the images of its hero as well as of its principal characters remain vivid and moving.[4]

[1] *Cf.* D. W. Robertson, junior, "The Doctrine of Charity in Mediaeval Gardens, a Topical Approach through Symbolism and Allegory". *Speculum* XXVI (1951), pp. 29–49, reprinted in *An Anthology of Beowulf Criticism, op. cit.,* pp. 165 ff.

[2] See Dorothy Whitelock, *The Audience of Beowulf* (Oxford, 1951). For a careful consideration of this matter *cf.* Herbert Wright, "Good and Evil, Light and Darkness, Joy and Sorrow in Beowulf", *Review of English Studies,* new series, VIII (1957), pp. 1–11.

[3] A powerfully challenging attack on the assumption of artistic values in the structure of the poem was made by Dr. Kenneth Sisam in his *The Structure of Beowulf* (Oxford, 1965). But this destructively realistic critical approach may seem to go too far in sweeping aside so briefly accepted current views.

[4] Some possible Irish influences have been speculated upon, as might be expected in early Christian Anglo-Saxon work. This has been sought in some of the folklore elements of the poem, in Grendel's ancestry, and in his dwelling under the mere. See James Carney, *Studies in Irish Literature and History* (Dublin Institute of Advanced Studies, 1957), especially Chapter 3 on "The Irish Elements in *Beowulf*".

CHAPTER 8

Cynewulf and the Christian Establishment

WITH THE POETRY of Cynewulf, and of those who employed the same type and style, we pass from the Christianized Germanic heroic verse of which *Beowulf* is the noblest expression to a kind of writing which was at once specifically religious, deliberately didactic, and even basically homiletic. While with Cynewulf and his school traditional metre and much of the formulaic character of the poetic diction remained, a new and quite definitely Christian genre of verse comes to prevail, which to some extent developed its own conventions and formulae of religious poetry without losing all in this regard that tradition had bequeathed. Whereas we may conjecturally connect the composition of *Beowulf* as we have it with the cultural centre of some kind of religious house, the makers of the Cynewulf poetry quite clearly belonged to monastic establishments, and must almost certainly have been themselves ecclesiastics with primarily Christian Latin education. The new Cynewulfian poetry, which seems to belong to the late years of the eighth and first half of the ninth centuries, was chiefly concerned with the lives and legends of saints, lessons from the Gospel story, or the adapting to Old English of the allegoric procedures of the Latin Christian fathers. Yet this clearly later verse expression of the fully established Christian Church, with its more sophisticated religious language grafted on to the still developing traditional diction, was indeed far from being merely didactic versifying. For in Cynewulf and his contemporary poets there are commonly to be noticed careful craftsmanship of often fine quality, narrative skill in the best *Beowulf* tradition, and occasionally a moving depth and intensity of lyric art. Reminiscences or echoes of *Beowulf* on the one hand show that this Cynewulfian poetry is definitely later than that poem, while on the other, its general respect for the earlier metrical rules indicate that it must have been composed before the relative licence associated with the verse developments of the tenth century. Moreover, since this poetry, which survives chiefly in the manuscripts known as the Exeter Book and the Vercelli Book, shows a number of forms characteristic of the West-Saxon of King Alfred's reign, it must have at least passed through a recension in his Wessex of the later ninth century, and therefore have been already in existence by then. For its language is clearly in origin a dialect other than that of King Alfred's kingdom, into whose early West-Saxon it must have been turned, though its surviving form is in the Classical Anglo-Saxon or Late West-Saxon of the Benedictine Revival period when the extant manuscripts were copied.

Of Cynewulf himself, who gives his name by convention to this type of poetry, we know nothing for certain beyond his name, and what may be inferred of his personality and education from four poems to which his name is added, apparently with the idea that readers or audience might by this emphasis be minded to pray for his soul. In the four poems which, because of the appearance of the author's name in runes in each, are commonly referred to as 'the signed poems of Cynewulf', we have the only undisputed canon of his work. For though all the poems of the Cynewulf school have at one time or another been attributed to this poet, it is now generally thought that metrical, linguistic, and stylistic tests have established that only the four pieces in whose surviving copies his name so emphatically appears can confidently be accepted as Cynewulf's: and indeed these poems all share certain characteristics not found to the same degree in any of the other Cynewulfian pieces.[1] The name (not properly 'signature' in view of its occurrence only in manuscripts much later than the author) was probably set out in runes because these symbols with their original associations of magic conveyed a feeling of auspiciousness; runes had in any case already been used for specifically Christian memorial inscriptions.

The four authentic poems of Cynewulf occupy in all 2600 lines. They are, in order of length, *Elene*, 1321 lines in the Vercelli Book, *Juliana*, 731 lines in the Exeter Book, *Christ II* or *The Ascension of Christ*, 426 lines, also in the Exeter Book, and *The Fates of the Apostles*, 122 lines in the Vercelli Book. Of these, three are hagiographical—*Elene*, *Juliana*, and *The Fates of the Apostles*—while *Christ II* is largely based on an Ascension homily of St Gregory the Great. Other poems belonging clearly to the Cynewulf group are *Andreas* (a poem on St Andrew), *Guthlac A* and *Guthlac B* (two poems on the life of St Guthlac), *Christ I* (a collection of Advent lyric hymns), *Christ III* (treating largely of the Last Judgment), *The Phoenix* (an allegorical handling of the traditional Phoenix legend and the "Earthly Paradise"), and the greatest of all Anglo-Saxon religious poems, *The Dream of the Rood*. Of these all are in the Exeter Book save *Andreas* (which immediately precedes *The Fates of the Apostles*) and *The Dream of the Rood*, which are both in the Vercelli Book. All in this group present a number of qualities also found in Cynewulf's authenticated work. But while the resemblances are very marked in *Christ I*, *Guthlac B*, and *The Dream of the Rood*, there are funda-

---

[1] See Satyendra Kumar Das, *Cynewulf and the Cynewulf Canon* (Calcutta University Press, 1942). *Cf.* Claes Schaar, *Critical Studies in the Cynewulf Group* (Lund Studies in English XVII: Lund, 1949).

mental differences which separate from Cynewulf *Andreas, Christ III, Guthlac A*, and *The Phoenix*. Let us look a little more closely at Cynewulf's canonical poems, and then cursorily at the rest of the group, varying the emphasis according to their respective literary merits.

Elene, by far the longest and most skilful of Cynewulf's poems, was evidently suggested by the emphasis on the Church Festival of the Invention of the Cross which became marked in England in the later eighth century. In heroic epic style at times reminiscent of *Beowulf* the poet traces the voyage of St Helena to the finding of the True Cross,[1] ending with a quite separate meditative Epilogue in which the author speaks of himself and his productive veneration of the Cross in elegiac tone, including a complex acrostic in which each of the runes which form his own name is employed as a meaningful word. This last can be seen as a kind of autobiographical statement, though probably the matter of the lines using the rune-names as words was merely dictated by the need to get in each of the symbols which make the name Cynewulf. Thus the rune for C, (CEN) means 'a torch', Y (YR) is a late rune, and could have almost whatever sense the context might require; N (NED) is 'necessity', E (EH) is a 'horse', W (WYNN) is 'joy', U (UR) should stand for the bison or aurochs, L (LAGU) is 'a stretch of water', and F (FEH) means 'wealth' or 'property'. Two of the runes, however, have been interpreted otherwise than in their normal significance: C (CEN) has been equated with the adjective *cene*, 'bold', and U (UR) as the Anglian form of the pronoun *ure*, 'our'. Giving the runic names their value in the acrostic passage, we may make a translation in which their verbal names are substituted for the actual runes of the manuscript:

> A wæs sæcc oð ðæt
> cnyssed cear-welmum, CEN drusende,
> þeah he in medu-healle maðmas þege,
> æplede gold. YR gnornode,
> NED gefera nearu-sorge dreah,
> enge rune, þær him EH fore
> mil-paþas mæt, modig þrægde
> wirum gewlenced. WYNN is geswiðrad,
> gomen æfter gearum, geogoð is gecyrred,
> ald onmedla. UR wæs geara
> geogoð-hades glæm. Nu synt gear-dagas
> æfter fyrst-mearce forð gewitene,
> lif-wynne geliden, swa LAGU toglideð,
> flodas gefysde. FEH gehwam bið
> læne under lyfte.
>
> (lines 1256–1270)

---

[1] Cf. *Elene* 225 ff., with *Beowulf* 205 ff. and 1903 ff.

Ever was there strife, until, beaten by the surgings of care, the *torch* [or the *bold man*, if CEN is taken as *cene*], was flagging, even though in the mead-hall he had been wont to receive embossed gold. The *horn* [giving a conjectural meaning to YR] lamented, and with *necessity* as a companion, that narrow rune, he endured an oppressive secret. Forward the *steed* adorned with wirework trappings proudly measured the ways in miles, speeding along in his pride. *Joy* has diminished, and sport with the passing of the years. The ancient pomp has passed away with youth. In days of yore *our* man [or the *bison* or *aurochs*] was a gleam of youth: but now have the days of old departed away with the passing of time. Life's joys are gone like as the *waters* driven by floods part asunder. To everyone is the possession of *wealth* a transitory thing beneath the sky.

In the beginning of this Epilogue, separated in the manuscript from the poem proper by the word FINIT, Cynewulf describes himself in a rhyming passage already quoted in Chapter 3 as old and ready for death, but having been comforted in the consciousness of his sins by a vision of the Cross, and how through the Cross he gained his power of song-craft. Doubtless Cynewulf was a man of ecclesiastical Latin culture though no special learning, who had been rewarded at times by patrons (poetically described as receiving embossed gold in the mead-hall), and was familiar with good horses. It is evident too that devotion to the Cross was a dominant feature of his spiritual life: and it is for this reason, and in the light of the vision of the Cross implied in this Epilogue, that *The Dream of the Rood*, which in style so often resembles Cynewulf, has frequently been attributed to him.

Elene, Cynewulf's most aspiring work, with its almost uniformly excellent craftsmanship, may well have been the work of the poet's maturest years. With it his next longest poem *Juliana* is in several ways in marked contrast. Its relative prosaicness or lack of poetic quality and its less original handling of its Latin source may suggest that it was the work of a much younger Cynewulf. It has been compared to a verse presentation of one of Ælfric's *Lives of Saints*: but though it lacks poetic feeling, it fairly steadily follows sound metrical practice. The name Cynewulf in its Epilogue is quite clear in three groups of runes, and is spelt in exactly the same way as in *Elene*. Here is the passage with letters this time:

> Geomor hweorfeð
> C Y ond N. Cyning biþ reðe,
> sigora syllend, þonne synnum fah
> E W ond U acle bidað
> hwæt him æfter dædum deman wille
> lifes to leane. L F beofað,
> seomað sorg-cearig.
>
> (lines 703–709)

C, Y, and N become sad. For stern is the giver of victories when, stained with sins E, W, and U await in terror what He will adjudge for them according to their deeds as a requital for life. L and F are trembling as they lie afflicted with grief.

One cannot here determine whether the groups of runes are intended merely to make up the name of the poet, or have some further significance. The fact that the name Cynewulf is spelt as CYNEWULF here and in *Elene*, but as CYNWULF in *Christ II* and *The Fates of the Apostles*, though it may help to date the poems on a linguistic point, does not seem to be seriously significant.[1] The spelling CYNWULF, however, looks like the Anglian version of a West-Saxon CYNE-WULF, and this may point to an Anglian origin for the poet himself. This view is confirmed by the forms of the opening lines of the *Elene* Epilogue, where the obviously intended rhymes are only to be clearly apprehended if Anglian forms are assumed to replace the Late West-Saxon of the Vercelli Book.

The matter of *Juliana* is closely taken from a popular Latin version of the legend of St Juliana, in which a crudely presented conflict between the Saint and the devil is set forth, as indeed are all poetical Old English heroes and heroines, with still recognizable Germanic features.

The first sets of verses in the Exeter Book, usually known collectively as *Christ*, comprising 1664 lines, present three rough structural divisions all dealing with aspects of the Gospel story of Christ: they are therefore generally referred to as *Christ* if the whole is regarded as a unity, or as *Christ I, II*, and *III* if the three parts are taken to be properly separate poems treating of different parts of a common subject. The first part, lines 1 to 440, consists of twelve lyric adaptations of antiphons mostly for Advent; and it has sometimes been thought that the whole tripartite poem *Christ* was originally intended for celebrations extending from Advent through Easter. *Christ I* has been edited separately as *The Advent Lyrics*.[2] *Christ II*, now commonly referred to as *The Ascension*, covers lines 441 to 866. The third poem, *Christ III* or *The Last Judgment*, is longer and more various in treatment, extending to almost 800 lines, from 867 to the end at 1664. These poems have a unity in general subject-matter, and it seems likely that the collector of the Exeter Book put them together for this reason. Opinion inclines to regard them as three separate pieces, though arguments from style and treatment which suggest this are by no means final, since they must of necessity be somewhat subjective. It is, however, agreed that for certain *The Ascension*—*Christ II*—is the authentic work of Cynewulf, and it is in this piece that his name in runes appears.

[1] See K. Sisam's British Academy Lecture, "Cynewulf and his Poetry" in his *Studies in the History of Old English Literature* (Oxford, 1953), pp. 2–6.
[2] Jackson J. Campbell, *The Advent Lyrics of the Exeter Book* (Princeton, 1959).

The passage, near the end of *The Ascension*, containing the poet's name is obscure, probably because of the difficulty of fitting the runes —and perhaps their meanings—into an intelligible context. The name is here spelt, as in *The Fates of the Apostles*, as CYNWULF, in the Anglian manner. It is not certain whether these runes stand merely for the poet's name, or are to be understood in their context each as the words they normally symbolize. Here follows the text with a rough but literal translation of the lines:

> Þonne C cwacað, gehyreð cyning mæðlan,
> rodera ryhtend, sprecan reþe word
> þam þe him ær in worulde wace hyrdon,
> þenden Y ond N yþast meahtan
> frofre findan. Þær sceal forht monig
> on þam wong-stede werig bidan
> hwæt him æfter dædum deman wille
> wraþra wita. Biþ se W scæcen
> eorþan frætwa. U wæs longe
> L flodum belocen, lif-wynna dæl,
> F on foldan.
>
> (lines 797–807)

(Before the judgment seat of Christ) then C [CEN the torch] shall quake when he hears the King, ruler of the skies, speak, uttering stern words to those who in days past had obeyed him but feebly in the world at the time when Y [YR the horn] and N [NED necessity] could quite easily have found consolation. There on that expanse of ground many a man shall be waiting wearily and in terror for what grievous torments will be adjudged to him in accordance with his deeds. W [WYNN the joy] of earth and its adornments shall be shattered. For long was U [UR the bison, or perhaps I] encompassed with floods of L [LAGU water] when there had been happiness in life and F [FEH wealth] on the earth.

The poem is notable for some bold and effective rhetorical images and metaphors, and its frequent allegorical manner is a clear reminder that Cynewulf belonged to a later and more definitely established Christianity than the poet of *Beowulf*. St Gregory's Ascension homily is adapted and adorned into an Old English heroic lay in which the whole of Christ's acts, from Incarnation to Judgment, are handled with vivid poetic feeling. As with all Old English poetry, the title is only a modern editorial convention: but the *Ascension*, since this occupies the predominant place, is as good a name as has been found. As in the Epilogue to *Elene*, Cynewulf has some use of internal or Leonine rhyme as a rhetorical device. Thus in lines 589 ff. internal rhyme appears with marked stylistic effect where we are told that as a result of Christ's coming each man may choose while here on earth the humiliations of hell or the joys of heaven, the light of lights or hateful night, the onrush of glory or the misery of darkness, joy with the Lord or lamentation with the devil, torment among the wicked or glory among the virtuous, life or death. Now, the rhyme-words in these lines need to be put into their Mercian or Anglian forms, as do those of *Elene* to be properly heard, and this, therefore, is again direct evidence that Cynewulf was a Mercian. Here is the Old English passage, with the rhyme words corrected accordingly:

> þæt nu monna gehwylc
> cwic þenden her wunað, geceosan mot
> swa helle *hænþu* swa heofones *mærþu*
> swa þæt *lehta leht* swa ða laþan *neht,*
> swa þrymmes *þræce* swa þystra *wræce,*
> swa mid dryhten *dream* swa mid deoflum *hream,*
> swa wite mid *wraþum* swa wuldor mid *arum,*
> swa lif swa deað.[1]

(lines 589–596)

The Fates of the Apostles is a short poem which begins with the conventional epic heroic formula and follows a Latin list with skeleton biographies of the Apostles, treating them as Germanic heroes and using the conventional epic diction along with the specifically Christian elements common to the Cynewulf school. It follows *Andreas* in the Vercelli Book, but is not connected with it otherwise, although earlier scholars were inclined to regard it as some kind of epilogue to *Andreas,* and hence to confer Cynewulfian authorship upon that poem by reason of the name of the poet in runes. It is not in any way remarkable as a literary performance, and with its own rather crude epilogue may well have been the product of Cynewulf's declining old age. In an elegiac epilogue to this poem, lines 88 ff., Cynewulf emphasizes that through the runes of an acrostic men may learn "who composed this poem": and he evidently regards the runes as a way of calling the reader or hearer to pray for the poet, who represents himself as meditating on approaching death. This time the runic symbols of the name, spelt CYNWULF, are arranged in an unparalleled order and grouping: F, W U L, and C Y N.

Speaking of Cynewulf, assuming only the four 'signed' poems to be genuinely his, Dr Kenneth Sisam sums up:

> He was a ninth-century ecclesiastic of cultured taste; very devout in his old age and probably always of a devotional cast of mind; not a great scholar like Bede but well versed in the Latin works that the educated clergy of those days used; not boldly original but unusually sensitive and pliant to the influence of Christian Latin models: and

[1] In the third line the Alfredian West-Saxon *ie* of *hienþu* is adjusted to an Anglian *æ* as *hænþu* so as to make an assonance with *mærþu.* In the next line Mercian *lehta* and *leht* are substituted for *leohte* and *leoht;* and *leohte* of the manuscript is taken as a genitive plural and so normalized to *lehta.* Similarly, *neht* replaces *niht.*

perhaps one may say, a man of letters, the first in English whose name and works are known.[1]

But this estimate is incomplete, since it leaves out of account Cynewulf's specifically poetic merits. In *Elene* he had used the heroic diction of the past with marked success: and indeed Cynewulf was generally a competent craftsman in verse. In *The Ascension* he showed at times impressive ability in what may be termed poetic rhetoric, and this piece has its moments of true lyric power. Passing from the heroic paraphrasing of Old Testament material of the Cædmonian school, Cynewulf seems to have led the way in a great expansion of religious verse, treating hagiographical and homiletic sources along with Gospel themes with freedom, and sometimes showing a very real poetic 'enlargement'. The definite revelation of the name of a poet with indications of his authentic works too marks a new departure amid the normal medieval anonymity among poets. The only poet before Cynewulf whose name we know (apart from the tradition of Aldhelm) is Cædmon. But this knowledge was preserved by Bede and not provided by Cædmon himself, nor can we point to any authenticated poem from him save only the nine-line *Hymn*.

The chief pieces which may be considered as representing a 'School of Cynewulf', because of their varying resemblance to the authentic works in versification, style, diction, and subject-matter, as well as in apparent date, have the following editorial titles: *Guthlac A*, *Guthlac B*, *Christ I*, or *Advent Lyrics*, *Christ III*, *The Phoenix*, *Physiologus*, *Andreas*, and *The Dream of the Rood*. Of these the first six are in the Exeter Book, and *Andreas* and *The Dream of the Rood* in the Vercelli Book. The two poems *Guthlac A* and *Guthlac B* seem to abandon the traditional practice by treating of an entirely English saint, the Mercian hermit whose Latin prose life by Felix of Croyland probably provided the material, along with oral tradition. *Christ I*, perhaps the most poetical of these Cynewulfian pieces, has already been noticed. It forms the first of the tripartite group *Christ*, usually regarded as three distinct poems by different authors. *Christ III*, which forms the last stage of *Christ*, is chiefly concerned with vividly portraying Doomsday. *The Phoenix* follows in its earlier part the Latin poem on the Phoenix of Lactantius, *Carmen de Ave Phoenice*, and in its latter portion allegorizes its theme in the traditional Latin Christian manner. Similarly *Physiologus* is Christian allegory based on legendary natural history, part of what is known as a 'Bestiary', and is adapted from the Latin *Physiologus*. *Andreas*, adapted from a Latin apocryphal book of the *Acts of SS. Andrew and Matthew*, is concerned with dramatic and sensational episodes of which St Andrew is the hero. *The Dream of the Rood*, though associated with the name of Cynewulf because of its sharing the subject of *Elene*, the True Cross, and for its often close

[1] K. Sisam, *loc. cit.*, pp. 27–28.

resemblances to Cynewulf in style and diction, is really a poem quite apart from the rest. Its outstanding poetic qualities, its creative originality, and its depth of feeling place it on an altogether higher level than the work of the Cynewulf school, with which it yet shares so much at least superficially. It is the portrayal of a vision in which the Cross is personified in a dream, to give the poet hope and strength.

Of these eight Cynewulfian poems, three especially have been claimed as authentic Cynewulf, though in no case with entire success. These are *Christ I*, *Guthlac B*, and *The Dream of the Rood*. Probably the strength of this claim is largely due to a subjective feeling among some scholars that they are, each in its way, superior to the other Cynewulfian poems, and therefore more likely to be authentic. Some who believe that all three parts of *Christ* are a unity, or that *Christ I* and *Christ II* are really one, naturally must regard these *Advent Lyrics* as true Cynewulf, since *Christ II* (or *The Ascension*) contains his runic 'signature'. Moreover, something of the intensely lyric quality of *Christ I* may seem to be close to similar excellences in the *Ascension*. *Guthlac B*, a better poem than *Guthlac A*, and with closer stylistic resemblances to the accepted Cynewulf pieces, has lost its concluding lines in the Exeter Book, though the amount of the missing end-piece can now only be guessed at. But the state of the manuscript has suggested to some competent judges that the missing portion was the size that would have allowed for the inclusion in it of Cynewulf's name in a runic acrostic on the lines of that in *Elene*. The opening and closing lines of *The Dream of the Rood* may seem to echo the thought of the Epilogue to *Elene*, and the fact that its basic theme, the Invention of the Cross, is treated also in *Elene* again suggests common authorship on a first view. With regard to the other Cynewulfian poems, there is less reason for ascribing any of them to the poet.

Guthlac A, which follows *Christ III* in the Exeter Book, begins with a kind of very free prologue of 29 lines, describing the happiness of the arrival of a faithful soul in heaven: and this exordium, with the concluding passage of exultation on Guthlac's reception into heaven, forms some sort of vague framework for the poem proper, which is a narrative of the Saint's hermit life and his fearful struggles with hordes of fiends who encompass his hill-dwelling to tempt him to destruction. The whole, consisting of 818 lines, is evidently intended as a separate and complete poem—at least, by the anthologist of the Exeter Book. The dramatic arguments between *Guthlac* and the devils, which form much of the subject-matter, are often lively: and the handling is not entirely conventional. But *Guthlac B*, which begins at line 819 of the joint *Guthlac* and ends with an evident lacuna at 1379, is a rather more impressive performance which often seems to be very much in the authentic style of Cynewulf, though it is far more dependent on Felix of Croyland's Latin *Life* than is *Guthlac A*. Its treatment of this source, too, seems very much to resemble Cynewulf's method in treating his Latin original as exemplified in *Elene*. It has a sort of exordium in a description of the Creation and the exile from Eden of Adam and Eve, with a discussion of the best kind of life for the good on earth, extending for some sixty lines. Then, it having been explained that the highest earthly life is that of the hermit saint, Guthlac himself appears at line 879, and the main matter of the poem which follows is the intense sufferings of Guthlac, his last illness and death, and his assumption into heaven. The Saint's valour in face of tremendous trials is described, with much of the traditional heroic diction applicable to a Germanic warrior: and the dialogues of the hermit with his disciple are done with considerable poetic power.

The Advent Lyrics of *Christ I* include some of the finest purely lyric passages in Old English religious poetry proper. But this poem is also of historical importance for the remarkable dramatic dialogue between Joseph and Mary on the question of the (to Joseph) bewildering mystery of her impending motherhood. This dialogue may seem to be the first use in the vernacular of that kind of liturgical antiphonal exchange which was to provide the beginnings of medieval drama. Drama originated in religious ritual: and as early as the ninth century there are records of monastic celebrations of Easter in which the angels and the three Marys sing an antiphonal Latin dialogue at the tomb of the risen Christ. Now, this tense conversation of Mary and Joseph (lines 164–214) comes near to expanding the idea of the liturgical dialogue added to the Easter Mass into a genuinely dramatic fragment.[1]

The Phoenix, separated in the Exeter Book from the truncated *Guthlac B* only by a verse fragment *Azarias*, covers 677 lines. It is in two complementary parts, the first 380 lines being a very free adaptation of the Latin poem on the Phoenix thought to have been the work of Lactantius, and the second a varied allegorical interpretation of the mythical material in accordance with Christian Latin practice. As already noted, the poem belongs to the Bestiary type, first introduced into medieval literature by the Latin *Physiologus*, or collection of fables of animals and birds allegorized to Christian didactic purpose, probably from the fifth century. The Phoenix, whose symbolic legend is told by Lactantius (apparently before his conversion) with little that is specifically Christian, is treated in the first part of the Old English poem, which freely adapts the Latin, with adjustments of phrase and implication so as to prepare the ground for the latter portion of definite Christian allegories. The mythical bird, originally an Egyptian creation especially associated with Arabia, later Chaucer's "Phenix of Arabie", becomes for the English poet an allegory of the redemption of man from the Fall, his resurrection, and later of Christ himself and the historical Resurrection. The allegories seem to be

[1] For the best full account of the liturgical origins of medieval drama see Karl Young, *The Drama of the Medieval Church* (Oxford, 1933).

from the usual Latin Christian tradition, though their detailed handling is probably the poet's own. The poem as a whole is very much in the manner of Cynewulf, and certainly belongs to his school; but in the absence of any runic acrostic with his name in it, there is not any definite evidence of Cynewulf's authorship. Moreover, in this poem, as in the others of this group, much of the apparent verbal suggestion of Cynewulf's diction should be accounted for only by the development in this literary period of many new common formulae of religious poetry, which were added to and developed from the formulaic language of earlier heroic verse. The most striking thing about *The Phoenix* for the historian of literature is the attitude towards nature shown in the description of the dwelling of the wondrous bird. For the poet provides a background in his choice of words of Germanic tradition for his "noblest of lands", *æþelast londa*, with which he renders the *felix locus* of the Latin. In amplifying with many phrases the rather simple Latin, the Germanic tradition is clearly emphasized by an exordium in which the Latin is expanded into the traditional Old English epic opening formula. Lactantius' words are only the one line:

> Est locus in primo felix oriente remotus.

This is replaced in the Old English by six lines in the traditional epic mode:

> Hæbbe ic gefrugnen þætte is feor heonan
> east-dælum on æþelast londa,
> firum gefræge. Nis se foldan sceat
> ofer middangeard mongum gefere
> fold-agendra, ac he afyrred is
> þurh meotudes meaht man-fremmendum.
>
> (lines 1–6)

Whereas the Latin merely says there is a happy place remote far in the East, the Old English may be translated:

> I have heard tell that there is, far in the Eastern regions, the noblest of lands that men have ever heard of. That district of earth is not approachable for many men throughout the world who dwell on the earth; but by the might of the Creator it has been placed far away from the doers of evil.[1]

As contrasted somewhat with the normal Anglo-Saxon attitude towards nature, with its subjective dwelling on storm, hardship, and sadness, we find in *The Phoenix* signs of independent pleasure in the happy contemplation of nature in her seasons; and there is here and

---

[1] The Latin text of Lactantius is printed as Appendix A in the valuable edition of *The Phoenix* by N. F. Blake (Manchester University Press, 1964). Here much illustrative and background material is conveniently to hand.

there in natural descriptions more colour than is usual. In expanding the brief Latin of the account of the paradisal home of the Phoenix, the English poet shows obvious pleasure in filling out a completely happy picture of smiling Nature, in perfect weather. As in Cynewulf's *Elene* Epilogue and his *Ascension*, internal Leonine rhymes and assonances are to be found in *The Phoenix*, employed as an occasional stylistic device with charming effect:

> Ne mæg þær ren ne snaw,
> ne forstes *fnæst*, ne fyres *blæst*,
> ne hægles *hryre*, ne hrimes *dryre*,
> ne sunnan hætu, ne sin-caldu,
> ne wearm weder, ne winter-scur
> wihte gewyrdan.
>
> (lines 14–19)

There harm is not in any way done by rain or snow, nor the breath of frost nor the blast of fire, nor the falling of hail nor descending hoar-frost, nor the heat of the sun nor lasting cold, nor hot weather nor winter storm.

The *Physiologus* mentioned above is represented in the Exeter Book by two allegorical beast-fables and a very incomplete fragment, treating respectively of *The Panther*, *The Whale*, and (apparently) *The Partridge*. *The Panther*, 74 lines, takes this creature as an allegory of Christ, *The Whale*, 88 lines, portrays its subject as the devil pretending to be an island to tempt sailors to land on it and be drowned as it submerges; and the whale's jaws symbolize hell. *The Partridge* is a fragment of only sixteen lines of a poem from which the last 80 or so lines seem to have been on a now-lost leaf. Its meaning is not clear; but it seems likely that it would have allegorized the partridge, so that we have in effect three poems from the *Physiologus*, representing respectively creatures of earth, sea, and air. The poems are very much in Cynewulf's manner, and Latin Christian in substance. But they have not the literary merits of *The Phoenix*, with which they naturally are linked by their bestiary subject-matter and method.

The longest poem of the Cynewulfian group by far is *Andreas*, which extends to 1722 lines in the Vercelli Book, in which it immediately precedes Cynewulf's *Fates of the Apostles*. It follows with some freedom and additions a Latin version of an originally Oriental-Greek *Acts of Andrew and Matthew in the Land of the Cannibals*. As in the case of the *Guthlac* poems, there is a prose version (two, in fact) in Old English of much of the material covered by the poem: but this can scarcely have any connection with *Andreas*. In the style of a traditional Anglo-Saxon hero, St Andrew goes to the satanically ruled cannibal land of the Mermedonians, where he rescues St Matthew from the direst imprisonment. Then, having converted the savages by means of a terrifying overwhelming flood, and in face of

fierce opposition by the devil, the hero, after spending a little time
longer (by special request of his converts) in Mermedonia, departs
from a now grief-stricken and pious land: and the poem ends with
the erstwhile cannibals singing as the Saint leaves their shore a hymn
to the glory of God. Of all the Cynewulfian pieces, *Andreas* has by far
the most frequent and obvious echoes of *Beowulf* in its heroic diction.
Indeed, it seems certain that this poet was often a conscious imitator
—not always with full understanding—of the *Beowulf* words, as well
as using freely the common epic formulaic diction. Generally the
craftsmanship of *Andreas* is rougher than is that of Cynewulf, though
there are some lively and vigorous passages, especially in the description of Andreas's sea voyage and of the gigantic flood which overcame the Mermedonians.

Of all this Cynewulfian group, undoubtedly *The Dream of the Rood*
demands the most attention, alike for its quite outstanding intrinsic
merits and for its historical importance. For it is one of the greatest
religious poems in English literature. At some time in the eighth
century, or possibly a little earlier, some continuous fragments of the
poem were cut in runes on the famous Northumbrian sculptured
stone cross at Ruthwell, in Dumfriesshire, which is one of the greatest
monuments to that leadership in the arts given to Western Europe by
the Northumbria of the age of Bede.[1] The poem, 156 lines, is in the
Vercelli Book, which also contains Cynewulf's *Elene*. The portions of
it carved in runes on the Ruthwell Cross must, most students agree,
be dated earlier than the life of Cynewulf himself, which would seem
to rule out that poet from authorship. Moreover, the runic fragments
of the poem being in the early Northumbrian dialect (while Cynewulf
seems to have been a Mercian), would also militate against its being
attributed to him. But the chief reason for rejecting Cynewulf as
author, despite the many remarkable resemblances in tone, style, and
diction to *Elene*, is that *The Dream of the Rood* is an original poem,
whereas Cynewulf's 'signed' poems are all based on established Latin
sources. It might seem odd that Cynewulf, having set his name to
four poems, should, if he had composed this piece which is so superior
in every way to his acknowledged work, have failed to indicate his
authorship by runes in his one really outstanding poem.

The title *The Dream of the Rood*, given to the poem by Benjamin
Thorpe in 1836 in his *editio princeps* of the Vercelli Book poems, has
sometimes since been replaced—following foreign editors in whose
languages there is no suitable word to distinguish rood from cross—
by *The Vision of the Cross*.[2] But in fact the poem deals with a rood,
and is a dream as well as a vision. For the Cross seen in the poet's
dream-vision, sometimes adorned with streamers, is clearly then a

---

[1] For details of the Ruthwell Cross see G. Baldwin Brown, *The Arts in Early
England* (Edinburgh, 1921), V. *Cf.* W. J. Collingwood, *Northumbrian Crosses of the
Pre-Norman Age* (London, 1927).
[2] *Cf.* the edition by Bruce Dickins and A. S. C. Ross, 4th ed. (London, 1954).

ceremonial symbol like that which in ecclesiastical language is technically called a *rood*.[1] In the first line the vision is spoken of as *swefna cyst*, 'the most exquisite of dreams': and no doubt we are to think of a vision that came during sleep: for *swefn*—'dream'—has the same root as the verb *swefan*, 'to sleep'. Such a dream-vision the poet Cædmon had encountered, as Bede narrates: so that this device was not strictly new in Anglo-Saxon. But the combination of this dream-vision with the Latin prosopopoeia by which the Cross is made to speak as a person was something quite original in Anglo-Saxon. The blend of dream with allegory in the poem is also for its time startlingly original. *The Dream of the Rood* is evidently the product of the cult of the Cross which, owing something to Irish influence, was strong in Northern and Western Britain in the later eighth century: but this special devotion to the Cross had clearly played a great part in the poet's personal development, so that what he expresses in this twofold literary device is alive with deep spiritual feeling.

The poem opens with an introductory account of the dream in which the poet beheld the Cross towering into the air, encompassed with light. The most beauteous of trees was adorned with gold, with precious gems at each of the four points of the Cross. This would be suggested by the Ceremonial Cross unveiled on Easter Day, as also by the thought of the actual Cross visited by countless pilgrims after its recovery from the Persians in the early seventh century, when it was adorned with so many precious gifts. 'Marvellous was that tree of victory' (*sige-beam*) at line 13 reminds us of the symbolic figure of Christ crowned in victory notable in the earlier Middle Ages. Terrified at the fair sight in the consciousness of his own sins, the poet yet could not but gaze on: and he had seen that through the gold on the Cross could be perceived the affliction which it had caused and suffered, as with its changing colours it began to bleed on the right side. Then, after this striking opening of 25 lines, the Cross begins to speak to the dreamer: and in 50 lines of most moving depth and simplicity the wood speaks a narrative of its life, from its first being cut down in the forest to the Crucifixion and beyond. Christ is portrayed as a young Germanic warrior, yet at once both victorious as divine and suffering all the torments and griefs as human. Here are some lines of the speech of the personified Cross:

> Feala ic on þam beorge gebiden hæbbe
> wraðra wyrda: geseah ic weruda God
> þearle þenian: þystro hæfdon
> bewwigen mid wolcnum Wealdendes hræw,
> scirne sciman. Sceadu forð eode,
> wann under wolcnum. Weop eal gesceaft,
> cwiðdon cyninges fyll: Crist wæs on rode.
>
> (lines 50–56)

[1] For this distinction see *The Oxford Dictionary of the Christian Church*, ed. L. Cross (Oxford, 1957), *s.v. Cross* and *Rood*.

Many things and cruel happenings have I suffered on that hill; I saw the Lord of hosts grievously stretched in pain. Darkness had covered the body of the Lord, that bright radiance, with clouds: the shadow of dusk had come forth beneath the skies [the darkness over the earth during the Crucifixion]. All creation wept in lamentation for the fall of the King. Christ was on the Cross.

This austere style, with the tremendous juxtaposition of the weeping universe with the stark half-line *Crist wæs on rode*, is unique in Anglo-Saxon poetry. There follows more speech by the Cross describing the burial of Christ by his disciples: and it is significant that they walk solemnly around the corpse singing a funeral dirge in the traditional Germanic manner. For Christ is the leader of his own comitatus of followers.

The later portion of the Cross's speech after the account of Christ's entombment, and the description of how men from all over the world now visit the symbol of his victory as pilgrims, is rather in the nature of a homily, and is therefore often considerably curtailed by modern anthologists. But the exhortation to service of the Cross and the promise of celestial aid are expressed with a tone of deeply moving sincerity which must have got well home to 'the business and bosoms' of its auditors. It is of interest to notice that the author of *The Dream of the Rood* evidently shared with Cynewulf a special devotion to the Cross and to the Blessed Virgin. For in this poem we find the earliest literary vernacular reference to that marked devotion to her which is particularly characteristic of medieval England. The Cross says:

> "Hwæt me þa geweorþode wuldres Ealdor
> ofer holt-wudu, heofon-rices Weard,
> Swylce swa he his modor eac Marian sylfe
> ælmihtig God for ealle men
> geweorðode ofer eall wifa cynn."
>
> (lines 90–94)

"Truly the Prince of glory who is guardian of the kingdom of heaven honoured me above all other trees: as likewise Almighty God honoured Mary herself before all men above every kind of woman."

The origin of *The Dream of the Rood* is quite obscure. Only some parts of the runic lines of the poem inscribed on the Ruthwell Cross now survive, so that we cannot determine how much of it was originally carved in eighth-century North Northumbria. The 156 lines in the Classical Late West-Saxon of the later tenth century in the Vercelli Book may have been an expansion of the original poem, perhaps especially in its later homiletic parts. But it includes forms of Alfredian West-Saxon which suggest that it shared in some kind of recension in King Alfred's time, or that the actual expansion of the poem as we know it was done then—probably as a result of the increased emphasis on the cult of the Cross which took place about that time through the Pope's gift to the King of a piece of the 'True Cross' in the year 885. Just as the Ruthwell Cross inscription seems too early for Cynewulf's authorship of the original poem, so too the expanded Vercelli text's archetype, if it was Alfredian, would be rather too late. The attribution of the Ruthwell fragments to a poem by Cædmon—the only other claimant to authorship—was encouraged by the fact that it is in a Northumbrian dialect, and that it has been dated, though without convincing evidence, as early as the late seventh century (Cædmon's time) by earlier investigators. *The Dream of the Rood* really stands quite by itself, as anonymous as it is unique. Its sources may be conjecturally glimpsed here and there in well-known Latin hymns like the *Vexilla Regis*, and in the tradition, seen in some Old English riddles later, of beginning with a statement of one having *seen* what follows (*ic geseah* 'I have seen'), and then a speech by the thing seen as personified.[1] But the whole conception of the poem is in any case profoundly original, and it stands as the great creative achievement of Anglo-Saxon religious poetry.

As with Cynewulf's *Elene*, *The Dream of the Rood* ends with a meditative pious epilogue as was usual. But like that of *Elene* also, its tone is elegiac and personal.

> "Nah ic ricra feala
> freonda on foldan, ac hie forð heonon
> gewiton of worulde dreamum, sohton him wuldres Cyning,
> lifiaþ nu on heofenum mid Heah-fædere,
> wuniaþ on wuldre; ond ic wene me
> daga gehwylce hwæne me Dryhtnes rod,
> þe ic her on eorðan ær sceawode,
> of þysson lænan life gefetige,
> and me þonne gebringe þær is blis micel,
> dream on heofonum, þær is Dryhtnes folc
> geseted to symle, þær is singal blis;
> and me þonne asette þær ic syþþan mot
> wunian on wuldre, well mid þam halgum
> dreames brucan."
>
> (lines 131–144)

"Few are the powerful men on earth who love me. But they have departed from the joys of the world and sought for themselves the King of glory. They live now in the heavens with the Father on high, dwelling in glory. And every day for my part I look for the time when

---

[1] Dickins and Ross in their edition (*op. cit.*, pp. 18–19), compare this convention of riddling, which was current in the Latin *aenigmata* of the time and later imitated in Old English. They mention Riddle 56 in the Exeter Book as an example, and suggest that the Cross may be the solution of this riddle, though it is more commonly taken to be a weaver's loom.

the Cross of the Lord which here on earth I have gazed at aforetime should fetch me away from this fleeting life and then bring me there where there is great happiness, joyful revelries in the heavens, where the Lord's people are seated at the feasting and where their blessedness is eternal. So that He may then place me where henceforth I may live in glory to enjoy great happiness with the Saints."

The diction here, as usual, contains echoes of the heroic past: and this picture of the Lord's people seated at the feasting natually calls to mind the Germanic Valhalla.

Old English religious poetry has so much in common, and its chronology is so uncertain, that its division for the sake of historical convenience cannot but be somewhat arbitrary and artificial. But the elegiac tone of the endings of *Elene* and of *The Dream of the Rood* may now suggest our passing to the discussion of those poems which come nearest in Old English to lyric, since these include the so-called Elegies.

CHAPTER 9

Lyric, Elegy, and Miscellaneous Minor Poems

THE ANGLO-SAXON POETIC MIND does not seem to have included those tendencies which produce lyric verse in any strict sense. The only poems which may come under this category are *Deor* and (to a less extent) *Wulf and Eadwacer*, discussed in Chapter 5 as verse in the Germanic heroic tradition. The stanzaic structure of *Deor* and its use of the lyric refrain are quite exceptional: and *Wulf and Eadwacer*, which makes some use of a refrain, also has the feature commonly associated with lyric of expressing deep love-emotion. If one thinks of the traditional association of lyric with music, as the etymological force of the word lyric suggests the quality of harp-music, then it becomes clear that, since the harp was normally the proper concomitant of the recitation of Old English verse, the Anglo-Saxons must have appreciated the musical elements in poetry. If we consider the term 'lyric' as implying in a general way the musical utterance of feeling in a limited personal expression of a single mood, then there are certainly lyrics in Old English verse. Yet it is true that the expression of lyric in Anglo-Saxon is only to be found in single poems or in passages of epic where the tone is 'elegiac'. The term 'elegy' in English poetry has commonly been used in two senses: (*a*) the expression of grief in studied verse for the death of a valued personality, or (*b*) the general meditation in solitude of what may be called universal griefs. Of the first type carried to excellence by universalized feeling, English literature has been very productive. The outstanding examples are Spenser's *Astrophell*, Milton's *Lycidas*, Shelley's *Adonais*, Arnold's *Thyrsis*, and Tennyson's *In Memoriam*. The second type provides England's most admired and best-known poem in its class, Gray's *Elegy written in a Country Churchyard*. It is *elegy* in Gray's sense that is the convenient term applicable in the classification of Old English poetry. Indeed, it is only in the elegiac mood in Gray's sense that lyric expression as defined above is usually to be encountered.

Fond as they were of contemplating nature in aspects that provoke feelings of sadness and the consciousness of mortal transitoriness, the Anglo-Saxon poets frequently introduced lyric elegiac passages into epic and narrative verse. Thus, for instance, we have the picture of the mood of misery of the father whose son has ended on the gallows in *Beowulf*, lines 2444–2462, and the words of the last warrior survivor of glorious race in the same poem, lines 2247–2266 quoted in Chapter 7. Both of these are in effect elegies which make pauses in a narrative context. Again we find elegiac expression of personal meditation in the Epilogue to Cynewulf's *Elene* and in the poet's individual utterances at the close of *The Dream of the Rood* noticed in the last chapter. In a sense the whole of *Beowulf* may be regarded as stemming from the idea of a funeral elegy. It might almost be said that in Old English the lyric mood is always the elegiac.

There are, however, some poems in Old English which are more or less complete in themselves as lyrics but to which the name 'elegy' has been commonly given. Of these the following, all occurring in the Exeter Book with titles invented by Benjamin Thorpe in 1836, may be termed 'The Elegies': *The Wanderer*, *The Seafarer*, *The Wife's Lament*, *The Husband's Message*, *The Rhyming Poem*, and *The Ruin*. The making of poetry was prominent among the liberal arts which an educated Anglo-Saxon aristocrat should be able to practise; and it is significant that the great 'Arthurian' king Hrothgar in *Beowulf* is described as himself composing elegiac verses on his own past to the harp's accompaniment (lines 2105—2114). The far-famed seventh-century East-Anglian king whose ship cenotaph was found at Sutton Hoo in 1939 was, it would seem, an accomplished performer on the harp; for his personal small harp was among the luxuriously rich treasures placed by his followers in his funeral ship.[1] In this group of poems the grief of exile, whether from native land or for the earthly pilgrim for the heavenly home, is a recurrent theme, as is also the remembering of vanished past joys and glories and the feeling of present desolation made endurable for the Christian poet only by thoughts of celestial happiness. But only three of the elegies are specifically religious. While *The Wanderer*, *The Seafarer*, and *The Rhyming Poem* are deeply Christian, *The Wife's Lament*, *The Husband's Message*, and *The Ruin* are not. *The Wife's Lament* and *The Husband's Message* are—besides being something like love-poems—nearer to the older Germanic tradition than any of the others of this group; and *The Ruin*, the first topographical poem in English, is an elegiac meditation on the ruins of an actual and once Roman city which has been convincingly identified as Bath.[2] While there is still a good deal of Germanic inheritance in the diction and style of these religious lyrics, they are also clearly the work of poets, probably ecclesiastics, who use the commonplaces of Christian Latin allegorical teaching and familiar Latin devices of rhetoric. There is thus much which *The Wanderer*, *The Seafarer*, and *The Rhyming Poem* share in substance with Anglo-Saxon homily,

[1] See J. B. Bessinger, "Beowulf and the Harp at Sutton Hoo", *Toronto University Quarterly* XXVII (1958), pp. 148 ff.
[2] See *Three Old English Elegies*, ed. R. F. Leslie (Manchester, 1961). This includes a full edition of *The Ruin*.

which looked back to the same Latin sources for method and illustrations.[1] The two apparent love-poems, on the other hand, seem to look back to some lost old Germanic legends, and in this way, perhaps, may be linked with *Wulf and Eadwacer*. To the historian of English literature *The Ruin*, which describes what seem to have been ruinous remains of Roman Bath, through the medium of a Germanic background and style, is of special importance as being apparently a pioneer in the poetry of places. Not that the idea of such a method of treatment was entirely new, for it had been used in Latin poetry much earlier, and such work as Alcuin's verses in praise of York at the end of the eighth century is probably earlier than the vernacular poem. *The Ruin* was to have a successor, though a quite inferior one, in Old English in a late poem in praise of *Durham*.

One feature shared by all the poems of this elegiac lyric group, though in varying degrees, is their high poetic quality. All of them contain verse of lyric power and deep feeling with some indications of technical skill, although structurally they must seem unsatisfying to modern readers. It should, however, be borne in mind that the virtues of construction, the architectonics of poetry, were not looked for by the Anglo-Saxons.

The Wanderer, 115 lines only but complete and convincing as a whole, is the finest of all the elegiac lyrics. Though its construction has seemed puzzling to modern readers, it follows a clear sequence of thought, with a definite beginning and end. Its main subject is the mind of an exile of noble birth, visiting many places in search of a leader whose comitatus he might join, since his own lord and all his former comrades are slain. Thinking of the desolation in the world as he sees it in his nostalgic loneliness, the poet comes on the ruins of some ancient citadel, 'the work of giants', presumably left by the Romans. Contemplating this and its past glories, he thinks of his own lost hall of noble revelry and heroism; and from such thoughts his mind passes to moralizing on the transitoriness of all things in the world, and so naturally to good advice and firm confidence in the grace and comfort of the Father in heaven, 'in which stands the whole of secure salvation for us'. *The Wanderer* is a misleading title, since the emphasis is on exile, and only incidentally on 'wandering'. A fitter title might be, as has been suggested, 'The Exile's Consolation"—or better, perhaps, "Thoughts of an Exile."

The Wanderer consists mainly of two parts, joined together by an intermediate series of moralizing gnomic verses, and the whole set within a framework of a short prologue and the pious concluding lines usual in such poems. But a conscious structure and sense of wholeness is suggested by the fact that the first and the final lines

---

[1] See J. E. Cross, "On the Genre of *The Wanderer*", *Neophilologus* XLV (1961), pp. 63–75, and "On the Allegory in *The Seafarer*", *Medium Ævum* XXVIII (1959), pp. 104–106.

each emphasize in the same word (*ar*) divine Grace. The prologue of five lines suggests the influence of the Celtic concepts of the hermits and of the Christian pilgrim or *peregrinus* who chooses exile among strangers for the love of God and as an act of penance:

> Oft him an-haga are gebideð,
> Metudes miltse, þeah þe he mod-cearig
> geond lagu-lade longe sceolde
> hreran mid hondum hrim-cealde sæ,
> wadan wræc-lastas. Wyrd bið ful aræd.

Oft-times the solitary thinker gains God's grace by waiting, and the mercy of the Creator, even though, sad at heart, for long he must needs stir with his hands in rowing the ice-cold sea across the paths of ocean and voyage in the tracks of exile. Fate is inexorable.

Here in the final sentence we have that identification of the pagan notion of fate (*wyrd*) with God which is common in Old English poetry—cf. *Beowulf*, line 455: *Gæð a wyrd swa hio scel*. Then comes the first major part of *The Wanderer* (lines 6–62) in which the exile speaks in the first person of his loss of lord and companions, the vanished joys of the mead-hall, his search for a new leader, and the physical and mental hardships he has endured. On the sea he falls into a reverie in which his lost comrades appear vividly before him once more, only to make his lonely misery the more poignant when they depart in silence. Meditating on his own trials, the poet then begins to reflect on how the departure suddenly from the banquet-hall of life of his former comrades reminds him of the general misery of the world. From this point onward the poem becomes more homiletically moralizing: and it is here that some critics, not liking at all the Anglo-Saxon love of moralizing, and the more emphasized influence of Latin Christianity, have sought to detect interpolations. As has been said, the second major part of *The Wanderer* is joined to the first by a series of gnomic verses of ten lines. Such moralizing recitations of pious platitudes, as they must seem to the modern reader, were a source of pleasure to the Anglo-Saxons:

> Swa þes middan-geard
> ealra dogra gehwam dreoseð ond fealleþ,
> forþon ne mæg weorþan wis wer, ær he age
> wintra dæl in woruld-rice. Wita sceal geþyldig,
> ne sceal no to hat-heort ne to hræd-wyrde,
> ne to wac wiga ne to wan-hydig,
> ne to forht ne to fægen, ne to feoh-gifre
> ne næfre gielpes to georn, ær he geare cunne.
>   (lines 62–69)

Thus every day this world is falling away and decaying. Indeed, a man cannot be wise until he has gained a vast deal of years in this world.

A prudent man should be patient. He must not be too passionate in heart nor too quick to speak, nor too weak as a warrior nor too inclined to act without thought, nor too timorous nor too joyful nor too greedy for riches; nor ever too eager in his boasting until he knows his powers for certain.

After a little more of this, the second major section (73–110) begins with reflections on the coming end of the world (a commonplace in Christian sermons). It is then that the exile begins to meditate on universal transitoriness as he contemplates the ruins of some stone-built Roman citadel:

> Woriað þa win-salo, waldend licgað
> dreame bidrorene, duguþ eal gecrong,
> wlonc bi wealle. Sume wig fornom,
> ferede in forðwege, sumne fugel oþbær
> ofer heanne holm, sumne se hara wulf
> deaðe gedælde, sumne dreorig-hleor
> in eorð-scræfe eorl gehydde.
>
> (lines 78–84)

The wine-halls are rotting and those who once ruled them are lying in death bereft of joys and revelries: for the noble band of young warriors have fallen in their pride by the wall. Notable men have been carried off by war on their journey hence. One was taken away by a bird across the depth of the sea: another the grey wolf has shared with death: and yet another was placed by a sad-faced warrior to hide in a cavern of earth.

This last catalogue of ways of death and disposal of the corpse is the echo of a well-known rhetorical device in Latin Christian poetry; but it is important to observe that this poet, while utilizing much that was commonplace in his Latin Christian culture, can make such material into moving and even exciting poetry. Contemplating this ruined citadel, the poet thinks of the revelries that once went on within its halls, and unconsciously his mind passes to his own lost hall of joys. For when he speaks of the walls being adorned *wyrm-licum*, 'with serpent-patterned shapes', (line 98) he is obviously thinking of a Germanic, not a Roman, setting.

Then follows after a few lines the most famous passage in *The Wanderer*, in which the rhetorical question is asked, again following a familiar Latin device, "Where are the vanished glories of the past?" But this so-called *Ubi sunt* literary homiletic device is here employed to produce a poetic effect unsurpassed in Anglo-Saxon:

> Hwær cwom mearg? Hwær cwom mago? Hwær cwom maþþum-gyfa?
> Hwær cwom symbla gesetu? Hwær sindon sele-dreamas?
> Eala beorht bune! Eala byrn-wiga!

Eala þeodnes þrym! Hu seo þrag gewat,
genap under niht-helm, swa heo no wære.

(lines 92–96)

Whither has departed the steed with his noble rider? Where has gone
the lord who once gave out treasure? Where are the joyful revelries
in the hall? Alack for the shining goblet! Alas for the warrior in his
corslet! Woe for the glory of the prince! How that time has passed
away, grown dark neath the shadow of night as if it had never been!

And there is more of the same quality.

The epilogue to *The Wanderer*, like its prologue, consists of five
lines which are, however, especially distinguished by being verses
of the lengthened or extended type such as are sometimes used for
stylistic effects. Here the gnomic manner of the middle juncture of
the poem is again employed, followed by the final sentence which
echoes the poem's beginning:

Wel bið þam þe him are seceð
frofre to Fæder on heofonum, þær us eal seo fæstnung stondeð.

Well shall it be for him who seeks for himself Grace and comfort with
the Father in the heavens, where stands the whole security and
salvation for us.

The Seafarer, found in the Exeter Book in 124 lines, belongs clearly
to the same genre as *The Wanderer*, with which it shares much in
tone as well as in the outstanding qualities of its poetry. But, unlike
The Wanderer, it seems as it stands very difficult to understand as a
complete unity in structure; and it is generally far more specifically
Christian. The first 102 lines have often seemed to be the whole
poem as originally intended—for this division, with its two major
sections, the one treating of the poet's hardships in voyaging and the
other mainly homiletic, would seem markedly parallel to *The
Wanderer*. But *The Seafarer* as we have it follows this intelligible
pattern with 21 lines (103–124) which are gnomic-homiletic commonplace matter of much inferior quality to the rest, which do not
seem at all clearly to fit in with the remainder of the poem, and are
textually sometimes corrupt or incomplete.

The first part of *The Seafarer*, lines 1–64, is a most vivid and
moving description of the trials and excitements of sea-voyaging, in
which the Anglo-Saxon love of the sea finds its outstanding poetic
expression, and the exile's alternating feeling of the pull of the sea
for the sailor and of its pains and terrors are displayed in lively
dramatic form which at times suggests a kind of dialogue of inner
voices. In the second part (lines 64–102) the voyager meditates more
widely on the basic defects of the life on land to which he had sometimes longed to return: and we are given a series of elegiac verses
then on the transitoriness of all earthly joys, the passing away of

ancient pomps and glories, and the vanity of mortal things. Then the poet thinks of the wider sea on which the pilgrim towards the heavenly *patria* may voyage ultimately, and of the value of leaving a glorious memory for posterity by means of noble deeds and warfare against the devil in this life. In the remaining portion of the extant poem, lines 103–124, we have a third section, if its genuineness is accepted, which is mostly of little marked poetic quality and is gnomic versifying of the kind which seems to have been commonplace in Old English poetry. Yet, as has been already said, one must remember that the Anglo-Saxons probably would like both the tone and matter of verses of the kind which literary critics of modern times would wish to reject.

The Seafarer is in many respects the most poetical of all the elegies; and this fact is supported by the attractiveness of the poem to several modern poet-translators, including Ezra Pound. Here is a characteristic piece of marine description in which the author speaks of his exile sufferings:

> Þæt se mon ne wat
> þe him on foldan fægrost limpeð,
> hu ic earm-cearig is-cealde sæ
> winter wunade wræccan lastum,
> wine-mægum bidroren,
> bihongen hrim-gicelum; hægl scurum fleag.
> Þær ic ne gehyrde butan hlimman sæ,
> is-caldne wæg. Hwilum ylfete song
> dyde ic me to gomene, ganetes hleoþor
> ond huilpan sweg fore hleahtor wera,
> mæw singende fore medo-drince.
> Stormas þær stan-clifu beotan, þær him stearn oncwæð
> isig-feþera; ful oft þæt earn bigeal,
> urig-feþera; ne ænig hleo-mæga
> fea-sceaftig ferð frefran meahte.
>
> (lines 12–26)

These things are unknown to the man to whom befalls the greatest happiness in the world: how I passed the winter in wretchedness and in poverty on the ice-cold sea in the tracks of exile, reft of my beloved kinsmen and with icicles hanging all around me. Hail was coming down in torrents. There I heard nought save the roaring of the ocean with its ice-cold waves. Sometimes I had as my music the song of the swan, and instead of the merriment of men there was the voice of the gannet and the cry of the curlew with the murmuring noise of the sea-gull in place of the drinking of mead in hall. There were storms beating there on the rocky cliffs where the sea-swallow with his ice-covered feathers gave answer. Very often the eagle with dripping wings would shriek around me. No protecting kinsman was there to comfort my desolate heart.

This species of poetic description, whether we may think of it as having symbolic significance or not, vividly portrays a sea-voyage in storm near to dangerous rocks; and the contrast of this detailed near-shore account with the more generalized references to seafaring on a wide ocean later in the poem has led some critics to believe that the poet intended to distinguish between the hard life of mortals on earth and the hoped-for wider voyage to the heavenly *patria* from which he is exiled through the sin of Adam. The latter part of *The Seafarer* begins, and indeed sets its tone, by contrasting 'the joys of the Lord' with life in the world:

> Forþon me hatran sind
> dryhtnes dreamas þonne þis deade lif,
> læne on londe.
>
> (lines 64–66)

There follows after a few lines a passage typically emphasizing in traditional Germanic style the memorial value of noble deeds, but with a most marked Christian slant:

> Forþon þæt bið eorla gehwam æfter-cweþendra
> lof lifigendra last-worda betst,
> þæt he gewyrce, ær he on weg scyle,
> fremum on foldan wið feonda niþ,
> deorum dædum deofle togeanes,
> þæt hine ælda bearn æfter hergen,
> ond his lof siþþan lifge mid englum
> awa to ealdre, ecan lifes blæd,
> dream mid dugeþum.
>
> (lines 72–80)

Truly it is best in the end for every man to leave a fame among those who shall speak of him afterwards, by bringing while he yet lives some good upon the earth before he must depart hence, by splendid deeds against the enmity of fiends and the devil, in such wise that the children of men may later praise him, and that his glory may then live for ever among the angels and that he may have joy in eternal glory with the heavenly hosts.

Here we have the traditional sentiment of the heroic past adapted to homiletic purpose. In its simple form *Beowulf* provides the best early example of this:

> wyrce se þe mote
> domes ær deaþe; þæt bið driht-guman
> unlifgendum æfter selest.
> (*Beowulf*, lines 1387–1389)

Let him who can gain glory before his death. That shall be the best for a noble warrior afterwards when he is dead.

There is much in the homiletic latter part of the poem that is closely paralleled in Hrothgar's long sermon in *Beowulf* (lines 1724–1769) which may suggest that the use of homily in elegiac poetry is not necessarily an indication of lateness of date, unless both *The Seafarer* and *Beowulf* sermons are to be taken out as later interpolations. *The Seafarer*, like *The Wanderer* in the passage already quoted (lines 80–84), employs the rhetorical device of cataloguing ways of death which Anglo-Saxon elegiac poetry must have obtained from a Latin tradition (lines 91–102). This practice had already been illustrated in *Beowulf* as part of Hrothgar's great sermon just cited (lines 1762–1769).

But *The Seafarer*, with its descriptions of stress and storm, also touches happily on nature's happier aspects at one point in a way which reminds us of the descriptions of the earthly paradise in *The Phoenix*:

> Bearwas blostmum nimað, byrig fægriað,
> wongas wlitigiað, woruld onetteð;
> ealle þa gemoniað modes fusne
> sefan to siþe, þam þe swa þenceð
> on flod-wegas feor gewitan.
>
> (lines 48–52)

The woodlands take on their blossoming flowers, and the flowers make fair the dwellings of men and make the plains beautiful. The world of nature becomes living. All these things urge the man eager in heart to depart on his journey when he thinks in this way, far upon the waves of the sea.

But these signs of the coming of spring then at once suggest to the poet the cuckoo, that season's harbinger whose notes may also recall feelings of bitterness and sorrow.

The elegiac tone found in *The Wanderer* and in passages in *Beowulf* is at its most effective in the latter part of *The Seafarer*:

> Dagas sind gewitene,
> ealle onmedlan eorþan rices;
> nearon nu cyningas ne caseras
> ne gold-giefan swylce iu wæron,
> þonne hi mæst mid him mærþa gefremedon
> ond on dryhtlicestum dome lifdon.
> Gedroren is þeos duguð eal, dreamas sing gewitene,
> wuniað þa wacran ond þas woruld healdaþ,
> brucað þurh bisgo. Blæd is gehnæged,
> eorþan indryhto ealdað ond searað.
>
> (lines 80–89)

The days are departed with all the pomps of the kingdom of earth. There are not now kings nor Caesars nor givers of treasure as once there were, when such men performed deeds of glory and lived in the noblest esteem. Fallen is all that mighty troop of warriors. Joyful revelries are gone away, and feebler men dwell upon the earth and pass their life in affliction. Their glory is laid low. The fine things of the world grow aged and wither.

Like *The Wanderer*, but more unequivocally, *The Seafarer* expresses the idea of penance and deliberate exile from everything on earth held dear, in a pilgrimage where all human ties are forsaken for the love of God. The concept of such a pilgrimage—peculiarly Irish, and hence passed on to the Anglo-Saxons through Irish Christianity—is touched on very clearly in the poet's feeling himself urged to visit the *land of strange peoples* across the sea:

> Forþon cnyssað nu
> heortan geþohtas, þæt ic hean streamas,
> sealt-yþa gelac sylf cunnige;
> monað modes lust mæla gehwylce
> ferð to feran, þæt ic feor heonan
> *el-þeodigra eard gesece.*
>
> (lines 33–38)

Indeed, the thoughts of my heart are now strongly stirring me: they press that I myself should strive to test the tumult of the salt waves. Every moment the mind's desire is urging my spirit to the journeying, that I far from hence should seek the *land of strange peoples*.

The choice of words in the phrase 'seek the land of strange peoples' suggests the Celtic idea of *peregrinatio pro amore Dei*. For the Old English *elþeodigra eard gesece* exactly echoes the usual prose rendering, as in the Alfredian version of Bede's *Historia Ecclesiastica*, of the Latin *Peregrinam ducere vitam*.[1] Moreover, the Old English word for pilgrimage in this sense, *elþeodignes*, probably looks back to the Irish *ailithre*, 'pilgrimage', with which it shares etymology.[2]

The homiletic piece known as *The Rhyming Poem* consists of 87 lines in the Exeter Book, in which it immediately precedes the allegorical *Physiologus* pieces. Its editorial title arises from the fact that it is the one complete poem in Anglo-Saxon which was evidently intended to be entirely in rhyme—in lines which, while alliterating in the usual way, at the same time link their two halves by means of internal rhyme. Such Leonine lines had been used occasionally singly as in *Beowulf* 1014 and *Maldon* 282 for stylistic effect, and by Cynewulf in the famous continuous passage opening the Epilogue

---

[1] The Old English of the Alfredian Bede has *on elþeodignesse faran*.

[2] The Old English *Elþeodig*, literally 'pertaining to alien peoples', has the elements *el* = Irish *aili* 'alien' and *þeod* = Irish *tir*, 'land', and these combine, with the normal Irish consonant-change, to form the compound *alilithre* which is the regular traditional word for 'pilgrimage' in this sense.

to his *Elene*. The suggestion for such devices seems to have come through a type of Latin hymn widely used in Western Europe, though it is possible that the blend of alliteration and rhyme may owe something to an early Irish practice. As the only Old English poem in rhyme throughout, the work might be thought of as a first anticipation of the passing over to regularly rhymed metre which characterized the Middle English period. But there is no clear evidence of late date, since the tone of the poem can be easily paralleled from *Beowulf* in Hrothgar's famous elegiac homily in lines 1724 ff. *The Rhyming Poem* is more likely to have been just a piece of bold experimenting. For the poet clearly found rhyme a very difficult medium, and often had to write very obscurely to get in the needed sounds. These rhymes frequently seem to have been defaced in the usual passage to the surviving West-Saxon recension, and they can at times be clearly restored by the substitution of Anglian forms. Here is a specimen of this alliterating and internally rhyming metre:

> Scealcas wæron *scearpe*, scyl wæs *hearpe*,
> hlude *hlynede*, hleoþor *dynede*,
> sweglrad *swinsade*, swiþe ne *minsade*.
>
> (lines 27–29)

This describes the joyful sound of music and poetry as a symbol of former happiness:

> Keen were the retainers as the harp sonorously shrilled; it sounded loudly as the voice [of the reciter] rang out: melodious was the music, nor did its power diminish.

The Rhyming Poem is a generalized homiletic sketch of the life of a prosperous and noble man who through sin was brought down in lonely humiliation to prepare for death, ending with the hope of Grace and heaven. The poet speaks in the first person, and the tone is very much like that of *The Wanderer* and *The Seafarer* in its elegiac dwelling on vanishing mortal glory, followed by misery and the need for penitence. The Book of Job has been suggested as a possible general source: but it is probable that the writer was using traditional Latin homiletic devices as with the other elegies. In particular, as in *The Seafarer*, the parallelism between man's life and that of the world passing into its last age is emphasized.[1] One may compare *The Seafarer* 89–90, already quoted:

> The noble things of the earth grow aged and wither away, just as now does every one throughout the world.

---

[1] The device of parallelism between man and the world, quite frequent in Old English homilies, has been thoroughly examined for elegiac poetry, especially for *The Rhyming Poem*, by J. E. Cross in an important paper, "Aspects of Microcosm and Macrocosm in Old English Literature", *Comparative Literature* XIV (1962), pp. 1–22, especially 11 ff.

In *Guthlac A* we read:

> Ealdaþ eorþan blæd æþela gehwylcre
> ond of wlite wendeð wæstma gecyndu;
> bið seo siþre tid sæda gehwylces
> mætræ in mægne.
>
> (lines 43–46)

The glory and all the noble things of earth grow aged and pass away from their beauty as do the natural qualities of crops and fruits. In the later age the strength of every seed shall be poorer.

and in *The Rhyming Poem:*

> Sumur-hat colað,
> fold-wela fealleð, feondscipe wealleð,
> eorð-mægen ealdaþ, ellen colað.
>
> (lines 67–69)

Cold grows summer's heat: the riches of the earth begin to fall away, and the enemy rages. The might of earth grows aged, and valour grows cold.

The difficulties of metre lead sometimes to textual obscurity, and there are gaps and mistranscriptions which make the poem seem almost like a series of word-puzzles. Yet there is both dignity and depth of feeling, and some of the lyric qualities of *The Wanderer* and *The Seafarer* are found here also.

As has been remarked earlier, the Anglo-Saxon temperament did not lend itself to the making of love-poetry, for which Britain had to wait till the coming of a strong lyric impulse from the Continent. *Wulf and Eadwacer*, discussed in Chapter 5 as a poem in the Germanic tradition, is the nearest thing to a love-lyric in Old English: but two other pieces in the Exeter Book, *The Husband's Message* and *The Wife's Lament*, also touch upon the sentiment of love. These three poems, then, constitute the whole of Old English love-poetry, with the possible addition of the lines on the return of a Frisian sailor to his wife intercalated into the gnomic verses or *Maxims* in the Exeter Book. These last, however, suggest rather the practical Germanic attitude toward marriage as described by Tacitus:

> Leof wilcuma
> Frysan wife, þonne flota stondeð;
> biþ his ceol cumen ond hyre ceorl to ham,
> agen æt-geofa, ond heo hine in laþað,
> wæsceð his warig hrægl ond him syleþ wæde niwe,
> liþ him on londe þæs his lufu bædeð.
>
> (*Maxims* I, lines 94–99) ASPR III, 160.

Her dear one is welcome to the wife of the Frisian when his vessel lies in harbour. His ship is come home with her man, her own provider of food. And she invites him in, washes his soiled garments, gives him fresh clothes, and grants him on land that which his love craves.

The Husband's Message (we do not know whether the man who sends the message is actually lover or husband) takes the form of an urgent plea sent by a trusted retainer from a man who has left his wife (or betrothed) to go into enforced exile overseas, but has now found fortune and wealth and honour, in which he bids the woman take ship to be happily reunited with him in surroundings worthy of her noble rank. To authenticate himself, the messenger brings a piece of wood on which his lord has carved runes to verify his true faith and loyalty. The poem occupies only 53 lines in the Exeter Book, some of which are hopelessly defective in the manuscript. Only in a loose sense may this poem be termed elegiac. Yet though its mood is hopeful, it has something of the common underlying suggestion of melancholy, as shown in its reference to the 'mournful cuckoo' whose notes sounding over the woodlands are to be the signal for the woman to take ship in the coming spring. One may compare the passage in *The Seafarer* in which the 'mournful cuckoo's' call seems to urge the sailor back to the sea:

> Swylce geac monað geomran reorde,
> singeð sumeres weard, sorge beodeð
> bitter in breost-hord.
> (*The Seafarer*, lines 53–55)

Likewise the cuckoo, with mournful voice, urges him; the herald of summer sings, boding bitter grief in the breast.

Reference to 'old vows' which the messenger says the couple had taken jointly[1] and to the carrying through of their love[2] may imply that they were betrothed, and the situation perhaps has some parallel with that of the lovers in *Waldere*. It has sometimes been suggested that both *The Husband's Message* and *The Wife's Lament* touch upon episodes from Germanic heroic tradition, but there is no way to determine the value of this conjecture.

The poem closes with a kind of epilogue in which is a runic inscription cut apparently on a piece of wood brought by the messenger who speaks the husband's (or lover's) words. It reminds one a good deal of Cynewulf's runic epilogues, such as that to *Elene*, and as usual with such runic acrostics, it is obscure to us now. It has often been thought that Riddle 60, which describes a piece of wood on which a message has seemingly been cut, meaning "for us two alone,"[3] should be regarded as the beginning of *The Husband's*

---

[1] *eald gebeot incer twega* (line 48).   [2] *freondscype fremman* (line 19).
[3] *for unc anum twam* (line 15).

Message, which it immediately precedes in the Exeter Book. It seems to describe wood with a runic inscription on it: and this might be the very piece of wood which the faithful retainer brings to the wife (or betrothed). But in that case there must be a prosopopoeia in which the whole of the poem is spoken by the personified wood. Riddle 30 seems to personify a piece of wood in several ways, but to emphasize it as a Cross, in a manner comparable with the prosopopoeia in *The Dream of the Rood*[1] : so that there is some support for supposing the personified piece of inscribed wood to speak the whole of *The Husband's Message* if Riddle 60 really was its intended beginning. But there are difficulties of inconsistency in this view. On the whole the more satisfying theory is that *The Husband's Message* is entirely spoken by the messenger, leaving Riddle 60 as a separate piece as printed in *The Anglo-Saxon Poetic Records*.[2] The runes seem to be some kind of symbolic asseveration of the distant lover's good faith, and the poem ends with his repeated declaration through the messenger that he would 'perform the pact and keep the troth of love as long as he lives, which you two in days of yore ofttimes spoke'.[3] *The Husband's Message*, mainly secular in tone like the other love-poems, has the usual Christian implications. Its interest is not very markedly poetic, for it lacks any of the lyric intensity of feeling to be found in *Wulf and Eadwacer* and in *The Wife's Lament*.

The title *The Wife's Lament*, like that of all Old English poetry, is merely editorial. But, unlike *The Husband's Message*, it appears an account from the wife's point of view of definitely marital misfortunes, so that Thorpe's title may properly stand. It is, by coincidence, of exactly the same 53 lines length as *The Husband's Message*, and has seemed to some to treat of the same couple. But it is not placed beside *The Husband's Message* in the manuscript, and on closer examination it does not show any real connection with it. Moreover, its tone is quite different. For here the wife, who speaks in her own person throughout, expresses her feelings of longing grief for her deliberately absent husband, and her present material misery, with far more intensity of feeling and some effective poetic imagery of lyric quality. In its contemplation of the sadness and longing misery of the wife, the poem thus shows the common elegiac tone and some lyric feeling.

The wife, as is clearly indicated by the grammar of the opening line, utters her 'lament' in her own person. She describes the departure of her husband to some distant region leaving her alone to seek in vain for some place in which to support herself. Then, turned against her by some of his kindred who wish to part them, her lord compels her to dwell in some desolate grove in a lonely

---

[1] Cf. Margaret Schlauch, "*The Dream of the Rood* as Prosopopoeia" in *Essays & Studies in Honor of Carleton Brown* (New York, 1940), pp. 23–24.
[2] III, p. 225.　　　　　　　　　　　[3] Lines 51–53.

cavern bereft of all friends: and it is here that she meditates on past happiness and present grief in material wretchedness. Some other man, it would seem, is at least in part the cause of this separation. She remembers the vows of lasting fidelity she and her lord had exchanged: and now their love is 'as if it had never been'. Vividly, though in general terms, the wife describes her present sojourn under an oak-tree in a cave-dwelling which is of ancient design. surrounded by high and painful towering rocks, with dark, narrow valleys overgrown with briars. Here she weeps as she thinks how there are other lovers on the earth who live in happiness and may share a couch:

> Þær ic sittan mot sumor-langne dæg,
> þær ic wepan mæg mine wræc-siþas,
> earfoþa fela; forþon ic æfre ne mæg
> þære mod-ceare minre gerestan,
> ne ealles þæs longaþes þe mec on þissum life begeat.
>
> (lines 37–41)

Here I must sit through the never-ending day bewailing my exiled travellings and my many hardships. For never can I rest from my heart's sorrow, nor in any way at all from the love-longing which has seized upon this life.

Then she thinks of her husband who may perchance by now be also in misery and sad grief for her. But finally her thought again returns to hopelessness, with the conclusion that 'grievous will it be for those who must wait in longing for the loved one.'

> Wa bið þam þe sceal
> of langoþe leofes abidan.

This poem is entirely secular in expression.

The Ruin, a piece of 49 lines as we have it immediately following *The Husband's Message* in the Exeter Book, entirely lacks its closing lines as well as being only fragmentary over nearly a third of its length: for lines 12–18 and the eight after line 41 are too incomplete in the manuscript for reconstruction of what is missing to be possible. The poem is clearly in the elegiac tradition, having affinities with the meditation on the ruined city of *The Wanderer* and the description of the thoughts of the last survivor in *Beowulf*.[1] But, unlike the elegies of Christian homiletic tendency, it lacks all religious or didactic reference: and while it shows the usual sadness for the loss of ancient glories and the consciousness of present decay, it has nothing of the imaginative personal utterance found in all the other elegies. The poet is gazing on the ruins of some once Roman city described as 'the work of giants' (*enta geweorc*) like the similar ruin of *The*

---

[1] Cf. *The Wanderer*, lines 75–107 and *Beowulf*, lines 2247 ff.

Wanderer 87, 'the ancient work of giants' (*eald enta geweorc*). On this scene of crumbling decay the poet meditates, considering the joys and rich treasures and warlike adornments of those who must once have dwelt there. But the elegiac meditation is quite general, and with nothing of the usual moralizing and Christian piety such as there is in *The Wanderer, The Seafarer,* and *The Rhyming Poem:* and the cause of everything in this scene of desolation is not God, but fate (*wyrd*). This impersonal tone makes *The Ruin* stand somewhat apart from other work of elegiac type. Another thing that seems to insulate it is the vivid concrete detail in descriptions which appear to be definitely prompted by things in a desolate ruin which the poet has seen with his own eyes. Indeed, his wall 'grey with lichen tinctured with red' (*ræghar ond read-fah*)[1] has suggested to recent investigators a still visible wall in the remains of Roman Bath on which the grey moss has acquired an orange-coloured stain through the effects of the red of the tiles which have crumbled from the roof. Certainly the vocabulary of *The Ruin* in its descriptive passages contains words of concrete detail not otherwise known, and an alternation between generalized description and detailed observation is a clear feature of the poem. It is remarkable that a piece so brief and fragmentary should yet even in its truncated state convey here and there some real poetic feeling.

The Ruin may in a very general way have been suggested by Latin topographical verses such as those of the sixth-century Christian poet Venantius Fortunatus on the devastation of Thuringia. It is in a sense the first example of topographical verse in English. It is related in its tradition probably to the classical Latin poems in praise of particular places such as Alcuin made for York in the early ninth century (though *The Ruin* is rather the obverse of the conventional *encomium urbis*). The only other Old English topographical poem is the very late fragmentary piece on Durham. The identification of the city of *The Ruin* as Bath has much to recommend it, though it must remain only an attractive hypothesis. The details of *The Ruin* which make it unique might well have been imaginatively constructed by the poet from ruins that he had himself seen: but recent archaeological examination of the poem in relation to Bath[2] seems strongly to support the identification. That the poem seems to have been originally in a Mercian dialect does not overthrow this view, for Bath was in Mercian territory in the eighth century, when the piece is thought to have first taken shape.

In view of the fact that Old English elegiac poetry was so much disposed to homily and moralizing, even in lyric passages, it seems

---

[1] For the argument see R. F. Leslie, *Three Old English Elegies,* op. cit., which treats fully of *The Ruin* along with *The Husband's Message* and *The Wife's Lament,* and presents the case for Bath in the Introduction, pp. 22 ff.

[2] See Leslie, *op. cit.,* for useful archaeological references.

appropriate to end this chapter with some reference to a number of short homiletic pieces which, though they seldom share the poetic merits of the elegies so far discussed, need some mention by the literary historian, and do not conveniently fit into any of the clearly recognized categories. Since the centres of literary culture in Anglo-Saxon England were naturally religious houses, relatively far more verse of didactic significance has survived than has that using less obviously Christian material. Only, perhaps, by an occasional fortunate accident would love-poems get themselves copied and preserved even incompletely, whereas venerated religious works like Bede's *Death Song* and *Cædmon's Hymn* survive in very many copies. The only poem apart from such specially valued pieces which has survived in more than one copy is the purely didactic verse-homiletic dialogue known as *Soul and Body*, which is preserved, though with much textual variation, in both the Exeter Book and the Vercelli Book. Any kind of secular literature which had no obvious didactic or religious value had far less chance of survival: and when an attempt was made in recent years to assess the losses from Old English literature of what had once existed the general conclusion was that much work of historical content has disappeared, but that much of an entirely non-didactic verse nature that might have been expected to survive was either never copied at all or was allowed to vanish through neglect.[1] Nor can we know how much poetry that existed only in oral tradition failed to be written down at all.

The Exeter Book, donated by the city's first bishop Leofric (who died in 1072) to Exeter Cathedral, in whose library it remains, is described in the list of his gifts as "one large English book composed in verse about all kinds of matters"[2]: so that it is not surprising to find in it a considerable number of miscellaneous minor pieces of verse which do not clearly fit any definite classification, though all are more or less didactic, and most are definitely religious. These poems, of which there are thirteen, generally treat of traditional themes of an edifying nature, vary a good deal in method and completeness, and seldom show any marked literary merit, though often they are of interest for the light they throw on life in Anglo-Saxon times. Unlike the poems hitherto noticed from this manuscript, several of them have had their titles editorially varied from time to time, in departure from the usual practice of accepting the superscriptions of Thorpe, which have become traditional. Generally in this book the texts discussed are as printed in *The Anglo-Saxon Poetic Records*, with the titles assigned by the editor of its third volume, though other readings are sometimes preferred.[3] Taking the Exeter Book as a basis, then, since it

---

[1] See R. M. Wilson, *The Lost Literature of Medieval England* (London, 1962).

[2] A facsimile of this manuscript with full introduction is *The Exeter Book of Old English Poetry*, ed. R. W. Chambers, Max Förster, and Robin Flower (London, 1933): the list of donations, etc., is given on pp. 11 ff.

[3] *The Exeter Book*, ed. George Philip Krapp and Elliott van Kirk Dobbie (Columbia University Press, 1936).

contains the main collection of minor religious poems, others of similar
or parallel theme or type found in other manuscripts will be mentioned
also as occasion arises.

The title *The Descent into Hell* is given to a poem dealing with the
traditional theme best known as 'The Harrowing of Hell' in 137 lines
in the Exeter Book. This is more appropriate to the piece than the
traditional one. For 'The Harrowing of Hell', a favourite medieval
homiletic theme based largely on the latter part of the Pseudo-
Gospel of Nicodemus, implies a conflict between Christ and Satan
in which the divine visitant violently worsted the devil, as well as
removing from hell the Patriarchs and pre-Christian holy men: but
the Exeter Book poem ends only with the welcoming of Christ by
Adam, and has no fighting. The same theme is handled in the
Junius Manuscript poem *Christ and Satan*, and is touched on in
Christ III and a little in *Christ I*, as well as in several prose sermons.
From the briefest reference to Christ preaching "to the spirits in
prison",[1] in the first Epistle of St Peter a tale vividly dramatized had
grown up of how Christ visited Satan's captives in hell between His
crucifixion and resurrection, and in heroic style 'harrowed' Satan
and his entourage. The Old English poem has much lively dialogue
and some dramatic eloquence, though hardly poetic power. The same
theme was again to be treated dramatically in a mid-thirteenth-
century poem, *The Harrowing of Hell*.[2] The poem clearly belongs to
the Cynewulf school.

The dialogue as a dramatic literary device had no doubt been
suggested to the Anglo-Saxon poets by Latin models, and its limited
use has been noticed already in several places. In a poem known as
Soul and Body, which appears in differing but closely related versions
both in the Exeter Book and in the Vercelli Book (this latter in a rather
less incomplete form), there is some approach to the dialogue form,
though the body, being dead, cannot reply to the reproaches of the
damned soul, which has to visit from hell its former habitation every
week for three hundred years. The virtuous soul also addresses its
body with kindness in the latter, incomplete part of the poem.
Here is something like the embryo of the dialogue-debate or dispute
which came to Britain from Latin tradition and was to be developed
fully only in Middle English. As with *The Harrowing of Hell*, the
theme of *Soul and Body* is treated more effectively as a debate in
Middle English.[3] The poem in Old English is a simple homily on
the results in the after-life of good or bad deeds. In *The Anglo-Saxon*

[1] 1 Pet. iii, 19: the Vulgate text has *in quo et his qui in carcere erant spiritibus
veniens praedicavit.*

[2] See *The Middle English Harrowing of Hell and Gospel of Nicodemus*, ed.
William Hulme (EETS ES 100: London 1907). *The Gospel of Nicodemus* was
translated into Old English; it is edited by S. J. Crawford (Edinburgh, 1927).

[3] See *þe Desputisoun bitwen þe Bodi and þe Soule*, ed. W. Linow (Erlangen,
1889).

Poetic Records the Exeter Book version is called *Soul and Body II*
to distinguish it from *Soul and Body I* of the Vercelli Book, printed
in Vol. II, with notes relating the two pieces on pp. 126-129.

Between *Guthlac B* and *The Phoenix* occurs a rather longer poem,
191 lines, versifying the prayer of Azariah and the three children's
song in the fire as narrated in the third chapter of the Book of Daniel
in the Vulgate version. It has been given the title *Azarias*. But this
material, which in the Vulgate occurs between verses 23 and 91,
is relegated to the Apocrypha in reformist English translations, though
the children's song as the *Benedicite* is sung in churches. Azariah's
prayer and this form of the *Benedicite* are found in the *Daniel* poem
in the Junius Manuscript in a second version in parts closely related
to the Exeter Book *Azarias*. Here they appear as lyric passages[1]
markedly different in style from the simple narrative epic of *Daniel*.
They—especially the prayer of Azariah—are so awkwardly fitted
into the Junius Manuscript poem as to suggest interpolation. Whether
the *Daniel* scribe added these lyric passages in this misplaced manner
to fill a gap from knowledge of the poem *Azarias* or the latter is
indebted to the *Daniel* poet is not certain. But it seems clear that there
were originally two separate poems of Azariah and the three children.
Azarias lacks a beginning which once stood in the Exeter Book.
But we cannot tell how much has been lost. As poetry, neither
Azarias nor the parallel *Daniel* passages have much literary merit
beyond a fair technical skill.

A set of five pieces found at various points in the Exeter Book have
been conveniently grouped together in *The Anglo-Saxon Poetic
Records* because of their general similarity of tone. They have had
varying titles, but those in *The Anglo-Saxon Poetic Records* are
generally acceptable. They are: *The Gifts of Men*, *Vainglory*, *The
Fortunes of Men*, *The Order of the World*, and *The Judgment Day I* (this
last figure to distinguish the poem from a longer metrical adaptation of
Bede's Latin poem on this subject of a much later date and in another
manuscript.[2]

The Gifts of Men, 113 lines, is a moralizing catalogue of human
characteristics set between a pious exordium and ending. *Vainglory*,
84 lines, is largely a homily against pride, prefaced by a prologue
of eight lines in the first person, and in a tone reminding one a little
of *The Wanderer* and *The Seafarer*—though it seems to lack any
structural relation with the sermon on the vanity of pride which
forms the main part of the piece. In the Facsimile edition of the

---

[1] See *Daniel*, lines 279-408.
[2] *The Judgment Day II* is versified in 306 lines from Bede's poem *De Die
Judicii*. It belongs to a group of five homiletic pieces, similar in theme to some
extent though much inferior in quality to the Exeter Book group, found in MS.
Corpus Christi College, Cambridge, 201. It is printed in ASPR VI, pp. 58 ff.

Exeter Book R. W. Chambers has the title *The Spirit of Men*[1]: but
it is primarily against pride that the homily is versified. *The Fortunes
of Men*—perhaps better known by its earlier title *The Fates of Men*—
is of 98 lines, and lists in the two distinct parts of the poem the miserable and the happy fortunes of men. Some of the happenings touched
on are of historical interest, especially the description of the poet or
scop sitting at his lord's feet playing his harp, loudly plucking its
strings with a plectrum and receiving fitting reward for his art.[2]
The Order of the World, better remembered as *The Wonders of
Creation*, of 102 lines, again has a kind of personal introduction, as
does *Vainglory*: but this longer opening (lines 1–37) is not so much
autobiographical as a mere device for the homilist to make his
exhortation seem more personal. The main part of the piece treats of
the Creation and of the happiness of the blessed, ending with conventional pious moralizing. This poem reminds one a good deal of
Cynewulf, as do the others of this group, in varying degrees, so that all
might loosely be described as of his 'School'. *The Judgment Day I*
has also much in common with the account of the Last Judgment in
Christ III, but the treatment here lacks the dramatic narrative
vigour of that poem.

In 94 lines a father is pictured as giving a lecture of ten precepts
to his son: and for this reason the piece has been entitled *Precepts*
in *The Anglo-Saxon Poetic Records*, and as *The Father's Instruction to
his Son* by Thorpe and others.[3] The poem is somewhat gnomic in
character, but was probably written as a contribution to Christian
education. In form it resembles *The Order of the World* with its
fictional opening situation.

A poem of 118 lines in the later part of the Exeter Book is called
Resignation by the editors of *The Anglo-Saxon Poetic Records*, by
Thorpe *A Supplication*,[4] and by others *The Exile's Lament* or *The
Exile's Prayer*. The poem has affinities in its references to exile with
The Wanderer and *The Seafarer*, and as in them the exile is probably
symbolical, and suggests the spiritual grief of a penitent exiled from
the celestial *patria*. The poem belongs to a later period than those
so far noticed in this chapter. It seems to have been influenced by
the Penitential Psalms, and largely takes the form and tone of a
personal prayer. It is thus rare in the degree of its subjectivity, and
though its prayer is personal there is nothing of the quasi-auto-
biographical approach of other elegiac poetry. The poet prays with
intense feeling as a guilt-laden sinner; but from line 88 the tone suddenly becomes more impersonal, rather in the gnomic style of the passage which links the two main sections of *The Wanderer*. The sea in

---

[1] *Op. cit.*, p. 40.
[2] See lines 80–85. *Cf.* C. L. Wrenn, "Two Anglo-Saxon Harps", *Comparative
Literature* XIV (1962), pp. 124–125.
[3] See R. W. Chambers in the Exeter Book facsimile, *op. cit.*, p. 40.
[4] *Ibid.*, p. 42.

this latter part of *Resignation*, on which the 'friendless exile' longs to journey, seems to play much the same symbolic part as in *The Seafarer*: but the manuscript is here often defective. The poem ends, unusually, with a piece of quite non-religious gnomic wisdom:

> Giet biþ þæt selest, þonne mon him sylf ne mæg
> wyrd onwendan, þæt he þonne wel þolige.
>
> (lines 117-118)

Yet indeed this is best, that when a man cannot himself change his fate, then he should endure it well.

Finally, following *The Descent into Hell* in the Exeter Book, are four very short religious pieces of little apparent consequence. These are: nine lines on Salvation through Almsgiving, a defective eight-line fragment of a dialogue or *Interrogatio* on the numbers in the army of Pharaoh, *The Lord's Prayer I*, which is a very economical paraphrase of the *Pater Noster* in eleven lines; and a defective 20-line *Homiletic Fragment II* offering spiritual comfort to one in great sorrow and ending with a reference to the Nativity. The *Pater Noster* paraphrase is numbered I because there are two further versions in other manuscripts and this appears to be the earliest.[1]

Along with the minor religious verse in the Exeter Book may conveniently be noticed a few similar pieces from other manuscripts. In the Vercelli Book[2] there is a poem of 47 lines, much on the lines of *Vainglory*, Homiletic Fragment I, formerly entitled *Falseness of Men*. In MS. Corpus Christi College, Cambridge, 201, among much important prose, there is a group of five religious pieces,[3] which occur together. These are the following: *The Judgment Day II*, *An Exhortation to Christian Living*, *A Summons to Prayer*, *The Lord's Prayer II*, and *Gloria I*. The *Judgment Day II*, a longer and more meritorious version of Bede's poem on this subject in the Exeter Book, contains 306 lines, and expands a good deal on Bede. *An Exhortation to Christian Living*, 82 lines, is of the same genre and tone as the Exeter Book *Precepts*. *A Summons to Prayer*, 31 lines, is of interest because of its type of 'macaronic' lyric metre, in which the second half of each line is in Latin while alliterating in the usual way with the Anglo-Saxon first half. This type of line is occasionally found in late Old English, as in the lines in praise of St Aldhelm[4] and became frequent in Middle English. *The Lord's Prayer II* runs to 123 lines and greatly enlarges on the matter of the *Pater Noster*. It is so numbered to distinguish it from the Exeter Book earlier

---

[1] The Lord's Prayer metrical versions II and III, which occur respectively in MS. Corpus Christi College, Cambridge, 201 and MS. Bodley, Junius 121, are edited in ASPR VI, pp. 70 ff. and 77 ff. respectively.

[2] ASPR II, pp. 59 f.

[3] ASPR VI, pp. 58 ff.

[4] ASPR VI, p. 97. On the macaronic lines to St Aldhelm see Chapter 4 (p. 58).

version, and from a third piece in the so-called *Benedictine Office*.
Gloria I, versifying the *Gloria Patri*, is again distinguished from a
Gloria II found elsewhere.[1] It is, like *The Lord's Prayer II*, much
expanded from its basic matter. In MS. Junius 121 in the Bodleian
Library is a piece of prose setting out some of the regular liturgical
offices, apparently for beginners in a religious house: and among
these offices are some pieces in verse,[2] along with some fragments of
Psalms. Here is *The Lord's Prayer III*, another version of *Gloria I*,
and the Apostles' Creed. All are in the usual Old English verse,
but with signs of some late licence: and they show relatively little
literary merit.

Two poems written for purely didactic purposes near the end of
the Old English period deserve mention for historical reasons rather
than for any quality they might possess as poetry, beyond their
metrical features. They are a *Menologium*, or versified ecclesiastical
calendar, and *The Seasons for Fasting*, which sets forth guidance for
fasting in Lent and the Ember-tides.[3] *The Menologium*, 231 lines,
is a mnemonic summary Church calendar showing the obligatory
feast-days of the year, and what they commemorate. It ends with the
statement that from its information one may learn the feast-days that
are obligatory "in the realms in Britain of the king of the Saxons".
The only English saint treated is Augustine, and it seems that
Canterbury was the centre from which this calendar emanated. But
the special attention given to *Lammas*, August 1st, when the harvest
is celebrated in thankfulness (*hlaf-mæsse* or 'Mass of the loaf'),
is specifically English: for this festival is not strictly ecclesiastical
but rather of natural origin. This mention of Lammas is the first of
the kind.[4]

The Seasons for Fasting, remaining unfinished at line 230, is
evidently intended for minor clergy, as it closes with a protest against
the practice of allowing the drinking of wine and eating of oysters
immediately after Mass. But the special interest of this purely
instructive poem is that it is divided into stanzas, consisting usually
of eight lines apiece. Now, this stanzaic structure at length is so far
unparalleled in Old English, though the short poem *Deor* may be
regarded as largely stanzaic. Historically the piece tells us a good deal
of Church practices at the beginning of the eleventh century, though
it is primarily an exhortation of the faithful to the proper observance
of the obligatory fasts, rather than a mnemonic like the *Menologium*.

[1] This 3-line piece is edited ASPR VI, p. 94 from MS. Cotton Titus D XXVII
in the British Museum.
[2] ASPR VI, pp. 74 ff. There is a full discussion of these poems in *The Benedictine Office*, ed. James Ure (Edinburgh, 1957), pp. 49ff.
[3] ASPR VI, pp. 49 and 98 respectively.
[4] Lammas, probably celebrating 'first-fruits', was very popular in England in
the Middle Ages, though it was never an official Church Feast in the technical
sense. Lammas is still remembered in Scotland as the day when rents are paid.

CHAPTER 10

Learning and Folk Poetry

UNDER THIS GENERAL HEAD may be considered a number of miscellaneous poems of very varied dates and origins, which have in common pleasure in the ingenious display of antiquarian learning, the preservation of partly Christianized traditions of empirical magic, elements of Germanic folklore, or the making and solving of verbal puzzles—probably first popularized under Irish influence. Thus the two incomplete poems known as *Solomon and Saturn* combine extensive antiquarian learning with features from a widely known folk-tale of Oriental origin, as well as with much magic; and again *The Rune Poem* records the significance of each of the symbols of the later runic system with some poetic embellishment, and with obvious antiquarian satisfaction. The *Riddles*, of which 95 survive in the Exeter Book, include adaptations from ingenious Latin riddles from the pen of St Aldhelm and some other ecclesiastics who shared something of his Irish love of learned puzzles, as well as pictures of daily life which echo much rustic folklore. The *Charms*, often belonging to the medical recipes of religious houses, show an empirical pre-serving of Germanic magic very roughly adapted to use by Christians in place of the older wizards. The gnomic pieces, which versify much popular lore and moral platitudinizing, clearly contain in fossilized forms elements of the traditional Germanic practice of a type of mnemonic versifying combining didactic aims with the kind of pleasure to be had from old-fashioned nursery rhymes. Usually these pieces are of historical or sociological rather than literary interest, though most of them include occasional short passages of poetic imagination or feeling.

The macaronic lines in praise of Aldhelm,[1] along with his Latin writings, have been discussed in Chapter 4. No doubt this kind of learned blend of English and Latin, with the combination of allitera-tion and internal rhyme, looks back in some sort to Irish influences. Belonging originally probably to the early tenth century, this incom-plete poem rather parallels *A Summons to Prayer* and the last lines of *The Phoenix*. Its use of learned and out-of-the-way terms and its learned echoes may lead on to some examination of two incomplete poems, apparently from the late ninth century, which survive, separated by a prose piece on the same theme known as *Solomon and*

[1] ASPR VI, p. 97.

Saturn. This intriguing group, with its associations of magic and Christian learning, survives in the late tenth-century MS. Corpus Christi College, Cambridge, 422. Part only of the first of the two poems exists also in MS. 41 of the same collection.

The two poems are evidently of differing authorship and attitude.[1] The first, and much the shorter—169 lines—treats in detail of the magical and exorcistic properties of the Latin version of the Lord's Prayer, taking the runes of the nineteen letters of the Latin alphabet needed to make up the whole *Pater Noster* separately with their symbolic meanings and powers: and the special significance of the palm is brought out in a study of "the palm-twigged *Pater Noster*". Saturn, a prince of the Chaldeans (who were so famous for magical lore), is learned in the same kind of wisdom as was Shakespeare's Prospero. He is doubtless related to the Germanic god Woden ultimately, as well as to some Germanic representative of the Roman god Mercury. He demands of the wise Solomon a full explanation of the special powers of the palm-twigged *Pater Noster*: and though this poem is in the form of the dialogue or *interrogatio* type, nearly all of it is occupied with Solomon's disquisition on the magical powers of the *Pater Noster*. The runes of the *Pater Noster* are marshalled against the devil, with the symbol R (RAD) leading:

> Đonne hiene on unðanc RAD ieorrenga geseceð,
> boc-stafa brego, bregdeð sona
> feond be ðam feaxe.

> (lines 98–100)

Furiously RAD [the rune R], prince of written symbols, drags at once the fiend by the hair.

In the second and larger part, which is a separate poem (lines 179–506) Saturn, now a different person from the Chaldean magician of the earlier piece, conducts a regular dialogue with Solomon, in which weighty and learned matters are canvassed: and it may be said that the dialogue form, inherited from Latin, is here fully employed. Moreover, here the suggestion of a dialogue debate, or *disputatio*, found rarely and only partially in Old English (as in *Soul and Body*), is fully carried through. In both poems Solomon, who represents Christian learning, and Saturn, who stands nearer to pagan and Oriental lore, hold a debate, though only in the second and superior piece is this idea fully realized. This second poem is on a higher literary level than the first, and shows some poetic feeling for Nature as well as imagination. After the first poem in the principal manuscript there is a fragment of verse that seems only loosely

---

[1] They are to be found in ASPR VI, pp. 31–48. There is a particularly scholarly and attractive separate edition, *The Poetical Dialogues of Solomon and Saturn*, ed. Robert Menner (New York, 1941).

apposite, followed by the gap of a lost leaf: then comes the fragment of a prose dialogue which adds a good deal to the traditional magical lore of the poems. This piece had not been published between its inclusion in John Kemble's learned survey edition *Anglo-Saxon Dialogues of Salomon and Saturn* of 1848[1] and its inclusion a century after in Menner's edition. Behind the poems of *Solomon and Saturn* there evidently lies a folk-tale of a contest between Solomon and some kind of demon, known in several European versions of the poem as Marculf; and there seems to be evidence of some more remote Jewish and Arabic influences in the development of this folk-tale, of which the Anglo-Saxon material provides the earliest known form. Indeed, these pieces furnish much material for the study of Old English and Germanic folklore, and the Christianization of Germanic magic.

Solomon and Saturn, which treats of the magical powers of the runes of the *Pater Noster* in its first part, ends this with an account of how runes may be employed to effect magical results when cut on the weapons of battle[2]: and in the second poem there is a good deal in the dialogue of ingenious riddling. Both these features, runic lore and riddling, are joined again in the *Rune Poem*, though this probably originated rather earlier than *Solomon and Saturn*. This piece, of 94 lines, survives only through a printing by George Hickes of 1705, as its only known manuscript was burned in the fire which destroyed so much of the Cotton collection in 1731, and its text seems to have been a good deal corrupted and manipulated.[3] It gives in a series of 29 metrical sentences the meaning, with some comments, of each of the runes of the Anglo-Saxon *futhorc* or list of runic symbols in a style often much the same as that of a riddle. Indeed, it may be that originally these sentences were intended as riddles, the answers to which were the respective rune-words: the runic symbols themselves appear not to have been in the original poem, but were added by Hickes from another manuscript. As it parallels much of the larger *Solomon and Saturn* poem in its riddling manner, so too the *Rune Poem* abounds in runic lore which is of immense interest to the historian and the folklorist. Thus at lines 10–11 we learn that an originally Germanic god OS—the name of the later Old English O-rune—'was the originator of all speech': we are reminded that according to Old Norse tradition it was Óðinn (Woden) who invented runes and the art of writing. From lines 13–15 on the rune RAD we learn the double meaning of this word. For RAD, literally "riding", originally referred to the rhythmic movement of a rider on horseback, and hence stands here for the rhythm of music:

---

[1] Printed for the Ælfric Society in three parts (London 1845–46, 1848). The prose dialogue is on pp. 178–192.

[2] Lines 161–169.

[3] ASPR VI, pp. 28–30, with bibliographical details on pp. xlvi–l.

RAD byþ on recyde rinca gehwylcum
sefte, ond swiþ-hwæt ðam ðe sitteþ on ufan
meare mægen-heardum ofer mil-paþas.

(lines 13-15)

The rhythm of music [RAD] is to every man a pleasant thing in a hall,
and riding [RAD again] is a very strenuous matter to him who sits
on a mighty powerful steed as he gallops over the miles.[1]

Besides the usual kennings, the *Rune Poem* occasionally shows flashes
of true poetic quality. Thus in his handling of the rune LAGU,
'water', the poet dwells with vivid feeling on sea-voyaging, somewhat in the manner of *The Seafarer*.[2] Here the ship—*brim-hengest*
'stallion of the sea'—'does not heed the bridle'.

Evidently this piece is in part the result of some antiquarian interest
in the scop, who revives for his purpose older material from Germanic tradition. Here too the ancient Germanic deity who appears as
Tiw in Old English and whose name survives in Tuesday makes
an appearance as TIR, the T-rune: the auspicious potentialities of
the arrowhead-shaped symbol of this war-god are emphasized,
though the exact form of the name has become assimilated to the
word *tir*, 'glory'.

Two heterogeneous collections of *Gnomic Verses* called *Maxims*
in *The Anglo-Saxon Poetic Records* survive, apart from occasional
examples intercalated into other poems, such as those which link
the two main parts of *The Wanderer* or occur as moralizing comments in
Beowulf. One of these, known as the *Exeter Gnomes* or *Maxims*,
extends to 204 lines in the Exeter Book, while the other, the *Cotton
Maxims*, only 66 lines, is so called because it occurs in a Cottonian
manuscript of the *Anglo-Saxon Chronicle* from the eleventh century,
Cotton Tiberius B I in the British Museum. The longer collection
of Exeter *Maxims* is edited in volume III of *The Anglo-Saxon Poetic
Records* as *Maxims I*, the shorter and possibly later Cotton collection
being edited in volume VI of this series as *Maxims II*.

Gnomic verses or gnomes are pieces of universally accepted knowledge in the form of versified sentences, including also aphorisms,
moral maxims, and pieces of traditional lore of the nursery rhyme
type. The *Cotton Maxims* consist of a series of gnomes or maxims
followed from line 54 by a kind of pious Christian epilogue which
shows something of the elegiac poetic quality:

A sceal snotor hycgean
ymb þisse worulde gewinn, wearð hangian,

[1] On the meanings of *rad* cf. Caroline Brady "The Old English Nominal
Compounds in *rad-*", *Publications of the Modern Language Association of America*,
LXVII (1952), pp. 538-572.
[2] Lines 63-66.

fægere ongildan þæt he ær facen dyde
manna cynne. Meotod ana wat
hwyder seo sawul sceal syððan hweorfan,
and ealle þa gastas þe for Gode hweorfað
æfter deað-dæge, domes bidað,
on Fæder fæðme. Is seo forð-gesceaft
digol ond dyrne; Dryhten ana wat,
nergende Fæder. Næni eft cymeð
hider under hrofas, þe þæt her for soð
mannum secge hwylc sy Meotodes gesceaft,
sige-folca gesetu, þær he sylfa wunað.

(lines 54–66)

Always a wise man ought to think of the turmoil of this world. A criminal should be hanged so as to pay handsomely for the wickedness that he formerly did to mankind. The Creator alone knows whither the soul must afterwards depart, and all the spirits who will go before God after their death-day, when they shall await judgment in the embrace of the Father. Mysterious and secret is the future. Only the Lord knows this, He who is the saviour and Father. No one shall come again hither to the dwellings of men who might be able of a truth to tell them of what kind is the nature of the Creator, and what are the dwellings of the victorious peoples where He Himself abides.

The interest of these gnomic verses is mainly in the light they may throw on native folklore and traditional patterns of thinking, though, like most Anglo-Saxon verse, they inextricably blend elements of ancient pre-Christian tradition with Christian piety. Typical maxims are the opening lines of *Maxims II*.

Cyning sceal rice healdan. Ceastra beoð feorran gesyne,
orðanc enta geweorc, þa þe on þyssan eorðan syndon,
wrætlic weall-stana geweorc. Wind byð on lyfte swiftust,
þunar byð þragum hludast. Þrymmas syndan Cristes myccle,
wyrd byð swiðost.

(lines 1–5)

A king should keep his realm. (Roman) citadels are visible from afar, those ancient dwellings in the work of giants. These ruined remains are wondrous fortresses of stone walls. Wind is the swiftest thing in the air: sometimes thunder is the loudest. Great are the glorious powers of Christ. Fate is mightiest.

The Exeter Gnomes, or *Maxims I*, are in three sections or *fitts* in the manuscript, and are even more heterogeneous than *Maxims II*. But they show no marked poetic quality. However, in them there are perhaps more of the gnomic traces of ancient oral tradition. They begin with the statement that 'skilful men are in the habit of making

alliterative verses': and from then on the compiler seems merely to
have set down whatever occurred to him of the heterogeneous gnomic
and sententious material he remembered. The mention of the
building of a ship, for instance, suggests to him the famous lines on
the return of the sailor to his Frisian wife (lines 94–99) which have
been noticed earlier as one of the very rare approaches to love-
poetry. *Maxims II*, which occur in the same hand as *The Menologium* and *The Anglo-Saxon Chronicle* in MS. Cotton Tiberius B I
as mentioned above, seem to have been regarded along with the
poetic Church calendar as a kind of preamble to the *Chronicle*: and
with their religious epilogue show a slight sense of form, whereas
Maxims I are a mere string of disconnected gnomic statements.

Both sets of *Maxims* must have been compiled by ecclesiastics,
in view of the Christian and sometimes learned piety which they
display beside the traditional lore. No dates can be assigned to them,
since much of the matter clearly is an inheritance from the earliest
Anglo-Saxon times and some of it is pre-Christian, while some of
the sententious moralizing is evidently of the period of the Old English
homilies of the tenth century. In the compilations of such mixed
material as appears in the extant texts we seem to have incomplete
and more or less casual collections of *memorabilia* assembled for
purposes of edification, both secular and religious. Though we may
not now detect much aesthetic appeal in these writings, it is to be
remembered that the Anglo-Saxons found genuine entertainment
as well as edification in the hearing of moral aphorisms and *senten-
tiae*, as is shown by their sporadic inclusion even in *Beowulf*.

The use of charms or magic incantations as remedies against
natural disasters, diseases, or hostile witchcraft, or as general pro-
tectives, was doubtless among the Germanic cultural inheritances
brought to Britain by the Anglo-Saxons. Following the advice of
St Gregory the Great to St Augustine of Canterbury to use latitude
in adapting pagan religious practices to Christian purposes, we find
preserved often in medical—especially herbal—recipes in religious
houses, in manuscripts of the tenth and eleventh centuries, some
twelve metrical charms intercalated among prose ceremonial directions and related matter. These *Charms*, in which commonly the
pagan traditional magic has been largely Christianized, while retaining
its basic character, naturally have little poetic quality that we can
now appreciate, since their primary purposes were practical and
curative. Their interest lies rather in their irregular metres, which
look back to oral traditions older than those of classical Anglo-
Saxon poetry, in their rare material for the student of cultural anthro-
pology, and often in an unexpected freshness and vitality. It is not
always easy to distinguish between these verse-incantations and their
prose accompaniment, but twelve *Charms* are usually recognized,
and these are printed with numbers from 1 to 12 instead of titles in

the *Minor Poems*, volume VI of *The Anglo-Saxon Poetic Records*. They appear, together with translations, prefaced by an essay on this type of magic, in Gottfrid Storms' *Anglo-Saxon Magic* (The Hague, 1948).[1]

The fullest of these *Charms* is an *æcer-bot* or 'remedy for cultivated land', found in MS. Cotton Caligula A VII in the British Museum. With elaborate prose ceremonial directions, it has four verse incantations against infertile land, which disaster might be the result of enemy witchcraft and poison. It is clearly an inheritance from ancient fertility cult practices, but is entirely Christianized externally while retaining its basic pagan magic. The Trinity is first invoked, with prayer to the Blessed Virgin: and the singing is then required of the *Sanctus*, *Benedicite*, and *Magnificat*, with three *Pater Nosters*. Evidently a priest is thought of as participating, as Latin names and phrases are employed, and Masses are to be sung later over selected representative sods from the affected land and its products. The names of the four Evangelists are also to be used for magical purposes. The sign of the Cross too is to be extensively employed. But some lines clearly recall the inherited pagan fertility rites, as in the famous line.

> "Erce, Erce, Erce, eorþan modor"

in which a goddess Erce is invoked as 'mother of earth'. The exordium of the incantation has a dignity which reminds one of a priest's prayer before celebrating Mass, and may indeed have been modelled on this:

> "Eastweard ic stande, arena ic me bidde,
> bidde ic þone mæran domine, ic bidde ðone miclan drihten,
> bidde ic ðone haligan heofon-rices weard,
> eorðan ic bidde and upheofon
> and ða soþan sancta Marian,
> and heofones meaht and heah-reced,
> þæt ic mote þis gealdor mid gife drihtnes
> toðum ontynan þurh trumne geþanc,
> aweccan þas wæstmas us to woruld-nytte,
> gefyllan þas foldan mid fæste geleafan,
> wlitigigan þas wanc-turf, swa se witiga cwæð
> þæt se hæfde are on eorþ-rice, se þe ælmyssan
> dælde domlice drihtnes þances."

> (lines 26–38)

"I stand at the East, and I pray for mercies. I pray the glorious Lord, the great ruler, the holy Guardian of the heavenly kingdom [in a formula reminiscent of *Cædmon's Hymn*]. I pray to the earth and

---

[1] The fullest study with text of the *Charms* is still F. Grendon, "*The Anglo-Saxon Charms*", in *The American Journal of Folk-lore* for 1909, reprinted separately for the second time (New York, 1930).

to heaven above and to the true Santa Maria, to the might of heaven and the sky above, that I may by the Lord's Grace open this magic charm with my teeth in firm mind. I pray that I may thus rouse up these crops for use in the world, fill this earth in firm faith, make beautiful these grassy plains, since the Prophet said that man should find mercy on earth who nobly distributed alms through the Lord's Grace."

Five of the *Charms* are in an Old English manuscript Herbal of the eleventh century, which includes a number of medical recipes with the incantations. These, in MS. Harley 585 in the British Museum, are often called by the Old English term *Lacnunga*, 'healings'. Of these the most interesting are the famous *Nine Herbs Charm*, and that apparently against lumbago caused by the action of witchcraft or elves. This, with the title "For a sudden stitch", is No. 4 in the edition of the *Charms* in ASPR VI.

First, in this fourth Charm, feverfew, nettle, and dock are to be boiled in butter; and at the end a knife covered in this concoction is to be applied to the afflicted part. But within this framework of a mixture of empirical knowledge and magic there are two incantations. In the first the witches are flatteringly described:

> Hlude wæran hy, la, hlude, ða hy ofer þone hlæw ridan,
> wæran an-mode, ða hy ofen land ridan.
>
> (lines 3–4)

Loud were they, yea, loud, as they rode over the hill: resolute they were as they rode over the land.

Then the magic of the refrain is used:

> "Scyld ðu ðe nu, þu ðysne nið genesan mote.
> Ut, lytel spere, gif ðu her inne sie"
>
> (lines 5–6)

"Now protect thyself and thou mayst escape this enmity: out, little spear, if thou beest herein."

Then in the second part the charmer describes how he stood beneath a linden shield and watched how those magic women prepared their devices and sent shrieking darts at the victim. The remedy is homeopathic, as he now sends a similar dart from his side and repeats the refrain: *Ut, lytel spere, gif ðu her inne sie.* Smiths at their wicked work are matched by the charmer with parallel methods and the refrain is again repeated. Whatever be the cause of the trouble, whether the shot of witches or gods or elves, and wherever the darts have penetrated, the incantation will be effective. Then finally the wizard who is working the magic commands the wicked spirit to flee to the mountain-top (the proper place for a witch), and cries to the patient: "Be thou whole; may the Lord give thee his help". In the end a knife is to be applied: and one is reminded of the rustic practice still occasionally to be met with in England of setting the blade of a knife covered in butter to a bruise. Much of the incantatory part of this charm is in epic style, which is exceptional in the *Charms*. The 'elf-shot' mentioned as a likely cause of the pain is paralleled in some remote rural areas of Northern England, where the flint arrow-head occasionally picked up is called an 'elf-shot', and one afflicted with lumbago is said to be 'elf-shotten'.

MS. Royal 12 D XVII in the British Museum is the oldest and most copious collection of medical recipes in Old English. It belongs to the tenth century. In it is one charm, against some kind of disease caused by a 'water elf'. The magic herbal treatment and incantation prescribed is called a *lǽcedom*, 'medical prescription'. This collection of medical lore has a manuscript title *Lǽceboc*, 'book of medicine'.

In MS. Corpus Christi College, Cambridge, 41, in the same hand that copied its portion of *Solomon and Saturn*, there are four charms. They deal respectively with the swarming of bees, the theft and the loss of cattle, and with magical protection on taking a journey. The seriousness with which magic under Christian auspices was treated by some ecclesiastics at least is suggested by the fact that this codex, which includes both part of *Solomon and Saturn* and four charms, is chiefly a copy of the Old English version of Bede's *Historia Ecclesiastica*. Of these charms the incantation for catching and keeping a swarm of bees, No. 8 in the *Minor Poems* text, is of most interest, and in several ways it parallels that against the stitch or lumbago. Witches have seduced the swarm of bees, who are possessed by them. So the charmer addresses the witch-bees flatteringly:

> "Sitte ge, sige-wif, sigað to eorþan:
> næfre ge wilde to wuda fleogan."
> (lines 9–10)

"Sit ye, victorious magic women: sink down to earth. Never flee wildly to the forest."

This is to be said as the bees are swarming away. Tribute is here paid to the immense universal magical powers of earth.

Of interest for its metre, which is something like the doggerel of a nursery rhyme, is the charm for getting rid of a 'wen' or tumour surviving in MS. Royal 4 A XIV in the British Museum, and numbered 12 in the printed text. It is in a very late eleventh-century hand with an almost early Middle English spelling, and begins thus:

> "Wenne, wenne, wenchichenne,
> her ne scealt þu timbrien, ne nenne tun habben."

"O wen, O wen, tiny little wen, here shalt thou not build nor have any dwelling."

With the exception of one version of a riddle of St Aldhelm which exists in early Northumbrian as well as in the Exeter Book, all the *Riddles* are in that manuscript, and there are ninety-five of them. They are of very varying character, date, and origin, and they touch upon almost every aspect of nature, the daily life of the Anglo-Saxon people, folklore and learning. They also make a good deal of use of the lore of runes. The *Riddles* vary greatly in length. St Aldhelm's Latin riddle *De Creatura* has been expanded and elaborated to make an Old English riddle of 108 lines (No. 40), whereas No. 76 consists of a single line—though this may be only the beginning of a lost riddle.

The practice of making ingenious riddles in Latin verse, which was highly developed among Alcuin and his associates during the Carolingian Renaissance at the close of the eighth century and in the early ninth, had arrived a good deal earlier in Britain with the Irish missionary teachers of the seventh. St Aldhelm, who probably inherited a love of strange knowledge and ingenious verbal gymnastics from his Irish master, included a series of a hundred Latin riddles in a letter on the art of metrics addressed to the Northumbrian king Aldfrith so famed for his learning at the close of the seventh century.[1] Bede practised the riddling art in Latin, as did his friend Eusebius and Archbishop Tætwine of Canterbury, his contemporary. Later in the eighth century St Boniface too practised this art. Often such Latin riddles were exercises in the metrical art merely; but many of them also provide much information on the daily life and customs of the time.[2]

The earliest surviving riddle in Old English is a free translation of one of St Aldhelm's century of *Aenigmata*, No. 33, on the *lorica* or mail-coat, which exists in an eighth-century version in the Northumbrian dialect in a ninth-century copy now in the University Library at Leiden. A version in the usual Late West-Saxon language also appears in the Exeter Book, where it is No. 35 among the first major group of *Riddles*. The Northumbrian so-called *Leiden Riddle* could be early enough to be the work of St Aldhelm; but its being Northumbrian and not West-Saxon would seem to preclude this possibility.[3] This *Leiden Riddle*, with its later version in the Exeter Book, looks back to the eighth century, and this may be taken as about the time at which the practice of vernacular riddling began: it would seem to have continued almost up to the time when the Exeter Book was brought together in its present form at the close of the tenth century. This riddle, in which St Aldhelm's elaborate lines on the *lorica* are simplified, retains much of the form that was to become

[1] St Aldhelm's *Riddles* are edited with translation by J. H. Pitman (Yale Studies in English, 1925).

[2] For a fine and thorough study of the Latin riddles of England and their influence, see Erika von Erhardt-Siebold, *Die lateinischen Rätsel der Angelsachsen* (Heidelberg, 1925).

[3] *The Leiden Riddle* is edited in ASPR VI, p. 109.

typical of the Old English *Riddles*. The subject of the riddle, a coat of mail (Old English *byrne*), speaks in its own person, describes its attributes—and what it is not—and then asks the listener to 'say what this garment is'. The prosopopoeia, inherited from Latin usage, is common in the *Riddles*, where it no doubt is employed in following the Latin models. Here is this riddle, in the Exeter Book version:

> "Mec se wæta wong, wundrum freorig,
> of his innaþe ærist cende.
> Ne wat ic mec beworhtne wulle flysum,
> hærum þurh heah-cræft, hyge-þoncum min.
> Wundene me ne beoð wefle, ne ic wearp hafu,
> ne þurh þreata geþræcu þræd me ne hlimmeð,
> ne æt me hrutende hrisil scriþeð,
> ne mec ohwonan sceal am cnyssan.
> Wyrmas mec ne awæfan wyrda cræftum,
> þa þe geolo god-webb geatwum frætwað.
> Wile mec mon hwæþre seþeah wide ofer eorþan
> hatan for hæleþum hyhtlic gewæde.
> Saga soð-cwidum, searo-þoncum gleaw,
> wordum wisfæst, hwæt þis gewæde sy."

"The wet plain, wondrous cold, first brought me forth from its inward parts. I do not know myself to have been worked over with a covering of the fleeces of wool, with hairs by supreme skill, in the thoughts of my mind. Wefts are not twisted for me, nor do I have a warp, nor does the thread resound for me in its crowded movements, nor for me shall the weaver's shuttle throb from any direction. Silk-worms have not woven for me with their fateful devisings, those which adorn the yellow royal robe with trappings. Nevertheless far and wide over the earth they call me a joyful garment before men. You who are cunning in skilful thoughts, speak wisely and in true words say what this garment is."

This use of prosopopoeia, by which a personified inanimate object is made to speak, is found in other Old English poems, notably *The Dream of the Rood*: and with this latter may be compared Riddle 30a and 30b, two versions of the same theme, which seems again to make the Cross, its subject, speak personally.

The Exeter Book *Riddles* are in two main groups, from 1 to 59, and from 61 to 95, these two divisions being separated in the manuscript by *The Wife's Lament*, a group of religious poems, *The Husband's Message*, and *The Ruin*. Riddle 60, treating apparently of a piece of wood bearing a runic message between two intimates, immediately precedes *The Husband's Message*, and is thus isolated from the main groups, unless one takes it as the introduction to *The Husband's Message*, as some have done. But, as has been suggested earlier, the 'Message' seems to have been carried by a trusted retainer and not to have been inscribed in runes on a piece of wood.

The subjects of the *Riddles* are very varied, as is their length and treatment. Natural phenomena are featured, such as tempest, winter, and ice; also weapons such as sword and bow, and things from life in hall such as the favourite honey-drink, mead, and the harp. Then there are the marvels of God's creation, such as sun and moon, and birds like the cuckoo and the raven. There are themes from varied aspects of the life of the time—a Bible codex, the worm that eats books, and the seller of onions. While most of these *Riddles* are ingenious exercises in the usual alliterative metre, occasionally there is true poetic descriptive power in dealing with Nature.

Indeed, most of the poetic power in the *Riddles* is found in descriptions of the sea. This theme, which in all its aspects is here and there touched upon in the *Riddles*, had always a special fascination for the Anglo-Saxon poets. We have already noticed the power of descriptions of sea-voyages in *Beowulf*, *Elene*, and *Andreas*, besides the outstanding qualities in *The Seafarer*: and it has been seen that almost the slightest opportunity seems to provoke the Old English poet to dwell on matters of the sea, so that there is an astonishingly wide and varied poetic vocabulary for all that pertains to it. A few of the more significant of the *Riddles* may now be looked at by way of clearer illustration.

The first three Riddles, as printed in *The Anglo-Saxon Poetic Records*, volume III (the Exeter Book), treat of storm in many aspects, but especially various types of sea-tempest. The third Riddle, which extends to 74 lines, has magnificent descriptions of storms at sea and of the battling of sailors and ships with them. Its images are bold and sharp-edged, and its 'flint-grey flood' becomes immensely vivid:

"Hwilum ic sceal ufan yþa wregan,
streamas styrgan ond to staþe þywan
flint-grægne flod. Famig winneð
wæg wið wealle, wonn ariseð
dun ofer dype; hyre deorc on last,
eare geblonden, oþer fereð,
þæt hy gemittað mearc-londe neah
hea hlincas. Þær bið hlud wudu,
brim-giesta breahtm, bidað stille
stealc stan-hleoþu stream-gewinnes,
hop-gehnastes, þonne heah geþring
on cleofu crydeþ. Þær bið ceole wen
sliþre sæcce, gif hine sæ byreð
on þa grimman tid, gæsta fulne,
þæt he scyle rice birofen weorþan,
feore bifohten fæmig ridan
yþa hrycgum. Þær bið egsa sum

æ̆ldum geywed, þara þe ic hyran sceal
strong on stið-weg. Hwa gestilleð þæt?"
(Riddle 3, lines 17–36)

"At times I [the storm] will stir up the waves from above and set in tumult its currents as I thrust its flint-grey flood on to the shore. The foam-crested wave wrestles with the sea-wall as it rears up, dark and fallow over the deep. Then darkly in its wake there comes on a mass of turbid water, so that the mountainous eddies smite together close to the shore. There the sound of a ship and the noise of its sailors is heard. Then for a moment the precipitous rocky cliffs seem to await the water's mighty onrush in their tumultuous mass as the huge swirling mole of water crashes its way on to the cliffs. There any ship may look for dire strife if in that grim hour the sea is carrying it, filled with human lives: for then it becomes utterly helpless and bereft of its life as, covered in foam, it rides the hills of the waves. Then it is that mighty terror is manifested to men whom I hear striving on the vast and stubborn seas. Who shall quieten that?"

As in the description of the voyage over the Red Sea in *Exodus*, the vocabulary and imagery are highly individual and often strange, so that no translation can be anything like exact. Yet something of the extraordinary vitality and power of this poet's storm-descriptions may be glimpsed.

Typical of these collections in general are the riddles of the swan (No. 7) and the cuckoo (No. 9), in which the well-known and traditional attributes of the birds are fancifully yet clearly set out in graceful short poems. In Riddle 14 the various uses of the horn, in peace and in war, for the mead-drinking in hall or at sea, are explained poetically, but with the echo of a very ancient folk-practice at the close. The listener is told in a formula as old as the Vedic Hymns of the ancient Hindus (in which riddles occasionally appear) *Frige hwæt ic hatte*: "Ask what I am called."

It was a recognized feature of a riddle that its solution might be difficult or that it could be the deliberate setting of a puzzle to test ingenuity. Hence the use of runes and the making of a cryptogram. No. 23, to which the answer is a bow, Old English *boga*, gives its solution in its first word: but this word is spelled backward, and with the *b* of *boga* replaced by *f* (a kind of interchange not unknown in early manuscripts). So the riddle begins: '*Agof* [*boga*] is my name'. Riddle 75, which is merely a one-line statement obviously referring to a hunting-dog, tells the reader (here a reader rather than a listener must be assumed) that: 'I saw a swift hound journeying as it was tracking.' But here the word for hound, Old English *hund*, is written backward and in runes: and there is the further complication— whether accidental or intended—that the word is spelled DNLH. If we replace the rune for L by a U, we get DNUH, or HUND backward. This last also provides an instance of the practice sometimes resorted to in the *Riddles* of stating the answer to the problem in the opening line. No. 47 is a famous illustration of this. It is on a book-moth, and opens with the statement that 'a moth ate words'. Like several others in the Exeter Book collections of a more academic kind, this is an adaptation from Latin, as it freely adapts the idea of Symphosius' Aenigma 16, *Tinea*.[1] Its word-play is a good instance of a common scholarly pastime then:

> Moððe word fræt. Me þæt þuhte
> wrætlicu wyrd, þa ic þæt wundor gefrægn,
> þæt se wyrm forswealg wera gied sumes,
> þeof in þystro, þrymfæstne cwide
> ond þæs strangan staþol. Stæl-giest ne wæs
> wihte þy gleawra, þe he þam wordum swealg.

A moth was eating words. That seemed to me a strange happening when I heard about that marvel, that the worm had swallowed the poem of a notable man, a glorious utterance which had given strength to the strong, like a thief in the darkness. The thieving visitant was no whit the wiser by having swallowed those words.

While the normal metre is used generally in the *Riddles*, all sorts of ingenious devices are to be met with in what may be termed 'sound-play', such as the use of onomatopoeia and the suggestion of a theme by choosing words that bring to the mind of the auditors the exact sound of what is being described. Riddle 57, though its exact solution may remain uncertain, is probably an example of deliberate onomatopoeia:

> Ðeos lyft byreð lytle wihte
> ofer beorg-hleoþa. Þa sind blace swiþe,
> swearte salo-pade. Sanges rope
> heapum ferað, hlude cirmað,
> tredað bearo-næssas, hwilum burg-salo
> niþþa bearna. *Nemnað hy sylfe.*

This air carries little creatures over the slopes of the hills. These have coats that are very dark, black or yellow. Copious in song, they travel in flocks and are birds with loud cries. They move among wooded headlands, and sometimes in the halls of men. *They name themselves.*

Now, the final sentence clearly tells us that the noise these birds make is at the same time the name by which they are known. As they fly they utter their name. The best suggestion so far made is that the birds are Cornish choughs. For Ælfric has left us in his *Grammar*[2]

---

[1] Symphosius's *Aenigmata* are to be found with translation of the Latin in *The Enigmas of Symphosius*, ed. R. T. Ohl (Philadelphia, 1928).

[2] *Ælfrics Grammatik und Glossar*, ed. Julius Zupitza (Berlin, 1880), p. 307 note. Here *ceo* is spelled *cheo: Cornicula cheo*, the common later orthography.

an Old English word *ceo*, 'chough': and one can well believe that the creatures of Riddle 57 cry something sounding like *"ceo, ceo, ceo"* as they fly.

No. 28, on the making of a harp, is an astonishing instance of suggesting the quality of the musical instrument by choosing repetitive sounds only very loosely related to meaning:

> Corfen, sworfen, cyrred, þyrred,
> bunden, wunden, blæced, wæced,
> frætwed, geatwed, feorran læded
> to durum dryhta.
> (Riddle 28, lines 4–7)

Cut and curved, turned round and dried, bound and twisted, bleached, softened, adorned and ornamented, brought from afar to the dwellings of noble warriors.

Folklore is plentifully touched on in these *Riddles*. The most poetical instance of this is in the Sun and Moon riddle, No. 29. But enough has been said to give some idea of the amazing variety of the Exeter Book collections. As is natural in pieces intended to provide puzzles and learned or popular ingenuity, there is a good deal that must remain obscure in these poems, since we lack the key which a knowledge of Anglo-Saxon daily life provided for the intended auditors or readers. The text too is often apparently corrupt: and especially in the latter group of *Riddles* there are *lacunae* and evidence of casual or hasty copying.

CHAPTER 11

Later Heroic Poetry and 'Occasional Verse'

THE ANGLO-SAXON HEROIC TRADITION evidently continued to be at least sporadically productive in its later period, though relatively little has survived. Some tolerably correct verse was still being written even up till the later tenth century by religious, apart from those on heroic themes now to be discussed. For at St Augustine's Abbey in Canterbury there appeared about that time the *Kentish Hymn* and the *Kentish Psalm*, surviving in a mixed West-Saxon and Kentish dialect in MS. Vespasian D VI in the Cotton collection in the British Museum.[1] The *Hymn*, 43 lines, which seems to be a carefully constructed composition, follows the rules of Beowulfian metre very well; and the *Kentish Psalm* which expands the Vulgate Psalm 50 (51 in the King James Bible), *Miserere mei Deus*, into 157 lines, has an introduction quite in the old heroic style and diction explaining David as the heroic penitent. Of heroic poetry proper, spanning the tenth century, three examples remain: *Judith*, *The Battle of Brunanburh*, and *The Battle of Maldon*. But that there were once heroic cycles, especially of the more popular kind, may be inferred from occasional references in Anglo-Latin writers. *Judith*, which presents in epic heroic style the exploit of the Hebrew heroine in slaying Holofernes and freeing her people from Assyrian oppression, belongs clearly to the heroic Anglo-Saxon tradition, although its subject-matter is taken from the Vulgate Bible. *The Battle of Brunanburh* is an exultant scop's glorification of the historic victory of King Athelstan in 937 over the Irish Norsemen and their allies. *The Battle of Maldon*, which is often thought of as the finest of Old English heroic poems, describes the battle at Maldon in 991 in which the East Saxons showed supreme heroism in the noblest tradition of Germanic valour when they were defeated by the Vikings.

Judith is in the Beowulf manuscript, Cotton Vitellius A XV, in which it immediately follows *Beowulf* in the same hand as the later portion of that poem. *Judith*, which extends, with an incomplete initial line, to 349 lines, has after the first fourteen a series of three Roman marginal numerals X, XI, XII, such as normally indicate the

---

[1] Edited in ASPR VI, pp. 87–94.

division of a poem into sections, or fitts: and from this arrangement it seems that the whole piece was originally conceived as having twelve fitts, each of about 100 or more lines, of which only the last fourteen and a half lines of fitt IX and fitts X, XI, and XII survive. Thus it would appear that the original poem ran to some 1200 or 1300 lines, of which little more than a quarter remains. This view is supported by the appearance of the manuscript which seems to indicate that a number of leaves, immediately preceding the truncated *Judith*, are lost. On the other hand, a similarity between the opening words of the poem as we have it and its closing lines—both of which emphasize the heroine's confidence in the Grace of God—might suggest that what we have is practically the whole poem, with the loss of only a few opening words, and that the apparent sectional or fitt numbers refer not to this poem alone, but to a larger group of which *Judith* was the last, for such an extension of the fitt-numbering to cover several poems can be paralleled.

While the appearance of the manuscript seems to indicate that only the last quarter or so of the poem remains, there are literary and aesthetic reasons for accepting *Judith* almost as it stands as a complete whole. *Judith* is a poetic dramatization of the crises or highlights of the career of the Hebrew heroine based on the Vulgate version of the Old Testament Book of Judith. Very freely adapting, contracting, expanding, and adding, the poet in the extant *Judith* begins with her planned visit to the camp of the Assyrian general Holofernes and ends with her triumphant return to her native city of Bethulia with the head of the slaughtered general, her rousing of her people to battle, and the glorious defeat and utter spoliation of the heathen foe by the Hebrews under her leadership. Judith's fine hymn of praise and thanksgiving for victory, which is in Chapter 16 of the Vulgate *Judith* and still has a place in the Roman Breviary, is not touched. The Latin material is only used from Chapter 12, verse 10 to the end of Chapter 15. Now, it may well be that, as with the poet of *Exodus*, the author of *Judith* deliberately selected that part of the heroine's life which lent itself to epic and vividly dramatic treatment. For it is difficult to see much material suitable for such a poem in the earlier chapters of the Book of Judith, or in its brief account of Judith's closing years. Had the poet in fact made the complete Book of Judith into a poetic whole, it is difficult to see how he could have avoided many dull passages: and from what we know of this poet he was not the man to have done this. He was a man of fine imagination and vivid dramatic sense who loved to use the epic heroic tradition at its best. But there can yet be no final judgment on the question of how much is lost from the surviving *Judith*.

Limiting the number of characters to three—Judith, Holofernes, and Judith's maid—the poet has given an impression of concentrated vigour and freshness. The images and the personalities are sharpened: Holofernes becomes a diabolical fiend and monster of cruel lust, while

Judith, 'a maiden beautiful as a fairy' (*ides ælfscinu*, 14), is given the most vigorous qualities of a saint. A canopy (*canopeum*) which was over the bed of Holofernes, mentioned in the Vulgate without comment (Chapter X, 19), is treated imaginatively by our poet. The Biblical account has simply:

> Now Holofernes rested upon his bed under a canopy, which was woven with purple and gold and emeralds and precious stones.[1]

The *Judith* poet entirely transforms the idea and expands it in a quite original way with a touch of Oriental knowledge:

> Þær wæs eall-gylden
> fleoh-net fæger ymbe þæs folc-togan
> bed ahongen, þæt se beado-fulla
> mihte wlitan þurh, wigena baldor,
> on æghwylcne þe ðær inne com
> hæleða bearna, ond on hyne nænig
> monna cynnes, nymðe se modiga hwæne
> niðe rofra him þe near hete
> rinca to rune gegangan.
>
> (lines 46–54)

There was a beautiful fly-net made all of gold thread hung around the bed of the general. This was in such wise that the evil creature who was leader of the warriors could look through upon every one of the children of men who should come into the room, while no one of the race of men could look in on him unless that proud one should have summoned some of those renowned warriors to come close to him for a private council.

Again, Judith in the prayer she makes as she prepares to kill Holofernes introduces an invocation to the Trinity, for which, of course, there is no basis in the Vulgate (lines 83–86). This last piece of definitely later Christianity reminds us of the generally later character of this poem. Its metre shows signs of later licence, with its occasionally introduced internal rhymes and its abundance of expanded verses. In fact the general style of this poem suggests a relatively late date—at least, that it is post-Cynewulfian.

The two most outstanding passages treat of Holofernes' drunken feasting, and of the battle in which the Assyrians are utterly shattered after Judith's return to Bethulia. Here we have the ancient epic heroic style at its very best: and either passage may be compared favourably with anything of the kind in Anglo-Saxon poetry. This is the account of Holofernes' feast:

---

[1] Chapter X, 21, in the King James Bible translation among the Apocrypha. The Book of Judith, concerning which St Jerome had doubts because of the absence of a Hebrew text, was accepted as canonical throughout the Middle Ages. It was relegated to the Apocrypha by the Protestant reformers, but remains in the Roman use.

Hie ða to ðam symle sittan eodon,
wlance to win-gedrince, ealle his wea-gesiðas,
bealde byrn-wiggende. Þær wæron bollan steape
boren æfter bencum gelome, swylce eac bunan ond orcas
fulle flet-sittendum; hie þæt fæge þegon,
rofe rond-wiggende, þeah ðæs se rice ne wende,
egesful eorla dryhten. Ða wearð Holofernus,
gold-wine gumena, on gyte-salum,
hloh ond hlydde, hlynede ond dynede,
þæt mihten fira bearn feorran gehyran
hu se stið-moda styrmde ond gylede,
modig ond medu-gal, manode geneahhe
benc-sittende þæt hi gebærdon wel.

(lines 15–27)

Then all those proud warriors, his bold comrades in the disaster which was to come, went to sit at the wine-drinking. There were deep drinking-bowls borne along the benches, and goblets and flagons were carried to the guests who were seated in the hall. Renowned warriors, doomed to death as they were, partook of that, although the mighty one, the terrible lord of men, had no expectation of his fate. Then Holofernes, giver of treasures of gold to men, was in exultant joy as the wine was poured. He laughed and roared, shouted and made vast noises so that the children of men could hear from afar how that tough-hearted one stormed and yelled as he became exuberant as the drink overcame him. Oft did he urge those who were seated on the benches to bear themselves like men in the drinking.

The account of the final battle, with all the panoply of traditional heroic diction, brings too the traditional birds of prey who hover over the field of slaughter:

Þæs se hlanca gefeah
wulf in walde, ond se wanna hrefn,
wæl-gifre fugel. Wistan begen
þæt him ða þeod-guman þohton tilian
fylle on fægum; ac him fleah on last
earn ætes georn, urig-feðera,
salowig-pada sang hilde-leoð,
hyrned-nebba. Stopon heaðo-rincas,
beornas to beadowe, bordum beðeahte,
hwealfum lindum, ða þe hwilum ær
elðeodigra edwit þoledon,
hæðenra hosp. Him þæt hearde wearð
æt ðam æsc-plegan eallum forgolden,
Assyrium, syððan Ebreas

under guð-fanum gegan hæfdon
to ðam fyrd-wicum. Hie ða fromlice
leton forð fleogan flana scuras,
hilde-nædran, of horn-bogan,
strælas stede-hearde; styrmdon hlude
grame guð-frecan, garas sendon
in heardra gemang. Hæleð wæron yrre,
land-buende, laðum cynne,
stopon styrn-mode, sterced-ferhðe,
wrehton unsofte eald-geniðlan
medo-werige; mundum brugdon
scealcas of sceaðum scir-mæled swyrd,
ecgum gecoste, slogon eornoste
Assiria oret-mecgas,
nið-hycgende; nanne ne sparedon
þæs here-folces, heanne ne ricne,
cwicera manna þe hie ofercuman mihton.

(lines 205–235)

At that the lean wolf in the forest and the dark-coated raven rejoiced. Those were the birds so greedy of slaughter. Both knew that the men of the fighting people intended to provide for them their fill in doomed men. And in their track there flew the eagle longing for carrion. Dark-coated, with dewy feathers and horny bill, it sang its song of battle. The warlike fighters advanced to the fray with vaulted linden shields which covered them. These were the Hebrew warriors who erstwhile had suffered the reproaches and scorn of the heathens. To the Assyrians it was grievously requited for all those things, after the Jews, under their banners of war, had advanced to the enemy war-camp. Then it was that they vigorously let fly their war-javelins, those serpents of battle from their bows of horn, those strong and firm arrows in storms. Loudly did those fierce men of battle rage as they sent their spears into the midst of the strong men. Furious were the warlike dwellers in the land against the hated race. Mighty men were stern in heart as the strong-hearted fighters went forward to arouse ungently from sleep their ancient foes now exhausted with drinking of mead. The men drew from their sheaths the brightly adorned swords as with finely tempered sharp-edged weapons they smote the warriors of the Assyrians, their wicked-minded enemies. Not one of the men of that army did they spare of living men, humble nor mighty, whom they might overcome.

No doubt this description of a battle is conventional to heroic poetry, in which such 'beasts of battle' as the eagle, wolf, and raven, are traditional: but it has here a vigour and a vitality unsurpassed anywhere in Old English. Similarly the account of the sending of the soul of the slain Holofernes to hell is conventional to religious verse, but again it shows wonderful freshness:

> Læg se fula leap
> gesne beæftan, gæst ellor hwearf
> under neowelne næs ond þær genyðerad wæs,
> susle gesæled syððan æfre,
> wyrmum bewunden, witum gebunden,
> hearde gehæfted in helle-bryne
> æfter hin-siðe. Ne ðearf he hopian no,
> þystrum forðylmed, þæt he ðonan mote
> of ðam wyrm-sele, ac ðær wunian sceal
> awa to aldre butan ende forð
> in ðam heolstran ham, hyht-wynna leas.

> (lines 111–121)

The foul basket of his carcass lay empty behind: his spirit had departed to another world deep beneath the steep cliff promontory, and there was drawn down to be bound with torments ever after, encompassed with serpents, chained in punishments, grievously fettered in the fire of hell after the journey hence. No need has he, surrounded with darkness, to hope that he may get from thence out of that hall of serpents: but there he must remain for ever and ever in that dark dwelling, eternally without ending, bereft of any hope of joys.

It is not possible to assign anything like an exact date to *Judith*. Its inclusion in the *Beowulf* manuscript suggests that at the close of the tenth century, when this was copied, the poem had already been in existence for a little time. While there are features of its style which remind one of Cynewulf, its metrical character and its tone seem to imply a relatively later date. The vigorous patriotic feeling perhaps parallels the growth of national sentiment which occurred in King Alfred's later years, and again in the early tenth century in the days of Edward the Elder and King Athelstan. The violent zeal against the heathen Assyrians displayed in *Judith* has seemed to many to owe something to these national upsurges against the Vikings. Indeed, Gregory Foster, who made a very thorough study of the poem,[1] believed that its inspiration was the sister to Edward the Elder, the famous "Lady of Mercia", the heroine who led the successful wars against the Danes which captured the Five Towns. This warlike woman, Æthelflæd, might easily have been linked in men's minds with the glorious deeds of the Hebrew Judith. Æthelflæd died in the year 918, so that this hypothesis would place the composition of *Judith* early in the tenth century, which fits well enough with its style and metre. If a date at about 900 or a little after be accepted, what is remarkable is the marvellous vitality and vividness in the application of the old heroic diction to the not very

---

[1] See T. Gregory Foster, *Judith, Studies in Metre, Language and Style* (Strasbourg, 1892).

impressive Vulgate material in such a way as to give the finest epic qualities of Anglo-Saxon poetry at this late date.[1]

It seems that the more settled life in England which followed the victories under Æthelflæd and Edward the Elder over the Danes, itself initiated some revival in courtly and cultivated circles of interest in the older style of heroic verse, with its formulaic diction: and it was no doubt following and developing from such a revival that the preserving of this older poetry as we have it in the four main manuscripts came about near the close of the tenth century, with the inspiration of the Benedictine movement associated with St Dunstan and his colleagues. It was probably because the annals of the *Anglo-Saxon Chronicle* during this period and after were generally meagre and lacking in vitality that poems were added in some of the *Chronicle* manuscripts dealing with events of special interest. While some of these are mere doggerel verse which cannot easily be distinguished from rhythmical prose, there are a few which deliberately follow the ancient traditions of style and diction, keeping carefully to the technical rules of metre, even in times when a very licentious popular fashion of verse was becoming common. These *Chronicle* poems imitating the ancient manner would appeal to a courtly audience or to cultured ecclesiastics with some antiquarian interests. Each of them deals with an event in history in which royal personages play noble parts: so that they may be thought of as belonging to the genre of the panegyric. They are, however, somewhat artificial in their studied revival of the older style and diction: and with their suggestion of a courtly appeal in often sophisticated tones, they are in some respects nearer to the poetry of the Norse skalds[2] than to *Beowulf*. Indeed, they have something in common with the Norse type of poem in praise of a great man called a *drápa*. This last is particularly true of the longest and best of the *Chronicle* poems, *The Battle of Brunanburh*.

This poem, as are all those to be noticed hereafter in this chapter, is edited among the *Anglo-Saxon Minor Poems*. Its 73 lines are an exultant ode of triumph, celebrating the battle in which the English heroes King Athelstan and his brother Edmund defeated in 937 Anlaf (Olaf), the Norse king of Dublin, who was supported by an army of Scandinavian-Irish, Scots, under their aged king Constantine, and Celtic Britons of the district of Strathclyde. As with the other *Chronicle* poems, it is evidently put in to replace the normal jejune annal. The poem abounds in phrases and formulaic expressions from the traditional earlier heroic poetry, in the use of the

---

[1] *Judith* is edited in ASPR IV, pp. 99–109. There is a useful separate edition by B. J. Timmer (London, 1952).

[2] For Skaldic poetry see Lee H. Hollander, *The Skalds* (New York, 1945). Texts are conveniently accessible in Gudbrand Vigfusson and F. York Powell, *Corpus Poeticum Boreale*, vol. II, *Court Poetry* (Oxford, 1883).

stylistic device of parallel variation, and in forms which were by the tenth century archaic or dialectal, but which were felt to be proper to a deliberate revival of the ancient ways of heroic verse, where such forms were probably part of a traditional poetic vocabulary. Of the 146 half-lines in *The Battle of Brunanburh* one-seventh had already occurred in earlier verse. As contrasted with the freer language and considerable metrical licence of the other principal war-poem of the later period, *The Battle of Maldon* (written at the very end of the tenth century), *The Battle of Brunanburh* is always deliberately faithful to the conventions of the older verse, which its author had evidently studied: and it is scrupulously faithful also to the exact classical rules of metre. Some air of artificiality is inevitable in a poem of this type written in a deliberately antique style, nor has it much significant historical value, since the poet is primarily concerned with national glory and making a fine-sounding panegyric of his heroes, rather than using any kind of detailed knowledge of actual happenings. Here again there is a contrast with *The Battle of Maldon*, in which the poet most successfully creates the impression of personal knowledge of his characters and their doings. What gives *The Battle of Brunanburh* its value is the extraordinary vitality and vigour which the poet manages to convey, even with such artificial means. For the literary historian too it is important as a reminder that the ancient ways of verse were effectively revived and cultivated at so late a period. But in fact this kind of courtly verse continued to be produced parallel with the free popular verse right up to the Norman Conquest, as the relative correctness of the *Chronicle* poem on the *Death of Edward the Confessor* clearly demonstrates. *The Battle of Brunanburh* begins thus:

> Her Æþelstan cyning, eorla dryhten,
> beorna beah-gifa, and his broþor eac,
> Eadmund æþeling, ealdor-langne tir
> geslogon æt sæcce sweorda ecgum
> ymbe Brunanburh. Bord-weal clufan,
> heowan heaþo-linde hamora lafan
> afaran Eadweardes, swa him geæþele wæs
> from cneo-mægum, þæt hi æt campe oft
> wiþ laþra gehwæne land ealgodon,
> hord and hamas. Hettend crungun,
> Sceotta leoda and scip-flotan
> fæge feollan, feld dænnede
> secga swate, siðþan sunne up
> on morgen-tid, mære tungol,
> glad ofer grundas, Godes condel beorht,
> eces Drihtnes, oð sio æþele gesceaft
> sah to setle.
>   (lines 1–17)

In this year King Athelstan, lord of men and giver of treasures of gold to warriors, side by side with his noble brother Edmund, gained in battle glory to last for ages by the blows they struck with their edged swords at Brunanburh. They clave the wall of shields, cutting through those linden battle-defences with their finely forged weapons. The sons of Edward, with what they had nobly inherited from their ancestors, once again defended in warfare against every foe their land, their treasure and their homes. Their furious enemies, the Scots and those who had landed in Viking ships, fell, doomed to death as they were. The field of fight was made dark with the blood of warriors after the sun, glorious luminary and candle of God the eternal Lord, in the morning had risen over the plains, until that magnificent orb sank to its resting-place.

The poem ends with an exultant historical flourish:

> Ne wearð wæl mare
> on þis eiglande æfre gieta
> folces gefylled beforan þissum
> sweordes ecgum, þæs þe us secgað bec,
> ealde uðwitan, siþþan eastan hider
> Engle ond Seaxe up becoman,
> ofer brad brimu Brytene sohtan,
> wlance wig-smiþas, Wealas ofercoman,
> eorlas ar-hwate eard begeatan.
>
> (lines 65–73)

Never yet did greater slaughter happen in this island, nor were more people slain with edged swords until now, as books tell us written by ancient historians, since the time when the Angles and Saxons came to Britain from the East, proud forgers of battle, across the wide seas, and conquered the Britons with glorious courage and gained for themselves their land.

We have no clear idea of just where Brunanburh was fought, save that it must have been in the north-west: nor has the poem characterization or topographic details as has *The Battle of Maldon*. But the poet clearly saw how politically important was this crushing defeat of the enemies of England even as he concentrated on general patriotism and the glorifying of his heroes.

That the poem is late, despite its antique diction, is indicated by the use in it of a purely Norse word, *cnearr*, for a ship.[1] King Athelstan had much contact with friendly Norsemen: and it is claimed in the saga of Egill the warrior poet that this Icelandic Viking along with some of his followers was at Athelstan's court,

---

[1] Old Norse *knǫrr* (earlier **knarru*).

and himself present actively at the battle of Vinheiði, which seems to be the same as Brunanburh.[1]

As *The Battle of Brunanburh* is largely a panegyric on King Athelstan, it seems likely that it was written soon after the battle, as he did not live for very long after that victory. Some sixty years later the much less historically significant fight between some Viking raiders, led by Olaf Tryggvason, later King of Norway, and the local Anglo-Saxons of Essex under a heroic leader became the theme of a poem, *The Battle of Maldon*, which has justly been celebrated as one of the very finest expressions of the Germanic heroic spirit that Anglo-Saxon poetry ever produced. This battle, briefly recorded in a *Chronicle* annal but without any verse, appears to have resulted in a poem soon after the event, which took place in August of the year 991. This was copied in a Worcester manuscript of the eleventh century, Cotton Otho A XII, which was destroyed in the fire in the Cottonian library in 1731. But the text had been copied in 1725, and was printed by the great Anglo-Saxonist Thomas Hearne in 1726 as an appendix to his edition of the Chronicle of John of Glastonbury. This somewhat inaccurate version is now the inevitable basis of the text of *The Battle of Maldon*, which runs to 325 lines, having lost, apparently, some 50 odd lines at its beginning and twice as much at its end. The poem, before the loss of a leaf at its beginning and two at its end, seems to have extended to somewhere near 500 lines.[2] It is not only, even in its surviving truncated form, the greatest heroic poem in Old English—since *Beowulf* is basically rather an elegy than an heroic poem proper—but it is also the only purely heroic poem which has survived. For the early fragments of *Waldere* and *The Fight at Finnsburh* are far too incomplete to be comparable.

What is especially astonishing about *The Battle of Maldon* is its depth and the fidelity of its expression to the whole of the ancient Germanic spirit. Indeed, all the ideals of the old Germanic noble warrior, and how they were carried out in practice, as described by Tacitus in his *Germania*—the heroism of war-leader and comitatus in their mutual loyalties, and the Germanic contempt for those who failed to live up to them in times of crisis—are put before us in this poem of the end of the tenth century in fresh simplicity, and in vivid dramatic speeches in traditional epic style. *Beowulf*, the greatest of Anglo-Saxon poems, had expressed these Germanic heroic ideas in the grand style, and with a wealth of archaic poetic diction; but its scope had been far wider, and its assimilation of Latin Christian culture with Germanic antiquarianism is found but little in *The Battle of Maldon*, where all is concentrated on the conduct of heroes

---

[1] *The Battle of Brunanburh* is edited with full apparatus and exceptional thoroughness by Alistair Campbell (London, 1938).

[2] The best edition is still that of E. V. Gordon (London, 1937).

in the crisis of battle. *Beowulf* again has a pervasive elegiac tone which is quite absent from the narrower concentration on heroic tragedy of *The Battle of Maldon*. While faithfully following the poetic inheritance of *Beowulf*, the later poem is written in an altogether simpler and rather more austere style in its use of the ancient poetic diction. Its language sometimes even suggests the colloquial. The metre, too, though never lapsing into the popular licence of the later Old English period, uses a good deal of freedom in sometimes relaxing the technical rules. In this last respect *The Battle of Maldon* contrasts with the careful correctness of *The Battle of Brunanburh* and the courtly poems of the later *Chronicle*.

The battle of Maldon, in which Byrhtnoth, leader of the Essex men, was slain with most of his followers, whom he led to face impossible odds in the old heroic spirit, was certainly an event in history, though not nationally important like that of Brunanburh: and the poet vividly conveys the impression of nearness to the fight and of personal knowledge of its details. He knows the names of the English warriors of most significance, and apparently none of those of their enemies: and Byrhtnoth too is a famous historical character piously commemorated. The chief characters' actual speeches are reproduced by the poet, though almost every one of them is on the traditional lines that can well be paralleled in *Beowulf*. The basis of this remarkably vivid air of historicity and verisimilitude, though sometimes even assumed to have been used by an eye-witness who provided the poet with his facts, has lately been called in question.[1] Just as some of the apparently closely historical Old Icelandic sagas have been discovered on exact examination to present a most skilful simulation of detailed history largely fabricated by the maker of the saga in its written form, so too it has been suggested that the poet of *The Battle of Maldon* has brilliantly simulated much of the seemingly historical detail, adjusting everything to the presentation of the noblest heroic traditions. But such skill in simulating history and producing so vivid an impression of verisimilitude, however unsatisfying to the historian, only adds to the literary excellence of the poet.

Though *The Battle of Maldon* is entirely concerned with the ancient heroic spirit, its hero, well remembered as a pious Christian, utters a prayer which is the one definite Christian element in the poem. Like Beowulf at the point of death giving thanks for the treasure he has won, he gives thanks for all the joys that he has met with in the world, following this with a petition for his soul's journey after death which reminds us of the stories of Old English saints whose souls were seen being carried to heaven by bands of angels:

"Geþancie þe, ðeoda waldend,

[1] See J. B. Bessinger, "*Maldon* and the *Óláfsdrápa*, an Historical Caveat", *Comparative Literature* XIV (1962), pp. 23–35.

ealra þæra wynna þe ic on worulde gebad.
Nu ic ah, milde metod, mæste þearfe
þæt þu minum gaste godes geunne,
þæt min sawul to ðe siðian mote
on þin geweald, þeoden engla,
mid friþe ferian. Ic eom frymdi to þe
þæt hi hel-sceaðan hynan ne moton."
(lines 173–180)

"I thank thee, Lord of peoples, for all those joys which I have lived through in the world. Now, O merciful Creator, I have the greatest need that thou shouldst grant blessing to my spirit, so that my soul may make its journey to thee, be carried into thy protection, O Prince of angels. To thee I make my prayer that the enemies from hell may not bring it low."

But the spirit of this great poem reaches its consummate expression in the speech of the aged companion of the English chief after his beloved lord has been slain:

Byrhtwold maþelode, bord hafenode
(se wæs eald geneat), æsc acwehte;
he ful baldlice beornas lærde:
"Hige sceal þe heardra, heorte þe cenre,
mod sceal þe mare, þe ure mægen lytlað.
Her lið ure ealdor eall forheawen,
god on greote. A mæg gnornian
se ðe nu fram þis wig-plegan wendan þenceð.
Ic eom frod feores; fram ic ne wille,
ac ic me be healfe minum hlaforde,
be swa leofan men, licgan þence."
(lines 309–319)

Byrhtwold, an aged man of his household comrades, raised his shield and shook his ashen spear as he spoke with full courage, and admonished the warriors: "Our minds must be the stouter, our hearts the bolder, our spirit the mightier as our power grows less. Here lies our lord all hewn about; our leader is on the ground. He who thinks of departing from this battle-play now shall for ever lament in misery. Old am I in years: but I will not go hence from the field, but mean to lie dead myself beside my lord who was so loved a leader."

An example of *The Battle of Maldon's* best manner in giving a speech on traditional lines which is exactly paralleled in *Beowulf*—because both poets are using the same cultural heritage—is that of Ælfwine as he reminds his comrades of the loyal promises they had made to their lord Byrhtnoth at feastings when boasts were rife, and of their duty to requite the many benefits they had received from a generous leader:

> Ælfwine þa cwæð, he on ellen spræc:
> "Gemunan þa mæla þe we oft æt meodo spræcon,
> þonne we on bence beot ahofon,
> hæleð on healle, ymbe heard gewinn;
> nu mæg cunnian hwa cene sy.
> Ic wylle mine æþelo eallum gecyþan,
> þæt ic wæs on Myrcon miccles cynnes;
> wæs min ealda fæder Ealhelm haten,
> wis ealdor-man, woruld-gesælig.
> Ne sceolon me on þære þeode þegenas ætwitan
> þæt ic of ðisse fyrde feran wille,
> eard gesecan, nu min ealdor ligeð
> forheawen æt hilde. Me is þæt hearma mæst;
> he wæs ægðer min mæg and min hlaford."
>
> (lines 211–224)

Then Ælfwine spake with valiancy: "Remember the times when oft we used to speak at the mead-drinking when we were wont to raise our loud boasts along the benches about stern strife as the warriors sat in hall. Now it will be put to the test who is truly bold. I will make known the worthiness of my ancestry to all, and that I was born of a mighty race among the Mercians. My grandfather's name was Ealhelm, a wise leader and notable in the world. Never shall the retainers reproach me among the people, saying that I am willing to go from this war-troop to seek my own home, now that my lord lies there, hewn to death in the battle: that is for me the greatest of evils. He was both my kinsman and my leader".

In fuller expression and less economy of language Wiglaf, Beowulf's faithful retainer, had exhorted his comrades to help their lord in his hour of need in words of striking similarity.[1] But it is not that here, and in a number of other passages, the poet is directly following *Beowulf*: it is rather that both poems are faithful expressions of the ancient heroic traditions in the traditional diction. *The Battle of Maldon*, being so much later, uses fewer kennings and conventional poetic epithets and is freer in metre, but the basic culture of the two is the same. The astounding thing is that at the end of the tenth century, when in so many ways the national English vitality seemed low in the midst of renewed Viking invasions, the poet of *The Battle of Maldon*, quite apart from the more courtly writing of *The Battle of Brunanburh* and the better *Chronicle* pieces, should have given such noble and moving expression to the ancient heroic spirit and shown it in action.

---

[1] *Beowulf*, lines 2631–2660.

Apart from the important poems so far dealt with in this chapter, leaving aside merely popular verse of no literary merit, such as some in the later *Chronicle*, the later significant poetry may be conveniently grouped together as 'occasional verse'. By this designation is meant sets of verses composed for particular occasions or to commemorate special events or famous places. Such poems are, naturally, more or less of the nature of panegyrics of persons concerned in the events celebrated or of a historic city admired by the poet. A group of such occasional poems, usually in courtly style and deliberately reviving traditional poetic techniques, was included at appropriate points, as already noticed, in the *Anglo-Saxon Chronicle*, much in the same way as was *The Battle of Brunanburh*. Three of these belong to the tenth century, and appear in their best guise in the Parker Manuscript of the *Chronicle*, the large codex bequeathed to Corpus Christi College, Cambridge, by Queen Elizabeth's first Archbishop of Canterbury, Matthew Parker, and numbered 173. The first of these, *The Capture of the Five Boroughs*, celebrates the final subjection of the five towns of the Danelaw and their districts held by the heathen Danes: Lincoln, Leicester, Nottingham, Stamford, and Derby. It covers only thirteen lines, and praises King Edmund's great victory in the year 942 in technically correct and agreeable traditional style. The next poem is a very brief general account in correct verse of the *Coronation of Edgar* at Bath on Whit Sunday 973. This event, apparently postponed for fourteen years after Edgar's accession to await the full acknowledgment of the West-Saxon king as an imperial ruler in most of Britain, was supported by all the notables of Britain, though the poet only mentions 'a host of priests and a great collection of monks'. This coronation, which is of great historic importance as being the first fully recorded church ceremony of the kind, and the basis of English coronation services to this day, is here given twenty well-turned honorific lines. The third of this group, which some think was produced by the poet of Edgar's coronation, treats of *King Edgar's Death* in 975. Its first twelve lines treat Edgar's death in excellent traditional metre and much of the old formulaic phrasing, but rather as if the earthly end of a saint were being set forth. Then, after that, the poem is extended to 37 lines by a versifying of the five other events of note which occurred in the same year as the King's death. This latter series of annals, while still correctly versified in quite traditional style, lacks the dignity and vitality of the actual account of the King's death, and is little more than the putting into traditional metre and diction of a set of the usual *Chronicle* annals. It has, indeed, been thought by some that only the first twelve lines are the work of one poet, the rest being a rather mechanical addition.[1]

In the British Museum Cotton MS. Tiberius B I of the *Anglo-Saxon Chronicle* are two further occasional poems not found in the

---

[1] See *The Battle of Brunanburh*, ed. A. Campbell, *op. cit.*, p. 36.

Parker Manuscript: they deal respectively with *The Death of Alfred*, son of Ethelred, in 1036, and *The Death of Edward* (the Confessor) under the date 1065. The poem on King Edward the Confessor is in correct traditional style, though very much influenced also by the literary practice of saints' lives. It celebrates the saintly king as being also a mighty potentate in 37 lines, ending with praise of Harold Godwinson as legitimate successor by Edward's wish. The poem has no marked literary merit. The remaining piece from the *Chronicle* which merits notice is 25 lines under date 1036 on the capture and savage murder of Edward's brother, Prince Alfred, by Earl Godwin and his agents. It begins in rhythmical prose, gradually developing into somewhat doggerel verse with internal rhymes or assonances and frequent disregard of the rules of alliteration. Like the other *Chronicle* pieces, it is in part a panegyric on the murdered prince. A comparison between the correctly composed poem on Edward the Confessor's death written some thirty years later and this very roughly phrased poem on Prince Alfred reminds us that the more traditional techniques of vernacular verse were in use right up to the end of the Old English period, existing latterly side by side with a more popular and freer style with much rough rhyming and declining alliteration, as exemplified in the Alfred poem.

Related to this kind of occasional verse is the poem in praise of a particular city, such as had been inherited with Latin culture from classical times. Of this type Alcuin has left us a long Latin poem in praise of the great ecclesiastics and holy men of his beloved York mentioned in Chapter 4, *De Pontificibus et Sanctis Ecclesiae Eboracensis Carmen*.[1] In a Cambridge University Library manuscript, Ff. 1. 27, from the twelfth century, along with Symeon of Durham's famous *History of the Church of Durham* in Latin is an Anglo-Saxon poem in praise of the city of Durham, with its cathedral, its memories of St Cuthbert, St Aidan, St Oswald, and other holy men, and its wondrous collection of sacred relics. This piece can be shown to have been composed as late as the early twelfth century, between the years 1104 and 1109; naturally, it shows marked traces of the spelling of its time, looking towards the transition to Middle English, yet it is still remarkably correct Anglo-Saxon traditional versification. But with it the known history of Old English poetry ends. This Durham poem, as remarked in Chapter 9, is the earliest English vernacular specimen of topographic verse. Before it only *The Ruin* (if it be taken as embodying an actual description of Bath) could be thought of as topographic: but clearly the main purpose of *The Ruin* is not of such a kind, whereas the poet of *Durham* intends primarily to touch on the geography as well as the historical memories of his chosen city. Even today one may recognize Durham from

---

[1] Included in J. Raines, *Historians of the Church of York and its Archbishops* (Rolls Series 71) I, pp. 349 ff. See also references in Chapter 4 (p. 67, note 2).

what is said in the poem—its swift-flowing river with wooded banks, the fish in its waters, and the great cathedral then newly risen. The translation of St Cuthbert's relics to Durham had just taken place when our poem was written. Accordingly the poet is exultant over the sacred greatness of his town, and here is none of the elegiac tone of *The Ruin*. Yet the interest of *Durham* is chiefly historical, for though unexpectedly well written technically in the traditional style, it lacks poetic merit of any other kind.

Another type of occasional verse probably suggested by Latin practices are the Prologues, Prefaces, or commendatory lines, of which only very few have survived. Of such work the earliest and most interesting are the sixteen lines of verse which introduce King Alfred's translation of St Gregory the Great's *Pastoral Care* after his prose Preface, and another set of thirty lines at its conclusion which serves as epilogue. Both the verse Prologue and Epilogue to the *Pastoral Care* survive in the best manuscript of this, probably Alfred's first attempt at translating, the Hatton MS. 20 in the Bodleian Library, Oxford, being actually written at the King's direction in the last decade of the ninth century. In these verses, therefore, we probably have a fairly authentic contemporary copy of King Alfred's earliest efforts at poetry; and they are also of considerable interest for the student of the history of English versification because they are the only surviving examples of the prosody of the late ninth century copied in a contemporary hand. The metrical Preface to King Alfred's *Pastoral Care* summarizes the story of how St Gregory's work was brought to England by St Augustine of Canterbury, and how the King, having translated it, ordered copies to be distributed to all his bishops. The verse of both Alfred's pieces is tolerable technically, though it does not employ the traditional heroic diction. The Epilogue to the *Pastoral Care* is merely a commendation of the importance and didactic value of the book. The twenty-seven lines of metrical Preface to Bishop Wærferth's translation of St. Gregory's *Dialogues* survives only in an eleventh-century copy, MS. Cotton Otho C I in the British Museum. Here it is stated that it was copied by the command of Bishop Wulfstan, to whom it was given by King Alfred. This 'Wulfstan' may be an error for Wulfsige, friend of Alfred and Bishop of Sherborne, in view of the fact that this bishop did in fact receive a copy of the King's earlier work, the *Pastoral Care*[1]: for there was no Bishop Wulfstan available at that time. Or perhaps the Wulfstan referred to is the early eleventh-century Bishop of Worcester whose name replaces the original in the late copy because he was especially well known in Worcester, from whence MS. Otho C I seems to have come. One cannot be sure who composed this metrical Preface,

---

[1] K. Sisam, "An Old English Translation of a Letter from Wynfrith to Eadburga (A.D. 716–7) in Cotton MS. Otho CI." in *Studies in the History of Old English Literature*, op. cit., pp. 201–203.

whether Bishop Wærferth or another. But whoever this was, he was no more of a poet than was Alfred himself, and provides merely a pious commendation of the *Dialogues* and praise of King Alfred. At the end of a version of the Alfredian Bede in MS. Corpus Christi College, Cambridge, 41, of the eleventh century, which also contains part of *Solomon and Saturn*, a scribe has added what is apparently his own metrical prayer inviting his aristocratic readers to pray for the book's copyist. It is printed in *Minor Poems*, p. 113. This is obviously a late performance, lacking the fair metrical accuracy of the pieces of the Alfredian period, and showing a good deal of improper licence. But the piece has interest as an early example of what became a very common practice, that of a copyist adding a prayer to his manuscript with a request for the prayers of his readers for himself.

In another eleventh-century manuscript in the Cotton collection, Claudius A III, is a little poem of eleven lines printed in *Minor Poems*, p. 97, commending a certain nobleman Thureth, who is said to have been responsible for the making of a beautiful book. The book, called a *halgungboc*, seems originally to have been a liturgical collection containing a Pontifical, or book of Sacramental offices for a bishop, and a coronation rite. For the word *halgung* might, since it literally means 'consecration', indicate equally a Pontifical or a coronation service; and since the manuscript in which Thureth occurs shows signs of once having included both Pontifical and coronation rite, *halgungboc* probably covered both. But this *halgungboc* is here personified by the same kind of prosopopoeia that we find in the *Riddles*: and we have prayers for the eternal well-being of Thureth, who had it made. This Thureth has been identified as a nobleman of the late tenth century whose name as Thored appears in a Surrey charter copied into the same manuscript as the poem: so that it can be dated fairly closely to the end of that century.

The metrical translation of texts, as distinct from the adaptations and free paraphrasing of Old English Biblical and hagiographical poetry, seems not to have been common; nor have verse translations of any marked poetic merit survived. The fragments of verse renderings of Psalms for the Church offices which appear in the *Benedictine Office* have been mentioned already in passing. These fragments of passages proper to the various offices in a Benedictine monastery are closely related to the only considerable body of metrically translated Psalms which is known in Anglo-Saxon, the so-called *Paris Psalter*. The only other verse translation is the late Kentish version of the Vulgate Psalm 50, *Miserere mei Deus*, noticed earlier in the chapter for its technical skill and effective art. Apart from such Psalter renderings, the only considerable attempt at metrical translation is the verse-rendering of the metrical portions of Boethius's *De Consolatione Philosophiae*, generally assigned to King Alfred.

The Paris Psalter, an early-eleventh-century manuscript now in the Paris Bibliothèque Nationale, is a fine piece of book production, though illustrations which once adorned it or were planned for it have been cut out, or are only represented by pen-sketches. It contains a prose version of the first fifty Psalms and verse translations of Psalms 51 to 150[1]: but the fragments of translation in the *Benedictine Office*[2] show that a complete version of the whole Psalter in verse once existed, since they include some adapted from a text clearly the earlier part of the Paris Psalter. This manuscript, as is usual with Psalter codices, includes the Canticles and prayers of the daily Offices, but these latter are not translated. The Latin of the Psalter appears opposite the Anglo-Saxon translations presented with elegance. The versification of the Paris Psalter is very free, especially in the matter of alliteration, nor does it show any poetic merit beyond what is occasionally carried over from the Latin. The limitations imposed by following the Latin in vernacular verse seem to have prevented any real success, as contrasted with the work of the poets who had been able to select and expatiate so freely in handling the Old Testament for the Cædmonian poems. The common practice in the Anglo-Saxon Church was to provide the Latin Psalter and Canticles with interlinear glosses, so that those ignorant of Latin who had to recite the daily Offices could follow the sense of what they were saying. The Psalter was especially frequently glossed because of its dominant position in the Church liturgies, especially in the regular daily Offices of a religious house. The Paris Psalter, then, stands out as unique for being an actual translation of the Latin instead of the common interlinear glossing. It would be interesting to know the purpose of this translation into verse—whether, for instance, these Psalms were recited instead of the Latin as being more helpful to less learned monks and laymen. Such verses might be thought to fulfil St Augustine of Hippo's idea that the threefold aim of Christian teaching was 'to teach, to give pleasure, and to persuade': *docere, delectare, flectere*.

Having turned the whole of Boethius's *De Consolatione Philosophiae* into Old English prose, it seems that King Alfred then took his own vernacular version as a basis for a verse rendering of the *Metra*, or metrical sections of Boethius's work, thus making in his final translation the same distinction between the prose and the poetical parts of the work as its Latin author had intended. The prose version of both Latin prose and verse survives in an early twelfth-century manuscript, Bodley 180 at Oxford. The verse rendering, with some losses or omissions, of Boethius's *Metra* survives only imperfectly in an eleventh-century manuscript in the British Museum Cotton Otho A VI, which was severely damaged in the fire in the

---

[1] The verse section is in ASPR V, pp. 3–150.
[2] See the discussion in *The Benedictine Office*, ed. J. Ure (Edinburgh, 1957), pp. 17 ff.

Cottonian Library at Westminster in 1731. But a copy of the entire
Old English translation of Boethius made by Francis Junius in the
later seventeenth century before the fire occurred enables some of the
damaged text to be reconstructed. Both the prologue in the Oxford
manuscript, which is entirely in prose, and the metrical prelude to
the verse renderings preserved from a lost leaf of the Cotton manuscript in Junius's copy state that King Alfred translated the *Metra*
into verse as well as prose. But since Otho A VI is of the tenth century
and the Oxford manuscript belongs to the early twelfth, there cannot
be absolute certainty as to Alfred's authorship of the verse renderings:
but a strong tradition and a good deal of external evidence make this
generally acceptable. The quality of the verse is not remarkable,
and for the most part merely puts the prose which Alfred had written
earlier into verse with minimal change. Moreover, since the verse
passages are only preserved in later and often clearly inaccurate
copies, this metrical Boethius cannot be judged as an authentic
specimen of King Alfred's technical skill, as can the metrical Preface
and Epilogue to his version of the *Pastoral Care*, which survive in
strictly contemporary form. In the metrical Prologue Alfred is said
to have wished to convey his matter to the people in poetic form to
make it more agreeable and to avoid tedium: and it does happen in
some passages that the beauty of Boethius's verses is expressed more
effectively in Alfred's verse than in his prose. Alfred had no marked
poetic gift, but we know that he did much to encourage the poetic
art. As Asser tells us, he was "Saxonica poemata die noctuque solers
auditor, relatu aliorum saepissime audiens, docibilis memoriter
retinebat".[1] Such a youthful training would give him the necessary
technical knowledge.[2]

[1] *De Rebus Gestis Ælfredi*, 22, 13–15.
[2] The Alfredian version of Boethius's *Metra* is edited in ASPR V, pp. 153–203.
The complete work is available in *King Alfred's Old English Version of Boethius*,
ed. W. J. Sedgefield (Oxford, 1899).

PART III

PROSE

CHAPTER 12

The Beginnings

ANGLO-SAXON PROSE, though much more of it has survived than the extant verse, is very largely non-literary. A great deal of it consists of translations or paraphrase from Latin originals. It developed much later and more slowly than poetry, since its aims were primarily utilitarian and practical rather than artistic, and its intended edification was far more direct and obvious than was that of verse, which strove to convey its teaching with the conscious aid of pleasure. Whereas prose was mostly addressed to a readership through the eye, poetry—at least in its earlier and more vital appeal—sought to work through the medium of an aesthetic attraction directed to an audience through its ears. Poetry arises in early times as a natural expression of men's feelings, and uses natural rhythms which grow and become traditional because they spring from a selection of the patterns of actual speech, from the rhythms of songs and dances, and from employing designs of formulaic phrases to suit the ethos of the people. Prose generally only comes into existence at a more sophisticated stage of cultural development. Poetry can grow up naturally long before the common use of vernacular writing, whereas prose will generally only grow among those who have the habit of writing, and it will not appeal at all widely until it can have an appreciative body of readers. Thus Homer long antedates Herodotus, and Ennius Cicero. Prose did indeed develop in the late Old English period to the achievement of qualities of literature proper with the aid of conscious art: but even at its best, since most of it was translated or carried over from Latin models, its merits could only be those of style. Prose could seldom attain to anything like originality in subject-matter or rhetorical arrangement, such as can be found in the freshness and vitality of the best of the poetry. Its interest to the historian—especially the social historian—and to the student of the development of the English language is often great. The art of verse-making grew up naturally from Germanic roots in England. It certainly owed much to the Christian Latin culture to which it was in many ways assimilated, but its foundations were on a native inheritance, whereas prose only grew from Latin models from practical necessity, to meet basically utilitarian and didactic ends. When it did later develop aesthetic qualities, this was chiefly in the art of the preacher, who cultivated stylistic attractions to hold the attention of his hearers. The homilies of the effective prose-writers of the Benedictine Revival period, Ælfric and Wulfstan, were written to be read aloud, and their use at times of the rhythmic devices of verse in this prose clearly indicates an appeal to the ears of the people such as had been made by early poetry. However, these homilies had to be read from manuscripts by those who delivered them without any of the advantages which the memories of the oral poetic tradition gave the poets. Most of the basic material of the homilies of the best writers was adapted or translated from Latin sources. Even in the one secular prose romantic tale which has survived, *Apollonius of Tyre*, we are given mainly a rendering of a Latin original, however attractively it is presented in the vernacular.

The study of Old English prose, then, for the reasons indicated above, must be for the most part a relatively non-literary one, concerned more with history than with aesthetics. It may therefore be presented in a work on Anglo-Saxon literature rather more broadly than the poetry. With the one possible exception of the saga-like interpolation in the *Chronicle* for 755, all prose that has survived from pre-Alfredian times is entirely non-literary. It was only when King Alfred's example and authority began to give some prestige to the making of prose that prose as a branch of English literature may be said to have had a beginning. Nevertheless, though Alfred had no clear tradition to guide him in his pioneering translations and original prefaces and interpolations, laws, charters, and glosses, while outside the sphere of literature properly considered, do afford some glimpse of prose development: and the short passage in the *Anglo-Saxon Chronicle* mentioned above, which seems to be an interpolation from a partly remembered oral saga-tradition, does have some literary quality.

When the Angles, Saxons, and Jutes first invaded Britain they must be supposed to have brought with them a considerable body of customary law orally preserved among their tribal elders. This, as it needed to be mnemonic, was handed down orally in formulaic style, in which alliterative patterns and occasional rhyming jingles were preserved in a very terse and economical prose. We know that some laws were committed to writing in the vernacular as early as the beginning of the seventh century in Kent, the first region to come under Christian influence, though these Kentish laws only survive in a copy made in the early twelfth century. Bede tells us in his *Historia Ecclesiastica* that King Ethelbert of Kent, among other beneficial acts, caused his laws to be written down in the

English language as royal decrees, and that these were still preserved in Bede's time and were still then in force.[1] These Kentish laws, because of the strong conservatism of the legal mind, can still probably be read basically unchanged (apart from their late Old English dress) in the great collection of legal documents made at Rochester in Henry I's time, which is now in Rochester Cathedral library, and is known as the *Textus Roffensis*. But nothing of these, the earliest English laws, made under direct Christian influence and that of Roman models, survives in any pre-Conquest text. For the earliest Old English laws in an actual near-contemporary form we must look to the Parker Manuscript which contains the *Anglo-Saxon Chronicle*. In this, Corpus Christi College, Cambridge, 173, we have King Alfred's laws with his Prologue, followed by the laws of the early eighth century West-Saxon king Ine which Alfred had used as an aid. This manuscript, dated to the beginning of the tenth century, provides us with something very near to the actual language used by the King. He tells us that they were produced after careful study of the Old Testament law as well as of Roman types. King Alfred's laws (those of Ine in the same manuscript are of course a copy made two hundred years after their first promulgation), are the only early examples preserved in any pre-Conquest manuscript. These two collections, the *Textus Roffensis*—which includes much other legal matter besides Ethelbert's decrees—and the Parker version of the laws of King Alfred and of Ine between them provide almost all that we have up till the death of King Alfred. A third legal collection in MS. Corpus Christi College, Cambridge, 383 of the later eleventh century provides much later legal material, especially laws drawn up under the influence of Archbishop Wulfstan in the early eleventh century. But by this time Anglo-Saxon laws had become rather more discursive in form, and read much like ordinary prose with a technical vocabulary; and many of them have the qualities of the vigorous style of Wulfstan the homilist. Notably this is true of some of those of King Ethelred the Unready and of Canute. But the early laws, as has been indicated, are only prose in a very limited and non-literary sense.[2]

Though Latin was always in common use among the ecclesiastics who conducted most affairs, the vernacular was continuously employed for legal and business purposes from the very earliest Anglo-Saxon times, as has been shown above: but the early vernacular laws have only survived partially in much later copies. The early charters (mostly for the conveyance of land) were written in Latin, with only

[1] Chapter 2, 5. The passage is translated in *English Historical Documents* I, p. 610.

[2] Most of the laws are fully edited in F. Liebermann, *Die Gesetze der Angelsachsen*, 3 vols. (Halle 1903–16). The earlier texts with translation and comments are in *The Laws of the Earliest English Kings*, ed. F. L. Attenborough (Cambridge, 1922). There is a useful bibliographical summary in *English Historical Documents* I, p. 351.

the boundaries and place-names shown in English. But from the eighth century vernacular charters begin to appear, though only from the tenth century do they show anything like passages of vernacular prose. As with the laws, very many of the charters survive only through copies made much later. The oldest charter which exists in an actual contemporary document is a grant of land in Thanet by Hlothhere, King of Kent, to a certain Abbot Brihtwold. It can be definitely dated 679: but its survival is a somewhat isolated case, and it is only from the ninth century that charters in Old English become at all frequent. From the mid-tenth century they become relatively abundant: and it is in these latter that we frequently find narrative passages of continuous prose setting forth the circumstances in which a particular estate came into the possession of the donor or testator. Hlothhere's charter just mentioned is, however, in Latin, with only English names in native form. The first charter written in continuous Old English is one made in Kent about the year 829 in which an important nobleman Oswulf with his wife grants land to the monastery of Christ Church, Canterbury.[1] A good example of the later narrative prose sometimes added to charters to justify or explain is one in which Eadgifu, daughter of King Edward the Elder, grants an estate to Christ Church, Canterbury, in the year 961.[2] Here an exciting story is told of the vicissitudes through which Eadgifu's property had passed, and how a creditor of her father sought to rob her of her rights, till, with the approval of King Edgar and the Witan and all the bishops, she finally 'with her own hands placed the title-deeds on the Altar' of the Abbey. As with the laws, however, such features belong rather to the general development of later prose than to an account of its beginnings.[3] The surviving early charters are always in Latin save for the names of places and witnesses. It is not till the ninth century that we find documents in continuous English that can in any sense be called pieces of prose.

From the beginning of the ninth century, too, we find a fairly continuous stream of vernacular wills. Like the charters, these sometimes contain interesting social and historical matter, and as in charters the testators sometimes vary with thoughts of their own the formulaic preambles.[4]

Related to the charters are the writs: but these only begin as they have survived in later times, from the reign of Ethelred the Unready. A writ is an official letter on a matter of administration sent to

[1] See *The Oldest English Texts*, ed. Henry Sweet (EETS 83: London, 1885), No. 37, pp. 443–444.
[2] Sweet's *Anglo-Saxon Reader* conveniently includes this charter, 13th ed., pp. 50–51.
[3] A convenient collection of charters, excluding the earliest, with translations, is found in A. J. Robertson, *Anglo-Saxon Charters* (Cambridge, 1939). Some earlier charters are in F. E. Harmer, *Select English Historical Documents of the Ninth and Tenth Centuries* (Cambridge, 1914). Translations are given.
[4] See D. Whitelock, *Anglo-Saxon Wills* (Cambridge, 1930).

a State officer with instructions which are to be made public, and with its authenticity proved by a seal appended to the parchment document. It must also carry the names of the king or high notable who sends it and of the recipient, and must always include a salutation or greeting. Some 120 of these Anglo-Saxon writs of accepted authenticity are preserved, from the early years of King Ethelred II till the Norman Conquest and a little beyond. They have a special interest for the literary historian, since the formula of the royal writ has remained substantially the same till our own day.[1] But the writs, like the laws and charters, use much formulaic language which can be shown, by means of comparison with parallels in other Germanic languages, to go back to an inheritance from an oral tradition. For laws, when they were only preserved in the minds of the tribal elders in ancient times, made much use of formulaic phrases, rhyme, or assonance and the pairing of words by alliteration, as well as the metrical pattern of two-stress phrases, which doubtless were valuable aids to the necessary memorizing. Charters and wills would follow the legal style. This is also true of the writ. But the special interest of the writ for the literary student is that its history helps to demonstrate the survival of ancient phrases and rhythms sometimes more fully. For although writs do not appear in their full technical form till the late tenth century, we can detect a clear line in the development of this type of epistolary form from the latest days of the Roman Empire of the West, and through Latin models to King Alfred. Alfred's famous *Preface* to his version of the *Pastoral Care* of St Gregory begins with the formal protocol proper to a writ, and is in all basic respects save for the absence of a royal seal a royal writ addressed to the bishop, directing him to take certain action concerning the copy of the book sent to him with the writ. We may compare Alfred's opening of this Preface with a royal writ of more than a century later, one in which King Canute in 1020 sends his official greetings and instructions to archbishops and various officials, both ecclesiastical and lay. King Alfred thus addresses Bishop Wærferth:

Ælfred kyning hateð gretan Wærferð biscep his wordum luflice ond freondlice; ond ðe cyðan hateð ðæt me com swiðe oft on gemynd. . . .[2]

Here is Canute's opening to his proclamation writ:

Cnut cyning gret his arcebiscopas and his leodbiscopas and Þurcyl eorl and ealle his eorlas and ealne his þeodscype, twelfhynde and twyhynde, gehadode and læwede, on Englalande freondlice. And ic cyðe eow þæt ic wylle. . . .[3]

[1] Writs are very fully discussed, edited, and translated in F. E. Harmer, *Anglo-Saxon Writs* (Manchester University Press, 1952).
[2] *King Alfred's West-Saxon Version of Gregory's Pastoral Care*, ed. Henry Sweet (EETS 45: London, 1871–72), p. 3.
[3] See Liebermann, *op. cit.*, I, 273–5: also Miss A. J. Robertson: *The Laws of the Kings of England* (Cambridge, 1925), pp. 140–45. On the genuineness of this royal proclamation with writ protocol cf. *Anglo-Saxon Writs*, p. 17 and pp. 169–70.

Both these letters begin by naming the royal sender and the recipient(s) with the addition of a formal greeting, and then change from the third to the first person in stating the King's thoughts and commands. This greetings formula with the naming of the persons concerned obviously goes back to the Latin official epistolary formula of 'A to B says salutation', *salutem dicit*. Clearly King Alfred was following an established tradition in this Preface: so that, although our surviving writs proper are all much later, we may legitimately infer from King Alfred's practice that the form of the writ—though not necessarily its accompaniment by a seal of authentication—was in continuous use from pre-Alfredian and probably quite early times. Alfred would, of course, also have been aware of the same type of formal opening of a letter in the New Testament, in the Epistle of St James. The King James Bible has here:

> James, a servant of God and of the Lord Jesus Christ, to the twelve tribes which are scattered abroad, *greeting*.

The Vulgate, which Alfred knew, has:

> Iacobus Dei et Domini nostri Iesu Christi servus, duodecim tribubus quae sunt in dispersione, *salutem*.

From very early times—at least from the early eighth century—the practice of literal translation in vernacular glosses inserted between the lines, usually above the Latin words, was in use. From the end of the eighth century there grew up a tradition of glossing the Psalter and common Canticles word by word.[1] Some translations of difficult Latin words were also compiled—the first glossaries, which were the ancestors of dictionaries. While earlier glosses seem to have been the interlinear rendering of hard Latin words, and the gathering of selections of these into glossaries, by the ninth century we find evidence of interlinear glossing so complete word for word as to amount almost to literal rendering of the Latin. Of this the first example is the so-called *Vespasian Psalter Gloss*, copied about the beginning of King Alfred's reign from a Mercian text into a fine and much older Latin Psalter and Canticles.[2] At this point it would seem that close and full glossing began to merge into the crudest actual translating. There are later similar full vernacular glosses, notably those of the *Lindisfarne Gospels* and the *Rushworth Gospels*, belonging respectively to two Northern dialects of the late tenth century.

What, it may well be asked, have these early laws, charters, and glosses, which are in fact non-literary, to do with the beginnings of Anglo-Saxon prose? It may be answered that in the language of such

---

[1] Cf. J. R. R. Tolkien, "Sigelwara Land", *Medium Ævum* I (1932), pp. 183–196.
[2] These Mercian glosses are in the British Museum MS. Cotton Vespasian A I edited in *The Oldest English Texts* and by Sherman Kuhn (Ann Arbor, 1965).

documents, with their mnemonic formulae and other related devices,
we have evidence of a tradition which had continued from the days
of oral transmission of customary law: and in the later examples we
see how such elements from oral tradition made their contribution to
the development of a continuous prose which was to become literary.
For instance, in the homilies of Archbishop Wulfstan, which were the
deliberate literary art of a man who had been much concerned with
the drafting of legal codes from traditional material, we see how
the early mnemonic devices—rhyme and assonance, alliterative
pairing of words of related meaning, the use of two-stress clauses
like those proper to verse—could be employed by a master for properly literary purposes.[1] Or again it might be argued that the making
of such early glosses did something to prepare the ground for that
art of translation proper which was to be a leading feature in literary
Old English prose.

In view of what is known of the early Christian missionaries among
the Anglo-Saxons, we should have expected that translation from
Latin into the vernacular would have begun early. But in fact no
prose translations have come down to us from a period earlier than the
end of the ninth century, when the example and active encouragement
of King Alfred produced a considerable body of translated
or adapted text-books. But, just as we learn from the authoritative Bede that there were written English versions of laws from
the earliest seventh century (though nothing has survived which is
pre-Alfredian), so too it is from the Bede circle that we learn that
at least by the close of the great teacher's life translation was being
practised. In a famous letter written in Latin by one Cuthbert, a
disciple of Bede, to a young religious colleague describing the last
days and death of his master, as he had himself witnessed it, we are
told how Bede was dictating to a young scribe the last of a translation into Old English of St John's Gospel and how he had insisted
on finishing the final verse of a chapter even while his dying breath
was failing.[2] Evidently, then, there was a vernacular version of at
least part of St John, presumably in the local Northumbrian of the
monastery, in existence when Bede died in the year 735. This
translation must have been a scholarly performance: but one cannot
guess at its literary quality.

As has been already observed, the glossing of the Psalter word by
word which went on from at least the end of the eighth century
amounted in the more complete versions almost to the crudest

---

[1] See A. McIntosh, "Wulfstan's Prose", *Proceedings of the British Academy*
XXXV (1949), pp. 109–142.
[2] This *Epistola Cuthberti*, in which the latest progress of the translation is so
vividly described, is edited in E. v. K. Dobbie, *The Manuscripts of Caedmon's
Hymn and Bede's Death-Song* (New York, Columbia University Press, 1937),
pp. 49 ff.

literal translation, and this probably prepared the way for Biblical translation proper. Yet the earliest vernacular Bible translation is only preserved from Alfredian times in the prose rendering of the first fifty Psalms which precede the verse translations of the remaining hundred in the *Paris Psalter*. What prevents any of the glossed Psalters from being regarded as translations in any proper sense is that, since they are word-by-word renderings, their syntax is entirely that of the Latin and in no way English. Looking, therefore, at what has in fact survived, it may be said that the verse translations of the Alfredian period, the *Paris Psalter's* metrical and major part and the Alfredian translation of Boethius's *Metra*, the metrical renderings and those in prose, in so far as they have survived, are approximately coeval, and date their beginnings from King Alfred's days. Yet, as has been shown, prose translation must have begun historically nearly two centuries before the now verifiable written records would have suggested. It might be tempting to regard the prose portion of the *Paris Psalter* as actually based on King Alfred's own work. For according to William of Malmesbury (writing in the early twelfth century), Alfred was engaged on a vernacular Psalter which he was prevented from finishing by death:

> Psalterium transferre aggressus, vix *prima parte explicata*, vivendi finem fecit.[1]

This 'prima pars' might be the first part of the prose Psalms of the *Paris Psalter*. But this is merely conjecture.

We have seen how traces of the various ancient mnemonic formulae survived in the language of laws, charters, and glosses written down much later. It may be that in narrative prose, too, ancient oral modes betray their existence at least once. There is a famous passage in the Parker Manuscript of the *Anglo-Saxon Chronicle* which looks like the interpolation of an older, saga-like narrative from oral tradition among the usually jejune annals of the pre-Alfredian record. This is the tale of the West-Saxon king Cynewulf and his avenging foe Cyneheard, which appears under the date 755. The usual annalistic entry of the slaying of King Cynewulf by Cyneheard appears under date 784 (786 is the actual year, as the *Chronicle* is here two years out in its reckoning):

> In this year Cyneheard killed King Cynewulf and 84 of his men with him.

But under date 755 (properly 757) we find a detailed account of this king's slaying (which actually took place in 786), with some indications of the events that had made the deadly feud that caused it. This vivid and dramatic tale, told with many of the stylistic features associated with the Old Norse historical sagas, stands out

[1] *De Gestis Regum Anglorum*, lib. II, 123.

alone among the normally brief factual annals which were regular in the *Chronicle* till King Alfred had it expanded into pieces of historical prose. This famous entry will show a number of saga-like features: the allusive and selective method, the colloquial language, the sudden passing from indirect to direct speech, the concise compression of its objective presentation, the dwelling on the crises of the dramatically told story. All these suggest that it was originally addressed to an audience who were already familiar with its subject-matter, and needed only to be entertained by the manner of the telling. To make its stylistic effect this piece should be seen as a whole, so that it is here quoted *in extenso*:

755. Her Cynewulf benam Sigebryht his rices ond West-seaxna wiotan for unryhtum dædum, butan Hamtunscire; ond he hæfde þa oþ he ofslog þone aldormon þe him lengest wunode. Ond hiene þa Cynewulf on Andred adræfde; ond he þær wunade oþ þæt hiene an swan ofstang æt Pryfetes flodan—ond he wræc þone aldormon Cumbran. Ond se Cynewulf oft miclum gefeohtum feaht uuiþ Bretwalum; ond ymb XXXI wintra þæs þe he rice hæfde, he wolde adræfan anne æþeling se wæs Cyneheard haten—ond se Cyneheard wæs þæs Sigebryhtes broþur. Ond þa geascode he þone cyning lytle werode on wifcyþþe on Merantune, ond hine þær berad, ond þone bur utan be-eode, ær hine þa men onfunden þe mid þam kyninge wærun.

Ond þa ongeat se cyning þæt, ond he on þa duru eode, ond þa unheanlice hine werede oþ he on þone æþeling locude, ond þa ut ræsde on hine ond hine miclum gewundode; ond hie alle on þone cyning wærun feohtende oþ þæt hie hine ofslægenne hæfdon. Ond þa on þæs wifes gebærum onfundon þæs cyninges þegnas þa unstilnesse, ond þa þider urnon swa hwelc swa þonne gearu wearþ ond radost. Ond hiera se æþeling gehwelcum feoh ond feorh gebead, ond hiera nænig hit geþicgean nolde; ac hie simle feohtende wæran oþ hie alle lægon butan anum Bryttiscum gisle, ond se swiþe gewundad wæs.

Þa on morgenne gehierdon þæt þæs cyninges þegnas þe him beæftan wærun, þæt se cyning ofslægen wæs, þa ridon hie þider, ond his aldormon Osric, ond Wiferþ his þegn, ond þa men þe he beæftan him læfde ær, ond þone æþeling on þære byrig metton þær se cyning ofslægen læg, ond þa gatu him to belocen hæfdon, ond þa þærto eodon. Ond þa gebead he him hiera agenne dom feos ond londes gif hie him þæs rices uþon; ond him cyþdon þæt hiera mægas him mid wæron, þa þe him from noldon. Ond þa cuædon hie þæt him nænig mæg leofra nære þonne hiera hlaford, ond hie næfre his banan folgian noldon. Ond þa budon hie hiera mægum þæt hie gesunde from eodon; ond hie cuædon þæt tæt ilce hiera geferum geboden wære þe þær mid þam cyninge wærun. Þa cuædon hie þæt hie þæs ne onmunden 'þon ma þe eowre geferan þe mid þam cyninge ofslægene wærun'. Ond hie þa ymb þa gatu feohtende wæron oþ þæt hie þærinne fulgon ond þone æþeling ofslogon ond þa men þe mid him wærun, alle

butan anum, se wæs þæs aldormonnes godsunu; ond he his feorh
generede, ond þeah he wæs oft gewundad.

The *Chronicle* entry for this year (the actual dates written in the margin are 755, 756, 757) continues in its ordinary style with the length
of King Cynewulf's reign, his genealogy, and the places of the burial
of both princes, proceeding straight on to the accession of his
successor.[1]

Besides the saga-like features of the style already mentioned in this
unique passage, other parallels to the saga are the constant beginning of clauses with 'and', the use of subject pronouns without indication of the persons intended (since an audience would know this
from their familiarity with the story), and the freedom granted the
exciting and moving incidents to make their powerful effects without any aid beyond the simple statement of what happened. The
Old Norse saga, as preserved in the classical exemplars, was a
narrative orally handed down by a semi-professional tale-teller or
saga-man, who reproduced this prose of a stylized oral tradition.
Originally narratives of historical events featuring famous characters
of Norway and Iceland in the tenth century, and made soon after the
events themselves, the classical sagas were written down considerably later, but with their manner and matter often conservatively
retained. It seems that since Christian Latin culture came to
Iceland only about the year 1000, the oral saga form had by that
time become so fixed and habitual that it survived the cultural
changes and was transmitted into writing when written literature
began nearly two centuries later. In Britain, on the other hand,
where Christianity and the consequent development of writing
achieved dominance in the seventh century, the ways of oral prose
had not then enough root, so to speak, to survive except in isolated
cases. This, however, is mere speculation. What does seem clear is
that the *Chronicle* entry for the year 755 shows an interpolated piece
of prose remembered and copied down from oral tradition. This
piece may thus be thought of as a unique suggestion of saga in early
Anglo-Saxon times accidentally surviving. This may perhaps indicate
that oral saga-type historical tale-telling once existed, and that in a
sense Anglo-Saxon prose began, as did poetry, with purely oral
transmission.[2] This account of the slaying of King Cynewulf of
Wessex, with its somewhat archaic language and a syntax which

[1] The text quoted is that of the Parker Manuscript of the *Anglo-Saxon Chronicle*
in Charles Plummer, *Two of the Saxon Chronicles Parallel*, 2 vols. (Oxford 1892–
1899). For the exact method of setting out the matter under dates, see *The Parker
Chronicle in Facsimile*, ed. Robin Flower and Hugh Smith (Oxford University
Press, London, 1941).
[2] See C. E. Wright, *The Cultivation of Saga in Anglo-Saxon England* (Edinburgh, 1939), esp. pp. 26–27. *Cf.* C. L. Wrenn, "A Saga of the Anglo-Saxons",
History XXV (1940), pp. 208–215. The passage is explained most fully by F. P.
Magoun junior, in "Cynewulf, Cyneheard and Osric", *Anglia* LVII (1933), pp.
361–376.

seems so reminiscent of the Old Icelandic sagas, is also historically important as being the first piece of narrative prose of any length in English, or indeed in any Germanic language. Viewed as the earliest extant literary prose, the Cynewulf and Cyneheard saga-piece may be considered as formally out of place and inserted clumsily in a way which is quite out of keeping with the rest of the pre-Alfredian *Anglo-Saxon Chronicle*. Kemp Malone writes of it:

> The annalist of 755, who tried his hand at narration, did a bungling job, though he had a stirring story to tell.[1]

But however out of place where it is apparently interpolated, it does have in itself some literary merit. It presents too in the conduct of the men on both sides of the feud a vivid and dramatic picture of that traditional Germanic heroic spirit and loyalty which we associate with the older poetry. But it is not, as some have thought, a prose version made from the material of a lost heroic lay; for its style, as has been shown, is clearly that of an oral prose. Again, whereas in the early laws and charters there is evidence of Latin influence, this unique *Chronicle* passage shows nothing of this, but gives the impression of a purely native tradition of language. No doubt the original interpolator used saga-matter which had grown up soon after the events described; and the scribe of the early part of the Parker Manuscript, who finished his work in the year 891 or shortly after, was using as copy an earlier document.

The upshot of all that has been said, then, on the beginnings of Anglo-Saxon prose, though of concern to the literary historian, goes only to confirm the generally accepted conclusion, that Old English literary prose begins with King Alfred, since all that went before was non-literary. Yet the *Chronicle* entry for 755 stands out as the solitary surviving exception to this: nor does it owe anything to Latin example or to translation. It is, in a sense, the pioneer piece of original literary Anglo-Saxon prose.

[1] Kemp Malone, *The Middle Ages*, vol. I of *A Literary History of England*, ed. Albert C. Baugh (New York, 1948), p. 100.

CHAPTER 13

King Alfred and Educative Prose

ALTHOUGH THE *Anglo-Saxon Chronicle*, the first original narrative prose in any Western vernacular, covers a period beginning with the invasion of Britain by Julius Caesar, its earliest portion, down to the year 891, was all copied by one scribe in the Parker Manuscript shortly after that date. In fact, it would seem that, apart from the special case of the interpolation of 755, the language of this first part is Alfredian. The early part of the Parker Chronicle, therefore, compiled and copied in King Alfred's scriptorium apparently at Winchester about the year 900, must be reckoned as prose of the age of Alfred. It is this, then, with King Alfred's own writings and those directed by him—and no doubt he himself instigated the turning of the early annals into a continuous history—that make up what we may term Alfredian prose.

Despite the large impress which King Alfred has left on later medieval tradition, especially for his work as an educator, we have relatively little exact knowledge of him as the first maker of literary prose. For what is known or may be plausibly inferred concerning him we have only three sources. These are first the account of Alfred's acts—mostly warfare—in the *Anglo-Saxon Chronicle*; secondly, the considerable amount of personal detail included along with the King's external acts in Asser's *Life*; and thirdly—the most significant of all—the statements and reflections included in Alfred's own prefaces, which he wrote himself for his various translations, and the explanations, expansions, and interpolations which he often added in the body of these works. The *Chronicle* says nothing whatever of Alfred's intellectual activities, nor does it mention his writings; it is only concerned to show his skill as leader and statesman, and by implication his sterling character. Asser, on the other hand, writes as one who for some years shared Alfred's life intimately, as his teacher and co-worker. Indeed, Asser treats his subject much in the traditional manner proper to the life of an outstanding saint. There is a good deal of what looks like the rhetorical exaggeration of the devoted enthusiast here, so that much of the inner personal development of the King as described by Asser may seem unacceptable to the scientific student. But Asser tells us a good deal of Alfred's literary growth and of his educative work, some of which is well supported by later tradition, beginning with William of Malmesbury in the early twelfth century. But it is from Alfred's own words alone that we can be sure of making the right foundation for our ideas of the King as writer and educator.

Though there is no proof of any direct connection of King Alfred with the *Anglo-Saxon Chronicle*, it is clear that the portion dealing with his reign, copied in the Parker Manuscript by scribes who wrote very soon after the events they narrate, takes on the character of narrative history, instead of the earlier merely annalistic style. The *Chronicle* seems to have originated in the bare record of isolated events placed opposite the dates entered in the margin of a parchment to enable the clergy to work out when Easter would fall in a given year: and the blank line against a date was conveniently filled with a note of some happening that would be helpful to memory. At some monastic centre, probably in the eighth century, such bare annals were collected, and added to locally thenceforth. Hence it is that we have seven manuscripts of the *Chronicle*, all based on a single archetype for the earlier entries, but diverging later in work done at Winchester, Abingdon, Worcester, and other cultural centres. King Alfred's genealogy stands in the Parker Manuscript, the oldest version, on its first leaf; and this fact alone may suggest that Alfred was the direct inspirer of this—or of a possibly earlier copy. Many circumstances point to Alfred as having had the *Chronicle* collected and compiled, and sending copies from his scriptorium to leading monasteries for maintenance and continuation. There are, too, some passages in the entries for his reign which show stylistic features which seem to be shared by parts of his undoubted translation of Orosius. But without any certainty as to just how much of the Alfredian Chronicle represents his own work, we know that it is with his reign that literary historical prose begins. There are only two periods when Old English prose in the *Chronicle* achieved any real literary quality. The one was the *Chronicle* for Alfred's reign, and the other its account of the reign of Ethelred the Unready. Between the Alfredian period and the later tenth century the *Chronicle* becomes for the most part jejune and no more than briefly annalistic. Of these two phases of literary activity in the *Chronicle*—which correspond with the two great periods of cultural renaissance associated respectively with King Alfred and with the Benedictine Revival under St Dunstan and his colleagues and immediate successors— the first suggests the creation of a straightforward narrative style, while the second (not represented in the Parker Manuscript) is characterized by conscious rhetorical art which owes something to Alfred's pioneering work.

There are vivid detailed accounts of Alfred's wars with the Vikings in the entries for his reign, notably that of a brilliantly conducted naval battle under date 896. Here is a brief illustration of the Alfredian historical prose, from the entry for the year 895:

Ond þa sona æfter þæm, on ðys gere, for se here of Wirheale in on Norðwealas, for þæm hie ðær sittan ne mehton; þæt wæs for ðy þe hie wæron benumene ægðer ge þæs ceapes ge þæs cornes þe hie gehergod hæfdon. Þa hie ða eft ut of Norðwealum wendon mid þære herehyðe þe hie ðær genumen hæfdon, þa foron hie ofer Norðhymbra lond ond Eastengla, swa swa seo fird hie geræcan ne mehte, oþ þæt hie comon on Eastseaxna lond eastweard on an igland þæt is ute on þære sæ, þæt is Meresig haten.

Ond þa se here eft hamweard wende þe Exanceaster beseten hæfde, þa hergodon hie up on Suðseaxum neah Cisseceastre, ond þa burgware hie gefliemdon, ond hira monig hund ofslogon, ond hira scipu sumu genamon.

Ða þy ylcan gere, onforan winter þa Deniscan þe on Meresige sæton tugon hira scipu up on Temese, ond þa up on Lygan. Þæt wæs ymb twa ger þæs þe hie hider ofer sæ comon.[1]

The importance of the *Anglo-Saxon Chronicle* is mainly as a basic historical document; and its various versions add to its value and interest. But our concern here being entirely with literature, the Parker text, the earliest manuscript and that most likely to bring us near to Alfred's own mind, has alone been discussed. The whole of the *Chronicle* as history, and the problems it presents, with an excellent translation, will be found in *English Historical Documents*, Vol. I. This collection, the work of Professor Dorothy Whitelock, puts the *Chronicle* in proper perspective.

Alfred's laws, included in the Parker Manuscript, have been touched upon in Chapter 12 in connection with the origins of literary prose in Anglo-Saxon. They are not in any strict sense literary. But, as has been said earlier, their use of the formulaic language of oral tradition did contribute to later and literary prose. Wulfstan, for instance, in his moving homilies of the early eleventh century, makes impressive stylistic use of some formulae inherited from ancient oral tradition conveyed through the laws. The Parker Manuscript laws, with the Latin heading *Leges Aluredi*, are in a mid-tenth-century hand, and were bound up with the *Chronicle* about that time.[2] They may well have been written under the King's direct supervision. Moreover, they are introduced by a long preamble in which passages from the Mosaic law are summarized, and the example of Roman law emphasized. This Prologue sometimes suggests Alfred's own style, as represented in his acknowledged works. The language of Alfred's Laws, too, seems basically of the

---

[1] The text for Alfred's reign is conveniently printed with necessary apparatus in *The Parker Chronicle* (832–900), ed. A. H. Smith (London, 1936).

[2] See N. R. Ker, *Catalogue of Manuscripts containing Anglo-Saxon* (Oxford, 1957), pp. 57–59.

Alfredian period, though of course much of it is traditional or taken over from predecessors.

The *Anglo-Saxon Chronicle*, then, and the Laws of Alfred, deserve mention together as our earliest evidence of King Alfred at work. Their inclusion together in the Parker Manuscript strengthens this hypothesis.

The *Anglo-Saxon Chronicle* was continued in a number of monasteries up to the Norman Conquest or near. The Parker version ends, after an almost blank series of marginal figures for the eleventh century, with the one-line annal of the death of Godwin in 1053, followed by an unfilled space after the figure 1054. For the later literary *Chronicle* prose one must look in other versions. For instance, the best continuous account of Ethelred's reign is in the C text of British Museum MS. Cotton Tiberius B I associated with Abingdon, and the magnificent story of Godwin's outlawry under the date 1048 is in the Peterborough version, MS. Laud 636 in the Bodleian Library. This last, the *Peterborough Chronicle*, was kept up at Peterborough through the period of transition from Old to Middle English, ending only with the death of Stephen in 1154; and its last contributor, for Stephen's reign, produced some remarkably vivid colloquial prose.

We learn from Asser, Chapter 89, that Alfred kept by him day and night, so as to be always at hand, a book which he wanted to call his *encheiridion*—which Asser defines as a handbook, *liber manualis*. In this evidently large manuscript he was wont to copy or have transcribed passages he found especially helpful and comforting. It contained 'flowers gathered from all sorts of masters', *flosculos undecunque collectos a quibuslibet magistris*, and kept growing till it was as large as a Psalter. It seems that these passages had with them also something of Alfred's own writing. For William of Malmesbury, in whose time the *liber manualis* (he again uses this title) was still extant, speaks of it: and he cites as evidence for the tale of St Aldhelm reciting vernacular verse in public 'Alfred's book', *liber Elfredi*, and states that Aldhelm's famous poem is commemorated by Alfred, *commemorat Elfredus carmen triviale*.[1]

Besides this lost *liber manualis*, we learn also from William of Malmesbury, as mentioned in the preceding chapter, that King Alfred died leaving an unfinished translation of the Psalter. This might be represented in the prose version of the first fifty Psalms included in the *Paris Psalter*.

Asser as a writer has already been discussed in the chapter on Anglo-Latin literature. But as he is generally regarded as a primary source for Alfred's life, he must again be looked at here. Apart from

---

[1] See *Gesta Pontificum*, lib. V, sections 188 and 190.

the rather confused account of Alfred as a constant semi-invalid, and the patterning of the King as a saint in an extreme way, what Asser tells us of his venerated master agrees pretty well with what Alfred himself relates in his own writings as regards his love of poetry and education. His zeal for the dissemination and conserving of vernacular poetry is attested by the fact that all the major manuscripts in which Anglo-Saxon poetry is preserved show some linguistic features which point to their texts having been copied into some kind of Alfredian West-Saxon, though their final form is much later. Alfred's educative aims are clearly set forth in the Preface to his version of the *Pastoral Care*, and emphasized by implication in the Preface to his Boethius translation. The general trend of Asser's statements may therefore be accepted, allowing for understandable exaggeration, though the details cannot be checked. Moreover, as has been indicated above, William of Malmesbury, a remarkably careful historian for his time, supports Asser at several points. From Asser the literary biography of King Alfred may be summarized as follows. He remained without ability to read till he was more than twelve, through the lack of concern of his parents and nurses (Chapter 22). On being shown by his mother a manuscript of Anglo-Saxon poetry with a most attractive illuminated first capital letter, and on the offer of the book as a reward for whichever of the brothers could understand and recite it first, Alfred took the book to a teacher who read it to him, and he then returned it, and recited the whole (Chapter 23). This seems to have been a feat of memory. In the same Chapter 23 we are told that Alfred had a book of Hours and the liturgical Psalms, gathered in one codex, constantly with him day and night throughout his life. In Chapter 71 Alfred, described as 'King of the Anglo-Saxons' (*Angulsaxonum rex*), persuades the Pope to exempt from taxes the hospice in Rome used by English pilgrims, *Schola Saxonum in Roma morantium*. His affability and welcome to all visitors is emphasized in Chapter 76; and there we are told of a kind of school of liberal arts at his Court, where sons of nobles were taught along with his own children. They learned diligently the humane arts (*artes humanae*) in both Latin and the vernacular, 'and Psalms and Saxon books—especially poetry', *et Psalmos, et Saxonicos libros recitare et maxime carmina Saxonica memoriter discere*. We learn in Chapters 77 and 78 of the King's gathering learned men to aid his literary and educative work, both from Mercia and from the Continent. He is said (Chapter 86) to have begun both to read and to translate Latin on the same day: and in Chapter 89 we read of the multifarious 'hand-book' already discussed. Alfred's love of the arts is strongly stressed in Chapter 91, where a picture of the King's renovating and building cities adorned with gold and silver and precious things may seem too emphatic to be historical, although there is other evidence of his love of aesthetically pleasing things in the Preface to his *Pastoral Care*. Of actual Anglo-Saxon writings we have direct evidence of Alfred's action in Chapter 77, where we learn that it was by the King's command that the Mercian Bishop Wærferth of Worcester translated St Gregory the Great's *Dialogues* most lucidly and with elegance.

The construction of Asser's work is erratic, as if he had made an original plan to celebrate the King after his death, and then decided instead to write all he knew between his first coming to England in 887 and the year 893, in which the work suddenly ends. Much of it, too, the fifty chapters from 26 to 75, is merely adapted from the *Anglo-Saxon Chronicle*: but to the historian these versions from the *Chronicle* sometimes have a special value, because it seems that Asser used a text which was in some respects better than those which have survived.

While what Asser tells us of Alfred's learning and writing agrees well with the King's own statements, there is yet uncertainty concerning the historicity of much of Asser, particularly his portrait of the King as something like a neurotic valetudinarian and a cloistered saint, in view of the immensely active and practically strenuous life which the *Anglo-Saxon Chronicle* and his actual achievements in war and statecraft show him to have led. V. H. Galbraith has in fact lately revived the view that Asser is in some sense a literary forgery made some century and a half after the date when the real Asser would have written. In his *An Introduction to the Study of History*,[1] Galbraith takes as a specimen of exercise in historical research the question "Who wrote Asser's *Life of Alfred*?" The chief points causing scepticism are (a) Exeter was not a diocese till 150 years after Asser is said to have received the see from King Alfred; (b) the Latin seems later than it should be, and shows Frankish influence; (c) there is a marked tendency to follow Einhard's famous *Life of Charlemagne*; (d) the muddled and incredible accounts of Alfred's perpetual illness in Chapters 75-76; (e) the fact that some suspect features fit very well with composition in the eleventh century, and do not fit Alfred's actual lifetime. The most promising candidate for the authorship of Asser's work is Leofric, Bishop of Crediton, who by skilful manœuvring had his bishopric transferred to Exeter in the year 1050, and thus became its first bishop. He seems to have been a Welshman despite his very English name, and had a good deal of Frankish training. It is suggested that Leofric, who is best known to students of Old English literature as the testator of the Exeter Book of Old English poetry to Exeter Cathedral in 1072, was the author. But, as Galbraith's rather lighthearted essay shows, the substitution of Leofric or any other eleventh-century author for Asser requires a good deal of unsupported speculation and creates its own difficulties, while getting rid of those inherent in the earlier Asser. Without discussing further this placing of 'Asser' 150 years or so later than the events it purports to describe—and current

[1] London, 1964, pp. 85-128.

historical scholarship seems to be tending that way—it should still be accepted that a writer in the eleventh century who also used a valuable Old English Chronicle for Alfred's reign must be regarded as having preserved valid traditions of King Alfred.[1]

The *Dialogues*, in which St Gregory the Great had collected a large number of stories of the miracles of holy men, of their visions, and of resulting pious homilies, were much in use in religious houses throughout the Middle Ages: and as Gregory was, for historical reasons, especially venerated in England (he it was who sent St Augustine of Canterbury to convert the Anglo-Saxons), the choice of this popular work as the first translation of King Alfred's reign was natural enough. That it was undertaken at the King's request by his Mercian friend Wærferth, Bishop of Worcester, we learn both from Asser and from its Prologue. Asser speaks of Wærferth, Bishop of Worcester, as a man most learned in divine Scripture 'who was the first to translate the books of Dialogues of Pope Gregory and his disciple the deacon Peter by royal command from Latin into the Saxon tongue': and he goes on to say that Wærferth did this 'sometimes putting sense from sense, and that it was interpreted with accuracy and most elegantly'.[2] The Prologue, in British Museum MS. Cotton Otho C I, consists of a prose piece in which Alfred speaks himself, and a verse passage in which a bishop expresses gratitude and praise for Alfred, who provided him with the copy which he is now sending to another bishop. The proper name in this verse prologue is written Wulfstan, which seems to have been written over a partly erased name. This latter may have been originally Wærferth, or as Dr Kenneth Sisam argues, Bishop Wulfsige of Sherborne.[3] But in any case the attribution to Alfred's direct ordering is clear. We know too from Asser, and from Alfred himself in his Preface to his *Pastoral Care*, that Wærferth was one of his principal friends and helpers in his educational work. The verses of this Prologue have already been touched upon in Chapter 11.

St Gregory's *Dialogues* take the traditional form of a discussion between the master and a beloved disciple Peter. Gregory in four books edifies his pupil, who asks brief questions on the Christian life in the world, with a flowing series of tales of miracles, including a long set of narratives about his beloved teacher St Benedict. The style is simple if florid, and no demands are made on the reader's intellect. Wærferth's translation is free but not often inexact; it omits a good deal, and adds occasionally. The style has been thought

[1] In the reprint of Stevenson's basic edition of Asser (Oxford, 1959), there is an essay by Professor Dorothy Whitelock summarizing recent work on the subject, and emphasizing her agreement with Stevenson's defence of the genuine Asser.

[2] Chapter 77, p. 62. All references to Asser are to *Asser's Life of King Alfred*, ed. William Henry Stevenson (Oxford, 1904; reprinted 1959.)

[3] See K. Sisam, "The Verses Prefixed to Gregory's Dialogues" in *Studies in the History of Old English Literature* (Oxford, 1953), pp. 225–231.

at times to have a good deal in common with that of the Alfredian Bede,[1] but it does show some individual quality.

Wærferth's rendering, though it compares favourably with the frequent clumsiness of Alfred's *Pastoral Care* and parts of the Alfredian Bede, is not of any marked literary quality. It has fewer errors than the other early prose translations, however, and sometimes achieves in its conversational parts a pleasingly colloquial simplicity, while at times it expands the Latin to greater vividness in illustration. The *Dialogues*, with their many extremely naïve accounts of miracles (often of a somewhat trivial character), have inevitably lost their appeal since the Middle Ages. But with their emphasis on the greatness of St Benedict in the second book, they would have a special attraction to the Anglo-Saxon religious public, and their simple and even credulous piety would accord well with what Asser tells us of King Alfred's own spiritual development. This work of the beloved St Gregory, the 'apostle of England', was evidently a basic book in religious education, so that it was entirely natural that King Alfred, before he himself could undertake anything of the kind, should require his special friend and early mentor Wærferth to carry through this translation. It survives only in later eleventh-century manuscripts, two of them long associated with Worcester, where the St Wulfstan of William the Conqueror's days was the great cultural conservator of vernacular ways and a special devotee of saints' lives. The *Dialogues* are primarily a series of holy tales which set the style for the conventional medieval hagiographers. Bede, Ælfric, and Wulfstan the homilist clearly all made use of them on occasion, though only, of course, of the Latin text.

Of Bishop Wærferth little is known save what Asser tells us, and Alfred's own reference to him. This latter, in the Preface to Alfred's *Pastoral Care*, shows that he was a personal friend of the King, and that it was to him that the sole surviving contemporary copy of this text was specially sent. Wærferth was consecrated Bishop of Worcester in 873. He was one of a group of four Mercian scholars who were among Alfred's educational helpers, and was, it would seem, the oldest of these. He became a member of the King's Court and household about the year 883, and his death took place in 915. His may claim to be the first of those translations from Latin which set Old English prose on the way to becoming literature.[2] The saints treated are Italian: and the common exegetical features are especially concerned with the immortality of the soul. The style of the Anglo-Saxon may be indicated by the following literal translation of Wærferth's opening lines, with their simple directness:

And so now to begin with, we may hear how the blessed and apostolic

---

[1] *Cf.* Simeon Potter, *On the Relation of the Old English Bede to Werferth's Gregory and to Alfred's Translation* (Prague, 1931).

[2] Waerferth's translation is found in *Bischof Werferths Übersetzung der Dialoge Gregors des Grossen*, ed. Hans Hecht (Hamburg, 1907).

Pope Saint Gregory spoke to his deacon whose name was Peter about the teaching and the virtuous lives of holy men, as a lesson and an example to all those who do God's will and love Him. Now the blessed St Gregory was talking concerning himself with these words, and said as follows. On a certain day it happened that I was much afflicted by the tumult and difficulty of some worldly reflections at a time before I had undertaken the business of a bishop.[1]

We have seen that Alfred was the driving force which brought about the creation of historical prose in the *Anglo-Saxon Chronicle*. Again in the work of Bishop Wærferth we may see Alfred as the instigator of the art of prose translation. Wærferth was evidently a better Latinist than other translators of the age, though he makes mistakes from time to time. But the translation of the *Dialogues*, which must have been the first of the series of vernacular works of education inspired by King Alfred, was intended, one must suppose, for the unlearned. Its tales of the casting out of devils and the raising of the dead by the power of the Mass were meant to have especially a popular appeal. Yet the King's educational ambitions needed as a basis something much more substantial: and he seems to have realized, as soon as he himself had acquired some knowledge of Latin and experience as a ruler, that the one necessary foundation for education as well as good government in a state was a well-trained priesthood. But this could only be made possible by the establishment of first-class bishops, who should have the knowledge and wisdom to develop such a priesthood. Hence it was, as it seems, that Alfred chose as the first book that he would himself translate a work, like the *Dialogues*, that originated with St Gregory the Great, but which dealt with the higher aspects of ecclesiastical education, and was addressed to bishops primarily—and through them to the creation of the best possible priesthood. Moreover, since all matters of higher administration in a Christian state were directed by ecclesiastics, Alfred saw that the better training of priests through their bishops would lead to the creation of something like an effective higher civil service. St Gregory the Great's book of directives to bishops, and through them to priests in general, was written soon after he became Pope, probably in 591. It treats bishops as 'shepherds of souls', and aims to show how in every circumstance of life a spiritual director should be able to deal with all human problems. Entitled *Liber Regulae Pastoralis*, and dealing with the 'cure of souls', the book is often named *Cura Pastoralis*: and Alfred himself calls it *Hierdeboc*, or 'shepherd book'. *Cura Pastoralis* is commonly translated *Pastoral Care*. Since the distinction between bishops and parish priests was not so clearly marked as later, St Gregory's book, which became a text-book for medieval bishops, was regarded in Old English times as in effect a kind of manual for the guidance of parish

---

[1] From MS. Cotton Otho C I, ed. Hans Hecht, *op. cit.*, pp. 2–3.

priests. Hence the choice of this work for Alfred's first essay in translation.

We do not know for certain the dates or even the chronological sequence of King Alfred's translations, but one gains an overwhelming impression from what is known of the background history that the *Pastoral Care* should be placed first. For the production of first-class bishops and parish priests was, as has been said, the prime requisite for all the educational developments which Alfred had in mind. The fact that Asser does not directly mention any of Alfred's translations, but only that of Wærferth, shows only that by the year 893 (when Asser ends) the King's own translations were not known. We should, of course, naturally expect that these were only accomplished in the latest years of his reign, when he would have gained, in intervals snatched from warfare and statecraft, the necessary learning and experience.

The five translations attributed to Alfred himself should be regarded, until further evidence comes to light, as produced in the following order: (*a*) *The Pastoral Care*; (*b*) Bede's *Ecclesiastical History*; (*c*) Orosius's *Histories*; (*d*) Boethius's *Consolation*; (*e*) St Augustine's *Soliloquies*. Beginning with the translation of the best text-book for the higher training of the priesthood, Alfred then takes up (or induces another to do this[1]) the translating of Bede's *Historia Ecclesiastica Gentis Anglorum*, which would provide a full and accurate knowledge of the history of England, with special reference to the development of Christian culture. Alfred would thus have produced in the vernacular a great historical text-book especially valuable for teaching the clergy the history of their own Church. The *Anglo-Saxon Chronicle*, which owes its existence in the best extant form to Alfred's impetus, may be supposed already by this time to have given the higher laity some knowledge of their country's past history. The third work of translation would seem naturally to have been the great historical text-book of Orosius, for this presented the history of the known world in a manner specially designed to strengthen Christian faith by showing history as—despite many terrifying disasters—the work of God's providence. This book, entitled *Historiarum adversum Paganos Libri VII*, was the work of Paulus Orosius, a priest of Spain, who, soon after the conquest of his country by the Arian Visigoths, wrote, at the request of his master St Augustine of Hippo, a history designed especially to refute the view that the troubles of Rome and of Christendom of that age were due to the replacing of pagan deities by Christ. Having thus ensured that a specifically Christian view of world history should be part of his educational scheme, as a vernacular text-book presumably intended for the educated laity, it seems that Alfred's next step was to provide a text-book of sound

---

[1] The surviving manuscripts of the Old English Bede, all relatively late, are now thought by most scholars to represent work not done by Alfred himself, though the King's dominant impulse must still be assumed to lie behind it.

philosophy suitable for educated Christians. Boethius's *Consolation of Philosophy* (*De Consolatione Philosophiae Libri V*), written early in the sixth century by a Platonist statesman and philosopher who was also a Christian (though this fact is only implicit in the *Consolation*, but demonstrated in his theological writings) was one of the dominant medieval text-books in Christendom. Finally, as the King's own thoughts tended more and more to concentrate on eternal matters and his spiritual well-being, he made a collection of what used to be called in the Middle Ages 'flowers culled from the Fathers' —passages of Christian thinking freely paraphrased and often employed as a starting-point for his own reflections. They were drawn chiefly from St Augustine's *Soliloquia*, but with something from St Gregory and St Jerome. This last work of Alfred, as well as satisfying the King's own need, provided educative matter for meditation for his readers.

It is, then, from Alfred's own writings that we may best learn of his personality, and of his educative aims and achievements. What we thus learn agrees in the main with what Asser had told us,[1] but the picture becomes more vivid, and a virile and practical excellence in the King which Asser's pietistic and confused exaggerations had rather obscured becomes clear. From Alfred's own prefaces and interpolations into his translations we know that he was deeply religious, and that he practised his Christianity; and from the Preface in particular to the *Pastoral Care* we have confirmation of at least some of Asser's account (in his Chapter 75) of the royal school in which sons of the nobility and of the upper middle classes were taught the liberal arts in both English and Latin, as well as religion. This Preface to the *Pastoral Care* translation, existing as it does in a contemporary manuscript, is the basic document for Alfred's objectives, as well as being his earliest undoubted writing. Though the best known of all, it merits special attention here. Alfred's literary aim was to make available, in simplified and acceptable form and in the native tongue, the best Latin Christian text-books. In doing this, with the addition of the original matter of his prefaces and interpolations, he may be said to have been the fountainhead of Anglo-Saxon prose, though his purposes were didactic, not primarily literary.

As remarked in the preceding chapter, the *Pastoral Care* Preface takes very much the form of a royal writ, in which directives are given to the bishops (each of whom receives a copy of the book) as to its use, and especially the educational aims the King has in view. Here is King Alfred's first original composition as far as is known: though it is also his best known work, its basic importance as well as stylistic features may justify its inclusion here in full:

Ælfred kyning hateð gretan Wærferð biscep his wordum luflice ond

---

[1] Chapters 77 and 78.

freondlice; ond ðe cyðan hate ðæt me com swiðe oft on gemynd, hwelce wiotan iu wæron giond Angelcynn, ægðer ge godcundra hada ge woruldcundra; ond hu gesæliglica tida ða wæron giond Angelcynn; ond hu ða kyningas ðe ðone onwald hæfdon ðæs folces on ðam dagum Gode ond his ærendwrecum hersumedon; ond hu hie ægðer ge hiora sibbe ge hiora siodo ge hiora onweald innanbordes gehioldon, ond eac ut hiora eðel gerymdon; ond hu him ða speow ægðer ge mid wige ge mid wisdome; ond eac ða godcumdan hadas hu giorne hie wæron ægðer ge ymb lare ge ymb liornunga, ge ymb ealle ða ðiowotdomas ðe hie Gode don scoldon; ond hu man utanbordes wisdom ond lare hieder on lond sohte, ond hu we hie nu sceoldon ute begietan, gif we hie habban sceoldon. Swæ clæne hio wæs oðfeallenu on Angelcynne ðæt swiðe feawa wæron behionan Humbre ðe hiora ðeninga cuðen understondan on Englisc oððe furðum an ærendgewrit of Lædene on Englisc areccean; ond ic wene ðætte noht monige begiondan Humbre næren. Swæ feawa hiora wæron ðæt ic furðum anne anlepne ne mæg geðencean be suðan Temese, ða ða ic to rice feng. Gode ælmihtigum sie ðonc ðætte we nu ænigne onstal habbað lareowa. Ond for ðon ic ðe bebiode ðæt ðu do swæ ic geliefe ðæt ðu wille, ðæt ðu ðe ðissa woruldðinga to ðæm geæmetige, swæ ðu oftost mæge, ðæt ðu ðone wisdom ðe ðe God sealde ðær ðær ðu hiene befæstan mæge, befæste. Geðenc hwelc witu us ða becomon for ðisse worulde, ða ða we hit nohwæðer ne selfe ne lufodon, ne eac oðrum monnum ne lefdon; ðonne naman anne we lufodon ðætte we Cristne wæren, ond swiðe feawe ða ðeawas.

Ða ic ða ðis eall gemunde, ða gemunde ic eac hu ic geseah, ær ðæm ðe hit eall forhergod wære ond forbærned, hu ða ciricean giond eall Angelcynn stodon maðma ond boca gefylda, ond eac micel menigeo Godes ðiowa; ond ða swiðe lytle fiorme ðara boca wiston, for ðæm ðe hie hiora nanwuht ongiotan ne meahton, for ðæm ðe hie næron on hiora agen geðiode awritene. Swelce hie cwæden: "Ure ieldran, ða ðe ðas stowa ær hioldon, hie lufodon wisdom, ond ðurh ðone hie begeaton welan ond us læfdon. Her mon mæg giet gesion hiora swæð, ac we him ne cunnon æfter spyrigean, ond for ðæm we habbað nu ægðer forlæten ge ðone welan ge ðone wisdom, for ðæm ðe we noldon to ðæm spore mid ure mode onlutan."

Ða ic ða ðis eall gemunde, ða wundrade ic swiðe swiðe ðara godena wiotona ðe giu wæron giond Angelcynn, ond ða bec ealla be fullan geliornod hæfdon, ðæt hie hiora ða nænne dæl nolden on hiora agen geðiode wendan. Ac ic ða sona eft me selfum andwyrde, ond cwæð: "Hie ne wendon ðætte æfre menn sceolden swæ reccelease weorðan ond seo lar swæ oðfeallan; for ðære wilnunga hie hit forleton, ond woldon ðæt her ðy mara wisdom on londe wære ðy we ma geðeoda cuðon."

Ða gemunde ic hu sio æ wæs ærest on Ebreisc-geðiode funden, ond eft, ða hie Creacas geliornodon, ða wendon hie hie on hiora agen geðiode ealle, ond eac ealle oðre bec. Ond eft Lædenware swæ same, siððan hie hie geliornodon, hie hie wendon ealla ðurh wise wealhstodas on hiora agen geðiode. Ond eac ealla oðre Cristena ðioda sumne dæl hiora on hiora agen geðiode wendon. For ðy me ðyncð betre, gif iow swæ ðyncð, ðæt we eac suma bec, ða ðe niedbeðearfosta sien eallum monnum to wiotonne, ðæt we ða on ðæt geðiode wenden ðe we ealle gecnawan mægen, ond gedon, swæ we swiðe eaðe magon mid Godes fultume, gif we ða stilnesse habbað, ðætte eall sio gioguð ðe nu is on Angelcynne friora monna, ðara ðe ða speda hæbben ðæt hie ðæm befeolan mægen, sien to liornunga oðfæste, ða hwile ðe hie to nanre oðerre note ne mægen, oð ðone first ðe hie wel cunnen Englisc gewrit arædan. Lære mon siððan furður on Læden-geðiode ða ðe mon furðor læran wille ond to hieran hade don wille. Ða ic ða gemunde hu sio lar Læden-geðiodes ær ðissum afeallen wæs giond Angelcynn, ond ðeah monige cuðon Englisc gewrit arædan, ða ongan ic ongemang oðrum mislicum ond manigfealdum bisgum ðisses kynerices ða boc wendan on Englisc ðe is benemned on Læden *Pastoralis*, ond on Englisc 'Hierdeboc,' hwilum word be worde, hwilum andgit of andgiete, swæ swæ ic hie geliornode æt Plegmunde minum ærcebis-cepe, ond æt Assere minum biscepe, ond æt Grimbolde minum mæsseprioste, ond æt Iohanne minum mæssepreoste. Siððan ic hie ða geliornod hæfde, swæ swæ ic hie forstod, ond swæ ic hie andgit-fullicost areccean meahte, ic hie on Englisc awende; ond to ælcum biscepstole on minum rice wille ane onsendan; ond on ælcre bið an æstel, se bið on fiftegum mancessa. Ond ic bebiode on Godes naman ðæt nan mon ðone æstel from ðære bec ne do, ne ða boc from ðæm mynstre—uncuð hu longe ðær swæ gelærede biscepas sien, swæ swæ nu, Gode ðonc wel hwær siendon. For ðy ic wolde ðætte hie ealneg æt ðære stowe wæren, buton se biscep hie mid him habban wille, oððe hio hwær to læne sie, oððe hwa oðre biwrite.[1]

It is evident that Alfred sent copies which were highly valued to every bishop; and we know that the Hatton Manuscript went to Bishop Wærferth, as it has a note in contemporary hand saying 'This book is to go to Worcester': *Ðeos boc sceal to Wiogora ceastre*. The verses prefixed to the *Pastoral Care*, already noticed in Chapter 11, confirm the manner of publication shown in the prose Preface, and add that the copies were needed because some bishops knew little Latin.[2] The immense value of the *æstel* sent with each copy of the work suggests that it was a jewelled bookmark whose gold, gems, etc., would give it fitting dignity. Alfred's educational plan is made sufficiently clear as a whole in this Preface. The translation was done mainly from his recollection of the explanations his scholar helpers had given him; and hence it is uneven and often confused or slavish, so that it has no literary merit. But the prose of the original Preface is indeed a landmark in literary history.

[1] From the Hatton text in *King Alfred's West Saxon Version of Gregory's Pastoral Care*, ed. Henry Sweet (London, 1871), pp. 3–9.
[2] For a full account of the publication see K. Sisam, "The Publication of Alfred's Pastoral Care", in *Studies in the History of Old English Literature*. op. cit., pp. 140–147.

The Alfredian version of Bede's *Historia Ecclesiastica*, probably the next work in the King's programme, was made not by the King himself but by one of his Mercian helpers, of whom Asser mentions four in his Chapter 77. The surviving manuscripts are late, so that the amount of direct connection with Alfred is not clear. Nevertheless, there is a strong tradition preserved in late Anglo-Saxon times that Alfred made a translation. It shows frequent omissions as well as misunderstanding of the Latin. Its value lies in the fact that it provides a readable Old English version of a basically important book, and that in relating the famous story of the poet Cædmon and his dream-vision, the Old English version provides a West-Saxon text of the *Hymn* in a way which adds something by way of native tradition not given in Bede's Latin.[1]

Alfred's version of Orosius's *Histories Against the Pagans* is a free treatment of the Latin, but written in a rather more literary prose than the *Pastoral Care* or the Bede. However, its chief interest lies in Alfred's many original additions and interpolations, since as a work of history Orosius's books have now very little value, though it was a widely used text-book in the Middle Ages. Alfred's eagerness to find out information for himself, and his wide general knowledge, were as Asser has remarked, real, and his additions to Orosius and his free exposition serve further to make this clear. Finding the introductory account of the geography of Europe very thin and vague as regards some central regions, Alfred added his own less inexact knowledge. A little later in his version he interpolated two vivid and detailed geographical descriptions of voyages in Northern Europe which he had obtained at first hand, as he tells us, from Ohthere, a Scandinavian, and Wulfstan, an Englishman. These explorers had visited the King, and from a vivid memory of their verbal narratives he has provided a piece of original prose which is direct, perspicacious, and clear, and includes lively sketches of some of the strange peoples encountered in those northern climes, and of their ways of living. These passages were abbreviated and modernized in Hakluyt's collection of Elizabethan voyages, and upon this excellent piece of writing the fame of Alfred's Orosius now chiefly rests. They appear in almost all collections of Old English for students.[2]

From a purely literary point of view, King Alfred's major work is his translation of Boethius's *De Consolatione Philosophiae*. This philosophical dialogue written by a widely gifted statesman in the imprisonment which preceded his execution was the most influential medieval text-book of ethics. In it the working of divine providence in relation to worldly disasters and tribulations is set forth in Latin of a somewhat classical style, and it had a special appeal for Alfred. For his own life, beset by every difficulty—in ruling his kingdom as

---

[1] See C. L. Wrenn, "The poetry of Caedmon", *Proceedings of the British Academy* XXXII (1946), pp. 277–296.

[2] See Sweet's *Anglo-Saxon Reader*, 13th ed. (Oxford, 1954), pp. 17–22.

well as through his intense physical ailments (if Asser is to be believed)
—had many parallels with that of the Roman statesman. Alfred
seems to have found the finer points of Boethius's Latin beyond
him: but as the basic ideas so much attracted him, he was able to
fill in with explanations and expansions designed especially for
Anglo-Saxon readers, and to intercalate many of his own personal
meditations. He added too an introduction in which the circumstances
of Boethius's life which led to the writing of his *Consolation* are
narrated. In the famous seventeenth chapter, which is almost entirely
Alfred's own addition, the King meditates on his life as a ruler, his
desires for his people, and the tribulations entailed. He reflects,
among other matters, that a king must have three kinds of subjects to
rule well: men of prayer, men of war, and men of work. Without
these three sets of tools, he cannot exercise his talents in virtuously
carrying through the duties of kingship which have been entrusted
to him. He concludes here:

> For every good gift and every power soon grows old and is heard of
> no more if wisdom be not in them. Without wisdom no faculty can
> be fully brought out: for whatever is done unwisely can never be
> accounted as skill. To be brief, I may say that it has ever been my
> desire to live honourably while I was alive, and after my death to
> leave to them that should come after me my memory in good works.[1]

As may be discerned even from this translation, Alfred here writes a
noble and impressive prose: and it is characteristic of him that he
ends with the expression of a typical ancient Germanic heroic
sentiment. Alfred evidently took special trouble over his Boethius,
for it has been found that many of his comments and explanations
are based on those Latin glosses which were so plentifully added in
the margins of manuscripts of the *De Consolatione Philosophiae*. He
shows here too that his intellect and knowledge had matured and
widened much by this time.

Alfred's was the precursor of a number of English translations of
the immensely admired Boethius, including those of Chaucer and
Queen Elizabeth I, though none of them until very recent times
recognized Alfred's work.[2] The surviving manuscripts are all late,
but there is plenty of evidence, both internal and external, of the
authenticity of the Old English—that it is King Alfred's own work.

The collection of freely rendered passages from St Augustine's
Soliloquia, together with reflections and meditations on them which

---

[1] The Old English version is available in *King Alfred's Old English Version of Boethius*, ed. W. J. Sedgefield (Oxford, 1899). Sedgefield's translation, *King Alfred's Version of the Consolations of Boethius Done into Modern English, with an Introduction* (Oxford, 1900) conveniently differentiates those portions of Alfred's text not in the Latin by using for them italic type. The extract quoted is adapted from this translation, p. 42.

[2] On the importance and far-flung influence of Boethius see Howard R. Patch, *The Tradition of Boethius* (New York, 1935).

he called 'blossoms' or 'blooms' (*blostman*), seems to have been King Alfred's last work. It is found only in a twelfth-century copy bound up since the sixteenth century with the Beowulf Manuscript, British Museum Cotton Vitellius A XV, and is known to have been the property of St Mary's Priory at Southwick, Hants, in the later thirteenth century. The work is complete, save for its last half-sentence, and a colophon definitely assigns it to Alfred:

> Here end the sayings that King Alfred had gathered from the book that in English we call . . .

The Preface clearly shows the impress of Alfred himself, and may well be thought of as a kind of farewell to his literary educational work, as that to the *Pastoral Care* had announced its beginning. Alfred tells us that he has been gathering all kinds of wood in the forest, and collecting tools for building, and that always when he has returned home with a burden thus gained he has longed to get more. Emphasizing the many different tools and materials needed for a sound and beautiful edifice, he begs those strong men who have many wagons to go to the same forest and fill them with the best and most fair building-materials. He prays that, because of the work he has done, he may find life less difficult than it has been, and see with the eyes of his heart both light for the way through this life and that which is eternal.[1] Like much of Alfred's Boethius where he added his own thoughts, this Preface provides a strong impression of his personality, as well as examples of his original prose, as distinct from translation.

The achievements of King Alfred for the literary historian are first that he in effect inaugurated original prose composition; secondly, that he laid some foundation for the art of translation; and thirdly that through his prefaces and interpolations he has provided us with the impression of an outstanding and attractive personality, a pioneer in education who has indirectly left us vivid autobiographical fragments. Later medieval references show him as remembered with veneration primarily as a teacher. To him, apparently as the highest authority the compiler could picture, were attributed the thirteenth-century collection of moral gnomic proverbial sayings known as *The Proverbs of Alfred*. Here we are given a picture of King Alfred addressing his counsellors at Seaford in a series of familiar proverbs and platitudes. Again, when the poet of *The Owl and the Nightingale* (*c.* 1200) wished to quote a proverb with an air of the highest authority he would introduce it with 'Alfred said'. One might almost say that the deepest memory of King Alfred in the centuries that followed was, as he might have wished, that of a great schoolmaster. Yet though not a great writer, he was our first begetter of literary

---

[1] This Preface is conveniently printed in *An Anglo-Saxon Reader*, ed. Alfred J. Wyatt (Cambridge, 1925) as "Preface to Alfred's *Blooms*". The whole is edited by H. L. Hargrove (Yale University Press, 1902), and better by W. Endter (Hamburg, 1922).

prose. Nor should it be forgotten that it was to the direct impetus which he gave to the preservation of Anglo-Saxon poetry that we owe the survival of almost all that was regathered in the Benedictine Renaissance of our poetical heritage.

Doubtless Alfred's impetus must have caused the writing of other prose translations in his later years, but these have not survived, except possibly the originally Mercian *Life of St Chad*. This work—preserved only in an early twelfth-century copy made at Worcester, but descended from a Mercian original of about A.D. 900—seems to be among the very few survivals which indicate a literary Mercian tradition before Alfred's time. For this *Life of St Chad*, based on a lost Latin homily following Bede's account of the Saint, seems to look back to an already existing Mercian homiletic tradition. We know, as has been already pointed out, that Alfred employed Mercian scholars as helpers in his educational work: it was evidently only from West Mercia that he could obtain in England products of sound Christian culture, as he indicates in the Preface to his *Pastoral Care*. The Alfredian Bede, again, seems to be based on work done by a Mercian. This *Life of St Chad*, then, along with the Alfredian Bede (especially in MS. Tanner 10 in the Bodleian Library), may point to the existence of some literary culture in the West Mercia of Alfred's time which had survived from the eighth century.[1]

That literary work inspired by Alfred may have been lost is suggested by what we learn, from both Asser and Alfred himself, of his pleasure in and work for the liberal arts. In the Preface to his *Soliloquies* from St Augustine there is a description of building-tools and constructions which shows a loving and technical knowledge of these things. Asser, in his Chapter 91, has a riotously rhetorical account of Alfred as a builder and renovator of fine cities, of his buildings (presumably churches), adorned with gold and silver, of his interest in preserving antiquity, and how he personally supervised his architectural works. What remains to this day of Alfred's artistic activity is due to him only in a general sense—in monuments whose making must have been the indirect effect of his inspiration and example. Two of these are outstanding: the sculptured slab at the Church of Codford St Peter, in Wiltshire, and the famous King Alfred jewel, in the Ashmolean Museum at Oxford. This latter, with its wonderful enamel and gold work, has been thought to be possibly the base of one of those immensely precious book-markers or *æstelas* which the King particularly mentions as sent to each bishop to accompany the copies of his *Pastoral Care*. The Alfred Jewel is inscribed with the words 'Alfred commanded me to be made', *Ælfred mec heht gewyrcan*, so that here the connection with the King is close and direct.

---

[1] See *The Life of St Chad, an Old English Homily*, ed. R. Vleeskruyer (Amsterdam, North-Holland Publishing Co., 1953), where the assumption of a pre-Alfredian Mercian prose tradition is strongly argued.

CHAPTER 14

The Benedictine Renaissance
and Sermon Literature

IN VIEW OF THE GREAT UNCERTAINTY of the dating of so many Old English literary monuments, the loss of so much that once existed, and the consequent apparent blank spaces in literary history, it is not possible to produce anything like a continuous narrative of the development of prose. Inevitably there appear gaps which may be either accidental or real. Broadly speaking, two great periods for prose stand out—the age of Alfred, and the Benedictine Renaissance—the one for its pioneering promise, and the other for literary works of conscious art. There seems to be an almost complete pause in the production of literary prose between the Alfredian period and the time of the revival under the impetus of St Dunstan and his collaborators and disciples. This pause covers about half a century, roughly from the beginning of the tenth century to about 960. Perhaps a basic cause of the general falling away of the arts of vernacular writing which followed Alfred's successful efforts may be found in the fact that Alfred did not produce a revival or rekindling of the religious houses. He himself seems to have founded only two new houses, at Athelney and Shaftesbury; and while Shaftesbury was to become a very important abbey, Athelney, first ruled by John the Old Saxon and filled with various foreign monks, was a decided failure. Unlike Edgar later, Alfred, amid the multifarious and exhausting cares of his kingdom, was not able to stir up and establish any discernible monastic revival. We learn from Asser, as well as from the Preface to the *Pastoral Care*, how religious houses were everywhere deserted or inactive.[1] As Dom David Knowles, the best authority in this field, puts it: "Thus all available evidence from the reign of Alfred points to a complete collapse of monasticism by the end of the ninth century."[2] He is definite that the monastic life in any productive sense disappeared from England between the times of the first Scandinavian raids at the close of the eighth century and the inauguration of St Dunstan as Abbot of Glastonbury in the year 940. As late as Athelstan's time, a few years before Dunstan's elevation—and Athelstan was a ruler who was often a munificent

---

[1] See Asser, Chapter 93.
[2] *The Monastic Order in England*, 2nd ed. (Cambridge, 1963), p. 33.

benefactor of the Church—"We are justified in regarding England in the reign of Athelstan as being wholly without any organized monastic life."[1] It may be, then, that without the continuing life-giving force of the religious houses as centres of culture, no revival or new pioneering enterprise of letters could spread its roots deeply or widely enough to produce lasting and stable results. Alfred had some good and learned bishops: but there is no record of any of them having displayed the dominating statesmanship of St Dunstan, neither does Alfred's educational scheme appear to have been based on monastic schools. Whatever the reasons—and there is not really enough evidence to be sure of the causes—it is the fact that from the end of King Alfred's work till the times of St Dunstan there is only a thin trickle of vernacular literature that has survived. Even the *Anglo-Saxon Chronicle*, which had achieved a very respectable level under Alfred's impetus, generally becomes thin and sporadic through most of the succeeding century, and when it does produce good prose, it is usually not the continuation of the Parker text of Winchester that provides literary pieces of prose, but rather chronicles kept up (though also sporadically) at Abingdon, Worcester, or Peterborough.

The period of the Benedictine Renaissance, in which the new vitality of the reformed Church permeated every aspect of art, was a time of something like florescence of prose of several kinds. But there can be no doubt that it is the sermon written with literary art to be read aloud or recited, whether to religious or to lay people, that is the dominant product in the literature of this age. Again, as is natural, a relatively large body of these homilies has come down to us in good manuscripts from what may with some reason be called 'a golden age of book production', though by no means all have yet been printed. During the reign of Ethelred the Unready, 978–1016, Ælfric and Wulfstan wrote homilies and didactic religious work of real literary merit, while occasionally among more popular sermons, such as those of the Blickling collection and the Vercelli Book, there are homilies which show both liveliness and attractiveness. Ælfric, however, was by far the most versatile and solidly learned writer of his age, as well as being the most artistic. He therefore merits special consideration.

Though he always did his work within the walls of religious houses, rather than as a public leader like the great Benedictine English saints, Ælfric for the literary historian is clearly the great figure of his age. By far the most prolific writer in the vernacular (though he also wrote much in Latin), he has left work in his native language of permanent value and influence in many fields, although it is as a homilist with a sense of style and of the literary art that his greatest contribution to the development of English prose has been

[1] Knowles, *op. cit.*, p. 36.

made. He has left three large collections of sermons, containing a great deal of theological teaching, for both the laity and the clergy, pastoral epistles written for bishops, a Latin–Old English grammar intended for boys in monastic schools (in which he shows himself to have been a remarkable pedagogue and a master of colloquial style), a scientific treatise on the seasons on meteorological lines, based on Bede's *De Temporibus Anni,* and a variety of Biblical translations. Like King Alfred, too—whose work he greatly admired—he has left us some vivid impressions of an attractive personality in a number of prefaces in both English and Latin. In his use of the native tongue for the rendering of theology and grammar Ælfric is of very great importance in the enrichment of his language and the exploitation of its wide potentialities to their utmost. Ælfric finds, as he tells us, that there are many English books containing many errors which simple people regard as wisdom; but that the only books of sound religious teaching available to those who do not know Latin are 'those books which King Alfred turned into English with wisdom'.[1] His vernacular books of religious teaching are, then, the first since King Alfred's time. But Ælfric is to be remembered not only as the great practical teacher of the Benedictine reform, but as the first English writer to produce didactic prose whose style and literary art make it still an aesthetic pleasure to read.

As a teacher of theology, Ælfric simply sought to make available to non-Latinists the orthodox Catholic doctrine accepted in his time. Basing his methods on those traditionally in use as they had descended from the exegetical precept and practice of St Augustine of Hippo—especially in his *De Doctrina Christiana*—he sought to make available in direct, simple, and often rhetorically attractive language the teaching of the Church and those 'evangelical doctrines' which were not to be had in English. He translated and adapted from the great Doctors of the Church homiletic guidance and scholarly exegesis: and always without thought of any originality or new intellectual departure. On the one hand, as Dom David Knowles states:

> We look in vain to Ælfric, and more vainly still to Byrhtferth, for an original, genial idea or for any of that intellectual self-possession and clarity of criticism that comes in with Anselm and Abelard.[2]

But on the other hand, to quote Dom David again:

> But in his diligent absorption of the inheritance of the past, in the sobriety and breadth of his teaching, in his responsiveness to all calls made upon him, in his strong national feeling and in the quiet life

---

[1] Old English Preface to his "Catholic Homilies" in *The Homilies of the Anglo-Saxon Church*, ed. Benjamin Thorpe (London, 1844–46), vol. I, p. 2. This will be referred to as 'Thorpe'.
[2] *Op. cit.*, p. 47.

passed within the walls of a monastery, he inevitably recalls his great forerunner [Bede] and is, when all his gifts are taken into the reckoning, one of the most distinguished figures in the history of Western theological learning in the centuries immediately before the renaissance of the eleventh century.[1]

Ælfric lived from about A.D. 955 to 1020. Born of a noble family, he was educated in the Old Minster at Winchester under his revered teacher St Æthelwold, who was Bishop of Winchester from 963 till his death in 984. Some time after being ordained priest at the usual canonical age of thirty, he was sent through the influence of noble and cultivated patrons to Cerne Abbas, in Dorset, where a Benedictine house was set up in 987; but he seems to have returned to Winchester after only a few years in that monastery. In 1005, through the same aristocratic influence, he was made the first Abbot of a new Benedictine house at Eynsham, in Oxfordshire, where he seems to have spent the remainder of his quiet and apparently uneventful life. Remaining within monastic walls, but always fully responsive to all the events happening outside, and directly aiming to forward the revitalizing work of the Benedictine leaders and their legacy of teaching, Ælfric might be described in modern terms as the unobserved literary propagandist of the Benedictine movement, who provided some of the basic documents for rekindling and widening among both laity and clergy the teaching and the practical guidance of the Church.

Of the many sermons of Ælfric that survive, most find their place in one or other of the three series which he designed for various purposes and preachers. The first two of these three series are known collectively as his *Catholic Homilies*, and were called by himself *Sermones Catholici*. (The third series is known as *Lives of Saints*.) About the year 990 he made a compilation of forty homilies to be used on the appropriate principal Holy Days as they came round in the ecclesiastical year. They were to be preached by means of copies to be circulated under the authority of Archbishop Sigeric of Canterbury, to whom the writer presents the volume in his Preface, written in both Latin and Old English. This series he followed up, as he had proposed in the Preface to the first, with a second collection of forty-five sermons to be used in the second and alternating years. While most of these eighty-five homilies are preached on Gospel texts, others treat of saints. Ælfric claims only to be a translator, following the Alfredian precept of 'sometimes word for word, sometimes sense from sense'—an idea King Alfred had taken from St Gregory the Great. But there is much more freedom in Ælfric's homilies in many places, and an individuality in much of the presentation of the traditional material chosen from the four great Doctors of the Church and occasionally from eighth-century orthodox explicators. The

---

[1] *Op. cit.*, p. 63.

method, following tradition, is one in which the whole of the Scriptural text is translated first, then a simple but full exegesis is given, leading to a discourse on the lessons to be drawn, and ending with a concluding exhortation.[1]

The next work, intended primarily to help the clergy in calculating the dates of future Easters and other movable Church Feasts, was Ælfric's revision and adaptation into the vernacular of Bede's little treatise *De Temporibus Anni*, which explains chronology in relation to the universe and its seasons. It is evident that Ælfric, like King Alfred, had something of an educational plan which should help both laity and clergy. Having provided homilies for the principal Church Feasts suitable for all, he had then turned to fill a particular need of the clergy with his *De Temporibus Anni*.[2]

The third book was his *Grammar*, in which he aimed to provide small boys with the elements of Latin grammar in their mother tongue so that Latin grammatical terms and classifications could be applied in such a way as to promote the early study of both languages. He fears, as his bilingual Preface declares, that the knowledge of Latin may grow cold and seem tedious

> as it came about during a few years earlier until Archbishop Dunstan and Bishop Ethelwold once more raised up this teaching among the monastic orders. But it is by no means just for this reason that I say that this little book may accomplish much in the matter of teaching: but it will be, nevertheless, a certain beginning if it is pleasing to anyone.[3]

Grammar was then, as the necessary basis to all the written arts, of supreme importance: and this work of Ælfric is the first study of grammar in any vernacular of Europe, as well as the first attempt to teach the elements of both Anglo-Saxon and Latin through the medium of a bilingual instrument. The material is, of course, traditional, an inheritance from Priscian and other later Latin grammarians. Ælfric is, he says, content to teach in the simplest way the rules he had learned at school in Winchester from his master Æthelwold, but the presentation is his own. The immense influence of this *Grammar* is indicated by the fact that it survives in far more manuscripts than any other Old English work.

The *Grammar* was intended for small boys, probably oblates in the monastery school, who must learn to speak Latin as well as write and read it. Hence there is a Glossary at the end of Ælfric's *Grammar*, lists of words which are equivalent to those in Latin, arranged under common heads for the purpose of being the more easily committed to memory. Thus there are collections of English words with their corresponding Latin, under such heads as 'names of parts

---

[1] The two series of *Catholic Homilies* are printed, with translations, in Thorpe.
[2] *Ælfric's De Temporibus Anni*, ed. H. Henel (EETS 213: London, 1942).
[3] *Ælfrics Grammatik und Glossar*, ed. Julius Zupitza (Berlin, 1880), p. 3.

of the body', 'names of birds', etc. Having mastered such a body of words suitable for everyday simple dialogue in Latin within the monastery, Ælfric proposed that the boys should use a Latin *Colloquium*, a traditional type of teaching manual in which the material is arranged as dialogue between the master and his boys treating of simple and familiar themes. Having provided this Latin *Colloquium*, but in a much more vivid and flexible and less formal shape than the traditional type, Ælfric—perhaps with help from some bright pupils—supplied a continuous interlinear gloss to the Latin. This gloss is a unique illustration of the familiar colloquial language of early eleventh-century Wessex. The Latin with its continuous gloss is known as Ælfric's *Colloquy*.[1] Ælfric here has the lively idea of making his matter more dramatic and lifelike by having each boy taking part in the *Colloquy* assume the character of a rural worker—ploughman, smith, fisherman, etc. The simple charm of the Latin is equalled by the grace and colloquial vigour of the English.

The fourth and final major work of Ælfric's educational plan[2] was his third collection of homilies treating in particular the sufferings and miracles of those saints who are especially honoured by monks, and who have their own services. This book of thirty-seven homilies, freely translated or adapted as before from the best authorities, is known as the *Lives of Saints*.[3] This collection was made between the years 993 and 998, at the request of the author's old friends and noble patrons Æthelmær and Æthelweard. The Preface, in both Latin and Old English, tells us this, and also definitely says that this book is the last that he will undertake in this kind. For Ælfric does not think it fitting that very many such writings should be turned into the vernacular, 'lest perchance the pearls of Christ should be viewed with disrespect': *ne forte despectui habeantur margaritae Christi*. Throughout his work there is always something of caution and a weighing of the consequences in making Latin books widely available to the laity: and there is a clear distinction in Ælfric's view between the needs of the clergy and those of the unlearned. He says again in this Preface that he will keep silent about the *Vitae Patrum* (an official collection) because there are things in it of subtle character which should not be put before the laity—and, indeed, he adds, some things in it which "we ourselves" cannot fully grasp. A deliberate curtailing of the prolixity of the Latin sources is emphasized here, and the directness and simplicity aimed at is also stressed.

In the English Preface the last part is in rhythmic free alliterative verse, which is a significant fact. For in these *Lives of Saints* many

[1] Ed. G. N. Garmonsway (London, 1939).
[2] For an account of the order of Ælfric's major works in an educational plan, see K. Sisam, "The Order of Ælfric's Early Books" in *Studies in the History of Old English Literature*, pp. 298–301.
[3] Edited as *Ælfric's Lives of Saints*, by W. W. Skeat (EETS 76, 82, 114: London, 1881–1900). This will be referred to as 'Skeat'.

of the sermons are in such metrical form—a practice occasionally resorted to already in the *Catholic Homilies* of the earlier collection. We have seen how the use of alliterative phrase and traces of metrical rhythm had survived in traditional material such as laws and charters. It would seem that, since ordinary people were accustomed to listening to the recitation of verse—but not, of course, of prose—there was some virtue of added attractiveness in a homily declaimed in the manner of poetry, and having basically the traditional suggestion of two-stressed rhythm and juxtaposed alliteration. We know that traces of this practice lasted far into the Middle English period, especially in legends of saints. The early thirteenth-century tale of *St Juliana* is clearly a descendant of this manner.

Ælfric wrote much else in the vernacular, but most of this is of historical rather than literary importance, although always he wrote an agreeable, direct, and clear prose. He translated many selected portions of the Bible, choosing what would best suit the needs of the laity. Thus he chose to treat of Old Testament patriarchs like Jacob and Isaac, with an obvious lesson to illustrate, or other characters like Esther, Judith, and Samson whose careers should stir up patriotic, unselfish zeal for the defence of the country against the heathen Vikings. Always the Biblical stories are told well, with artistic adjustments and abridgments to make them the more effective to an Anglo-Saxon audience. Much of this Biblical translation is collected in what is known as *Ælfric's Heptateuch*. This odd title was invented by the first editor, Edward Thwaites, who issued the work from the Oxford Press in 1698. This *Heptateuch* comprises parts of seven books of the Old Testament (hence the name)—from Genesis, Exodus, Leviticus, Deuteronomy, Numbers, Joshua, and Judges. Ælfric provided effective vernacular teaching on the nature and proper uses of the Scripture in his *Preface to Genesis* and his *Treatise on the Old and New Testament*. These are conveniently printed along with the Biblical versions just mentioned in the Early English Text Society's edition of the Old English *Heptateuch*.[1]

Ælfric's work as a translator is unique for his time in that he obviously gave a great deal of thought to the methods to be employed and the objects aimed at. In his *Preface to Genesis* he discusses the differences between Latin and English in the matter of word-order and tone, and adds:

Æfre se þe awent oððe se þe tæcð of Ledene on Englisc, æfre he sceal gefadian hit swa þæt þæt Englisc hæbbe his agene wisan, elles hit bið swiðe gedwolsum to rædenne þam þe þæs Ledenes wisan ne can.[2]

---

[1] *The Old English Version of the Heptateuch, Ælfric's Treatise on the Old and New Testament and his Preface to Genesis*, ed. S. J. Crawford (EETS 160: London, 1922).
[2] *Ælfric's Heptateuch*, op. cit., pp. 79–80.

He who translates or teaches from Latin to English must always so order matters that his English preserve the special qualities of that language [*his agene wisan*]. Otherwise it will be most misleading to read for anyone who is not acquainted with the special qualities of Latin.

It was not for nothing, too, that Ælfric came to be traditionally known as "Grammaticus". For he was especially interested in matters of language and good usage: and there are manuscripts of his works that show careful correction evidently made under his supervision. One of these, MS. Royal 7 C XII in the British Museum, which includes the first series of his *Catholic Homilies*, shows clear signs of his personal attention, and contains notes of corrections or changes required which are in his own handwriting.[1] It is difficult to assess the debt of the literary language to Ælfric. For on the one hand his handling of theological, and to some extent of scientific, subjects brings out his remarkable ability to make his native language a fitting vehicle to convey his meaning to the simple people for whom he largely wished to provide; on the other his *Grammar* provides a set of Old English terms to express the Latin ones, and to convey the Latin concepts which would have been entirely new. His *Catholic Homilies*, in the exposition of traditional orthodox Catholic doctrine on such difficult mysteries as the Trinity and the Eucharist, often furnish the language with the necessary immediately intelligible terms by the expedient of coining new compound words from native elements. Ælfric also developed a flowing style adjusted as needed by the expert use of various rhetorical devices inherited from Latin, so that his prose can reflect subtly and vividly all the changing aspects of his subjects. Had not the Norman Conquest supervened, English might have been established as a first-class literary prose medium many centuries before this in fact occurred. But the Norman Conquest did sweep away most of this potentiality because its prolonged effects caused the atrophy of those inherent powers in the language—particularly the capacity for making new compounds to express new concepts—which Ælfric had so brilliantly exploited. One cannot say, therefore, that his writings left any strong permanent traces on the language of literary and intellectual prose, though the grace and strength of his best work become at once apparent to those who will read it in his Anglo-Saxon.

There is clearly interest for the literary historian in Ælfric's *Grammar*, with its new use of the vernacular, in his *Colloquy*, for its illustration of the colloquial speech of his time, and in his translations, both Biblical and scientific, as in his *De Temporibus Anni*. In his prefaces and introductions again there is the interest of his attractive personality and the clear and direct exposition of his

[1] See K. Sisam, "MSS. Bodley 340 and 342: Ælfric's *Catholic Homilies*" in *Studies in the History of Old English Literature*, pp. 173–174 and footnote.

objectives. But it is above all as a homilist that his reputation as a maker of literature has come to him. It is desirable, therefore, to look a little more closely at his two great collections, the *Catholic Homilies* and the *Lives of Saints*.

The *Catholic Homilies* cover the major Feast Days of the Church, and therefore embrace a considerable variety of themes, each of them requiring differing methods of treatment; and Ælfric, with his wide learning and flexible tone, presents us accordingly with a multitude of stylistic variations, yet always following tradition and the best authorities, while adding constantly his own illustrative matter so as to bring his material into a form which would vividly come home to his hearers, whether monks or laymen. One of these sermons—that for the Assumption of St John, which was quoted at the end of Chapter 3 for its form—has often been pointed out as an excellent example of Ælfric's manner at its best for its simple and dignified rhetoric. Another, that for the Holy Innocents, is superb in its art of moving pathos. Both these homilies are conveniently printed in Sweet's *Anglo-Saxon Reader*.[1] Here is a characteristic piece of pathetic rhetoric from the homily for the Nativity of the Holy Innocents.

Of the infants slain by Herod, we read:

> Hi wæron ðæs Hælendes gewitan, ðeah ðe hi hine ða gyt ne cuðon. Næron hi geripode to slege, ac hi gesæliglice þeah swulton to life. Gesælig wæs heora acennednys, for ðan ðe hi gemetton þæt ece lif on instæpe þæs andweardan lifes. Hi wurdon gegripene fram modorlicum breostum, ac hi wurdon betæhte þærrihte engellicum bosmum. Ne mihte se manfulla ehtere mid nanre ðenunge ðam lytlingum swa micclum fremian swa micclum swa he him fremode mid ðære reðan ehtnysse hatunge. Hi sind gehatene martyra blostman, for ðan ðe hi wæron swa swa upaspringende blostman on middewearde cyle ungeleaffulnysse, swilce mid sumere ehthysse forste forsodene.

These two sermons from Ælfric's first cycle of *Catholic Homilies*, on the Assumption of St John and on the Nativity of the Innocents, are, though in very different manner, expositional narratives. Others in this first series are more basically instructional; and of these the outstanding example is Ælfric's sermon on the doctrine of the Trinity, No. XX in Thorpe's edition, entitled *On the Catholic Faith* [*De Fide Catholica*]. Having in the immediately preceding homily dealt with the *Pater Noster*, Ælfric points out that one should pray with the Lord's Prayer, but confirm one's faith with the Creed. He then takes the matter of the Athanasian statement of orthodox Trinitarian doctrine as his theme, and produces by far the most simple, direct, and intelligible description and illustration of the doctrine of the Trinity that is to be found in any part of medieval

[1] 13th ed., pp. 57–74. In Thorpe, Vol. I, Nos IV and V.

English literature. His material, even most of the illustrative comparisons, is, as almost always with Ælfric, traditional or taken from ecclesiastically well authorized sources. But the effect of his homely and pellucid way of setting them out is difficult to parallel for strength and impression of sincerity. Here is a sample of this style:

> Seo sunne ðe ofer us scinð is lichamlic gesceaft, and hæfð swa-ðeah ðreo agennyssa on hire: an is seo lichamlice edwist, þæt is ðære sunnan trendel; oðer is se leoma oððe beorhtnys æfre of ðære sunnan, seo ðe onliht ealne middangeard; þridde is seo hætu, þe mid þam leoman cymð to us. Se leoma is æfre of ðære sunnan, and æfre mid hire; and ðæs Ælmihtigan Godes sunu is æfre of ðam Fæder acenned, and æfre mid him wunigende; be ðam cwæð se apostol, ðæt he wære his Fæder wuldres beorhtnys. Ðære sunnan hætu gæð of hire and of hire leoman; and se Halga Gast gæð æfre of ðam Fæder and of ðam suna gelice; be ðam is þus awriten, "Nis nan þe hine behydan mæge fram his hætan."

> (from *De Fide Catholica*, Thorpe, I, Vol. 282).

Ælfric's thirtieth homily of his first cycle, *On the Assumption of Blessed Mary* [*De Assumptione Beatae Mariae*], is an outstanding example of the instructional sermon combined with a deeply felt and impressive devotional simplicity. The Feast of the Assumption was already in the England of Ælfric's time one of the greatest festivals of the year; and England was distinguished in Western Europe for its keen early devotion to the Blessed Virgin. The occasion—August 15th, at the height of summer—therefore called for a major homily. But, on the other hand, there were many popular legends current, even in vernacular books, which Ælfric regarded as erroneous; and always he would unite a very cautious guarding against heresy with deeply felt devotion. In this sermon he begins with a warning against over-emphasis on physical miracles, and cites as his authority for what should be believed about Our Lady's Assumption into Heaven a letter of St Jerome on this subject. Then with almost passionate persuasion he draws his hearers to adoration of her whom he regards as 'the most precious treasure, and Queen of all the world', *þone deorwurðan maðm, ealles middangeardes cwene*: and he bases belief in her Assumption on a rational interpretation from the Incarnation. He ends with exhortation to prayers for the help of Mary's intercessions. He exhorts his readers to a simple belief in the fact of the Assumption, but without any attempt to understand the mystery of its occurrence. Ælfric's strength as a homilist— and this is true too of his prose style—lies in the blending of plain rational argument, in the simplest and most natural language, with a sincerely felt and moving devotion, and a sense of divine mysteries which draw faith but transcend full human understanding.

An example of a piece of theological exposition among the instructional sermons is that in the second cycle of *Catholic Homilies* known as *On the Sacrifice on Easter Day* [*De Sacrificio in Die Pascae*]: for this is Ælfric's most effective bringing of the basic significance of the Eucharist to the people. This, the fifteenth in this series, is by far the best known of Ælfric's sermons, not for its literary merits but because of the controversial use to which it was put by the Elizabethan Protestant reformers, who believed it could be taken as (to quote the words of the *Dictionary of National Biography*) "a sermon against transubstantiation". Probably because of its supposed value as a polemic, this homily, in which Ælfric had so carefully sought to steer a course of orthodox Catholic doctrine so as to avoid the extremes of differing heresies, was the nucleus of the first book printed in England in the original Anglo-Saxon, and with special Anglo-Saxon type produced for the occasion. Published under the direction of Archbishop Parker and his Anglican group, with a strongly Protestant preface by John Foxe, the author of the *Book of Martyrs*, it is entitled *The Testimonie of Antiquitie shewing the auncient fayth in the Church of England touching the sacrament of the body and bloude of the Lord here publikely preached, and also receiued in the saxons tyme, aboue* 600 *yeares agoe*, and was printed in London by John Day in the year 1567. Ælfric thus has a historical interest for the part his Easter sermon played in the Elizabethan revival of Anglo-Saxon studies.

This famous homily, which shows Ælfric's remarkable power of combining clear and simple exposition of doctrine with fervent expression of that faith which must supplement the intellectual processes, presents in fact not any variation from accepted doctrine as regards the Mass, still less any protest against authoritative teaching. It shares the general dedication of this second cycle of *Catholic Homilies* to Archbishop Sigeric, and the Latin Preface to this collection especially emphasizes the preacher's anxiety to avoid error: the Archbishop is begged to remove from these sermons 'any taints of wicked heresy' if he finds them, since Ælfric would rather be reproved by him than through incautious persuasiveness be praised by the ignorant.[1] In this sermon he seeks to include and explain both the symbolist and the realist emphasis in the Eucharist. The Council of Rome which condemned the unduly symbolist views of Archdeacon Berengar of Tours did not take place till 1050, half a century after the writing of this sermon: and neither the word nor the metaphysical concept of transubstantiation existed till a couple of centuries later, although of course the basic doctrine was part of ordinary teaching. Ælfric, while explaining that the divine elements are received in the Eucharist as a symbolizing (*getacnung*), and that this is done spiritually (*gastlice*), not bodily (*lichamlice*), so perhaps seeming to indicate the reformist belief, goes on to cite two miracles from the *Vitae Patrum* and St Gregory the Great's *Dialogues*

---

[1] Thorpe, *op. cit.*, Vol. II, pp. 1–2.

in which doubters of the carnal reality of the body and blood of Christ in the Mass were granted a vision of their physical presence as the priest performed the sacrifice.[1] Indeed, the Old English words *gastlice* and *lichamlice* do not quite correspond to our 'spiritually' and 'bodily' because they imply less materiality than those terms would indicate, with something like an element of personality. With several homely illustrations, Ælfric concludes:

Soðlice se hlaf and þæt win, ðe beoð ðurh sacerda mæssan gehalgode, oðer ðing hi æteowiað menniscum andgitum wiðutan, and oðer ðing hi clypiað wiðinnan geleaffullum modum. Wiðutan hi beoð gesewene hlaf and win, ægðer ge on hiwe ge on smæcce; ac hi beoð soðlice æfter ðære halgunge, Cristes lichama and his blod ðurh gastlicere gerynu.[2]

Truly the bread and the wine which are consecrated through the Mass by the priests appear as one thing to human intelligences externally, while inwardly they cry plainly another thing to faithful hearts. Externally they are visible as bread and wine both in colour and in taste: but after the consecration they in truth become Christ's body and his blood through a mystery of the spirit [*þurh gastlicere gerynu*].

The simple clarity and moving sense of the divine mystery combine to produce masterly stylistic effects in this sermon; and no doubt after Ælfric's skilful blending of emotive effects with appeals to simple reasoning, his auditors would readily have accepted his exhortation:

You are not to meditate upon how it [the miracle of the Mass] is done, but to keep in your faith the fact that it is so done. [*Ne sceole ge smeagan hu hit gedon sy, ac healdan on eowerum geleafan þæt hit swa gedon sy.*][3]

Ælfric's series of sermons on the *Lives of Saints*, his fourth and last work of educational translation, treats of those saints especially who are honoured by monks, since in the *Catholic Homilies* those whose festivals are held in general veneration by 'this famous nation', *gens ista caelebris*, had been dealt with. Even when addressing a clerical audience, Ælfric uses the native tongue: but he evidently had doubts as to the propriety of so much vernacular writing. For he ends his Preface by stating that he is resolved to make this his last work in this kind. There were a number of cults of individual saints in the England of the great Benedictine period, and it is with these in mind that the *Lives of Saints* were produced for the benefit of the many monks whose Latin was scanty, even in this revitalized age. The use of a poetic prose resembling free verse and using

[1] Thorpe, *op. cit.*, Vol. II, pp. 272–273.
[2] *Ibid.*, p. 268.
[3] *Ibid.*, p. 272.

alliteration and a looser type of traditional verse-rhythm, of which the latter part of the Old English Preface to this collection is an example, is a marked feature of the *Lives of Saints*. One may wonder how it should have come about that Ælfric chooses to employ this method much more in this series of homilies addressed to monks primarily than in the *Catholic Homilies*, which were intended for quite general audiences. It may be that experience had encouraged Ælfric to use this type of prose much more freely by this time because its echoes of ancient poetic tradition had been found to afford audiences greater pleasure. For Ælfric believed that the providing of pleasure was a subordinate element of value in the teaching process, as St Augustine had taught. However, not all the *Lives of Saints* collection as we have it is concerned with saints. Some of the *Lives* are general sermons evidently addressed to popular audiences. One, for instance, No. XVII, is on the *Greater Litany*, but is chiefly concerned with the sins of popular superstitions such as witchcraft and divination. Indeed, it has a sub-heading 'Concerning Auguries', *De Auguriis*, and shows Ælfric's intimate knowledge of the superstitions of the rural lay population, such as that connected with sneezing.[1] Its language is homely yet agreeable in its simplicity. Another, No. XVIII, is, as its author says, a small treatise of lessons to be drawn from existing passages in the Book of Kings, *Sermo Excerptus de Libro Regum*, and includes a well told story of Jezebel and of Naboth's vineyard.[2]

An excellent example of Ælfric's use of the poetical rhythmic type of prose in the *Lives of Saints* is his narrative sermon on St Edmund, the martyred King of East Anglia, No. XXXII in the collection. It opens with a short prologue in plain prose, in which Ælfric sets out the authority he is translating with vivid and convincing detail. A certain learned Benedictine monk named Abbo, he says, had come over to England from his monastery at Fleury, in France, on a visit to St Dunstan at Canterbury three years before the Archbishop died. (This gives us the exact date of 985 for Abbo's receipt of the tale.) Then St Dunstan related to his visitor the story of Edmund's martyrdom, just as he had heard it when a very young man from the lips of a very aged man who had been St Edmund's sword-bearer. We are further told that the slaying of Edmund by the Danes took place when King Alfred was twenty-one years old, thus fixing the date of that event to the year 870. It is further explained that Abbo (the Latin form of his French name Abbon), on returning home wrote down all that he had learned from the Archbishop in Latin, and that it is from this that Ælfric is translating. Now, Abbo's *Passio Sancti Edmundi* is extant, and as he was the most authoritative scholar of his time, this was clearly the ideal

---

[1] Skeat, *op. cit.*, Vol. I, pp. 364 ff.
[2] *Ibid.*, pp. 384 ff.

source-material.[1] After this masterly exordium—probably intended especially for the priest who was to use the homily—the narrative proper proceeds in Ælfric's type of poetical prose, employing the rhythmic and alliterative devices described in Chapter 3.[2] Despite the vernacular blend of the popular and the traditional heroic, Abbo's Latin is rendered with a keen colloquial flavour and a sense of drama. Ælfric also puts in homely and occasionally even lively touches, as for instance in his description of the robbers who were miraculously prevented from stealing the treasures which the pious had left at the shrine of the Saint. While these thieves were at work breaking in, one with a file working round the locks, another trying to dig under the door, and a third with a ladder seeking to force open the window, all were suddenly struck motionless, each just as he was in that moment. But Ælfric vivifies the scene with a phrase not in the Latin: 'each as he stood becoming rigid with the tool he was using in his hand', *ælcne swa he stod, strutigende mid tole*. This verb *strutian* is found nowhere else in Old English, and was evidently colloquial, having the sense 'to stand out rigidly or stiffly'. It is the ancestor of modern *strut*, but was used in Elizabethan times of the stiffly outstanding ruffs on a robe.[3]

As the *Lives of Saints* are primarily intended for the festivals of those whom monks in England especially honour with offices, a number of English saints are included: Saints Etheldreda, Oswald, King of Northumbria, and Swithin, besides St Edmund the Martyr. In dealing with these native characters Ælfric is particularly successful, and in handling Saints Etheldreda and Oswald, with Bede as basic authority, he is able to illuminate his material by the use of some traditional knowledge.

Ælfric, as the learned theologian of the Benedictine Revival, in addition to his important educational work in providing sermons and teaching material for the clergy, was evidently in great demand among bishops for aid with the writing of pastoral letters, and sometimes more recondite learned works, in both Old English and Latin. Thus it was that he wrote pastoral letters on occasion for Wulfstan, Bishop of Worcester and Archbishop of York,[4] and also drew up for the Church canons for the administration of ecclesiastical policy generally, and also a code of conduct for the individual cleric. There is, too, a curiously academic little treatise on 'false gods', *De Falsis Deis*, which relates the origin of the ancient classical deities and their supposed Germanic parallels, with some emphasis on Danish forms. This out-of-the-way homily is in free verse rhythm,

[1] Abbo's narrative, along with much other material on St Edmund, is included with translation in Lord Francis Hervey, *Corolla Sancti Edmundi* (London, 1907).
[2] Cf. Sweet's *Anglo-Saxon Primer*, revised N. Davis, 9th ed. reprinted (Oxford, 1957), pp. 81–87. Printed properly as verse in Skeat, *op. cit.*, Vol. II, pp. 314–334.
[3] See under '*Strut*' in the *Oxford English Dictionary*.
[4] Both Latin and Old English Pastoral Letters are in *Die Hirtenbriefe Ælfrics in Lateinischer und Altenglischer Fassung*, ed. B. Fehr (Hamburg, 1914).

and was evidently first composed in Latin and then translated.[1] But such works are scarcely relevant to a consideration of Ælfric in the history of literature. They have, however, another kind of interest in the light they throw on the Benedictine movement of the time, and on its educational success. There were, for instance, at this time actually laymen with a knowledge of Latin, as is indicated by the work of Æthelweard, Ælfric's friend and patron, who translated from the *Anglo-Saxon Chronicle* into Latin (though of a somewhat barbarous form).

It is evident that Bishop Wulfstan relied much on Ælfric for basic material. Two of his homilies, Nos. IX, *De Septiformi Spiritu*, and XII, *De Falsis Deis*, are mainly his own re-writing of Ælfric's works with the same titles,[2] and it has been plausibly argued that the prose matter of the so-called *Benedictine Office* was the work of Ælfric which Wulfstan revised and adapted.[3] Ælfric's *De Falsis Deis*, which Wulfstan took over, survives in seven manuscripts, so that it was clearly of wide interest despite its rather austere and schoolmasterly tone. The *De Septiformi Spiritu*, a homiletic treatise on the sevenfold gifts of the Holy Spirit, taken over as Wulfstan's ninth homily, is a simple but careful theological tractate which seems especially to have interested the Elizabethan Anglo-Saxonist theologians: for the manuscript, Cotton Tiberius C VI of the British Museum has much interlinear glossing of that period.

Wulfstan, the other famous Anglo-Saxon homilist, was a contemporary of Ælfric, and as mentioned above was aided by him in the preparation of some of his writings, and of official publications for the guidance of the clergy. Wulfstan, born in East Anglia and with connections with Ely, was a Benedictine monk like Ælfric; but unlike him he was to become a most influential statesman and drafter of laws as holder of the highest offices in Church and State. He was Bishop of London from 996, and held the see of Worcester along with the Archbishopric of York from about 1003 to 1017, when he divested himself of the Worcester bishopric in order to devote himself to the northern archbishopric, which he held till his death in 1023. He was the trusted adviser of King Ethelred and of his successor Canute, and in this capacity drew up codes of laws issued by both kings. As an experienced statesman and jurist he drew up a collection of directives setting forth the duties of all sorts and conditions of people in a Christian kingdom, both clerical and lay, as well

---

[1] Only partly in print, particularly its account of the origin of Saturn in J. Kemble's compilation *Salamon and Saturn*, Part 2 (London, 1847), pp. 120–125 with translation. Most of the text is included in the best manuscript of the *Lives of Saints*, British Museum MS. Cotton Julius E VII, fols. 238–240: also in MS. Corpus Christi Coll., Cambridge, 178, fols. 142–163.

[2] See *The Homilies of Wulfstan*, ed. Dorothy Bethurum (Oxford, 1957), for texts and discussion.

[3] See *The Benedictine Office*, ed. James M. Ure, *op. cit.*, pp. 34–43.

as defining the proper position of the Sovereign in relation to the State. These, to which Thorpe gave the name *Institutes of Polity*, have been referred to as the oldest 'courtesy book' in Western Europe, and they, copied sporadically into several manuscripts chiefly Corpus Christi College, Cambridge, 201, have every mark of Wulfstan's style, though they are not formally attributed to him. They constitute something like an embryonic treatise on Anglo-Saxon polity.[1] But these *Institutes of Polity*, which to the historian may well turn out to be Wulfstan's most significant work, have not yet been fully edited, so that until their proper shape is determined their literary qualities can hardly be profitably discussed.

In so far as their reputation continued in the post-Norman era, both Ælfric and Wulfstan seem to have been remembered mainly as sermon-writers (though Ælfric as grammarian also was not forgotten). During the twelfth century, as long as Anglo-Saxon continued to be at all understood (chiefly in the more conservative and remote West Midlands) the homilies of both were being copied, notably at that great Old English cultural centre Worcester. In the Elizabethan Anglo-Saxon Renaissance, however, while Ælfric received controversial fame through the Protestant publicizing of his supposed teaching on the Eucharist, Wulfstan, who hardly ever wrote anything that could properly be called theology, remained unnoticed. But, despite the importance to historians of his part in the legal codes of Ethelred the Unready and of Canute, his practical canons for the use of his clergy, and his *Institutes of Polity*, it is as a homilist that his literary name has been made. In the standard edition of Professor Dorothy Bethurum these sermons number only twenty-one, and most of them are rather brief: so that quantitatively Wulfstan's output of homilies seems small in comparison with that of his helper in the Benedictine reform, Ælfric. Whereas the simple monk provided sermons for all major Feast-days and ecclesiastical occasions, and definite didactic material in grammar and science, Wulfstan preferred to address his sermons to the widest possible public, and therefore to deal with large general topics with little reference to the Church's calendar or individual saints. He preferred to make his sermons exhortatory rather than instructional in what was often Ælfric's narrower sense. Whereas Ælfric wrote homilies to be used by the rural priests especially, Wulfstan carefully made his general exhortations to the nation so phrased and worded as to be most apt for actual delivery. Indeed, the best of them suggest that he in effect listened to their sound and pointed their style direct to the ears of an audience. Wulfstan was above all in his sermons a practical but fervently pastoral bishop, ever conscious of the wider duties of a public Church leader. He had Latin learning, though he made use of Ælfric for his more exact knowledge and

[1] Printed with translation in Benjamin Thorpe, *Ancient Laws and Institutes of England*, Vol. 2 (London, 1840).

literary qualities. But he was clearly a trained and accomplished orator, as his contemporary reputation shows; and he carefully wrote his sermons following the best Latin examples, while possessing the special gift of being able to make them simulate all the features of spontaneous utterance. Though, like Ælfric, he cultivated a rhythmic prose,[1] and could make most effective use of the traditional internal rhymes and alliterative phrases, he had not Ælfric's poetic sensitiveness. His only two extant pieces of verse (though their place in the Wulfstan canon has not been finally proved), are the poems *The Coronation of Edgar* and *The Death of Edgar*, which are found under dates 959 and 975 respectively in the *Anglo-Saxon Chronicle* in the "D" version thought to have been copied at Evesham or Worcester. While these show moderate competence, they have no serious poetical qualities. One can well see the clear difference between Wulfstan's prose rhythm and that of Ælfric by comparing the homilies *On False Gods* and *On the Sevenfold Pattern of the Holy Spirit*, numbered XII and IX in the Oxford edition, with Ælfric's treatment of the identical themes, which, as noticed earlier, the Bishop appropriated. Keeping the matter, and even the wording, unchanged for the most part, Wulfstan adds intensifying adverbs to adjectives here and there, and replaces some verbs with more forceful equivalents. On the one hand, as a bishop making a public declaration Wulfstan sometimes tones down or makes more dignified Ælfric's occasionally very homely vocabulary; but on the other, he substitutes his own speech-rhythm for Ælfric's, and reinforces the drive and vigour of the language by choice of more emphatic words. A good example of this is the sermon *De Falsis Deis* already mentioned as Wulfstan's version of an Ælfric homily. Here the story of the origin of the ancient classical deities from outstanding men under devilish instigation in the island of Crete is told. It is printed from the best Ælfric manuscript, Cotton Julius E VII, in Kemble's *Salamon and Saturn*,[2] and the same material reappears in Wulfstan's homily No. XII as noticed above. The story is simply and well told in both passages, and there is little difference in the wording, but the few changes that Wulfstan has made are significant. The same is generally true of the respective statements of Ælfric and Wulfstan on *De Septiformi Spiritu* already mentioned.

Wulfstan's relatively small output of sermons is classified by his latest editor Dorothy Bethurum under four heads: (*a*) eschatological, dealing largely with the need to remember the end of the world as foreshadowed in Scripture; (*b*) the Christian faith, treating of the Creed and *Pater Noster*, baptism, the Christian life, the gifts of the Holy Ghost, and the dangers of false gods; (*c*) archiepiscopal matters

---

[1] See A. McIntosh, "Wulfstan's Prose", *Proceedings of the British Academy* XXXV (1949), pp. 109–142.

[2] *Op. cit.*, pp. 120 ff., to be compared with *The Homilies of Wulfstan*, ed. D. Bethurum, *op. cit.*, pp. 221 ff.

such as the consecration of a bishop, the dedication of a church, rules for the conduct of religious and the reconciliation of penitents; and (*d*) evil days, dealing with the shocking wickednesses in the England of Ethelred the Unready and the Danish devastations. These sermons do not usually, as do Ælfric's, set out a full text to be treated or celebrate a Feast-day,[1] but are more exhortatory or episcopally pastoral in character, handling matters of public concern rather than any detail, and providing little of the kind of traditional exegesis commonly offered by Ælfric.

It may seem, therefore, odd that Wulfstan's most famous homily— indeed, the only one which is at all known except to specialists— is a long piece which in several ways is uncharacteristic of Wulfstan as we know him historically.[2] This is also one of the few to which Wulfstan seems to have set his name: for unlike Ælfric, who speaks in his own person in his prologues and prefaces, Wulfstan only occasionally acknowledges his work under the pen-name of *Lupus* (suggested by his actual name). This sermon, No. XX in Professor Bethurum's edition, has in the best manuscript, Cotton Nero A I in the British Museum, in near contemporary hands, the Latin heading: "Sermo Lupi ad Anglos quando Dani maxime persecuti sunt eos quod fuit anno millesimo XIIII ab Incarnatione Domini nostri Iesu Cristi'. This 'sermon of the Wolf to the English', preached and evidently distributed for reproduction by the Archbishop in the year 1014, when the evils and miseries of England between Ethelred and the Danes were at their critical worst, is couched in impassioned and fervent language, has much contemporary and historical detail, and uses the most pointed and emphatic language in painting contemporary vices. It is these features which are uncharacteristic of the Archbishop, who normally avoids detail, is restrained in language, and uses little purely emotive rhetoric. Yet this sermon shows many of Wulfstan's mannerisms, such as beginning without text or explanation, and the address to 'beloved men', *leofan men*. This manuscript, Cotton Nero A I, is evidently a kind of memorandum book kept by the Archbishop, for it contains, besides a number of his undoubted homilies, parts of the *Institutes of Polity*, drafts of legal codes made by him, and various ecclesiastical regulations. It also includes some matter which is actually in Wulfstan's own hand.[3]

The homily is widely circulated because of its very frequent inclusion in selections intended for beginners. It is also included

[1] Thorpe omitted the often long vernacular translations of the text preached on by Ælfric, as being superfluous, in his edition of the *Catholic Homilies*.

[2] For the best historical account of Wulfstan himself see Dorothy Whitelock, "Archbishop Wulfstan, Homilist and Statesman", *Transactions of the Royal Historical Society*, 4th Series, XXIV (1942), pp. 25–45.

[3] See N. R. Ker, *Catalogue of Manuscripts containing Anglo-Saxon* (Oxford, 1957), pp. 211 and 215.

among the translations in *English Historical Documents*, Vol. I.[1]
It is certainly a magnificent piece of moving prose rhetoric of a
kind to stir the deepest feelings of an audience: and, unlike Wulfstan's normal style, it has passages of even poetic appeal. At its
beginning the terrible state of England in anarchy and civil war
suggests to the preacher thoughts of the end of the world as shown
in Gospel portents:

> Leofan men, gecnawað þæt soð is: þeos world is on ofste, & hit
> nealæcð þam ende, and þi hit is on worlde a swa leng swa wyrse; and
> swa hit sceal nyde ær Anticristes tocyme yfelian swyðe.

Here is part of the description from the same homily of the state of
the country:

> La, hu mæg mare scamu þurh Godes irre mannum gelympan þonne
> us deð gelome for agenum gewirhtum? Ðeah þræla hwilc hlaforde
> ætleape & of cristendome to wicinge wurðe, & hit æfter þam eft
> gewurðe þæt wæpengewrixl wurðe gemæne þegne & þræle, gif
> þræl þone þegen fullice afille, licge ægilde ealre his mægðe; and gif
> se þegen þone þræl þe he ær ahte fullice afille, gilde þegengilde. Ful
> earhlice laga & scandlice nydgild þurh Godes irre us sind gemæne,
> understande se þe cunne, & fela ungelumpa gelumpð þisse þeode oft
> & gelome. Ne dohte hit nu lange inne ne ute, ac wæs here & hæte on
> gewelhwilcan ende oft & gelome, and Engle nu lange eal sigelease &
> to swiðe geyrgde þurh Godes irre, & flotmen swa strange þurh Godes
> þafunge þæt oft on gefeohte an fealleð tyne & twegen oft twentig, &
> hwilum læs, hwilum ma, eal for urum sinnum. And oft tyne oððe
> twelfe, ælc æfter oðrum, scændað & tawiað to bismore micclum þæs
> þegnes cwenan & hwilum his dohtor oððe nydmagan, þar he on locað
> þe læt hine silfne rancne & ricne & genoh godne ær þæt gewurde.
> And oft þræl þone þegn þe ær wæs his hlaford cnit swiðe fæste
> & wircð him to þræle þurh Godes irre. Wala þare yrmðe & wala þare
> worldscame þe nu habbað Engle, eall for Godes irre. And oft twegen
> sæmen, oððe þri hwilum, drifað þa drafe Cristenra manna fram sæ
> to sæ ut þurh þas þeode gewilede togædere, us eallum to worldscame,
> gif we on eornost ænige scame cuðe oððe a woldan ariht under-
> standan. Ac ealne þone bismor þe we oft þoliað we gildað mid weorð-
> scipe þa þe us scændað. We him gildað singallice, & hi us hynað
> dæghwamlice.[2]

This passage illustrates how Wulfstan here succeeds in impressing
his hearers, not by any properly stylistic effect, but by the horrific
accumulation of vivid detail. Evidently the terrible crisis of the
year 1014 caused the Archbishop to depart from his normal restraint

---

[1] *Op. cit.*, No. 240, pp. 854–859.
[2] From the text of *The Homilies of Wulfstan*, ed. D. Bethurum, *op. cit.*, pp.
263–264.

and episcopal manner. The sermon ends with a moving exhortation, not without tenderness, 'to crawl prostrate to Christ':

> Uton creopan to Criste & bifigendre heortan clipian gelome & geearnian his mildse. Uton God lufian & his lagum filigan, & gelæstan swiðe georne þæt þæt we beheton þa we fulluht underfengon, oððe þa þe æt fulluhte ure foresprecan wæron. And uton word & weorc rihtlice fadian & ure ingeþanc clænsian georne, & að & wed wærlice healdan & sune getriwða habban us betweonan buton uncræfton. And utan gelome understandan þone micclan dom þe we ealle to sculon, & beorgan us georne wið þone weallendan bryne helle wites, & geearnian us þa mærða & þa myrhða þe God hæfð gegearwod þam þe his willan on worlde gewyrcað. God ure helpe, Amen. *Sit nomen Domini benedictum, et reliqua.*[1]

It was natural that the Benedictine Renaissance should produce a large amount of vernacular religious literature for the practical purposes of the movement for Church reform and revitalization. Of this native prose the homily, as one would expect, was the outstanding feature. But from a literary point of view only men of very high attainments were likely to provide sermons of lasting aesthetic appeal. So it is that only Ælfric and Wulfstan have left homilies that seriously concern the literary historian, although there is varied historical interest in the anonymous work of many others. Though a vast number of Old English manuscript sermons of all kinds occur, many of them are still unpublished. They are seldom attributed to specific authors, and often one homilist has made copious use of the work of another, as Wulfstan did with Ælfric: and again the same homily was often reproduced with changes unacknowledged in a different manuscript. Two sets of homilies, apart from those of Ælfric and Wulfstan, must be mentioned, though neither has marked literary merit in itself. These are the *Blickling Homilies* and the *Vercelli Homilies*.

The *Blickling Homilies*—so called because for long the manuscript was in the library of Blickling Hall, in Norfolk—is an incomplete collection of eighteen sermons and a fragment, evidently intended for a cycle to cover the major Saints- and Feast-days of the ecclesiastical year. A note in one of the homilies speaks of the date 971 as current, which indicates the time when at least some of the copying was done. The manuscript is now in the collection of William H. Scheide in Titusville, U.S.A. It was printed with translation by Richard Morris in 1880.[2] It is a remarkable contrast to the work of both Ælfric and Wulfstan, both of whom it probably antedates by a few

---

[1] From the text of *The Homilies of Wulfstan*, ed. D. Bethurum, *op. cit.* pp. 265–266.

[2] *The Blickling Homilies of the Tenth Century*, ed. R. Morris (EETS 58, 63, 73; London, 1880). There is a facsimile of the manuscript with elaborate introduction by Rudolf Willard in *Early English Manuscripts in Facsimile*, Vol. X (Baltimore, London, and Copenhagen, 1960).

years. The language of the *Blickling Homilies* is considerably different in vocabulary from that of the Benedictine preachers, as well as in style. It lacks the traditional elements of rhythm, alliteration, assonance, etc., but on the other hand is often more poetic in its choice of florid and highly coloured metaphor. No. IX, for instance, is a glorifying of Christ's life on earth under the title of 'Christ the Golden-Blossom', *Crist se Goldbloma*: and in the sermon on the Annunciation Gabriel addresses Mary thus:

> The redness of the rose sheds its radiance upon Thee: and the whiteness of the lily shines on Thee: and let Christ's bridal bower be adorned with all the varied blossoms that the earth brings forth.[1]

Another contrast with the more authoritative and scholarly homilists is the extremely popular tone of the Blickling authors. Endless popular superstitious embellishments, often crudely materialistic in character, appear in the traditional stories. Thus the Assumption sermon, No. XIII, consists of a whole series of clearly superstitious fabrications taken largely from Oriental tradition, and the Blessed Virgin has a bodily assumption in great detail as well as a quite separate ascent into heaven of her soul, of which the stupendous whiteness is repeatedly emphasized: and the hearers are treated to lengthy and detailed speeches from a large cast. In fact this treatment of a great Festival, lacking all reference to its deeper significances, is just the kind of work to which Ælfric objected in his own sermon on this theme:

> Nevertheless there are yet erroneous books both in Latin and in English, and undisciplined men read them.[2]

Again, the sermon on the important Feast of Saints Peter and Paul, No. XV, is turned towards mere popular narrative of an endless and hard-fought contest between St Peter, aided by St Paul, and Simon the sorcerer. The sermon on the Dedication of St Michael's Church, No. XVII, shows entertainingly the Archangel himself coming to dedicate his church in person, and the homily ends with an account of how St Michael showed St Paul round some of the sights of hell in a localized echo of the apocryphal *Visio Pauli*. This last, however, has a special interest for its apparent reminiscence of the description of Grendel's mere in *Beowulf*. St Paul, in his vision of hell, sees in the Blickling Homily a lake overhung with frost-covered trees of immense depth, with the black souls of the damned hanging to the branches ready to drop a vast distance into the dark mysterious water. This, while generally in line with the *Visio Pauli*, presents here a detailed picture not in any known version and seeming even verbally to echo the *Beowulf* picture.[3] Did the Blickling homilist

[1] Ed. Morris, pp. 6–7.
[2] See Thorpe, *op. cit.*, Vol. I, p. 444.
[3] Compare the edition of Morris, pp. 209–211 with *Beowulf*, lines 1357 ff.

here deliberately remember his *Beowulf*? The sermon for Easter Day, No. VII, is almost entirely taken up with a popular and dramatic narrative of the harrowing of hell and Christ's violent battle with Satan as he rescues the Patriarchs. The interest of the *Blickling Homilies*, then, is mainly for the often entertaining picture they provide of the kind of popular beliefs which might be exploited by a less educated preacher. They are often also good examples of what was probably successful popular rhetoric with little discipline of language.

The *Vercelli Homilies* are so called because they occur in three groups in the Vercelli Book. There are twenty-three of them, but they are not arranged in any way to suggest an ecclesiastical cycle like those of Ælfric or the *Blickling Homilies*. They are rather (though not consistently) geared to serve as sermons in support of the festivals associated with the poems which give this manuscript its importance. It seems that the Vercelli Book—probably put together in the late tenth century, perhaps at Worcester—was designed as a mixed body of religious prose and verse suitable primarily for greater occasions of the Church's year. But it seems to have grown gradually, and without any clear final plan. Its sermons, dealing with the Passion, the seasons of Advent and Christmas, Lent, Rogation-tide, and such inevitable themes as the Last Judgment and the need for repentance, may be linked to some extent with the six poems of this manuscript. Thus the poems *Andreas* and *Fates of the Apostles* which follow the first group of five homilies suggest the Feast of St Andrew as well as a Festival of the Twelve Apostles which used to be kept in May, and also All Saints' Day. The two poems *Soul and Body* and *Falseness of Men* which follow the second group of homilies, VI to XVIII, go well with the several sermons on penitence and doomsday specially appropriate to Lent. *The Dream of the Rood* and *Elene*, which occur between the eighteenth homily and the nineteenth, suggest the Festivals of the Invention of the Cross and the Exaltation of the Cross, and may also be linked with homilies on Christmas. The homily on St Guthlac which ends the manuscript after the third group of sermons, XIX to XXII, was probably likewise intended for that saint's festival.[1]

The *Vercelli Homilies* are of varied authorship and origin, some of them being only copies or adaptations of others found elsewhere. They are generally translations or adaptations from Latin, with a preference for the more popular sources, nearer to the *Blickling Homilies* in attitude than to those of Ælfric and Wulfstan. Apart from

---

[1] The poems of the Vercelli Book from vol. II of *The Anglo-Saxon Poetic Records*, ed. Dobbie (Columbia University Press, 1942). The prose homilies were published only in part by Max Förster, *Bibliothek der angelsächsischen Prosa*, Vol. XII (Hamburg, 1932). For a complete view of the contents of the whole manuscript see the facsimile with full introduction by Max Förster: *Il Codice Vercellese con Omelie e Poesie in Lingua anglosassone* (Roma, 1913).

their being placed in what was perhaps originally an attempt at a prose and verse devotional anthology, there is not much literary interest in these sermons, except for the Guthlac piece which stands by itself at the end. This piece of prose, based largely on two chapters of the eighth-century *Vita Sancti Guthlaci*, by Felix of Croyland, describing mainly a fight between the hermit saint and two devils, may be nearly a century earlier than the complete Old English prose version of this Latin *Life*, which appears in MS. Cotton Vespasian D XXI in the British Museum. Guthlac evidently had a considerable cult, and is the only English saint treated of in the Vercelli Book.[1]

The Benedictine movement in England produced a great deal of valuable didactic writing, sometimes of literary merit: but apart from the work of the major homilists and some of Ælfric's writings, most but not all of its best work appears, as was to be expected, in Latin. The great personalities of this period, Saints Dunstan, Æthelwold, and Oswald of Worcester, while directing the educative work of the Church and making full use of those who could write well in the vernacular, themselves mostly wrote only in Latin. Indeed, even in the case of Ælfric, some of the best writing, such as Ælfric's devoted life of his old teacher St Æthelwold of Winchester, is only in Latin.

---

[1] The eleventh-century prose *Guthlac*, along with the Vercelli piece, is found in *Angel-sächsische Prosaleben des Heil. Guthlac*, ed. Paul Gonser (Heidelberg, 1909). The Vercelli fragment shows a language nearer to the lost Old English archetype than does the Vespasian version, and is evidently part of a once complete *Life*.

CHAPTER 15

Later Didactic Prose and the Beginnings of Romance

ANGLO-SAXON PROSE is undoubtedly not only the best of its age in Europe, but its products as literature generally are in advance by several centuries of those of other vernaculars. This must be attributed to the syntactic and lexical resources which the language had developed, and to the nature of the works for which it came to be employed. In Ælfric's time it was the only native prose which had developed a language which could express the ideas of theology and philosophy, could deal with scientific and technical subjects, and had begun to provide entertainment as well as edification. It had learned to develop excellent simple rhetoric by deliberate conscious art; and the historical narrative prose which had grown up from simple annals under the inspiration of King Alfred became in the best prose of the later *Anglo-Saxon Chronicle* a medium unparalleled till that date for effectiveness and attraction. The greater sermon-writers were by no means alone in their agreeable uses of rhetoric. We find too in this latest period of Anglo-Saxon prose the beginnings of the employment of this vehicle for the purposes of a fiction which should combine something like romantic entertainment with that moral edification which the Anglo-Saxons always enjoyed. It was also in this age that the art of translation, which had grown from interlinear glossing to continuous prose, came to fulfilment in the development of translation as a literary art—which was what Ælfric had desired in the *Preface to Genesis* cited in the previous chapter. On the state of the England which the Normans conquered, R. W. Chambers has provided convenient authentic documents in his *England before the Norman Conquest*[1]; and in his *On the Continuity of English Prose* he has shown what was the literary inheritance which the Anglo-Saxons were able to pass on by means of their prose to succeeding ages.[2] These and related matters will be the concern of the ensuing chapter.

The development of a vernacular prose able to express the exact sciences as then understood had been carried forward by Ælfric in

[1] London, 1928.
[2] *On the Continuity of English Prose from Alfred to More and His School,* (EETS 186: London, 1932, reprinted 1957).

his version of Bede's *De Temporibus Anni*. But there was a more specialized scientific writer with a wider scientific knowledge in a monk of the monastery of Ramsey, one Byrhtferth, who lived about Ælfric's time or a little earlier, and like him spent all his life in studious cloisters. Byrhtferth, however, unlike Ælfric, was evidently educated under direct Continental influence from the great Benedictine movement of Fleury; and he clearly had come under the influence of Abbot Abbo of Fleury, who taught for two years at Ramsey at St Oswald's invitation. Whereas Ælfric's development was through the school of St Æthelwold of Winchester, Byrhtferth's was by means of a wider Continental inheritance, though he was clearly devoted to St Dunstan and his ideals. Byrhtferth wrote for the most part in Latin on his special interests of mathematics, physics, and philology, though he was also concerned with the explication of the Scriptures. His only surviving work in Anglo-Saxon is a large and very various collection of scientific material dealing especially with matters of computus, using some Latin with his Anglo-Saxon, with many digressions on natural phenomena, astrology, the fixing of Easter, or simple homiletic advice. This is complete in MS. Ashmole 328, of the eleventh century, in the Bodleian Library, Oxford. It is known as *Byrhtferth's Manual*,[1] or in Old English *Handboc*, Latin (Greek) *Encheiridion*. It is possible that the idea of this *Manual* may have come to Byrhtferth through the lost *Encheiridion* which King Alfred kept in constant use; for the monk of Ramsey was in the tradition of Alfred and Ælfric. Byrhtferth was regarded by his contemporaries as the leading mathematician and astronomer, though his Latin works have been little noticed since his commentaries on four works of Bede were published in the Cologne Bede of 1612.

It cannot be said that Byrhtferth's Old English prose is remarkable for its literary qualities. However, in its use of the native vocabulary's potentialities for scientific purposes it shows some skill, and in this regard makes a contribution to the development of the language. Two homilies of advice to young clerics at the end read quite attractively. Byrhtferth's best work in Latin is probably his lively and careful writing on the great men he had himself known—St Dunstan, whose *Life* he seems to have written as "B. Presbyter", and St Oswald of Worcester.

Of what might very loosely be termed scientific prose of the Benedictine period there is a great deal in the shape of herbal and medical books which combine much folklore and Christianized magic and some charms with empirical information on the properties of herbs with all kinds of medical prescriptions. There is an Old English version of a Latin herbal attributed to Apuleius (of the *Golden Ass*). This *Herbarius Apuleii*, attributed in the best manuscript, Cotton Vitellius C III of the British Museum, to one

---

[1] *Byrhtferth's Manual*, ed. S. J. Crawford (EETS 177: Oxford, 1928); a second volume, of commentary, was never produced.

'Apuleius the Platonist who got it from Esculapius and from Charon the centaur who was Achilles' master', is illustrated with many coloured drawings. Like other works of the kind, this herbal and the medical books in late Old English, though of no literary significance, are immensely valuable to the social historian for the vivid light they throw, through their accounts of diseases and the remedies prescribed, on the everyday life of the Anglo-Saxons of their time. This herbal, along with most of the Old English medical and herbal collections, was included in a three-volume omnibus work entitled *Leechdoms, Wortcunning, and Starcraft of Early England,* ed. Oswald Cockayne (London, 1864–66).[1]

In the same manuscript with the *Herbarius Apuleii* is a treatise called *Medicina de Quadrupedibus,* setting forth the properties of animals and all their parts which can be extracted and employed medicinally. It is evident that many monasteries and other religious houses collected medical and related recipes for practical use. One such, known as *Bald's Laeceboc* (book of medicine) from a former owner of the manuscript who has left his name, is the best compilation of the kind, showing a blend of empirical and magical recipes with a number of those *Charms* which were noticed as verse in Chapter 10. The whole work appears in Cockayne's vast collection as *Laeceboc.*[2]

The developments in the literary art of prose seen in the writings of Ælfric and Wulfstan are paralleled in much of the historical writing of the later *Anglo-Saxon Chronicle,* which often shows a polished yet simple style with effective use of rhetorical devices. The Parker Chronicle, with its often blank or sparse later entries, is here the exception: for the "C" (Abingdon), "D" (Worcester), and "E" (Peterborough) versions all supply many excellent examples of historical narrative.[3] The outstandingly moving style of Wulfstan's *Sermo ad Anglos,* with its marked prose rhythm and its use of rhyme and alliteration, is again paralleled in the "C" version's account of the martyrdom by the Vikings of Archbishop Ælfheah (St Alphege) under date 1011, which matches Wulfstan's heaping up of horrific detail, stirs the heart by its rhetoric, and breaks into a kind of free verse in its lament for the imprisonment of the Archbishop. As late as the year 1048, in the "E" or Peterborough text of the *Chronicle* in the account of fighting at Dover and the banishment

---

[1] *Cf.* George Flom, "On the Old English Herbal of Apuleius, Vitellius C III", *Journal of English and Germanic Philology* XL (1941), pp. 29–37.

[2] An excellent facsimile of this *Laeceboc* was edited by Cyril E. Wright as *Bald's Leechbook,* vol. V of *Early English Manuscripts in Facsimile* (London, Baltimore and Copenhagen, 1955).

[3] For the different versions and their relationships see *English Historical Documents,* Vol. I. There is an excellent translation with introductory matter in G. N. Garmonsway, *The Anglo-Saxon Chronicle* (London, 1953).

of Earl Godwin, we find simple yet eloquent historical prose—according to Henry Sweet

> One of the noblest pieces of prose in any literature, clear, simple, and manly in style, calm and dignified in tone, and yet with a warm undercurrent of patriotic indignation.[1]

The later *Chronicle* is at its best almost continuously for the long reign of Ethelred the Unready, 978–1016, which was one of the most terrible periods in English history, yet corresponded to the best period of the later Benedictine movement. Here the chronicler writes with some intellectual concern as well as personal feeling for the moving events he records: he is interested in relations between cause and effect and the meaning of history, in a way which suggests that historical writing proper—which must include the art of literary presentation—has arrived in England.

We may take, then, the "C" version of Abingdon, MS Cotton Tiberius B I in the British Museum, to illustrate by some translated examples the later historical prose. Part of the entry for 994 shows the blend of simple and lucid prose with a strongly underlying warmth of feeling:

> Her on ðissum geare com Anlaf and Swegen to Lundenbyrig on Nativitas Sanctae Mariae mid IIII and hundnigontigum scypum, and hi ða on þa buruh fæstlice feohtende wæron, and eac hi mid fyre ontendon woldan, ac hi þær geferdon maran hearm and yfel þonne hi æfre wendon þæt him ænig buruhwaru gedon scolde. Ac seo halige Godes Modor on þam dæge hire mildheortnesse þære buruhware gecydde, and hi ahredde wið heora feondum, and hi þanone ferdon, and worhton þæt mæste yfel ðe æfre æni here gedon meahte on bærnette and hergunge and on manslyhtum, ægþerge be þam særiman, and on Eastseaxum, and on Kentlande, and on Suðseaxum and on Hamtunscire, and æt neaxtan namon him hors, and ridon him swa wide swa hi woldan, and unasecgendlice yfel wyrcgende wæron. Þa gerædde se cyning and his witan, þæt him man to sende, and him behet gafol and metsunge wiðþonðe hi þære heregunge geswicon.[2]

It was in this year that Anlaf and Swegen came to London on the Feast of the Nativity of St Mary, with ninety-four ships: and they kept on stoutly fighting against the town, and further, they wanted to set it on fire. But there they encountered greater disaster and pain than they had ever expected that any townspeople might have done them. For on that day God's Holy Mother manifested her compassion to the townspeople and delivered them from their foes. So the

---

[1] See Sweet's *Anglo-Saxon Reader*, 13th ed., p. 90.
[2] The Chronicle for Ethelred's reign is conveniently printed with translation and notes in Margaret Ashdown, *English and Norse Documents Relating to the Reign of Ethelred the Unready* (Cambridge, 1930). Here from p. 42.

Vikings went away from thence and wrought the greatest evil that ever any plundering army could have done, in burning and looting and slaughter of men, both along that sea-shore and in Essex and in Kent and Sussex and Hampshire. And at last they took their horses and rode all over the country as they pleased and continued to work every sort of unspeakable evil. Then the King and his counsellors decided that they should send to them, and he promised them tribute and supplies on condition that the Vikings should cease from plundering.

Under the year 999 the eloquent exasperation of the chronicler is well shown in this passage about the King's plans for preparing great sea and land forces against the Danes:

Ac þa ða scipu gearwe wæron þa ylcodan þa deman fram dæge to dæge, and swencte þæt earme folc þæt on ðam scipon læg, and þa swa hit forðwerdre beons ceolde swa wæs hit lætre fram anre tide to oþre, and a hi leton heora feonda werod wexan, and a man rymde fram þære sæ, and hi foron æfre forð æfter. And þonne æt ðam ende ne beheold hit nan þing seo scypfyrding ne seo landfyrding, buton folces geswinc, and feos spylling and heora feonda forðbylding.[1]

But when the ships were ready, then the authorities kept putting things off from day to day: and the wretched people who were on the ships were afflicted with toil: and always as things should have been more forward, so they were made later from hour to hour: and all the time they were letting the enemy troops grow mightier, and all the time they kept on retreating from the sea, and the Vikings kept on advancing in pursuit. And then in the end the fleet and the land forces accomplished nothing save toil and misery for the people, and wasting of money and the encouragement of the enemy.

Under the date 1003 we read in a more familiar, and even colloquial style, of the treachery and well-known trickery of a certain English leader named Ælfric:

Þa gegaderede man swiðe micle fyrde of Wiltunscire and of Hamtun-scire, and swiðe anrædlice wið þæs heres werd wæran. Þa sceolde se ealdorman Ælfric lædan þa fyrde, ac he teah ða forð his ealdan wrencas; sona swa hi wæron swa gehende þæt ægðer here on oþerne hawede, þa gebræd he hine seocne and ongan hine brecan to spiwenne and cwæð þæt he gesicled wære, and swa þæt folc becyrde þæt he lædan sceolde; swa hit gecweden ys: 'þonne se heretoga wacað, þonne bið eall se here swiðe gehindrad.' Þa Swegen geseah þæt hi anræde næron, and þæt hi ealle toforan, þa lædde he his here into Wiltune, and hi þa buruh geheregodon and tobærndon, and eode him þa to Searbyrig, and þanone eft to sæ ferde, þær he wiste his yð-hengestas.[2]

[1] *English and Norse Documents Relating to the Reign of Ethelred the Unready*, p. 44.
[2] *Ibid.*, p. 48.

Then a very mighty English army was gathered together from Wiltshire and from Hampshire who were full of resolution against the Viking plunderers. It then became the duty of ealdorman Ælfric to lead the English army, but it was then that he displayed his old tricks. For immediately when they were so near that each host could gaze upon the other, Ælfric pretended to be sick and began to spew violently, and he said that he was ill, and thus he betrayed the people that he ought to have been leading. Thus it was said: 'When the leader of the host grows feeble, then is the whole host utterly frustrated.' When Swegen saw that they were not resolute and that they all were scattering, he led his army to Wilton, and then utterly looted and burned the town. And then Swegen went to Salisbury, and from thence travelled to the sea once more where he knew that his horses of the waves were.

In this passage, with its citation of what was evidently a familiar proverbial saying, it is interesting at the same time to notice the use of a traditional poetic term for the Danish war-ships: *yð-hengestas*, literally 'stallions of the waves'.

The moving account of the murder of Archbishop St Alphege by the Danes because he would not raise money for his own ransom from his tenants, under date 1011, which is concerned with much the same period and type of theme as Wulfstan's *Sermo ad Anglos*, shows the chronicler's rhetorical prose at its height, and often bordering on poetry. Here is the lamentation over the saint's imprisonment from the "E" or Peterborough text of MS. Laud 636 in the Bodleian Library:

Wæs ða ræpling, se ðe ær wæs heafod Angelcynnes and Cristendomes. Þær man mihte ða geseon yrmðe þær man oft ær geseaah blisse on þære earman byrig, þanon us com ærest Cristendom and blis for Gode and for worulde.[1]

Rhetorical passages of this kind, and the account of the murder of St Edward which shortly follows, since they are illustrations of style, are not translated here. Perhaps the high-water mark in rhetorical prose in this kind, merging into exalted, if very free, verse, is the Peterborough Chronicle's account of the murder of St Edward the Martyr under date 979:

Her wæs Eadward cyng ofslagen on æfentide æt Corfes geate on XV.Kı Apr. And hine man bebyrigde æt Wærham butan ælcum cynelicum wurðscipe. Ne wearð Angelcynne nan wærsa dæd gedon, þonne þeos wæs syððan hi ærest Bryton land gesohton. Men hine ofmyrðrodon, ac God hine mærsode. He wæs on life eorðlic cing. He is nu æfter deaðe heofonlic sanct. Hine nolden his eorðlican magas

wrecan; ac hine hafað his heofonlice Fæder swiðe gewrecen. Þa eorðlican banan woldon his gemynd on erðan adilgian; ac se uplica Wre-
cend hafað his gemynd on heofonum and on eorðan tobræd. Þa þe
nolden ær to his libbendum lichaman onbugan, þa nu eadmodlice on
cneowum abugað to his dædum banum. Nu we magon ongytan þæt
manna wisdom and smeagunga and heora rædas syndon nahtlice
ongean Godes geðeaht.[1]

As the elements of verse technique here are so loose and inconsistent,
no attempt has been made to set out any part of it metrically, though
the use of alliteration and of verse-rhythm sporadically will be easily
apparent. The author of this passage evidently believed, like Wulfstan, that the miseries of England were the direct punishment for
widespread wickedness.

It seems likely that much other historical prose of the later Old
English period was written, though the great leaders of Church
and State usually wrote in Latin. We know, for instance, that
Ælfric's friend Æthelweard, who made a Latin translation from the
Anglo-Saxon Chronicle, used a good version other than those which
have survived.[2] Much probably perished in the neglect of Anglo-
Saxon of the later Middle Ages and the dispersion of the monastic
libraries at the dissolution under Henry VIII; and whereas Anglo-
Saxon homilies and other religious works continued to be read and
copied through most of the twelfth century, secular prose, including
the historical, was apparently allowed to fall into oblivion. The
Anglo-Saxon Chronicle, therefore, in its various versions, stands
alone as the monument to the historical prose of its time. But it has
been shown that its merits are great and varied, and that it was very
much a pioneer in Europe.

Until the Benedictine reforms began to affect literature, it seems
that poetry in England had had the entire monopoly of fiction.
Prose being primarily and in origin utilitarian, its use for the provision of entertainment must naturally have been a relatively late
development. It may be that some Oriental influences are connected
with the beginnings of prose romance which occurred in the later
tenth century. For Greek influence, which had always had at least
an indirect impact on Anglo-Saxon culture—as can be seen as early
as the Sutton Hoo baptismal spoons—received some impetus through
contacts with Constantinople at this time, through contacts with the
Greek religious houses in Rome, and possibly from the Greek-
cultured principality of Slavic Kiev. Certain it is that the Anglo-
Saxon fiction which appeared in the days of St Dunstan had its
material from Latin versions of originally Greek and Oriental-
influenced sources. While two of these fictional pieces, the *Letter*

[1] See Plummer edition, Vol. I. p. 123.
[2] See *The Chronicle of Aethelweard*, ed. A. Campbell (Edinburgh, 1959),
Introduction, p. xxxiii.

of Alexander to Aristotle and *Wonders of the East*, are of little strictly literary merit (though of historical interest), the third, the tale of *Apollonius of Tyre*, though only surviving in a longish and a short fragment, is something approaching a masterpiece in its kind. It may be that the anarchy and wretchedness of Ethelred the Unready's reign prevented the florescence of this new kind of prose, for we have no further examples of prose fiction in what remained of the Old English period. What we have in the three surviving examples of this late Old English prose fiction is, in effect, the indirect result of the far-flung medieval influence of late Greek romance introduced to England through Christianized Latin sources. All are, in varying degrees, translations or adaptations of Latin texts, though the immediate sources cannot be exactly identified.

Here may be very briefly noticed examples of the imitation of Latin instructional dialogue in Old English prose, which are at the same time definitely fictional and blend Germanic with Latin Christian culture. Along with the two poems *Solomon and Saturn* discussed in Chapter 10 and there mentioned with them occur parts of two prose dialogues of debate as question and answer between Solomon and Saturn first published in Kemble's *Anglo-Saxon Dialogues of Salomon and Saturn*, part 2, of 1847 and reprinted with some discussion by Robert Menner in his edition of these poems (pp. 8-10, 55-56, and 168-171). Here the Oriental influence in magical elements is clear too. These dialogues find a very close parallel or imitation in *Adrian and Ritheus*, printed from MS Cotton Julius A II in Kemble's collection mentioned above (pp. 198 ff). This short piece of prose is a dialogue between the Emperor Hadrian and a sophist philosopher, in which questions are asked such as "How long was Adam in Paradise?" or "Why is the sun red at evening?"

Wonders of the East, taken from a Latin collection of *Mirabilia* of ultimate Greek origin, is an account of all kinds of Oriental and fabulous phenomena seen by travellers as strange and often miraculous. *Alexander's Letter to Aristotle* is evidently of the same general origin as *Wonders of the East*, and makes use of some of the same material. It purports to be a long journal-letter in which the great Alexander describes to his old teacher Aristotle the marvellous things he has met in his far-extended campaigns and his feats of prowess and the repute he has earned. It is England's first vernacular contribution to the vast medieval heroic romance cycle on Alexander. He is one of the greater heroes of medieval romance, which starts from Latin echoes of Greek tales. There is, for instance, in Middle English a vast verse-romance known as *Kyng Alisaunder*, in which the second part treats much of the fabulous and supernatural features of life in India of the kind described by Alexander the Great in the Old English *Letter*.[1] Both *Wonders of the East* and

---

[1] The Middle English *Kyng Alisaunder* was edited with a volume of elaborate commentary by G. V. Smithers (EETS 227, 237: Oxford, 1952-57).

Alexander's Letter to Aristotle are in the Beowulf Manuscript, Cotton Vitellius A XV of the British Museum. As they are copied by the same hand as the first part of *Beowulf*, they cannot be dated later than the close of the tenth century. But there is some evidence which indicates that they were probably based on adaptations from the Latin sources made in West Mercia about the time of Alfred the Great. The inclusion, however, of this pair of echoes of Oriental romance in the Beowulf Manuscript suggests that their present form may be attributed to the period of the Benedictine Renaissance. Neither work is of literary interest as prose, since the style is generally crude or ordinary—particularly uncouth is some of *Alexander's Letter*. But the appearance in England of these examples of Oriental influence, anticipating in a sense what was to happen a little later through the effects of the Crusades, is certainly of concern to the literary historian.

It has been plausibly suggested that the Beowulf Manuscript goes back to the idea of compiling a sort of *liber monstrorum*, or book of marvels, designed for entertainment along with the usual edification. For this prose fiction is primarily concerned with fables and marvellous phenomena, and *Beowulf* could be regarded as also a poem of marvels in view of its supernatural monsters. The desire for such a compilation of pleasurable secular prose and verse, which could be at the same time not incompatible with Christian edification, would not have been an impossibility in a culture dominated by that artistic if austere lover of literature St Dunstan. Further, the opening of the Beowulf Manuscript with a prose legend of St Christopher (its first portion is missing) seems to strengthen this hypothesis: for St Christopher was a giant of supernatural origin descended from the cannibals with dog's heads known as *Cynocephali*, or in Old English *healf-hundingas*, 'half-dogs'.[1] These *healf-hundingas* are mentioned both in *Alexander's Letter* and in *Wonders of the East*. This latter set of Old English *Mirabilia* may have had some popularity: for it appears in a second manuscript, Cotton Tiberius B V of the British Museum, from the late eleventh century, with rather crude coloured drawings to illustrate its marvels. Here it follows parts of a translation from Bede's *De Temporibus Anni* as if it were regarded as having some scientific interest. The Latin *Mirabilia* which are translated here are given in full, neatly divided into sections with the appropriate Old English renderings following each.

The Old English *Apollonius of Tyre* also belongs, with *Wonders of the East* and *Alexander's Letter to Aristotle*, to prose fiction—representing Greek romance, however, rather more directly. It is a translation of a Latin text based on the third-century *Historia Apollonii Regis Tyri*, which itself was clearly adapted from a late Greek romance of about the same period. This *Historia* has Greek

[1] For argument for this view see K. Sisam, "The Compilation of the *Beowulf* Manuscript", in *Studies in the History of Old English Literature*, pp. 65 ff.

words and ideas in it, and represents a love-romance of late Greek culture from Asia Minor to some extent overlaid with Latin Christian civilization. Some version of this was evidently translated into Old English in a copy from which the mid-eleventh-century surviving text was copied into MS. Corpus Christi College, Cambridge, 201, where it follows a large quantity of Wulfstan's homilies and laws. This tale of virtuous love and adventure in its Old English dress probably belongs to the late tenth century in its lost archetypal form. It covers, in its present truncated state, some fourteen folios of manuscript: a first part of eleven folios followed without indication by a lost quire of parchment, and a concluding fragment of less than three folios. What we have is therefore less than half of the original, whose size may be guessed from Latin texts showing the character of the lost exact source. *Apollonius of Tyre* has been edited with full apparatus by Peter Goolden.[1]

The story of Apollonius, originating in a late Greek love-romance of probably highly sophisticated kind, acquired some features of Latin Christian culture through being rendered into the Latin of the later Roman Empire while retaining its grace and lively presentation of romantic love in a way which was to point towards the medieval *amour courtois*, or 'courtly love'. No doubt the Christian elements added in its Latin transfer would render it an acceptable entertainment to a tenth-century Anglo-Saxon, or it may owe its preservation to its having got palaeographically into an association with the work of Archbishop Wulfstan. While it is written in a clear but light and easy style which is often idiomatic in rendering the Latin, the English *Apollonius* does not pretend to be anything other than a translation. When he came to the end of his Latin tale the vernacular writer added a little epilogue which reminds one of both Alfred and Ælfric:

> Here ends both the misery and the good fortune of Apollonius of Tyre, let him read it who will. And if anyone reads it, I pray that he do not blame this translation, but that he conceal whatsoever in it is blameworthy.[2]

Apollonius of Tyre in Old English may possess some claim to be called the first English novel, although one can trace no direct influence from it on the Middle English users of the same material. The tale got into the immensely popular and influential medieval collection of *Gesta Romanorum* (where it is No. 153), and it was from this version that both French and English adaptations were made. In Middle English several versions of the story are known, but the one which came to be really influential was that which forms most

---

[1] "The Old English Apollonius of Tyre", in *Oxford English Monographs* (Oxford, 1958).
[2] Ed. Goolden, *op. cit.*, p. 42.

of the eighth book of Gower's *Confessio Amantis*.[1] Almost all European languages have versions of this vastly popular tale, but it was in England that it had the most significant developments. Besides Elizabethan versions of the novel type, Shakespeare's *Pericles* uses part of the Apollonius story in some of the finest writing of his later romantic period; however, much of other parts of the play may have come from different hands. Taking the character of Marina from *Pericles*, the eighteenth-century dramatist Lillo made his *Marina*, and in the twentieth century T. S. Eliot made the spiritual elements in Marina dominate his own poem under her name.

The handling of the Latin by the maker of the Old English *Apollonius*, while it does not often depart from the matter it is translating, and only occasionally paraphrases, contracts, or expands, is excellent in that he has produced a masterpiece in an exactly appropriate prose style. He has also maintained a vivid if not at all subtle presentation of his human characters, with a tone of courtesy and sympathy with romantic love which cannot be paralleled till the days of the Middle English romances. It is, as far as prose is concerned, a first English contribution to 'the literature of escape', while at the same time its tone is one of unobtrusive Christian ethics. As contrasted with the fiction of Oriental fable and marvels discussed earlier, *Apollonius of Tyre* presents a world of real human beings, though remote and romantic. The conveying to an Anglo-Saxon of so many ideas from the Greek and Latin world of the later Roman Empire is often achieved, using idiomatic or new-made yet natural Old English phrases that completely disguise the fact of translation. Thus, for instance, the Anglo-Saxon conception of torment in hell is suggested aptly by rendering the Latin *Tartarea domus* by *cwic* (*ciwic-suslene*) *hus*, 'house of living torment'. The tone of *Apollonius* may remind us at times of the high romance of *The Faerie Queene* in its treatment of terrifying adventure and of faithful love. Of some of this prose fiction its author might almost have said "Fierce warres and faithfull loues shall moralize my song." There are homely scenes like that between the shipwrecked prince Apollonius and the fisherman who saved his life, or the dealings of King Arcestrates with the three 'learned men' who came as suitors for his daughter, in which there is a touch of English humour.[2] Almost throughout one is struck by the fact that we have here so clear, simple, and natural a prose, which yet rarely departs from a close following of the Latin.

It is laid down in a Church canon of the end of the tenth century which is recorded in vernacular translation that

> On Sundays and days when Mass must be said, the priest is to tell the people the meaning of the Gospel in English, and about the

[1] Ed. G. C. Macaulay (Oxford, 1901), Vol. 2, Book VIII, lines 271 ff.
[2] Ed. Goolden, *op. cit.*, pp. 30–34.

Lord's Prayer and the Creed as often as he can, for the kindling of zeal among men, that they may know how to learn and to hold firmly their Christianity.

A warning is then added that "dumb dogs cannot bark", and of the danger of damnation to those who neglect this duty.[1] It is evident, therefore, that some Bible translating was practised in the times of St Dunstan. As early as the time of Bede, we have seen that some vernacular translation existed, though till the tenth century most translation seems to have taken only the form of more or less continuous glossing. The popular aspect of translation during the Benedictine reform period is suggested by the fact that Ælfric protested against erroneous apocryphal vernacular books, and that one of the especially popular Latin works of this kind, the so-called *Gospel of Nicodemus*, was translated, and survives to be edited in the twentieth century.[2] This pseudo-Gospel of a pseudo-Nicodemus is the source of part of the legend of St Joseph of Arimathaea, and contains the immensely popular narrative supposed to be related by the two sons of Simeon, of Christ's descent into Hades and rout of Satan and his angels known as 'the Harrowing of Hell', of which there are Old English versions in both prose and verse.

Ælfric's Bible translations have already been mentioned. But, as was pointed out, he translated only portions of Scripture for particular purposes, and latterly gave up further work of this kind through doubts as to the wisdom of placing large amounts of vernacular work before a lay public. He seems to have thought that the rendering of the Scripture normally read in Church in the vulgar tongue would be best left to the discretion of the priests concerned, and devoted most of his attention to the homiletic exegesis of extended Gospel texts required for festivals and days of obligation. Yet his *Preface to Genesis* shows that he had given much thought to the best methods of translation, and what he has left us, though not usually of his best vernacular writing, shows both skill and lucidity.

The one outstanding contribution of the Benedictine Renaissance to Bible translating was the *West-Saxon Gospels*, produced originally as a continuous gloss for which the basic text is not extant, but surviving in at least six manuscripts in which the Gospels appear as straight prose. These *West-Saxon Gospels*, translated probably near the end of the tenth century at a monastery in South-west England, have been most highly praised by Kemp Malone. Of them he writes in his survey of the literature of the Old English period

The translation, idiomatic but faithful to the Vulgate text, bears comparison with the Authorized Version of 1611 in literary quality.[3]

[1] See Thorpe's *Ancient Laws and Institutes of England*, Vol. 2, pp. 350–351.
[2] Ed. S. J. Crawford (Edinburgh, 1927).
[3] Kemp Malone, *The Old English Period* in *A Literary History of England*, ed. Albert C. Baugh, Vol. I (New York, 1948), p. 104.

On the other hand, George Anderson in his *Literature of the Anglo-Saxons* can see nothing of value in these Gospels save that they are a beginning:

> It is in no sense comparable to the Wyclif translations of the fourteenth century or the excellent performances of the sixteenth.[1]

The truth is that the *West-Saxon Gospels*, which are the first complete Biblical translation of considerable size, are generally a lucid and fairly idiomatic but close rendering of the Vulgate Latin, but with a good deal of variation in style which does not rise to literary excellence. But the Wycliffite rendering of the Gospels, often far too close to the Latin to be lucid or even always intelligible, is rather clumsy in style, and if a comparison with the Anglo-Saxon version were worth making it would be found that the *West-Saxon Gospels* are in every way better.[2]

Something is known of the places of copying of the main manuscripts, but the origin of that archetypal text from which all appear to be descended is obscure, beyond the fact that it must have been in Wessex. The Cambridge University Library version, for instance (pressmark Ii. 2. 11), is an Exeter book which is recorded among the gifts of Bishop Leofric, who died in 1072, to Exeter Cathedral. The Oxford text, Hatton 38 in the Bodleian, clearly came from Canterbury, as its markedly Kentish dialectal trend seems to indicate. MS. Corpus Christi College, Cambridge, 140 was copied at Bath: for it includes a prayer for himself by a scribe Ælfric of the monastery of Bath with the statement: "Ego ælfricus scripsi hunc librum in monasterio baþðonio et dedi brihtwoldo preposito". This inscription has led to the belief that Ælfric, monk of Bath, was the translator of the *West-Saxon Gospels*: and it was even at one time supposed that this translator might have been Abbot Ælfric himself. But as this statement is that of a scribe rather than a translator and it occurs only at the end of St Matthew's Gospel, it seems only that one Ælfric of Bath was the copyist of this Gospel: and in fact each Gospel is in a different hand. The Bodleian Library copy, MS. Bodley 441, which seems to be the earliest (but is considerably defective), was the text chosen for the printed edition of these Gospels produced by John Foxe under Archbishop Parker's direction as *The Gospels of the Fower Evangelistes* (London, 1571). It may be concluded, then, that the Benedictine reform movement had created by the end of the tenth century a competent and effective translation of the Gospels into the by then general literary West-Saxon, and that the multiplying of copies indicates that this translation was established in

---

[1] George K. Anderson, *The Literature of the Anglo-Saxons* (Princeton University Press, 1949), p. 351.

[2] *The West-Saxon Gospels* were edited by J. W. Bright, 4 vols. (Boston, 1904–10). The Wycliffite version may be conveniently seen, along with the main post-Reformation translations, in *The English Hexapla of the New Testament* (London, 1841).

wide use in the eleventh century. *The West-Saxon Gospels*, however, did not continue to be copied beyond the early twelfth century, and there is no evidence that they exercised any influence on later English versions. They remain as an illustration of how efficiently and naturally Anglo-Saxon could be employed on the Bible before the Norman Conquest, though their chief interest must be historical rather than strictly literary.

During all this time the practice of glossing the Psalter and Canticles, since they were used in almost every Office, remained. Some of these were continuous. Indeed, the continuous gloss became more widespread in this period. The best of these continuous interlinear glosses occasionally provide fairly readable Anglo-Saxon translations, though they hardly attain to the level of really competent rendering like *The West-Saxon Gospels*. A good example of the continuous interlinear gloss of this time (following a practice which had survived since the Mercian *Vespasian Psalter Gloss* of the mid-ninth century) is the *Salisbury Psalter*. This is conveniently accessible in an Early English Text Society edition.[1] The manuscript, now in Salisbury Cathedral Library but originating probably from Sherborne in the later tenth century, is a fine example of this type of codex.

As the Church in England developed under the impetus of St Æthelwold, Ælfric's beloved master, and his co-workers, the needs of a priesthood (in many cases still very weak in Latin) for vernacular manuals of all kinds began to be met by the production of all kinds of translations and adaptations of the accepted Latin text-books. Of these, the so-called *Benedictine Office* has been mentioned earlier.[2] Archbishop Wulfstan was apparently the prime mover in its production, using material provided by his collaborator Ælfric as a base. It provides for monks not yet proficient in Latin the matter of their monastic services in simple, lucid prose, with verse employed for some passages from the Psalter and some special liturgical prayers.

The *Benedictine Rule* was translated into clear and fairly idiomatic prose in a version thought to be a copy of an original translation by St Æthelwold himself, but apparently adapted to the use also of nuns. The Old English appears separately after the Latin, chapter by chapter, and is not a continuous gloss but a piece of competent prose. It is in the Latin text that there occur some feminine forms which suggest use for a convent.[3]

For the guidance of priests in the hearing of confessions and the assigning of correct penances to their people, manuals were provided

---

[1] Ed. Celia Sisam and Kenneth Sisam (Oxford, Early English Text Soc., no. 242, 1959).
[2] Ed. J. Ure (Edinburgh, 1957).
[3] *Die angelsächsischen Prosabearbeitungen der Benedictinerregel*, ed. A. Schröer (Hamburg, 1885).

in the vernacular, so that every priest without enough Latin might have a 'Confession-book', *scrift-boc*, to carry him through his parish work. These works often dealt very fully with every kind of sin, so that from them it is possible to learn much of the daily lives of the later Anglo-Saxons. Their interest is, of course, primarily for the social historian or the pastoral theologian: but they usually again show the language being used with clarity and efficiency. The idea of such 'penitentials' and 'confessionals' had come to England through the Irish Celtic Church: and this was reinforced from Frankish Latin sources in the Benedictine reform period. Two of these practical manuals, wrongly attributed to Archbishop Egbert of York of the eighth century, were evidently in wide use: the so-called *Confessionale Pseudo-Egberti* and the *Penitentiale Pseudo-Egberti*. These also show the language being effectively applied to another technical use.[1]

Doubtless all these works for the clergy were purely practical in the aims of their translation, nor was there much art in their production. They were means to an end, and often had to be made and copied with great speed. Apart therefore from the efficient employment of the native language, one should not expect to find in them aspects of literature proper. In the prose of the later Anglo-Saxon period it is to the *Anglo-Saxon Chronicle* and to the romantic beginnings in *Apollonius of Tyre*, apart from the masters of homily, that we must look for prose literature.

Looking back over what we have of Old English prose, one finds, as with all literary cultures, that its achievement is not to be compared in aesthetic appeal to that of the poetry whose flowering preceded it. Yet its achievement is still not by any means unimpressive. Historical prose was a creation of the Anglo-Saxon genius far in advance of the rest of Europe. The art of the sermon in the hands of its best performers had reached some outstanding levels, and in some sort furnished an anticipation of that lasting excellence in preaching which was to be a marked feature of English writing. The novel in embryo is suggested by *Apollonius of Tyre*, and this attractive prose also begins to show some of those qualities of romantic courtesy which were to flower in *Sir Gawain* and in Spenser. But it remains true that for the reader on the look-out for the aesthetic pleasures of melodic rhythm clothing matter of vivid appeal, or for the catharsis of the moving and heroic tragic epic, or for the kind of universal appeal to the feelings we get from Gray's *Elegy*, it is to the verse rather than the prose of the Anglo-Saxons that he must go. The barrier of linguistic change made so much deeper by the Norman Conquest inevitably cuts us off from many of the Old English ways of

[1] See *Das altenglische Bussbuch* (*sog. Confessionale Pseudo-Egberti*), ed. Robert Spindler (Leipzig, 1934); also *Die altenglische Version des Halitgar'schen Bussbuches* (*sog. Penitentiale Pseudo-Egberti*), ed. Josef Raith (Darmstadt, 1964).

expression; but far more impassable are the barriers which cut off Old English thought-patterns and feelings. Yet, as was shown in Chapter 2, there is in fact some continuity from Anglo-Saxon poetry as well as from its prose; nor did the Norman Conquest mean a complete cessation of prose. Ælfric's homilies were being used and copied through the twelfth century, until their language ceased entirely to be comprehensible. The historical prose of the *Anglo-Saxon Chronicle* in at least one place was able to bridge the transition from Old to Middle English in the *Peterborough Chronicle*, whose account of the reign of King Stephen provides some prose of the best quality.

There is little profit in attempting to estimate the relative greatness of a literature, or to compare its merits with those of others. A comparative study will not necessarily enable the student to appreciate the intrinsic qualities of a literature the better. Of the literature among the Germanic peoples, only that of medieval Iceland is of commanding stature. But its florescence was somewhat later than that of the Anglo-Saxons, and it seems likely that the older Norse heroic poetry was younger than that of England. In France the twelfth century produced a magnificent literary garden; but this again came after the Anglo-Saxon period. The Slavic literary developments of the Kiev state were again only becoming apparent near the close of our period. Only in the Arabic culture of Islamic Spain might parallels to some of the Old English excellences be found: but this would be a far-flung and speculative undertaking. The Crusades which were to bring so many Oriental additions to the culture of Western Europe only began thirty years after the Norman Conquest. The appreciation of Anglo-Saxon literature, therefore, should stand on its own feet, and find itself in the receptiveness and aesthetic capacity of those who will have the energy to approach its subject. It is hoped that this journey through Old English writing may have stimulated the student of English literature to pursue its early productivity with vigour as well as exactness. Such an effort, exacting though it must be, will certainly be rewarding.

SELECT BIBLIOGRAPHY

NOTE. The lists which follow are arranged as far as possible in alphabetical order under the four headings:

(*a*) *Bibliographies*
    (1) General works which include Anglo-Saxon
    (2) Those specially concerned with the Anglo-Saxon field

(*b*) *Historical Background*

(*c*) *Texts*
    (1) Verse
    (2) Prose

(*d*) *Literary History and Criticism, including Metre*
    (1) Literary histories and general works
    (2) Criticism (including translations).

Many books and articles recorded in the footnotes are not here repeated unless of major importance. Notes are added on occasion.

(*a*) BIBLIOGRAPHIES

(1) GENERAL

Annual Bibliography of English Language and Literature published for the Modern Humanities Research Association (Cambridge).

Annual Bibliography, Publications of the Modern Languages Association of America (New York). This since 1956 has a wide international coverage.

The Cambridge Bibliography of English Literature, Vol. 1 (Cambridge, 1941), Vol. 5 Supplement (Cambridge, 1957).

RENWICK, WILLIAM L., and ORTON, HAROLD: *The Beginnings of English Literature to Skelton, 1509*, 2nd ed. (London, 1952).

The Year's Work in English Studies, annually since 1921 (Oxford).

(2) SPECIAL

BONSER, WILFRID: *An Anglo-Saxon and Celtic Bibliography, 450–1087* (Berkeley, California, 1957). Especially necessary for Old English-Celtic cultural relations.

KER, N. R.: *Catalogue of Manuscripts containing Anglo-Saxon* (Oxford, 1957). Very full and exact descriptions of manuscripts and their contents.

ZESMER, DAVID and GREENFIELD, STANLEY: *Guide to English Literature through Chaucer and Medieval Drama* (New York, 1962). Includes excellent Old English bibliography by Stanley Greenfield.

(b) HISTORICAL BACKGROUND

ASHDOWN, MARGARET: *English and Norse Documents relating to the Reign of Ethelred the Unready* (Cambridge, 1930). This includes translations with the texts.

BLAIR, PETER HUNTER: *An Introduction to Anglo-Saxon England* (Cambridge, 1956).

CHADWICK, H. M.: *The Origin of the English Nation* (Cambridge, 1907).

CHADWICK, H. M. and CHADWICK, NORA K.: *The Ancient Literature of Europe*, vol. 1 of *The Growth of Literature* (Cambridge, 1932).

CHAMBERS, R. W.: *England before the Norman Conquest* (London, 1928).

CLARKE, MAUD G.: *Sidelights on Teutonic History* (London, 1911).

CRAWFORD, S. J.: *Anglo-Saxon Influences on Western Christendom* (London, 1933).

DUCKETT, ELEANOR: *Anglo-Saxon Saints and Scholars* (New York and London, 1947).

GODFREY, JOHN: *The Church in Anglo-Saxon England* (Cambridge, 1962).

HODGKIN, R. H.: *A History of the Anglo-Saxons*, 2 vols., 3rd ed. (Oxford, 1953). This third edition has a valuable appendix on the Sutton Hoo archaeological finds by Rupert Bruce-Mitford. The period covered extends only to the death of Alfred.

KNOWLES, DOM DAVID: *The Monastic Order in England*, 2nd ed. (Cambridge, 1963).

LEVISON, WILHELM: *England and the Continent in the Eighth Century* (Oxford, 1946).

MITCHELL, BRUCE: *A Guide to Old English* (Oxford, Blackwell, 1965). An excellent beginner's book with much on the language.

ROBINSON, J. ARMITAGE: *The Times of St Dunstan* (Oxford, 1923).

SCHÜTTE, GOTTFRIED: *Our Forefathers*, 2 vols. (Cambridge, 1929–33). This is a translation by Jean Young from the Danish *Vor Folkegruppe Gottjod*: valuable for all aspects of Germanic origins.

SMALLEY, BERYL: *The Study of the Bible in the Middle Ages*, 2nd ed. (Oxford, 1952).

SOUTHERN, R. W.: *The Making of the Middle Ages* (London, 1953).

STENTON, SIR FRANK W.: *Anglo-Saxon England*, 2nd ed. (Oxford, 1947).

THOMPSON, A. HAMILTON: *Bede, his Life, Times and Writings* (Oxford, 1935). A collection of valuable essays by various hands.

THORPE, BENJAMIN: *Ancient Laws and Institutes of England*, 2 vols. (London, 1840). All documents are translated.

WHITELOCK, DOROTHY: *English Historical Documents, I. 500 to 1042* (London, 1953). This includes nearly all the Old English historical prose, especially Chronicles and laws, and the chief Latin authorities, with bibliographical notes and introductions, excellent translations of all documents, but no original texts.

WHITELOCK, DOROTHY: *The Beginnings of English Society*, Pelican History of England, II (Baltimore and London, 1952). Excellent sociologically, and makes use of the Old English literary monuments.

(c) TEXTS

(1) VERSE

Alcuin: De Pontificibus et Sanctis Ecclesiae Eboracensis Carmen in *Monumenta Alcuiniana*, ed. Wattenbach and Dümmler (Berlin, 1873), pp. 80 ff. Translation in J. Raine: *Historians of the Church of York and its Archbishops* (Rolls Series, No. 71), Vol. 1, pp. 349 ff.

The Anglo-Saxon Poetic Records, ed. George Philip Krapp and Elliott van Kirk Dobbie, 6 vols. (New York and London, 1931–54). This is a complete collection of the extant Anglo-Saxon verse, with Introductions, Bibliographies, and summary commentary on each edited text.
Vol. I   The Junius or Cædmonian Manuscript
Vol. II   The Vercelli Book
Vol. III The Exeter Book
Vol. IV   The Beowulf Manuscript
Vol. V   The Paris Psalter and the Meters of Alfred's Boethius
Vol. VI   The Anglo-Saxon Minor Poems.
References in this book are usually to these editions, though other readings are sometimes employed.

Andreas and the Fates of the Apostles, ed. Kenneth R. Brooks (Oxford, 1961).

Beowulf, ed. Fr Klaeber, reprinted with Supplement (Boston and London, 1950). The most thorough and authoritative edition; it contains related poems and much background material.

Beowulf, an Introduction to the Study of the Poem with a Discussion of the Stories of Offa and Finn, by R. W. Chambers; 3rd ed. with Supplements by C. L. Wrenn (Cambridge, 1959; reprinted 1963). The most readable and humane work of its kind. Its supplements, including Bibliographies, bring it up to 1957.

Beowulf, ed. C. L. Wrenn (London, 1953; 2nd ed. reprinted 1961, 1966). This seeks to present the poem chiefly to the literary student.

Beowulf and Judith, ed. Dobbie, vol. IV of *The Anglo-Saxon Poetic Records* (New York, 1953; London, 1954). This, as do the other editions named, includes a bibliography, but the fullest is in Chambers's *Beowulf, an Introduction* noted above.

An Anthology of Beowulf Criticism, ed. Lewis Nicholson (University of Notre Dame Press, Indiana, 1963), hereafter referred to as ABC. This consists of a reprint of eighteen important papers dealing with every aspect of the poem.

Beowulf Manuscript Facsimiles

A revised edition of J. Zupitza's *Beowulf* Autotypes for the Early English Text Society, referred to as EETS hereafter: with new collotypes and

Introduction by Norman Davis (Oxford, 1959). There is a new facsimile in collotype as vol. XII of *Early English Manuscripts in Facsimile: The Nowell Codex*, edited with very exhaustive Introduction by Kemp Malone (Copenhagen, Baltimore, and London, 1963).

Beowulf Translations

By J. R. Clark Hall into prose, revised by C. L. Wrenn with Introduction, etc., and preface on metre by J. R. R. Tolkien (London, 1950). The best verse rendering is by Charles W. Kennedy: *Beowulf, the Oldest English Epic, Translated into Alliterative Verse* (New York, 1940).

The Battle of Brunanburh, ed. Alistair Campbell (London, 1938).

The Battle of Maldon, ed. E. V. Gordon (London, 1937).

Cædmonian Poems, edited as vol. 1 of *The Anglo-Saxon Poetic Records* by George P. Krapp: *The Junius Manuscript* (New York and London, 1931).

The Cædmon Manuscript of Anglo-Saxon Biblical Poetry, Junius XI in the Bodleian Library, ed. Sir Israel Gollancz for the British Academy (London, 1927). This is a complete facsimile with full introduction and apparatus.

The Poetry of Cædmon, by C. L. Wrenn, in *Proc. of the Brit. Acad.*, Vol. XXXII (1946), pp. 277–295.

The Manuscripts of Cædmon's Hymn and Bede's Death Song, ed. Elliott van Kirk Dobbie (New York, 1937). This is a complete study with all the known manuscripts.

The Anglo-Saxon Charms, by F. Grendon (New York, 1930). This is a very thorough edition and general study.

Anglo-Saxon Magic, by G. Storms (The Hague, 1948). This includes an edition of all the *Charms* with translations.

Christ I, edited as *The Advent Lyrics of the Exeter Book* by Jackson J. Campbell (Princeton University Press, 1959). This has translations facing the texts and a full apparatus.

Christ and Satan, ed. Merrel D. Clubb (New York, 1925).

Cynewulf's Poems

Apart from their inclusion in *The Anglo-Saxon Poetic Records* editions of the Exeter Book and the Vercelli Book, separate editions of value are:

Elene, by Pamela Gradon (London, 1958)

Fates of the Apostles, along with *Andreas*, by K. Brooks (Oxford, 1961).

Juliana, by Rosemary Woolf (London, 1955).

Critical Studies in the Cynewulf Canon, by Claes Schaar (Copenhagen, 1949).

"Cynewulf and his Poetry", by K. Sisam in his *Studies in the History of Old English Literature* (Oxford, 1953), pp. 1–28.

Deor, ed. Kemp Malone (London, 1933).

The Dream of the Rood, ed. Bruce Dickins and A. S. C. Ross, 4th ed. (London, 1954). Some valuable matter also in W. Bütow: *Das altenglische "Traumgesicht vom Kreuze"* (Heidelberg, 1935).

Elegies

Three Old English Elegies, ed. R. F. Leslie (Manchester University Press, 1961). Contains editions of *The Wife's Lament, The Husband's Message*, and *The Ruin*.

Exeter Book, edited as vol. III of *The Anglo-Saxon Poetic Records* by Elliott van Kirk Dobbie (New York, 1936).

Exeter Book Facsimile. The Exeter Book of Old English Poetry with Introductory Chapters by R. W. Chambers, Max Förster and Robin Flower, Printed and Published for the Dean and Chapter of Exeter Cathedral (London, 1933).

Exodus, ed. Edward Irving (Yale University Press, 1953).

The Finn Fragment or Fight at Finnsburg. Included in all editions of *Beowulf*, and in vol. VI of *The Anglo-Saxon Poetic Records—Minor Poems*, ed. Dobbie (London and New York, 1942).

The Later Genesis, ed. B. J. Timmer, 2nd revised ed. (Oxford, 1954). This includes the Old Saxon fragments partly translated into Old English. Still valuable is Fr Klaeber: *The Later Genesis and other Old English and Old Saxon Texts relating to the Fall of Man*, 2nd ed. (Heidelberg, 1931).

Gnomic Poems

The *Exeter Gnomes* are included as *Maxims I* in the Exeter Book volume of the *Anglo-Saxon Poetic Records*, and the Cottonian gnomic verses in the *Minor Poems* volume as *Maxims II*.

Gnomic Poetry in Anglo-Saxon, ed. Blanche C. Williams (New York, 1914).

Guthlac Poems, edited in the Exeter Book volume of the *Anglo-Saxon Poetic Records*, but no satisfactory separate edition.

Husband's Message. See under "Elegies".

Judith, ed. B. J. Timmer (London, 1952). Also in Dobbie's *Beowulf* and *Judith* as noted above.

Juliana. See under "Cynewulf's Poems".

Junius Manuscript Facsimile. See under *"Cædmon"*.

The Battle of Maldon, ed. E. V. Gordon (London, 1937). A particularly good work.

"Maxims." See under "Gnomic Poems".

The Phoenix, ed. N. R. Blake (Manchester University Press, 1964). Includes the text of the Latin source.

The Old English Elene, Phoenix and Physiologus, ed. Albert S. Cook (Yale University Press, 1919).

The Old English Physiologus with a Verse Translation by James Pitman, ed. Albert S. Cook (Yale University Press, 1921).

The Riddles of the Exeter Book, ed. Fred. Tupper (Boston, 1910).

The Rhyming Poem, edited in the Exeter Book volume of ASPR.

The Ruin. See under "Elegies".

The RunePoem, edited by Bruce Dickins in *Runic and Heroic Poems of the Old Teutonic Peoples* (Cambridge, 1915). A useful comparative study and includes parallel Old Norse pieces. Also edited in the *Minor Poems* volume of the *Anglo-Saxon Poetic Records.*

The Seafarer, ed. Ida Gordon (London, 1960).

The Poetical Dialogues of Solomon and Saturn, ed. Robert Menner (New York and London, 1941). A very fine work which includes a wide background of relevant knowledge.

Anglo-Saxon Dialogues of Salomon and Saturn, ed. John M. Kemble, 3 parts (London, 1845, 1847, 1848). This studies all the related folklore and still has value.

The Vercelli Codex Facsimile. Edited by Max Förster, published only in an Italian translation: *Il Codice Vercellese con Omelie e Poesie in Lingua Anglosassone a Cura della Biblioteca Vaticana con Introduzione del Prof. Dott. Massimiliano Foerster* (Roma, 1913). This somewhat reduced facsimile with apparatus in Italian includes both prose and verse, with a valuable Introduction.

Waldere, ed. F. Norman (London, 1936).

The Wanderer, edited in Exeter Book volume. Still valuable is the edition with translation included in *Anglo-Saxon and Norse Poems,* by Nora Kershaw (Cambridge, 1922).

The Wanderer, ed. R. F. Leslie (Manchester University Press, 1966).

Widsith, ed. Kemp Malone (London, 1936).

Widsith, ed. Kemp Malone, being vol. XIII of *Anglistica* (Copenhagen, 1963). This is a considerable expansion and revision of the preceding edition, with new and sometimes impressive speculations.

Widsith, a Study in Old English Heroic Legend, by R. W. Chambers (Cambridge, 1912). A classic in its kind.

The Wife's Lament. See under "Elegies".

Wulf and Eadwacer edited in the Exeter Book volume of ASPR. There is a valuable study of this poem by Kemp Malone: "Two English Frauenlieder" in *Studies in Old English Literature in Honor of Arthur G. Brodeur* (University of Oregon Press, 1963), pp. 106–128.

(2) PROSE

Ælfric's Works

In alphabetical order, with criticism:

Catholic Homilies in Benjamin Thorpe: *The Homilies of the Anglo-Saxon Church,* 2 vols. (London 1844–46). Translations face the texts.

Colloquy. 2nd edition by G. N. Garmonsway (London, 1947).

De Temporibus Anni, ed. H. Henel for EETS (Oxford, 1940).

Grammar and Glossary. Ælfrics Grammatik und Glossar, ed Julius. Zupitza (Berlin, 1880).

The Old English Version of the Heptateuch, edited for EETS, O.S. 160, by S. J. Crawford (London, 1922). Includes treatise on the *Old and New Testament* and the important *Preface to Genesis.*

Lives of Saints, ed. W. Skeat for EETS, Parts 1 and 2, 1881, Parts 3 and 4, 1900. Translations face the texts.

Pastoral Letters. Die Hirtenbriefe Ælfrics in altenglischer und lateinischer Fassung, ed. B. Fehr (Hamburg, 1914).

DUBOIS, MARGUERITE-MARIE: *Ælfric, Sermonnaire, Docteur et Grammairien* (Paris, 1914). This is a full and elaborate treatment.

WHITE, CAROLINE: *Ælfric, a New Study of his Life and Writings* (Yale University Press, 1898). Still generally reliable.

Note. Some of Ælfric's homilies are found separately in miscellaneous collections, e.g. *Angelsächsische Homilien und Heiligenleben*, ed. B. Assmann (Kassel, 1889). Includes the important treatment of the celibacy of the clergy, *Be clænnysse*. Ælfric's numerous as yet unedited homilies are to be published in 2 vols, edited by John Collins Pope for the EETS as *Uncollected Homilies of Ælfric* (1967–68.)

Æthelweard

The Chronicle of Æthelweard, ed. Alistair Campbell (London, 1959).

King Alfred's Writings

St Augustine's Soliloquies, ed. Henry L. Hargrove (Yale University Press, 1902). A better edition by W. Endter: *König Alfred der Grosse, Bearbeitung der Soliloquien des Augustinus* (Hamburg, 1922).

Bede's *Ecclesiastical History*, edited for EETS O.S. 95 and 110, by T. Miller (London, 1890–98). Also edited by Jacob Schipper: *König Alfreds Übersetzung von Bedas Kirchengeschichte* (Leipzig, 1889).

Boethius's *Consolation of Philosophy*, ed. W. J. Sedgefield (Oxford, 1899). Translation by Sedgefield (Oxford, 1900).

Gregory's *Pastoral Care*, edited for EETS O.S. 45, by Henry Sweet (London, 1871). Includes translation.

Orosius' *Histories* (*Historiarum adversum Paganos Libri VII*), edited for EETS O.S. 79, by Henry Sweet (London, 1883). Includes the Latin text.

King Alfred's Laws

See *English Historical Documents*, op. cit. Old English text is best in F. Liebermann: *Die Gesetze der Angelsachsen*, 3 vols. (Halle, 1903–16). Old English text with translation by F. L. Attenborough: *The Laws of the Earliest English Kings* (Cambridge, 1922).

The Anglo-Saxon Chronicle. Edited by Charles Plummer: *Two of the Saxon Chronicles Parallel*, 2 vols. (Oxford, 1892–99). *The Parker Chronicle* (823–900), ed. A. H. Smith (London, 1935). Translations by G. N. Garmonsway (London, 1957) and in *English Historical Documents, I*, noted earlier. Facsimile of the *Parker Chronicle and Laws*, edited for the EETS by Robin Flower and Hugh Smith (London, 1941).

Apollonius of Tyre, ed. Peter Goolden (Oxford, 1958).

Asser's Life of King Alfred, ed. W. H. Stevenson (Oxford, 1904). A second edition with additions by Dorothy Whitelock (Oxford, 1959). For serious questioning of the authenticity of Asser see V. H. Galbraith: *An Introduction to the Study of History* (London, 1964), Part 3, "Who wrote Asser's Life of Alfred?", pp. 88 ff.

AUGUSTINE. See under "King Alfred's Writings".

Bede's Historia Ecclesiastica Gentis Anglorum, ed. Charles Plummer: *Venerabilis Baedae Opera Historica* (Oxford, 1896). For the Old English version see under "King Alfred's Writings".

The Benedictine Office, ed. James M. Ure (Edinburgh University Press, 1957).

"Benedictine Rule". *Die angelsächsischen Prosabearbeitungen der Benedictinerregel*, ed. A. Schröer (Hamburg, 1885).

The Blickling Homilies, edited for the EETS, O.S. 58, 63, 73, by Richard Morris (London, 1880). Translations facing texts. Facsimile of the manuscript edited by Rudolf Willard as vol. X in *Early English Manuscripts in Facsimile* (Baltimore, Copenhagen, and London, 1961).

BOETHIUS. See under "King Alfred's Writings".

Byrhtferth's Manual, edited for the EETS, O.S. 177, by S. J. Crawford (London, 1929).

Gildas

De Excidio et Conquestu Britanniae, edited by T. Mommsen in *Monumenta Germaniae Historica, Auctorum Antiquissimorum* XIII (Berlin, 1898). Translation in John A. Giles: *Six Old English Chronicles* (London, 1848). A useful edition by Hugh Williams in *Cymmrodorion Record Series*, 3 (London, 1899–1901).

GREGORY. See under "King Alfred's Writings".

Gospels

The Gospels in West-Saxon, ed. J. W. Bright, 4 vols. (Boston, 1904–10).

The Gospel of Nicodemus, ed. S. J. Crawford (Edinburgh, 1927).

"Lives of Saints". See under "Ælfric".

Life of St. Chad, an Old English Homily, ed. R. Vleeskruyer (Amsterdam: North-Holland Publishing Co., 1953).

Two Lives of St. Cuthbert, ed. B. Colgrave (Cambridge, 1940).

Felix's Life of St Guthlac, ed. B. Colgrave (Cambridge, 1956).

Prose Life of St Guthlac: Das Prosa-Leben des Heiligen Guthlacs, ed. P. Gonser (Heidelberg, 1909).

Life of St Oswald of Worcester, ed. B. Colgrave (attributed to Byrhtferth), edited in J. Raine's *Historians of the Church of York and its Archbishops*, op. cit., Vol. I.

Leechdoms

Leechdoms, Wortcunning and Starcraft of Early England, 3 vols., ed. O. Cockayne (London, 1864–66). This includes most of the Old English medical works, the *Medicina de Quadrupedibus* and the *Herbarius Apuleii*, with much learned discussion; though this is sometimes now out of date.

Bald's Leechbook in facsimile, vol. V of *Early English Manuscripts in Facsimile, op. cit.*, ed. Cyril Wright (London, 1960).

"Miscellaneous Homilies": See Assmann's collection under "Ælfric".

NICODEMUS. See under "Gospels".

OROSIUS. See under "King Alfred's Writings".

Regularis Concordia, ed. Dom Thomas Symons (London, 1953). This covers both Latin and Old English versions, with a translation. It is the authoritative code of liturgical practice and way of life for all the English religious houses agreed at King Edgar's great Council of Winchester in 972, and probably drawn up by St Æthelwold.

"*Soliloquies* of St Augustine". See under "King Alfred's Writings".

Solomon and Saturn, Prose Dialogues, edited in J. M. Kemble's *Salomon and Saturn, op. cit.*, pp. 178–192: and as an Appendix to Menner's *Poetical Dialogues of Solomon and Saturn*, op. cit., pp. 168–171. The Kemble *Dialogue* is only known from the Beowulf Manuscript, Cotton Vitellius A XV.

Vercelli Homilies, edited (1st half only) by Max Förster: *Die Vercelli-Homilien I*, vol. XII of Grein-Wülker's *Bibliothek der angelsächsischen Prosa* (Hamburg, 1932).

WÆRFERTH (Bishop of Worcester): Translation of Gregory's *Dialogues: Bischof Werferths von Worcester Übersetzung der Dialoge Gregors des Grossen*, ed. Hans Hecht, vol. V of Grein-Wulkes's *Bibliothek des Angelsächsischen Prosa* (Hamburg, 1907).

"West-Saxon Gospels". See under *Gospels*.

Wonders of the East, edited in *Three Old English Prose Texts in MS. Cotton Vitellius A XV*, for EETS O.S. 161, by Stanley Rypins (London, 1924).

Wulfstan

The Homilies of Wulfstan, ed. Dorothy Bethurum (Oxford, 1957). *Sermo Lupi ad Anglos*, ed. Dorothy Whitelock (London, 1939, 2nd ed., 1952). There is particularly valuable information in Dorothy Whitelock's "Archbishop Wulfstan, Homilist and Statesman", *Transactions of the Royal Historical Society*, 4th Series XXIV (1943), pp. 25 ff.

A very thorough technical work on Wulfstan is Karl Jost: *Wulfstanstudien* (Bern, 1950).

(d) LITERARY HISTORY AND CRITICISM, INCLUDING METRE

(1) LITERARY HISTORIES AND GENERAL WORKS

ANDERSON, GEORGE K.: *The Literature of the Anglo-Saxons* (Princeton, 1949). Chiefly useful for its very full bibliographical information.

BAUGH, ALBERT C.: *A History of the English Language*, 2nd ed. revised (London, 1952). Its chapter on Old English covers the ground, especially on the social side.

BRANDL, ALOIS: *Geschichte der altenglischen Literatur* (Strassburg, 1908). The most reliable of its kind.

BROOKE, STOPFORD A.: *English Literature from the Beginning to the Norman Conquest*, 2 vols. (London, 1898).

The Cambridge History of English Literature, Vol. I (Cambridge, 1907). Some of its seven chapters on Old English have permanent value.

CHADWICK, H. M.: *The Heroic Age* (Cambridge, 1912).

DUCKETT, ELEANOR S.: *Anglo-Saxon Saints and Scholars* (New York, 1947).

———: *Alcuin* (New York, 1952).

EARLE, JOHN: *Anglo-Saxon Literature* (London, 1884). Very scholarly and readable despite its age.

ELLIOTT, RALPH W. V.: *Runes* (Manchester University Press, 1959). A careful and effective account of the Anglo-Saxon runic inscriptions, and a good introduction to the subject. It includes the Ruthwell Cross inscription which lies behind *The Dream of the Rood*.

GIRVAN, RITCHIE: *Beowulf and the Seventh Century* (London, 1935).

GREENFIELD, STANLEY: *A Critical History of Old English Literature* (New York University Press, 1965). A brief but fresh and well documented sketch.

KENDRICK, THOMAS D.: *A History of the Vikings* (London, 1930).

———: *Anglo-Saxon Art to A.D. 900* (London, 1938).

KENNEDY, CHARLES W. L.: *The Earliest English Poetry* (New York and London, 1943).

KER, W. P.: *Epic and Romance* (London, 1896).

———: *Medieval English Literature* (Oxford, 1912).

LAWRENCE, WILLIAM W.: *Beowulf and Epic Tradition* (Cambridge, Mass., 1928). Very valuable still.

MALONE, KEMP: "The Old English Period", in *A Literary History of England*, ed. Albert C. Baugh, Vol. I (New York, 1948). A brief but well-documented and stimulating survey.

Metre

The following selection is suggested as most useful to the student.

BLISS, ALAN J.: *The Metre of Beowulf* (Oxford, Blackwell, 1958). A brief and concentrated defence of Sievers's basic view.

LEHMANN, WINFRED PHILIP: *The Development of Germanic Verse-form* (Austin, Texas, 1958). This includes a good comparative account of Old English versification in its Germanic background.

POPE, JOHN C.: *The Rhythm of Beowulf* (Yale, 1942). This is a very thorough description of the basic theory of Old English metre now widely accepted. It includes an excellent history of the study of its subject.

SCHIPPER, JAKOB: *A History of English Versification* (Oxford, 1910). Its two chapters on Old English are clear and effective.

SIEVERS, EDOUARD: "Zur Rhythmik des altgermanischen Alliterationsverses," in *Paul-Braune's Beiträge zur Geschichte der deutschen Sprache und Litteratur*, Vol. X (Halle, 1884). This is the basic statement of what was for long the received view, and is followed by most books on the subject till Pope.

SLAY, D.: "Some Aspects of the Technique of Composition of Old English Verse", in *Transactions of the Philological Society*, (London, 1952).

SISAM, KENNETH: *Studies in the History of Old English Literature* (Oxford, 1953). A collection of outstanding technical essays, especially on *Beowulf*, Cynewulf, and Ælfric.

TEN BRINK: *Early English Literature*, Vol. I, translated by H. M. Kennedy (London, 1883). Some of this still has value, though it is often out of date.

WARDALE, EDITH E.: *Chapters on Old English Literature* (London, 1935).

(2) CRITICISM (INCLUDING TRANSLATIONS)

What follows is only a limited selection of individual writings and translations which have some special value. A few items on Sutton Hoo are included.

ANDERSON, O. S. (later ARNGART): *The Seafarer, an Interpretation* (Lund, 1937).

BARTLETT, ADELINE C.: *The Larger Rhetorical Patterns in Anglo-Saxon Poetry* (New York, 1935).

BLOMFIELD, JOAN: "The Style and Structure of *Beowulf*", *Review of English Studies* XIV (1938), 396–403.

BONE, GAVIN: *Anglo-Saxon Poetry* (Oxford, 1943). A selection of poetical translations, with a lively essay.

BONJOUR, ADRIEN: *The Digressions in Beowulf* (Oxford *Medium Ævum Monographs*, 1950).

BOWRA, SIR MAURICE: *Heroic Poetry* (London, 1952).

BRODEUR, ARTHUR G.: *The Art of Beowulf* (Berkeley, California, 1959).

BRUNNER, KARL: "Why was *Beowulf* Preserved?" *Études anglaises* VII (1954).

CHAMBERS, R. W.: *On the Continuity of English Prose*, for the EETS (London, 1932, reprinted 1957).

DU BOIS, ARTHUR E.: "The Unity of *Beowulf*", *Publications of the Mod. Lang. Association of America* XLIX (1934).

GIRVAN, RITCHIE: "The Medieval Poet and his Audience" in *English Studies Today*, ed. G. Bullough and C. L. WRENN (Oxford, 1951).

——: "Finnsburuh", in *Proc. Brit. Acad.* XXVI (1941).

GLUNZ, HANS: *History of the Vulgate in England* (Cambridge, 1933).

GORDON, IDA: "Traditional Themes in *The Wanderer* and *The Seafarer*". *Review of English Studies*, New Series V (1954).

GORDON, R. K.: *Anglo-Saxon Poetry*, 2nd ed. revised (London, Everyman's Library, 1954). Translations.

GRATTAN, J. H. G. and SINGER, CHARLES: *Anglo-Saxon Magic and Medicine illustrated specially from the Semi-pagan Text Lacnunga* (London, 1952). Texts from British Museum MS. Harley 585 with translations.

GREENFIELD, STANLEY: "The Formulaic Expression of the Theme of 'Exile' in Anglo-Saxon Poetry". *Speculum* XXX (1955).

HOTCHNER, CECILIA A.: *Wessex and Old English Poetry with Special Consideration of The Ruin* (Lancaster, Pennsylvania, 1939). This seeks to show that the elegies are of West-Saxon origin.

KASKE, ROBERT E.: "*Sapientia et Fortitudo* as the Controlling Theme of *Beowulf*", *Studies in Philology* LV (1958), 423–456. Included in ABC.

KENNEDY, CHARLES: *Old English Elegies Translated into Alliterative Verse with a Critical Introduction* (Princeton, 1936).

——: *Early English Christian Poetry Translated into Alliterative Verse with Critical Commentary* (Princeton, 1952).

MAGOUN, FRANCIS P.: "Oral-Formulaic Character of Anglo-Saxon Narrative Poetry", *Speculum* XXVIII (1953), 446–467. Included in ABC.

MALONE, KEMP: *Ten Old English Poems put into Modern Alliterative Verse* (Baltimore, 1941).

MORGAN, EDWIN: *Beowulf, a Verse Translation into Modern English* (Addington, Kent, Hand and Flower Press, 1952). One of its two introductory essays on the art of translation is excellent.

PATCH, HOWARD R.: *The Tradition of Boethius, a Study of his Importance in Medieval Christian Culture* (New York, 1935).

PONS, ÉMILE: *Le Thème et le Sentiment de la Nature dans la Poésie Anglo-Saxonne* (Paris, 1925).

SCHLAUCH, MARGARET: "*The Dream of the Rood* as Prosopopoeia", in *Essays in Honor of Carleton Brown* (New York, 1940).

SMITHERS, GEOFFREY V.: "The Meaning of *The Seafarer* and *The Wanderer*", *Medium Ævum* XXVII and XXVIII (1957–59).

SPAETH, J. DUNCAN: *Old English Poetry* (Princeton, 1922). Translations of *Beowulf* and a large collection into alliterative verse.

STANLEY, E. G.: "Old English Poetic Diction and the Interpretation of *The Wanderer, The Seafarer* and *The Penitent's Prayer*", *Anglia*, Vol. LXXIII (1956).

Sutton Hoo and Archæology

The following is a short selection of works which have a bearing on archaeology in relation to Anglo-Saxon literature.

BESSINGER, J. B.: "*Beowulf* and the Harp at Sutton Hoo", in *Univ. of Toronto Quarterly* XXVII (1959), pp. 148–168.

Bruce-Mitford, Rupert: *The Sutton Hoo Ship-Burial*, Provisional Guide (British Museum, 1947, and later reprints).
——: "The Sutton Hoo Ship-Burial, Recent Theories and some Comments on General Interpretation", *Proceedings of Suffolk Institute of Archaeology*, Vol. XXV, Pt. I (Ipswich, 1949). Valuable for possible light on *Beowulf*.
——: "The Sutton Hoo Ship-Burial", appendix to 3rd ed. of R. H. Hodgkin's *History of the Anglo-Saxons*, Vol. 2 (Oxford, 1952), pp. 698–734 and notes pp. 749–56. This is the best short account, and covers well the relations of Sutton Hoo with *Beowulf*.
Green, Charles: *Sutton Hoo: the Excavation of a Royal Ship-burial* (London and New York, 1963).
Martin-Clarke, D. Elizabeth: *Culture in Early Anglo-Saxon England* (Baltimore, 1947).
Sisam: Kenneth: *The Structure of Beowulf* (Oxford 1965).
Wrenn, C. L.: "Sutton Hoo and Beowulf", in *Mélanges de Linguistique et de Philologie in Memoriam Fernard Mossé* (Paris, 1959), pp. 495–507. Included in ABC.
Wrenn, C. L.: "Two Anglo-Saxon Harps", *Comparative Literature*, Vol. XIV (1962).

Timmer, Benno J.: "Wyrd in Anglo-Saxon Prose and Poetry", in *Neophilologus*, Vol. XXVI (1940–41).
Tolkien, J. R. R.: "Beowulf, the Monsters and the Critics", in *Proc. Brit. Acad.* XXII (1936). Most persuasive and widely influential. Included in ABC.
Whitelock, Dorothy: *The Audience of Beowulf* (Oxford, 1951). Particularly valuable on the historical side.
——: "The Interpretation of *The Seafarer*", in *The Early Cultures of North-West Europe*, ed. Sir Cyril Fox and Bruce Dickins (Cambridge, 1940).
Woolf, Rosemary: "The Devil in Old English Poetry", *Review of English Studies*, N.S. IV (1953).
——: "Doctrinal Influences on *The Dream of the Rood*", *Medium Ævum*, Vol. XXVII (1958).
Wright, Cyril E.: *The Cultivation of Saga in Anglo-Saxon England* (Edinburgh, 1939).
Wright, Herbert: "Good and Evil; Light and Darkness; Joy and Sorrow in *Beowulf*", *Review of English Studies*, N.S. VIII, (1957), 1–11. Included in ABC.
Wyld, Henry Cecil: "Diction and Imagery in Anglo-Saxon Poetry", in *Essays and Studies by Members of the English Association*, Vol. XI (London, 1925).

Index

The material found only in footnotes is not included in this index; nor was it thought necessary to record here titles and authors of modern works of criticism, since these are covered by the Bibliography.